Managing
Human Relations

PHILLIP V. LEWIS

Professor of Management

Abilene Christian University

Managing Human Relations

KENT PUBLISHING COMPANY
Boston, Massachusetts
A Division of Wadsworth

Senior Editor: John B. McHugh

Text Designer/Production Editor: Nancy Phinney

Cover Designer: Armen Kojoyian

Production Coordinator: Linda Siegrist

Kent Publishing Company
A Division of Wadsworth, Inc.

Printed in the United States of America

1 2 3 4 5 6 7 8 9 — 87 86 85 84 83

Library of Congress Cataloging in Publication Data

Lewis, Phillip V.
  Managing human relations.

  Includes bibliographies and index.
  1. Organizational behavior. 2. Personnel management.
I. Title. II. Title: Human relations.
HD58.7.L48 1983   658.3   83-137
ISBN 0-534-01428-3

CONTENTS

CHAPTER 7

Listening, Interviewing, and Conferring   140

CHAPTER 8

Making Decisions   162

─────────── CHAPTER 9 ───────────
Motivation and Morale   183

─────────── CHAPTER 10 ───────────
Employee Counseling and Discipline   206

PART 3

Challenges in Managing Human Relationships   231

CHAPTER 11

Grievances and Union-Management Relations   233

CHAPTER 12

Absenteeism and Turnover   259

─────── CHAPTER 13 ───────
Alcoholism and Drug Abuse 284

─────── CHAPTER 14 ───────
Prejudice and Discrimination 298

─────── CHAPTER 15 ───────
Performance Objectives and Appraisals 321

CHAPTER 16

The Stress of Change and Conflict   347

PART 4

Human Relationships and Your Future   373

CHAPTER 17

Values, Ethics, and Social Responsibility   375

CHAPTER 18

A Look into Your Future   398

to
MARILYN LEWIS

who continually fills my life
with a loving human relationship

PREFACE

Whether personal or formal, human relationships control the organization and affect its productivity and maintenance. This book was written to explore the impact of productive human relationships on organizations.

Productivity is the catchword of the 1980s. Today's managers are struggling with unprecedented productivity problems. The way they are conducting business now may not meet future challenges. Managers and employees must find new ways to develop the skills needed to facilitate change. For this reason *human relations*, that is, the study of human relationships, needs to be reemphasized as a source for developing these skills.

This book was also written to reacquaint managers with the human relations field. For the last four decades research studies have suggested that *good* human relationships increase corporate productivity. Unfortunately, too few managers pay attention to these studies. At a time when international competition is intense and innovation is high, human relations is needed more than ever. At a time when American organizations need revitalization and workers are demanding a better quality of work life, human relations is imperative. Human relations may in fact be the only low-cost means of increasing personal and corporate productivity. For example, how much would it cost a manager to say good morning to those who work for her or him? to give someone a needed pat on the back? to listen to the needs of people?

Human relationships are vital because they promise to alleviate critical productivity problems at a time when solutions seem difficult to attain.

Perhaps the first step to improving business productivity is improving human relationships. The improvements managers make in their human relationships will improve such human relations areas as trust, job satisfaction, performance, quantity and quality, absenteeism and turnover, motivation and morale, stress, and communication. This book shows how to establish and maintain productive human relationships, that is, how to manage human relationships.

 Textual Format

Managing Human Relations is divided into four major sections. The *first* section introduces you to the world of human relations. You will learn why people work, why we study human relations, how organizational climate affects working relationships, and what makes a group effective. The *second* section presents skills essential to managing productive human relationships. These skills are time management, leadership, communication, interviewing, and decision making. The *third* section describes major problems interfering with productive human relationships. These problems involve motivation and morale; employee counseling and discipline; grievances and unions; absenteeism, turnover, and job restructuring; alcoholism and drug abuse; prejudice and discrimination; performance appraisal; and the stress of change and conflict. Instructions for overcoming these problems are provided here. Finally, the *fourth* section invites a look into your future and the job you desire. The development of sound values and ethics as good business practice and as a manager's social responsibility is encouraged.

These areas are discussed with one aim in mind—to help you manage the human relationships in your chosen career. Therefore, you will want to study each chapter carefully. Work the question sections, solve the cases, and add to your in-class learning with outside readings and on-the-job practice.

 Acknowledgements

Very few projects in life are the result of singular effort. This book is no exception. Therefore, I'd like to thank the following people for their critical reviews and suggestions: Fred C. Sutton, Cuyahoga Community College; Allen Appell, Skyline College; Jim Lee Morgan, West Los Angeles College; Robert L. Markwith, American River College; Richard Gradwohl, Highline Community College; Linda Sarlo, Rock Valley College; Linda Jean Brown, College of Marin; Steven C. Branz, Triton College; Warren R. Plunkett, Wright College; and Peter L. Irwin, Richland College. Other reviewers deserving thanks include: Peter F. DiGiampietro, Earl E. Baer, Michelle Gradwohl, and

Jonathan Cobb. There are other reviewers, as well, whom I am unable to name, but you know who you are, so thanks.

Special thanks is due to Joseph T. Straub, Valencia Community College. Joe provided most of the cases, vignettes, world-of-work examples, and end-of-chapter applications. Most of the success of this book stems from Joe's insightful contributions.

Also, I would like to thank the various editors at Wadsworth and Kent Publishing Company who were associated with this project during its development—John Mahaney, Marshall Aronson, Keith Nave, and Jack McHugh. Thanks are also extended to the editorial and production staff of Kent Publishing Company. A thank-you is also deserved by Kathy Dorr for her faithful typing of the manuscript.

And, of course, I would be remiss if I did not thank my wife Marilyn for suffering with me through the moments of frustration one often faces during the creative phases of writing. To her I dedicate this book. Thanks also to my two sons Brook and Blair who probably wonder why Dad sometimes spends so much time at the typewriter.

1

An Introduction to Human Relations

1

Human Relations and Business

When you complete your study of this chapter, you should be able to:

1 Understand why people work and what their attitudes are,
2 Explain why human relations needs constant study,
3 Explain how misperceptions lead to human relations problems,
4 Discuss the chief determinants of perception,
5 Contrast social and work relationships, and
6 Practice the techniques for improving human relationships.

─────────────── OPENING CASE ───────────────

For Pauline Trimble work seemed to be a necessary evil. Determined to send her oldest daughter to an expensive private college, she took a job as a bookkeeper in a large department store to pay the tuition and other expenses. The job, a nine-to-five routine, became a long-term prospect when her younger daughter completed high school and wanted to follow in the older sister's footsteps.

After both children had finished college, Pauline realized she had been working ten years, half the time required to collect a substantial pension from her employer. To ensure a comfortable retirement for herself and her husband, she decided to spend a second decade in the same job. It is highly organized work that presents little variety or challenge, but demands an orderly person like Pauline who pays attention to detail.

Recently Pauline had an experience that caused her to reflect on the years she has spent as a bookkeeper. Her older daughter, now married and with a child of her own, wrote, "I've always appreciated the sacrifice you made to put me through school, Mom, and I'm going to do the same for your grandson Jack. Can you offer any advice?"

Seeing her daughter approach the same decision she had made twenty years before gave Pauline mixed feelings. She thought about the reasons she had remained a retail store bookkeeper for half her productive working years and wondered what advice she should give her daughter.

───

Do human relations need study?

During the last half of the twentieth century the field of human relations has gained stature in both business and society. Before the 1930s the human side of organizations was not emphasized as was the technical side. Behavioral science was marked by simple assumptions and solutions about how people formed relationships or behaved in these relationships. Such an approach was inadequate. A shift in emphasis was needed to understand human behavior in business organizations. The age of human relations dawned and the need for human relations competencies became apparent.

Awakenings are still needed for human relations, however. We still need a fresh look at what is happening inside business. The following question must be given a contemporary answer: How do supervisors and managers develop human relations competencies?

Because people are extremely complex systems, this question has no simple answers. However, Part I of this book, "An Introduction to Human Relations," is a start for understanding and dealing with the people problems supervisors and managers face in this decade. It will provide human relations knowledge and competency to assist you toward becoming a member of the management team. We begin in this first chapter by viewing the world of work and why human relations is needed.

Not Everyone Loves to Work

A lot of people in this world (both men and women) would relate to Pauline's feelings. They don't want to work and resent having to. Yet they do it. Sometimes they work out of necessity, and sometimes they work for luxuries. But they work, and they hate it. For example, studies at the University of Michigan show worker dissatisfaction at the highest point in a decade. Opinion Research Corporation of Princeton, New Jersey, portrays deepening discontent among American workers from 1950 to 1977. One research study dealing with a psychological evaluation of over 180,000 people indicates 80 percent of these people go to work reluctantly every day.[1] How can managers expect first-rate performances from employees who apparently don't like or believe in what they are doing? How can supervisors encourage healthy human relationships in such an environment?

The World of Work

Why do people work? Why are *you* planning to work? Is your field of study or career choice one you can really enjoy for the rest of your life? If *you* make the wrong career choice, chances are good in a few years you will be miserable with what you are doing. As we saw above, most people are not happy in their work. But, if the majority of people detest the work they do, why do they keep on doing it?

Why do I need to work?

Problems at Work

Researchers place emphasis on understanding why people work and how they relate to co-workers. They want to know what problems workers face. Unfortunately, human relations is still an emerging field. Thus, a systematic understanding of *all* the factors at work is not yet within grasp. The influences affecting attitudes, interpersonal relationships, and productivity are complex, to say the least. For example, what are the best ways for a supervisor to handle motivation and morale? organizational development and change? discrimination and prejudice? labor relations? performance appraisal and employee counseling? occupational stress?

What are some of the problems I'll face on the job as a manager?

This book deals with all these problems, as well as other dramatic human relations problems facing today's managers. The point is this: Problems are numerous and always present. However, their effect can be minimized and their occurrence predicted. Part of the secret is to realize that many of these problems arise because of changing attitudes toward work.

———————————— Why People Work ————————————

People generally work to enhance their life styles, but work may be either pleasure or drudgery. Part of the solution to negative attitudes about work is understanding the forces within the work environment. Human relations can provide such understanding. Work can be viewed as useful, practical, and purposeful. However, most people work for these seven reasons: habit, money, security, personal identity, pleasure, power, and escape.

Is the Puritan work ethic alive and well?

HABIT.   People work either because they are expected to or because they expect it of themselves. The habit of working provides meaning and order to life. A stigma is attached to unemployment. There is a fear of not knowing what to do next. And, of course, many of us are products of the Puritan work ethic, which teaches us that a person who does not work does not eat. We have been reminded it is by the sweat of the brow we are to bring forth the fruit of our labor. We have been taught that the fruits of hard work are almost always profit and honor. However, work is not only a means to an end; it can be the end for many people. Although we may have departed somewhat from the ideas of our Puritan ancestors, work still has value for the masses.

MONEY.   The desire for money in our society is an obvious reason for working. Money is important, not just for what it can buy, but because it often is concrete evidence of how well a person is doing. Research shows it is increasingly irrelevant in terms of need motivation, but very few people will work for nothing. Consider successful movie mogul Frank Price, chairman and president of Columbia Pictures. His four-year contract with the firm, effective in 1981, reportedly pays a $600,000 annual salary and at least $2 million in other annual cash payments including a $500,000 guaranteed performance bonus.[2] No doubt, money is one of Mr. Price's reasons for working.

How important is money to the average worker?

Unless people have a charitable reason and support elsewhere, they work for money. And money can motivate them toward higher productivity if it does increase with increased effort. Today's inflationary rates and uncertain economy also cause many women to work so that their family can afford a house. The second income has become vital. Money may not be the most important thing in the world, but as the saying goes, it sure beats what comes in second.

SECURITY.   People also work for economic security—having money coming in regularly, company benefits, retirement funds, and stock options. They may feel secure because they do not have to decide what to do with their time. Also, they seek the psychological security of knowing they have a job to do (unlike the apprehensive person in the unemployment line).

People seek security in familiar surroundings and freedom from strangeness. They also attempt to avoid physically hazardous situations. In gratifying this security need, however, people tend to maintain the status quo and follow reassuring behavior patterns. They use their current wages to buy food for today and provide for tomorrow.

PERSONAL IDENTITY.   Some people seek work in which they can make a meaningful contribution to life. They rebel against meaningless tasks and seek reasons for their work. They want to feel their job is important, and they like to see the benefits of a given task. It provides them with a personal identity at work and in their social world. For example, after initial introductions, the next question is nearly always, "And what do you do?"

PLEASURE.   People often do not associate pleasure and work. Pleasure is what occurs after the five o'clock whistle or on weekends. But many people do work because they enjoy it. They find work both pleasant and relaxing. They even whistle while they work. They view problems as challenges, not hindrances. They enjoy their colleagues, and they constantly seek ways to improve the work climate and their human relationships. Such people really enjoy living, also. For example, an independently wealthy married couple loved sailing. Although they had a generous lifetime income, they worked as a full-time crew on luxury charter boats, which enabled them to see most of the world, meet many fascinating people, and do the most pleasurable work they could imagine.

Can work be fun?

A refreshing motto in the executive dining room at Carlson Companies, the firm that owns Radisson Hotels, reads: "Lest you forget, our sole purpose here is to make money. However, let's have some fun while we are doing it." The president and sole stockholder, Curt Carlson, who is reported to compensate his top executives handsomely, celebrated one record-setting year by taking thirty-seven top managers and their spouses on a trip around the world.[3]

POWER.   Power is often the force that keeps people working. Many people are constantly seeking influence and the ability to induce others to behave in a desired fashion. They may not have sought work initially to acquire power, but they relish it once they have gained a powerful position. Such power may be obvious coercion or subtle persuasion. It may be verbal or nonverbal.

Several sources of power affect human relationships.

What are the sources of power?

- Direct control of task-environmental rewards is a source of power.
- Control of the rewards associated with friendly interaction is a source of power.
- The greater the personal attraction of other group members is to a single individual, the greater the power of that individual is.
- Control of punishment will be a source of power (a) when the conditions of punishment are clearly specified and (b) when compliance can be observed. Punishment-based power (a) will not lead to interpersonal liking and (b) will inhibit the exercise of power based on interpersonal attraction.[4]

Power tends to feed on itself. It can motivate some people to higher performance levels because they seek further advancement and greater power. That is, desire for power may not attract people to entry-level positions, but it tends to retain them once they have advanced up the organizational hierarchy.

ESCAPE.   Many people work to escape from the boredom of staying at home all day with children, parents, or daytime television. They want to make contact with the outside world. Escaping to another location, others choose jobs deliberately to get away from deteriorating relationships. Furthermore, it is now much easier to take care of a house with the advance of household conveniences. Many complain, "There's nothing for me to do at home! I *need* my job to make me a person, to give me variety and challenge."

———————————————— Attitudes Toward Work ————————————————

Can you have a job without the work?

As already mentioned, not everyone likes to work. One of the reasons for this situation is one's attitude toward work. And workers' attitudes affect not just themselves but the whole organization. An organization succeeds or fails not only because of the people who work in that organization but also because of these people's attitudes toward work. It seems many people want jobs but not work. They want the pay, security, fringe benefits, and so forth, but they don't want the responsibility of working for them. There is a world of difference between going to work for a salary, however, and going to work for an organization. Attitudes toward work will both govern people's progress and affect the attitudes and progress of their co-workers. Society is complex and technological. Jobs are broken down into small specialties that do not offer involvement in the whole job process. The result? Fewer and fewer people delight in their work. But right attitudes about work result in success; wrong attitudes about work result in mediocrity or failure. Work can be a tiresome chore and a burdensome responsibility, or it can be a challenging opportunity for growth.

Human Relations

Labor history has been altered by strikes, turnovers, and unproductive behaviors. Creativity, efficiency, productivity, and profitability have been affected. Such work changes have occurred because supervisors and managers did not recognize their influence on their followers. When interpersonal relationships are dehumanized, there is no social reward in the work. Employees become apathetic toward their work and do as little as they can. Some have even grown antagonistic and sabotaged operations to protest dehumanizing or impersonal treatment. When managers pay little attention to motivation and make hasty decisions without examining the assumptions underlying those decisions, their employees become passive or hostile toward them.

Human Relations Defined

Some people have defined human relations as management, leadership, or education. Certainly it includes these, as well as much more. For example, some might suggest human relations is doing to others what *you* would have them do to you. Others might say it is doing to others what *they* would have you do to them. It would be difficult to improve on either goal for living. The key is to realize when one's relationships are humane and when they are something less. For our purposes, **human relations** can be defined as the study of how people treat one another. This treatment may take place in a social or a work situation.

What is "human relations"?

human relations

    A few years ago Barbra Streisand popularized a song called "People," in which she told us how lucky people are who need people. This sentiment is so true you might wonder why most people don't get along better. However, some people have a very difficult time relating to others. Human relations seem simple enough, but practicing humane relationships is exceedingly difficult. However, unless we plan to become hermits, we will each need people, and they will need us. All people, especially those who desire a management position, need to learn all they can about how to treat others. Even if you do not seek a career in management, you will be spending most of your future years in some sort of an organizational environment working and socializing with other people just like you, who need other people. Therefore, one of the first goals in human relations is to become more sensitive to the needs and feelings of other people.

Why Study Human Relations?

Productivity is directly affected by employee intentions—intentions that result from the way employees are treated at work. For example, if you were to check productivity rates in the United States over the last decade, you would

Why do I need knowledge of human relations?

find a decline. We have the ability to match any nation in technology, but no longer can we match a nation like Japan in productivity. In fact, some would say we are approaching a serious problem in world power and domination because of our mediocrity in quality and production. Some would even claim that Japan is the new master.

FIGURE 1.1
Human Relations
Quiz

	Yes	No	Sometimes
1. Do you give *all* people the dignity to which they are entitled?	___	___	___
2. Do you know your own motivations? That is, are you aware of the actions you take in a given situation?	___	___	___
3. Do you try to make everyone with whom you work or associate feel important?	___	___	___
4. Do you understand others? That is, are you sensitive to *their* needs and motivations?	___	___	___
5. Do you communicate frequently with others about matters that affect them directly or indirectly?	___	___	___
6. Do you give praise when praise is due?	___	___	___
7. Do you delegate as much authority and responsibility as you can, within the framework of the task assignment?	___	___	___
8. Do you meet your appointments promptly so others will not have to wait for you?	___	___	___
9. Are you helpful to those who need your assistance?	___	___	___
10. Do you make tasks challenging?	___	___	___
11. Are you flexible in your behavior towards others?	___	___	___
12. Do you set a good example in your behavior by doing unto others as you would hope someone would do to you?	___	___	___

No doubt many factors could be singled out as the cause for low productivity. But one of the causes is the lack of emphasis on human relationships. This is one reason for human relations. Supervisors and managers must learn to create a positive working climate, an environment where people can satisfy their individual psychological and social needs as well as the organization's needs. This is not to imply that emphasizing human relations is a panacea for low productivity. Certainly such things as antiquated production facilities in some industries account for some of our dilemma.

Jobs differ in the skills they require, but nearly all jobs require social contact with humans. This is a second important reason for human relations. In fact, human relations is vital to successful development in any work activity requiring interpersonal contacts. This is a third reason.

Therefore, as you study human relationships, answer a very basic question as honestly as you can: How do you get along with other people when things are going well, and also when everything nailed down seems to be flying apart?

Do you enjoy working with other people?

If your answer is similar to many other people's, it is a timid, mediocre "OK, I guess." Others may wish to get by on shallow relationships and surface accomplishments. Ideally, you want to take your skills and knowledge and succeed with people regardless of your chosen career. Therefore, to gain insight about what you think about working with others, stop reading and respond to the questionnaire in Figure 1.1. Then begin reading again.

If you answered eleven or twelve questions yes on the questionnaire you have a high interest in human relationships; go buy another copy of this book for a friend. If you answered eight to ten yes, you have some interest; four to seven, little interest; one to three, no interest (go sell this book and drop the course).

It is important to know how we affect others through our behavior and attitudes. It is especially important to understand the potential influence we can exert over others. Without this self-awareness we may see ourselves quite differently than others see us. Whatever a person's personality is, it plays an important role in understanding how people behave. Also, understanding attitude weaknesses toward others alerts one to begin some sort of an improvement program.

However, one other insight is beneficial to improving social and work relationships. It is obvious in life that not everyone agrees. People differ because their perceptions differ.

How Do You Perceive the World?

Different people watching the same situation can see things differently. Naturally we see what is real; *they* miss the point. People see what they want to see, hear what they want to hear, and believe what they want to believe.

Why doesn't everyone see things the same way I do?

Unfortunately, reality is so infinite people have difficulty understanding it. Perceptions are not uniform. There are three sides to every story—yours, mine, and the facts. What is real to you is real—to you. But people truly interested in human relations will try to see, hear, and believe things as they really are. Being big enough to admit that none of us has the true picture, at least they will try to respect someone else's point of view.

———————————————————— Perceptual Problems ————————————————————

perception

The meaning of perception pertains to the function it plays. **Perception** is a process of interpreting data, that is, making sense out of incoming information. It involves observation, selection, organization, and interpretation of stimuli. For perception to occur some stimulus must be present. Our response to that stimulus depends on the structure of our sense organs— how we see, hear, and feel. Some perceptual problems are stereotyping, inferring, distorting, mind closing, and projecting.

Are you prejudiced against someone or something?

STEREOTYPING.   We have all been taught to perceive in certain ways. Because of these teachings, we have formed certain concepts we feel we can rely on regarding other people. Therefore, we may harbor harmful prejudices about others and even ourselves. We may or may not be aware of these prejudices. But prejudiced people often perceive stereotype features because they expect to perceive them. And no matter where they go, they will find others to share their stereotypes, prejudices, and biases. Unfortunately, this reinforces stereotypes as truths. Such stereotyping allows quick and easy classification of others, but such preconceptions are assaults on the dignity of people. For example, do you know people who believe, erroneously, that:

- persons with red hair have violent tempers,
- sports car owners are temperamental,
- bald-headed males are exceptionally virile,
- students who wear glasses are more academically inclined,
- persons with Irish surnames tend to be heavy drinkers, or
- overweight persons have jolly dispositions?

Such judgments disregard any distinctions among people. Stereotyping leads to problems in human relationships—problems that should not exist in an enlightened society.

Do you know a fact from an inference?

INFERRING.   Many people tend to judge others and situations without the facts. In doing so, they mistake inferences for facts. Facts are possible only after observation through one or more of the five senses and are limited to what was actually observed. Inferences can be made at any time because they go beyond observation. For example, you could see an apple and, because it smells good, infer it is good. But when you bite into it, it has a worm. Usually only a limited number of factual statements can be made after observation, but an unlimited number of inferential statements can be made. We must all occasionally make inferences, but we should know when we are inferring and not dealing with facts.

The story and quiz in Figure 1.2 will allow you to see how clearly you can distinguish between facts and inferences.[5] Read the story and assume everything you read is true. Don't memorize the story. You can look back at it during the quiz.

Did you answer all of the statements with don't-know? You should have, for none of the statements can be answered true or false with absolute certainty. If you missed any of the items on this quiz, go back, reread the story, and see where you inferred a point incorrectly. You can see how very easy it is to mistake inferences for fact. And that's what gets us into trouble with people. We infer these statements or actions to mean one thing, but they mean something entirely different. Incorrect inferences can destroy good human relationships.

DISTORTING. Because people select perceptions consistent with their self-concept, they can distort ambiguous information to fit their ideas, beliefs, and opinions. One way to see this process is illustrated in Figure 1.3. Take a quick look at it now. What do you see? Make a decision before reading further.

Figure 1.3 has been referred to as the Peter-Paul goblet. Did you see Peter and Paul? or just a vase? As stated earlier, we construct perceptions to make sense of incoming data. Since incoming data have no inherent meaning, they are open to various perceptions based on past experiences. Some information can be clear but some can be ambiguous. Whatever the information, it will be perceived according to the intent of the perceiver. Therefore, the central principle of perception is simplicity. Sometimes we don't immediately see what's intended because of distortion and ambiguity. Many human relations problems occur because we distort what we see and hear.

Why do we sometimes distort what we see and hear?

MIND CLOSING. Another perceptual problem occurs when people close their minds. They know what they know and that's all they want to know. General semanticists refer to this closed-minded attitude as "allness." It is a process of thinking your words or statements cover *all* that can be said about a given subject and not recognizing the details left out. Do you know anyone like this?

Obviously we can never repeat all the details that could be said about a given subject. Who would listen? So in all our communications with others we select some details and omit others. We also select the things to see, sense, or perceive; and in so doing, omit details. The limits of our nervous

What happens when you close your mind to new or different information?

A business person had just turned off the lights in the store when a college student appeared and demanded money. The cash register was opened, and the contents of the drawer were scooped up. The man sped away. A member of the law enforcement agency was notified.

True, False, or Don't Know?	T	F	?
1. A man appeared after the owner turned off the store lights.	_____	_____	_____
2. The robber was a college student.	_____	_____	_____
3. The person who opened the cash register was the owner.	_____	_____	_____
4. The business man scooped up the contents of the cash register and ran away.	_____	_____	_____
5. After the student, who demanded the money, scooped up the contents of the cash register, he ran away.	_____	_____	_____
6. Although the cash register contained money, the story does not state how much.	_____	_____	_____
7. The robber demanded money.	_____	_____	_____
8. The robber opened the cash register.	_____	_____	_____
9. After the store lights were turned off, a woman appeared.	_____	_____	_____
10. The robber did not take the money with him.	_____	_____	_____
11. The robber did not demand money of the business person.	_____	_____	_____
12. The business person opened a cash register.	_____	_____	_____
13. Taking the contents of the cash register with him, the man ran out of the store.	_____	_____	_____
14. The story concerns a series of events in which only three persons are referred to: the business person, a student who demanded money, and a member of the police force.	_____	_____	_____

FIGURE 1.3
A Perceptual
Distortion Problem

system make it impossible to *know* all, much less, *say* all. Therefore, we must remember the et cetera. Because there is always more than what we say, one of the human relations attitudes to foster is open mindedness. A closed mind creates barriers to understanding. It makes one rigid, unteachable, and narrow. Unlock your mind, throw away the key, and remain open to the et cetera.

PROJECTING. A final perceptual problem concerns the tendency to project feelings into the evaluation of others. This is similar to a mirror effect because instead of seeing someone else one actually sees oneself. That is, as people see undesirable traits in themselves, they project these traits into others. Then they do not have to admit that these undesirable traits exist in themselves. To improve human relations, however, one must realize that emotions often are affected by, and an understanding of the self is shaped by, feelings of inadequacy in some aspect of the personality. Therefore, try not to perceive similar qualities in others. Look for the best in every person. Understand your own feelings as well.

Why is it easier to see the faults in others than in ourselves?

———————————— Determinants of Perception ————————————

What causes people to perceive the way they do? Why do we form correct or erroneous perceptions about others? At least six perceptual determinants deserve attention: heredity and environment, peer pressure, snap judgments, halos and tarnished halos, self-fulfilling prophecy, and bosses and co-workers.

HEREDITY AND ENVIRONMENT. Any differences in perception between ourselves and others can be attributed to differences in background. The early influence of our family (their class, ethnic status, values, place of residence) and our sex have had considerable effect on who and what we are. These things also cause us to look at the world differently than anyone with a dissimilar background. Sometimes even those reared in the same family see things differently because of changes in age and status of parents when children are born.

Can you say "no" to group pressure?

PEER PRESSURE. Just as our family exerts pressure on us to perceive our world the way it does, so do our friends. Sometimes the desire for peer acceptance is so intense people go along with the group, regardless of where it is headed. Often these people have low self-concepts and don't feel secure with the self, if their goals or values are out of step with those of the majority. In fact, peer pressure in the later teen years is often more powerful than family pressure.

SNAP JUDGMENTS. A snap judgment is a direct, uncontrolled, immediate response to a situation—a reaction without thinking. For example, have you ever jumped to a conclusion before someone finished telling you a story? Or made a decision before you had all the facts? Or solved a problem before you knew what the real problem was? If so, you were guilty of making a snap judgment or an unsupportable decision. Snap judgments are akin to inferring.

Have you polished your halo lately?

HALOS AND TARNISHED HALOS. Have you ever assumed some people were good or bad because of their associates? The halo effect causes someone to assume a person who is good at one thing, or who associates with those who are good at that thing, to be good at something else. For example, a person with an excellent attendance record may be viewed as a high producer and quality worker. Someone who is aggressive may be seen as a person with high energy, dominance, and achievement. Or, a friendly person may be considered generous and warm. The converse is also true; there can be a tarnished halo effect.

Are you fulfilling your expected destiny?

SELF-FULFILLING PROPHECY. Similar to the halo effect, self-fulfilling prophecy suggests that a person's prediction of another's behavior will come true. For example, people who are seen as failures, as the worst at anything they do, probably will fail. People seen as successful, as the best at whatever they do, will probably succeed. People become who they think they are, and their friends or acquaintances do also. For example, in our opening case, if Pauline Trimble had been viewed or viewed herself as a corporate climber she would have had a totally different perspective. She would have received special opportunities and become a good manager because of expectations.

Instead, she viewed her job as a dead-end position, got less attention, and tended to lose hope. She had only a job, not a career.

SUPERVISORS AND CO-WORKERS.   Supervisors and co-workers tend to see problems from different vantage points. For example, a supervisor may see a new automated system as saving labor costs and as strengthening the company. The co-workers may see the new equipment as a threat to their jobs. Or, the employee who comes to work early and is the last to leave may see himself or herself as a hard worker able to really get into a problem. The supervisor may see this person as unable to get her or his work done on time. If we can learn to control our perceptions and to see things as they really are, both work and social relationships can be enhanced.

Social and Work Relationships

Human relations includes two aspects, social and work. Both are affected by one's perceptual skills. The first situation is perhaps the most familiar to persons who have not yet started their working career.

Social Relationships

Social relationships are contacts with people outside the working environment. Besides the basic social unit, the family, they include memberships in church groups, school or civic clubs, recreation teams, interest groups, and so forth. Each of these groups, especially the family, determines our social perceptions and attitudes. The key factors in these groups, from a human relations standpoint, are the ways one perceives, relates, and interacts with others. Sometimes, to win the attention, time, and cooperation of others, we must become interested in *them*. People usually are not interested in either you or me. They are interested in themselves. That concept is easy to illustrate: When we look at a group photograph we are in, whose picture do we look for first? People are primarily interested in themselves. Is there a way to get people to like us as we attempt to improve our social relationships? Yes, if we follow Dale Carnegie's six rules listed in Exhibit 1.1.

The building of social relationships also will enhance your relationships at work. Thus, Carnegie's six rules apply in or out of business.

social relationships

How can I become more people-oriented?

Work Relationships

Work relationships are those involving contacts with people in the working environment. People fail on the job daily because they can't deal satisfactorily with its social and human conditions. Many people who get fired from a job are, no doubt, fired because they can't get along with others. They are

work relationships

EXHIBIT 1.1
---

1 **Become genuinely interested in other people.** Put yourself out to do things for others—things that require time, energy, unselfishness, and thoughtfulness.
2 **Smile.** You must have a good time working with people if you expect them to have a good time working with you. If you don't feel like smiling, force yourself to smile. Act as if you were already happy, and that will tend to make you happy.
3 **Remember a person's name is to him or her the sweetest and most important sound in the English language.** When you are introduced to someone, remember that person's name and call it easily; by doing so you pay the person a subtle and very effective compliment. Forget or misspell the name, and you place yourself at a sharp disadvantage.
4 **Be a good listener. Encourage others to talk about themselves.** The people you talk to are a hundred times more interested in themselves and their wants and problems than in you and your needs. To be an interesting conversationalist, be interested; be an attentive listener.
5 **Talk in terms of the other person's interests.** Talk to people about their likes and interests and they will listen to you for hours and probably become your friends.
6 **Make the other person feel important—and do it sincerely.** Almost everybody you meet feels superior to you in some way. A sure way to other people's hearts is to let them realize you sincerely recognize their importance in their little world.[6]

How important is human relations to job success?

unaware of their effect on a group. They do not understand the needs, abilities, and reactions of others. Their communication and behavior are not directed toward achieving work objectives. Thus, human relations unites people at work and motivates them to function cooperatively and productively. For example, three employees of a landscaping company worked so well together that they seemed almost synchronized. However, they all enjoyed horticulture work, attended the same church, lived in the same neighborhood, and had the same hobby—racing a jointly owned stock car. Their social and work relationships united them in an especially effective way.

Work relationships are rather complex because of certain economic and psychological requirements not essential to social relationships. Most businesses are also more complicated than social clubs or educational groups. Organizations are run *by* people, *on* money, and (in the case of companies) *for* profit. Regardless of profit or funding, however, countless organizations are far less effective than they could be because managers at all levels disregard the role of human relations.

--- CONCLUSION ---

How an organization designs jobs, provides challenges, sets open or closed policies and recognizes achievement affects the working climate. The climate in turn affects behavior. That's what we'll be discussing in Chapter 2. If the climate allows workers to meet basic needs and realize self-esteem, they are apt to be more satisfied and motivated. And there is a spinoff effect. One relationship affects others; work affects social life, and vice versa. The more we learn in one area, the more we can apply those lessons in other areas. And people who practice improving relationships will be happier on the job, have happier co-workers, and be more productive.

KEY TERMS

Human Relations: the study of how people treat one another.
Perception: a process of interpreting incoming information.
Social Relationships: contacts with people outside the working environment.
Work Relationships: relationships with people in the working environment.

QUESTIONS

1 Reread the opening case.
   a. Do you believe it's possible to psych yourself into a positive frame of mind about a job? If so, would you recommend that to Pauline? Why or why not?
   b. Consider the slogan, "Every job is important here." As a supervisor, what might you do to make employees like Pauline believe that?
   c. Would you criticize Pauline for the way she has invested half her working life? If so, what else might she have done? What would you suggest she do now?
   d. What advice should Pauline give her daughter? Be specific; provide reasons for your answer.
2 Respond to one higher manager's remark: "At my level the paycheck becomes a status symbol. I rarely worry about my personal spending."
3 "My job is as big or small, as important or insignificant, as I want to make it." How does this attitude affect one's success in a chosen field? at a particular level in an organization?
4 List at least three jobs in which the jobholder's self-image and attitude toward the work may significantly affect performance. Why?
5 Discuss how you might perceive the following incidents *in*correctly, and why:
   a. man running down a crowded sidewalk,
   b. automobile being driven down a main street at night with its headlights out,
   c. a scream, "Stop, thief!" coming from a pet shop,
   d. a daughter coming in at 3:00 A.M. despite promises to be home by midnight, and
   e. a luxury car double-parked in front of a food stamp office.
6 Do you believe that applying sound human relations techniques with co-workers would help you in your social and family relationships too? Why or why not?

7 It has been said, "Reality is what is real to *you*." How does that concept relate to an individual's perception?

8 Discuss the significance of effective human relations in each of the following jobs:
   a. research scientist working on a new type of plastic,
   b. advertising copywriter,
   c. used car salesperson,
   d. night shift custodian in a large office building,
   e. college football coach,
   f. nationally ranked chess player,
   g. ocean-going hydroplane racer,
   h. professional tennis player,
   i. pediatrician, and
   j. lead vocalist for popular rock group.

9 Describe how the work attitudes of at least two of the following people influence their job satisfaction and likelihood of success:
   a. co-worker,
   b. parent,
   c. brother or sister,
   d. supervisor,
   e. close friend,
   f. well-known local, and
   g. business owner.

---------------------------- CASES ----------------------------

Case 1.1

John Chesley, a college student, works as a summer employee on the production line of an auto assembly plant. His father, who has twenty-three years of service with the company as a plant manager, arranged for John to be hired.

"It will be good experience to work at the bottom of the ladder for a while," he emphasized. "I know you're majoring in management, but you ought to see things from the workers' view, too."

Recently the company installed several robots. Some are programmed to paint auto bodies; others work in the foundry pouring molten steel; one installs light bulbs in dashboard panels. The topic of robot assembly is a sensitive one with assembly line workers. Although the union contract provides retraining rights for anyone who is displaced by a robot, most employees feel their jobs will eventually be jeopardized.

"I think these robots are a pretty impressive idea," John remarked during a lunch break one day. "Think of all the dangerous, dirty jobs they'll be doing. Also, I hear they cost less than $10 per hour to operate, while the average hourly labor cost for us fellows is around $21. If they help management keep the price of cars down and do undesirable or dangerous jobs at the same time, it seems to me we ought to think more positively about them."

"That's easy for you to say," grunted Chuck Radford, a twenty-five-year assembly line veteran. "You're a college kid working part-time during the summer, and your old man's been a manager for years. In a couple or three years you'll be making half again as much as many of us and working with your mind instead of your muscles. I say management plans to use those robots to do away with us working stiffs. The handwriting is on the wall."

Case Questions

1 Contrast John's and Chuck's points of view using each of the five determinants of perception.
2 Do you believe John should try to sell his co-workers on the long-term merits of robot assembly? Why or why not?
3 What might higher management do to reconcile the problem of perception that appears in this case?
4 How might John benefit from his experience in this job? How might his co-workers benefit from their association with him?

RESUME

Case 1.2

Name: Sean Reilly   *Marital Status:* Divorced

Address: 1620 Waverly Drive   *Age:* 42
           Boston, MA 02116

Position Applied For: Warehouse or production line superintendent

Education: Bachelor of Arts in Physical Education,
             University of Mississippi, 1966

Work Experience:
     • Assistant physical education teacher, Westview High School, 1966–1968
     • Retailing management trainee, Interco Department Stores, 1968–1970
     • Owned landscape maintenance company, 1971–1975
     • Salesperson, Weatherall Aluminum Siding Company, 1977–1979
     • Foreman, Above-All Roofing Company, 1979–1983
Hobbies: Karate, hiking, pistol shooting, chess
References: Furnished on request

Case Questions

1 Read the above resume and list the determinants of perception that influenced you.
2 How could you guard against the influences you listed in (1) above?
3 Assume you are a personnel manager and this applicant has applied for work with your firm. What questions would you ask to attempt to obtain a clear picture of what he has done and if he would be a suitable employee?

———— NOTES ————

1. Zig Ziglar, *See You at the Top* (Gretna, La.: Pelican Publishing, 1976), p. 306.
2. "Columbia Film Unit Chief Rewarded for His Success," *Wall Street Journal,* 23 September 1981, p. 39.
3. Roy Rowan, "Rekindling Corporate Loyalty," *Fortune* (9 February 1981): 54–56.

4. Barry E. Collins and Harold Guetzkow, *A Social Psychology of Group Processes for Decision Making* (New York: John Wiley and Sons, 1964), p. 139.
5. Adapted from William V. Haney, "The Uncritical Inference Test, Story C" (San Francisco: International Society for General Semantics, 1967).
6. Dale Carnegie, *How to Win Friends and Influence People* (New York: Simon and Schuster, 1936), p. 103.

SUGGESTED READINGS

Ritti, R. Richard, and Funkhouser, G. Ray. *The Ropes to Skip and the Ropes to Know.* Columbus, Ohio: Grid Publishing, 1977, 1982.

Chapman, Elwood N. *Your Attitude Is Showing.* Palo Alto, Calif.: Science Research Associates, 1977.

Terkel, Studs. *Working: People Talk About What They Do All Day and How They Feel About What They Do.* New York: Pantheon Books, 1974.

2

Human Relations at Work

When you complete your study of this chapter, you should be able to:

1 Understand the organizing process and discuss the major principles of good organization,
2 Compare formal and informal organizations,
3 Discuss the reasons for informal organizations,
4 Explain how formal and informal organizations can coexist,
5 Explain how organizational climate affects employees, and
6 Describe the organizations of the future.

--- OPENING CASE ---

Edwina Jackson went to work for Applied Products, Inc., as a computer programmer during its first year of operation. The company, which was very small when she started, has grown impressively during the last eighteen years. Its work force and the sophistication of its formal organization grew accordingly.

Edwina has been with the company longer than anyone else except the owners, which gives her a certain status and pride. She's also proud of her ability to deal with people, often remarking, "I can get along with anybody."

Her conscientious work and dedication to the company were rewarded with promotions as the organization grew, and she now manages the entire data processing department and reports to the vice president of finance. Her department, nicknamed the nerve center, interacts closely with every other area of the firm.

Edwina supervises more than twenty-five people, many of whom are part-time college students working toward a computer science degree. In the last year she has begun to feel she is losing control of her people and her job. There have been several incidents where she misunderstood or was not aware of the capabilities of newer, more complex equipment, and several of her college-educated subordinates have made program changes without her approval and knowledge.

Not long ago she overheard several members of her staff griping about fossils who had been grandfathered into jobs without staying abreast of the state of the art in new computers. They also complained about losing three respected programmers who resigned within the last eight months, pushing the department's turnover ten percent higher than the industry average.

According to a recent rumor, the company's vice president of human resources and Edwina's supervisors think that data processing should be set up as an autonomous department headed by a vice president who would report directly to the company president. This news compounds Edwina's concern about preserving her place within an organization that has become very different from the closely knit one she entered years ago.

--- Who in the Hierarchy Are You? ---

Because you will spend so much of your life within organizational structures, you need to understand such environments. You need to know where you fit in the structure, who all the others are in the hierarchy, and how all can work together productively. And, of course, if you reach your personal goals while the organization reaches its goals, you will be doubly rewarded. Such understandings are important, also, because it is our society's organizations—business, industry, government, education—that give meaning and direction to what people do. Without organizations havoc would reign as people worked toward conflicting goals or with incompatible objectives.

Also, to know how to relate to others, one must know who has the authority, who is responsible, and who belongs where. These are some of the problems Edwina Jackson was facing. "Where do I belong?" To help you gain a perspective of where you and others fit into the organizational scheme of things we'll begin by defining *organization*.

The Organizing Process

The tendency to organize seems to be a basic part of our personalities. Since the beginning of time people have banded together for one reason or another, but basically to achieve goals. Therefore, an **organization** is any group of people who have a primary goal and operate as a unit to achieve that goal. Each person communicates and contributes action to accomplish the goal, and each person's work within an organization is impossible or meaningless apart from the work of others. Each person relates to all other members and contributes toward the others' objectives. This relatedness within the organization is yet another reason for studying human relationships. Anyone interested in people and their working relationships must understand the organization.

What is an organization?

organization

Organizational Goals and Objectives

The above brief explanation of organizations and their importance implies people who work together need structure. They need a system that coordinates efforts. Therefore, most organizations establish certain goals and purposes to predict and integrate people's behavior. One of the obvious goals is to make a profit. To achieve that goal, one must reach other goals, for example, efficient production of goods and services, effective structure, and proper authority and responsibility.

What are the goals of an organization?

To understand how organizations set and meet goals one must understand organizational structure. There are two types: formal and informal. Either may stand out in an organization, depending on whether it is a profit or nonprofit group, but, usually the two coexist.

The Formal Organization

Most managers create formal systems of authority and responsibility necessary for group work. There is a vertical authority structure that defines boss-worker relationships. That hierarchy also defines the lines of authority

*How is a **formal** organization structured?*

formal organization

from top to bottom and the formal channels of communication. Generally there are four levels in the hierarchy: top management (president and vice presidents), middle management (department heads and superintendents), first-line management (supervisors), and the workers. Therefore, a **formal organization** consists of clear lines of authority, responsibility, and delegation. Figure 2.1 depicts a typical formal organization.

Closely related to the vertical authority structure is the horizontal structure. It consists of people who are equal in authority. These individuals may be peers, colleagues, or fellow workers throughout the organization. Whereas the vertical hierarchy explicitly defines the rules and regulations to direct member activities, the horizontal structure coordinates those activities. Typically, the horizontal levels deal not only with task coordination, but also with problem solving, information sharing, and conflict resolution. There tends to be much more horizontal than vertical communication.

To illustrate how the formal organization works, let's consider four principles: group goals, division of labor, chain of command, and efficiency and effectiveness.

--------- Group Goals ---------

Every organization should have a set of clearly defined goals toward which it is working. This is the first principle of good organization. Without goals there can be no measurable results. Several major goals have already been mentioned. A knowledge of any organization's goals provides insight about that group's productivity. For example, if the owners, members, and clients of an organization are benefiting from the goals and if a profit is being generated, the organization is probably successful and thereby productive. If these situations do not exist, the organization is probably not productive or successful.

What happens if an organization succeeds in meeting its goals and objectives?

Attaining organizational and personal goals is not always easy. However, if the organizational process is carried out properly and if the structure is designed suitably, several results should occur.

- Available resources (human and mechanical) will be used most effectively.
- Directional and operational goals and procedures will be determined clearly, and energies will be devoted to their achievement.
- An orderly hierarchy in which people are meaningfully related will result. Individual responsibilities and authority will be clear. Communication networks will be devised and maintained.
- Workers will benefit from planned superior-subordinate relationships in which every worker receives essential support and direction.
- Group and individual activities will become more rational, stable, and predictable.
- Treatment of individual workers may become more democratic, because patronage and favoritism tend to be reduced.

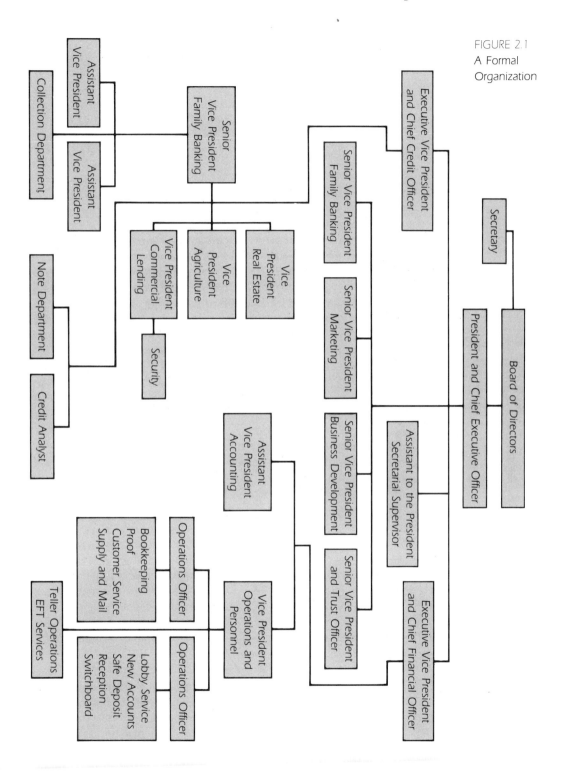

FIGURE 2.1
A Formal
Organization

- Reasonable work loads will be assigned. Individuals will be selected on the basis of ability to perform expected tasks. Simplification and specialization of job assignments will be more effective.[1]

If the organization's goals are integrated with the employees', employees are more likely to work enthusiastically and purposefully. All of us ask, "What's in it for *me*?" Therefore, setting goals and then working toward their accomplishment is enhanced by a second principle of good organization, the division of labor.

Division of Labor

Division of labor is concerned with allocating tasks among people and organizational units. It is a problem of who should be assigned what task. For example, any job assigned should be phrased so employees can picture the results of their work. Also, the jobs should include a challenge.

Whenever an organization consists of many people and jobs to do, the division of labor is necessary. Thus, two basic concepts need amplification because of their relationship to work assignments: task specialization and homogeneous assignment.

Should I specialize or be a Jack or Jill of all trades?

TASK SPECIALIZATION.   To achieve the highest level of productivity, an organization requires task specialization. Not everyone involved in a job can or should do the same thing. Therefore, specialization confines the work of each employee to a single function; for example, a computer programmer should not be responsible for filing. Part of the reasoning behind such specialization is that productivity increases when a work group has a single, planned and directed activity to work toward. This idea is known as unity of direction. Because there often is one best way to divide a task so it can be performed faster, people behave more productively as their tasks become specialized. However, too much specialization may result in less pride of accomplishment, make work monotonous, and affect individual growth.

Consider the tongue-in-cheek story of a customer who asked a salesperson for directions to the shoe department and was asked, "Left or right?" Highly specialized work like that of locomotive firemen may be adversely affected by technological change (in this case, the diesel locomotive) that renders their specialty obsolete. Thus, jobs should be designed to allow workers some flexibility, originality, or initiative to achieve their own personal goals, as well as the organizational goals.

Why must one group always have to depend on another group?

HOMOGENEOUS ASSIGNMENT.   The second division-of-labor principle deals with interdependence. One worker's efforts depend on another's. If one is not performing up to expectations, the other's job will suffer. This interdependency applies not only to workers in one department but also to departments within the organization, to parent and branch offices, to an organization and its subsidiary companies, or to an organization and the economy. For example, sales and marketing depend on production and advertising, and vice versa. Although some groups must occasionally function independently, these are rarities. Most groups are mutually dependent. Without this interdependence, organization is impossible.

---------------------- Chain of Command ----------------------

A third principle of good organization affirms the need for as few managerial levels as possible between top management and the workers. All organizations are based on hierarchical systems. Those at the top direct those at the bottom. Therefore, the closer those two levels are to each other, the greater will be productive output. There are three concepts related to the chain of command: unity of command, span of control, and delegation.

UNITY OF COMMAND.   In unity of command each person is accountable to *only one* person. Productivity results as each worker reports to one supervisor rather than several supervisors. Problems can arise when two supervisors give conflicting advice about what to do, how to do it, and whom to report to.

SPAN OF CONTROL.   The second concept is concerned with managers supervising only the number of people they can effectively control. This number depends on the ability of the manager, the needs of the workers, and the work being performed. Many management authorities suggest no one should supervise more than five or seven people whose work interlocks. The National Industrial Conference Board provides seven variables that determine how many people a manager can successfully direct. (*See* Exhibit 2.1.)

How many people should I supervise?

---------------------- EXHIBIT 2.1 ----------------------

1   Competence of superior and subordinate
2   Degree of interaction between units or personnel being supervised
3   Extent to which supervisors must carry out nonmanagerial responsibilities and demands on their time from other people and units
4   Similarity or dissimilarity of activities being supervised
5   Incidence of new problems in supervisor's unit
6   Extent of standardized procedure within organization
7   Degree of physical dispersion of activities[2]

Most spans of control in today's business world are larger than organizational theorists recommend. Whatever the size of the group supervised, however, spans of control affect the shapes of organizations. (*See* Figure 2.2.)

What is the difference between a tall and a flat organization?

FIGURE 2.2
Tall Versus Flat
Organizations

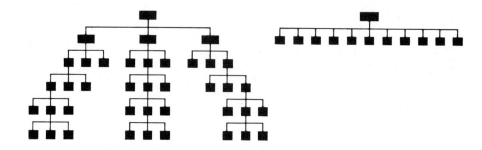

For example, tall (vertical) organizations encourage a smaller span of control. A tall organization is one with several layers in the vertical hierarchy. Managers supervise only a few subordinate managers. A flat organization (horizontal) has fewer layers, and its managers supervise many subordinate managers. Flat organizations reduce the number of levels and increase the span of control.

Tall organizations encourage face-to-face contact between manager and worker. The number of levels increases the number of communication channels. However it also increases the possibilities of communication breakdown and encourages workers to become supervisor-oriented. Thus, it is possible for workers to be more concerned with pleasing the supervisor than with meeting goals (although usually these two factors go together).

Flat structures, on the other hand, reduce the number of face-to-face contacts and give more freedom and independence to workers. However, flat organizations require workers to be self-motivated and self-controlled. This creates information overload for the manager.

DELEGATION.   The third concept related to the chain of command is delegation of authority and responsibility. It is often a direct result of supervision in tall organizations. Every organization needs someone in a high position to direct its daily activities and to assign work, responsibility, and authority. That's what delegation is all about. It works best though when it occurs level by level throughout the organization.

*When should I
delegate
responsibility?*

Many supervisors don't delegate, because they think they can do the job better than the worker. They lack confidence in the worker. Some supervisors do not feel secure in their positions or in their ability to teach someone else how to perform. Some just don't want to take the risk. Such obstacles to delegation might be removed if supervisors knew more about workers' abilities, skills, knowledge, needs, and so forth.

As the scope and size of business has increased, so has the need for delegation. Thus managers must choose between centralizing or decentralizing decision making, control, and authority. However, they must realize that ultimate responsibility lies with the higher levels. This realization will, for example, prevent top management from blaming assembly line workers for a production failure that brings a product liability suit.

Centralization Versus Decentralization.   In a centralized organization, decisions are made at the top. People in the lower levels are not encouraged to participate in decision making. Delegation is at a minimum. The advantages of centralizing authority and responsibility include formulating uniform decisions, standards, and policies and eliminating duplication of effort. One of the biggest disadvantages of centralization, however, is the reduction of a sense of belonging among the workers. Workers' skill and knowledge is easily rejected by management.

Should my organization be centralized or decentralized?

In decentralization, top management makes fewer decisions. Responsibility and authority are delegated downward to the smallest units practicable throughout the organization. Of course, there is a need for controls and communications to ensure that everyone is working toward acceptable goals. Some advantages of decentralization include allowing workers to better use their skills and talents, developing personnel for new supervisory positions, and increasing a sense of participation. Disadvantages include lack of uniform decisions, standards, and policies. Decisions may take longer because of the number of people involved, and coordination is more difficult. However, departmental decisions are often made more quickly because fewer people are involved.

The decision to centralize or decentralize affects organizational climate. From a human relations viewpoint, decentralizing is preferred over centralizing the management processes. However, from a managerial perspective, centralization is tempting. Moderation is probably the key. Excess in either direction is detrimental. Some compromise between the rigidity of no delegation and the possible anarchy of total delegation must be sought. Managers should delegate to those who need and can handle authority and responsibility.

Problems in Delegation.   The idea of moderation in delegation is important, especially if a supervisor tends to assign work that a worker cannot handle. Five problems result from such delegation, all associated with the formality required by organizational structure. They are responsibility without authority, the Peter Principle, overlapping authority, gaps in authority, and misuse of the exceptions principle.[3]

Is it possible to delegate more work than a person can handle?

1. *Responsibility Without Authority.* Have you ever been assigned a job to do but not the power to do it? Maybe you had a job but limited authority. Many graduate teaching assistants feel this way at times. Or perhaps you were told always to "check with me first." If so, you probably felt very frustrated. Unfortunately, many supervisors assign responsibilities without giving the authority. A person who is given directions should receive the power to accomplish the task.

Is the last rung on the ladder of success labeled "incompetence"?

2. *Peter Principle.* Have you ever been in a position you were not able to handle? People sometimes have the responsibility to do a job but not the ability. The Peter Principle says that people will rise to a level of incompetence in their jobs. Workers are often promoted to supervisors, and supervisors to managers. Each level requires more responsibility, and people may or may not be competent at the new job. If they are competent, they will be promoted to a higher level. Such promotions continue until the people reach the job in which they are incompetent. Then no other promotions will be offered them. They have risen to their level of incompetence.

3. *Overlapping Authority.* Have you ever been assigned a job to do and found that someone else is assigned a similar job that conflicts with yours? If so, your supervisor committed the error of assigning overlapping authorities. Clashes between you and the other person may have occurred because of the confusion, and the supervisor had to resolve these problems.

4. *Gaps in Authority and Responsibility.* Have you ever been given one assignment and your co-worker a second, but no one was assigned the third job necessary for successful completion of the activity? This does happen through oversight or negligence, and when it does occur workers often face some very acute problems.

5. *Misuse of Exceptions Principle.* Has anyone ever given you a job to do and then said something like, "Don't call me unless you've got a problem"? That's the exceptions principle. The supervisor delegates the job but doesn't want to be bothered unless some exceptional circumstance arises. This principle can be misused by a supervisor who fails to define clearly what are considered regular and routine duties and what are considered exceptions.

--------------------------- Efficiency and Effectiveness ---------------------------

Can I be efficient without being effective?

efficiency

effectiveness

The fourth and final principle of good organization deals with efficiency and effectiveness. These two concepts are often used synonymously, although they are different. They encompass all of the preceding principles and correlatives, since one of management's objectives is to reach its goals.

The distinction between efficiency and effectiveness is often described accordingly: **Efficiency** is doing things right; **effectiveness** is doing the right things right. Clearly, to do the wrong thing in the most efficient manner possible (e.g., scrubbing a floor with a tooth brush) is a waste of time. The results are nonproductive. Effectiveness is choosing the right goals and reaching them. Efficiency assumes the choice of right goals and looks for the best way to achieve them. For example, efficiency is doing an assigned job in a way that makes the most economical use of labor, time, and material. Both effectiveness and efficiency are valuable concepts, but effectiveness may be more important. At least it should precede efficiency. How can you find the best way to reach a goal if you don't know what the goal is? If you don't know where you're going, any road will take you there.

The Informal Organization

In any working situation there is a formal structure and an informal structure. *How does an informal*
The formal organization is represented by organizational charts, clear outlines *organization differ*
of authority and responsibility, and definite delegation of duty. Studies re- *from the formal*
peatedly show, however, that groups depart from formal tasks and hier- *organization?*
archies to create other channels of communication and dependence. Certain
persons are attracted to others because of proximity, task, common interests,
personality, or social class. Thus the informal organization is not represented
in the traditional hierarchical system. An **informal organization** does not **informal**
consist of clear lines of authority, responsibility, and delegation. **organization**

    Informal organizations consist of people who lunch together or drink
coffee together, of cliques within the office, and of common-interest groups;
their members work as autonomous units, small groups of people with
special interests, and large groups of people with similar interests. The larger
the informal organization, the harder it is to control.

Why Managers Prefer the Formal Organization

Any group within an organization that exists for unofficial reasons is classified
as an informal organization. Of course, some managers would prefer that *Which organization*
such an entity not exist. They prefer the formal organization, regardless of *do managers prefer?*
how clumsy it might be. One of their reasons for preferring the formal to
the informal may be that the informal organization is so closely identified
with the grapevine. However, informal communication is a part of corporate
life and is used by good managers.

    The **grapevine** is a communication system meandering back and forth **grapevine**
across organizational lines and carrying messages that have no official sanction. This communication system is fast, influential, and flows in all directions. Some studies indicate over 80 percent of the messages generated within
an organization are sent through the grapevine. It provides insights into
workers' and supervisors' attitudes, provides a safety valve for emotions,
and spreads information. However, the grapevine also can spread rumors,
untruths, and scuttlebutt. The four most typical methods of spreading information by the grapevine are identified in Exhibit 2.2 as the single-strand *How does the*
chain, the gossip chain, the probability chain, and the cluster chain. (*See also* *grapevine work?*
Figure 2.3.)

    Because the grapevine always exists and cannot be destroyed, man-
agers must learn to adapt to and control it. They can do these things by
opening up the formal communication channels, fighting rumors with positive presentations of facts, preventing employee idleness and boredom by
designing better jobs, and developing long-term credibility in managerial
communications. Since the grapevine exists to provide employees with information quickly, supervisors should satisfy this need by getting the information out.

--- EXHIBIT 2.2 ---

1   The **single-strand chain** is a serial method of spreading information. One person tells another person who tells another person, and that person tells another person who tells another person, and so forth.

2   The **gossip chain** consists of one person telling everyone else. For example, one person hears a rumor about a particular change in the working process and informs all his or her friends at the coffee break or during the lunch hour.

3   The **probability chain** works in accordance with the laws of probability. For example, one person communicates randomly with two other people, and they pass on the information in the same random manner. The primary difference between this method and the single-strand chain is the random pattern created by the communicators.

4   The **cluster chain** is perhaps the most frequently observed grapevine method of transmitting messages. The information is communicated by one person to two or three others, who in turn pass the message along to two or three, who then do the same, and so forth.

--- Why Informal Organizations Exist ---

Is the informal organization necessary?

The informal organization exists for the same reason the formal organization exists—to satisfy the needs of people. Three major needs are satisfied by the informal organization: social interaction, communication, and help on work-related problems. Since informal organizations are found in all formal organizations, managers must recognize these needs.

SOCIAL INTERACTION.   People need to be recognized, to have status, and to relate to other workers. They have social needs, which they expect the organization to satisfy. For example, most people prefer to work with people with whom they can be friends or at least feel comfortable. Most formal structures stifle social affiliation. However, the needs for affection,

FIGURE 2.3
Grapevine Chains

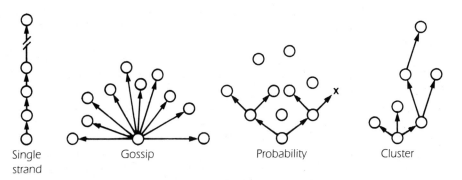

Single strand   Gossip   Probability   Cluster

Keith Davis, "Management Communication and the Grapevine," *Harvard Business Review* (September–October 1953): 43–49.

acceptance, belonging, and esteem must be dealt with. Satisfying these social needs makes the job and the human relationships more pleasant.

COMMUNICATION.   Formal organizational membership creates a need for information among workers, a need not often satisfied through formal channels. And just as the organization consists of formal and informal structure, so does it contain formal and informal communications (as shown in Figure 2.4). Formal communication follows the accepted hierarchical pattern, upward or downward, and is often given greater consideration and more careful examination than informal messages. Examples of formal communication are orders, directives, policies, and goals and objectives.

Informal communications furnish emotional and social support to group members and provide task coordination. Despite the great interdependence of various functions in the organization, formal communications are often inadequate. Thus, workers erect their own channels of communication—channels not prescribed by the formal organization. Examples of informal communication are intangible facts, opinions, suggestions, and suspicions. Communication will be discussed in depth in Chapter 6.

HELP ON WORK-RELATED PROBLEMS.   Managers have an obligation to help employees with problems that interfere with job performance. If supervisors or managers refuse to become involved with their people, complaints about the work environment will be widespread. Employees seek not only fair pay for fair work but also a high-quality working environment. They seek a supervisor who is understanding and sensitive to their needs and their situation. Help can come in a number of ways. For example, the supervisor who practices communication, is friendly and thoughtful, listens and shows confidence, communicates openly, and recognizes trouble when it arises is often viewed as concerned and helpful. The supervisor who doesn't speak to or listen to employees, displays a lack of trust in their abilities, withholds information, or engages in crisis management is often viewed as uninterested.

How can managers help their people?

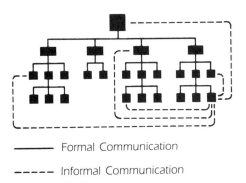

——— Formal Communication

- - - - - Informal Communication

FIGURE 2.4
Formal Versus
Informal
Communication

The primary goal of a supervisor's help is constructive behavioral change. For example, an employee may not have the necessary skills to solve a problem. The supervisor therefore attempts to understand, support, and respond appropriately to the employee. By doing so the supervisor helps reduce the employee's feeling of intensity, gathers information needed for the best solution to the problem, and helps the employee discover the solution. Such a helping relationship can occur only within a climate of trust.

Organizational Climate

organizational climate

How does the organizational climate affect working relationships?

It should be obvious by now that organizations affect personnel. In fact, the **organizational climate** is almost like a barometer, indicating how employees feel about specific managerial practices. Employees may feel relaxed, or driven, uptight, and under suspicion. The climate consists of the interpersonal and environmental factors that shape behavior and motivation. The organizational climate is that set of characteristics which describes an organization. The organizational climate distinguishes one organization from another, endures over a period of time, and influences people's behavior. Thus different climates stimulate different motivation and result in different performance and human relationships.

For example, after an especially tragic McDonnell Douglas DC-10 crash in Chicago cast doubt on the integrity of the plane's assembly, McDonnell Douglas's production workers rallied behind their work and their company impressively. Approximately 80 percent of those who built the plane decided to buy McDonnell Douglas stock. T-shirts, buttons, bumper stickers, and decals declaring "I'm proud of the DC-10" appeared spontaneously throughout a California assembly plant. The idea, which originated with a DC-10 inspector who moonlighted customizing T-shirts, grew into a wave of informal employee support that was reported in news media across the country.

Knowledge of organizational climate can provide a manager with information of how employees feel about other group members, about management, and about the organization. Throughout this book emphasis will be placed on improving the environmental conditions of the organization, especially as they relate to human relationships. Specific techniques will be shown for creating the proper climate. Instruments will be provided for measuring job satisfaction and dissatisfaction. If managers are aware of their organization's climate and can create or maintain the proper climate, they may increase the performance potential of their employees and thus of the organization.

The key appears to be *trust*. For example, managers who are supportive, friendly, and helpful have the most cooperative attitudes with their

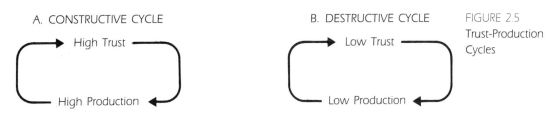

A. CONSTRUCTIVE CYCLE

High Trust

High Production

B. DESTRUCTIVE CYCLE

Low Trust

Low Production

FIGURE 2.5
Trust-Production
Cycles

Adapted from William V. Haney, *Communication and Interpersonal Relations— Text and Cases* (Homewood, Ill. Richard D. Irwin, 1979), pp. 13–15.

work groups. They are genuinely interested in their people; they are sensitive and considerate. They are confident of their employees and expect high performance. Because of these attitudes, we may conclude high trust stimulates high productivity, and high productivity reinforces high trust. The opposite is also true: low trust stimulates low productivity, and low productivity reinforces low trust. This is diagrammed in Figure 2.5.

How can I improve the climate in my department?

———————————— Trusting Versus Nontrusting Climates ————————————

In a trusting, supportive climate, employees respond positively to their supervisor's confidence in them (Figure 2.5A). When the supervisor places trust in the employee, the employee attempts to justify the supervisor's faith by an acceptable response. Thus a self-perpetuating cycle is started.

What happens when I don't trust my employees?

In a nontrusting climate, the supervisor fails to provide a supportive relationship. The employee responds with minimal compliance and resentment. Low productivity reinforces low trust, and this system likewise becomes self-perpetuating (Figure 2.5B).

———————————— Changing an Unhealthy Climate ————————————

Can anything be done to change an unhealthy, nonsupportive climate into a healthy, supportive climate? Yes. First, the employee could respond to the low-trusting supervisor with high productivity. If the employee is strong and mature enough to do this, the supervisor should eventually respond with high trust (Figure 2.6A).

Another approach depends on the supervisor's ability to respond to low productivity with high trust (Figure 2.6B). A supervisor who can do this without causing the employee to think she or he is being manipulated *should* be able to break the nonsupportive cycle and move to a high trust/ high productivity cycle. (Certainly, this procedure will not work in *every* situation.)

Again, the key to the supervisor's ability to maintain or create a supportive emotional climate is *trust*. The supervisor must win the respect

What is the key to a healthy climate?

FIGURE 2.6
Changing Unhealthy
Climates

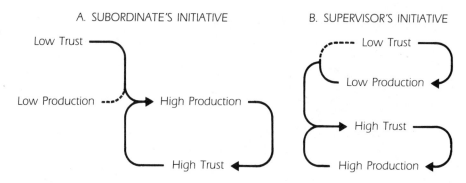

Adapted from William V. Haney, *Communication and Interpersonal Relations—Text and Cases* (Homewood, Ill. Richard D. Irwin, 1979), pp. 13–15.

of employees, develop mutual feelings of confidence between management and employees, and open clogged communication lines. Some amount of risk is involved in trusting others. Reaching out to other people may seem risky, but it usually results in goal attainment and personal growth. Certainly it builds strong relationships among people who risk and share together. Not everyone is willing to risk or to trust; that is why we often find conflict within organizations.

─────────────── Organizations in Conflict ───────────────

By comparing the formal and informal organizations, one can see that the needs of the formal organization and the needs of workers don't match. For example, in an informal system:

- The organization is viewed as a living and feeling organism, not as a machine;
- Provision is made for relevant decision making by the members of the organization;
- Mutual confidence, not obedience, is the basis for cooperation;
- Face-to-face groups rather than persons in assigned places are the units of organization;
- Leadership is person-centered instead of task-centered; and
- Communication includes appropriate feedback opportunities instead of flowing only one way.[4]

Are formal organizations compatible with the average employee's goals and objectives?

Formal organizations emphasize surface skills and material aspects of the job. Employees are expected to be submissive, passive, and dependent. That is, mature adults are expected to behave in immature ways. Therefore, formal organizations' requirements are incompatible with employees' life goals. Such organizations create barriers to the effective integration of worker and organization energies by ignoring the human need for growth. The organization's needs for productivity, control, and systematized authority relationships thwart employees' needs for growth and independence. As a result many workers become frustrated.

Although there are some advantages to formal organizations, there are some obvious disadvantages also. These organizations can be out of step with employee needs. That is why an emphasis on the human facets of organizations began to develop. Supervisors were encouraged to adopt humane management techniques that would reflect a greater appreciation of employees' social growth. Effective managers of formal organizations consider the functioning of human systems.

--- CONCLUSION ---

When the formal and the informal organizations work together in harmony, the overall structure operates efficiently, and human relationships function effectively. The two structures must coexist; peaceful coexistence is preferable to conflict and chaos. Supervisors can do much to foster peace by employing humane management techniques.

For example, some firms have aligned their organizational needs with employees' needs in the area of child care.[5] Recent statistics show that nearly half of all mothers with children under six years of age are employed. As traditional family ties change and older relatives like grandparents are less available to look after children, employers will begin to consider company-sponsored child care facilities.

A producer of heart pacemakers in Freeport, Texas, decreased turnover 23 percent within its mostly female, 400-person work force during the first year of operating a company day care facility. Although the company pays three-fourths of the weekly day care cost, management believes reduced absenteeism more than offsets the expense. Two-thirds of the human resource managers in a recent Harris survey believe day care will be a regular fringe benefit of the large employers by 1986.

--- KEY TERMS ---

Organization: any group of people who have a primary goal and operate as a unit to achieve that goal.

Formal Organization: the clear lines of authority, responsibility, and delegation within an organization.

Efficiency: doing things right; a term often used synonymously with productivity.

Effectiveness: doing right things right.

Informal Organization: subgroups within an organization that do not have clear lines of authority, responsibility, and delegation.

Grapevine: a communication system meandering back and forth across organizational lines and carrying messages that have no official sanction.

Organizational Climate: how employees feel about specific managerial practices; the environment within an organization.

QUESTIONS
---

1 Reread the opening case.
  a. Discuss the informal reasons why Edwina thinks a reorganization may take place.
  b. Suggest what higher management could do to help Edwina regain control of her people and her job.
  c. What potential problems may arise between Edwina and the type of subordinates she supervises?
  d. What implications does this case have for organizations that grow faster than anticipated? for employees like Edwina?

2 Defend the following comment: "Without goals or objectives, there's no need for an organization. Even informal organizations have goals."

3 Recall informal organizations you have belonged to in college, at work, or elsewhere. List some of their goals as you perceived them. Would you say most members of these groups perceived these goals the same way as you? Why or why not?

4 List at least three ways in which a company's informal organization may actually enhance the success of the formal one. Propose three ways that an informal organization may counteract the objectives of a formal one.

5. Discuss the reasons why managers are sometimes reluctant to delegate. What would you suggest to these managers? In times of rapid expansion, what problems may arise for the manager who prefers not to delegate?

6 Contrast efficiency and effectiveness. Give at least two examples of actions that are
  a. efficient but not effective,
  b. effective but not efficient, and
  c. both efficient and effective.

7 Describe a trusting versus a nontrusting organizational climate. What employee reactions can management expect in a nontrusting climate? What two approaches may be used to convert this climate to a healthy, trusting one?

8 Discuss the need for specialized tasks in an organization. What problems may arise if tasks are overly specialized?

9 A purchasing agent for a large auto manufacturing company orders left-hand taillight lenses two weeks late. Considering the concepts of homogeneous as-

signment and interdependence (and using your imagination), construct the disastrous chain of events that could occur because of that single error.

10   What actions might employees take when their organization ignores unity of command, thus causing them to report to more than one immediate supervisor?

11   List at least three variables that determine how broad a manager's span of control should be in a given situation. How would you describe the relationship of delegation to span of control in tall versus flat organizations? Which organization probably develops the most promotable subordinates, and why?

12   Sketch the operation of the following types of grapevine:
   a.   single-strand chain,
   b.   gossip chain,
   c.   probability chain, and
   d.   cluster chain.

13   What can managers do to control the spread of rumors through the informal communication channels in (12)?

14   Is an employee or a supervisor more likely to initiate action that would convert a nontrusting organizational climate to a trusting one? Why? Describe the possible results if the other party doesn't reciprocate.

CASES

Greg Poston, president of Poston's Office Equipment, Inc., has lived the great American dream. Founded in 1938 on a shoestring, his firm grew and now sells more than $40 million worth of merchandise annually.

Case 2.1

Greg's sense of family responsibility runs strong in his business. His children worked in the company during high school and college, and they now appear on the formal organization chart as vice presidents of personnel, finance, store operations, and marketing. Greg Junior, who recently earned his master of business administration degree, is vice president for administration and planning.

Recently young Greg began thinking about applying the chain store concept to retailing office supplies and equipment. Because the company is financially solid, it could afford to lease space in five surrounding shopping centers and open a satellite store in each. His father's response to the idea was less than enthusiastic, however.

"You know we're in business to make money, son," he said, "but our whole family lives comfortably off this company already. Expansion like that makes me a little uneasy. I've always been glad that I could see every person who works for us by walking through our store once a day. Scattering things out like you suggest— well, it's risky. We won't be able to stay on top of things. I never wanted to be the Sears, Roebuck of office equipment, I just wanted to build a profitable little company."

"Dad," Greg Junior countered, "you've got a terrific asset in all us kids. You sent us all through college, and we've accumulated lots of ideas and ambitions for this company in the process. We've talked this idea over among ourselves, and we think several well-placed satellite stores would double our profits within just three years! We're old friends with the local bankers, and they know how profitable we've been. We could raise money with a telephone call! Hey, give us the chance to apply ourselves to the fullest. Each of us could run a branch store if you like, so there would be family in each one. Eventually one of our competitors is going to beat us to the punch. Here are my financial estimates and a list of proposed store sites and everything else you'll need to make a decision. Read it over during the weekend, will you? We could become the giant of office equipment retailing in this state!''

Case Questions

1 Which internal organization principles will become most important to this company if Greg Senior agrees to open up branch stores? Why?
2 How might employees react to the idea of creating branch stores? How would you handle their reactions?
3 Prepare an announcement and information program to prepare employees for such a move.
4 Using chapter information and your imagination, construct an organization chart for this company if it opens five branches.

Case 2.2

Christine Owens, a retailing management trainee for Swingline Stores, just got her first big break. After working four years in progressively more responsible jobs, she has been selected to replace a retiring store manager.

Her store has been considered a problem store for several months. There have been many customer complaints about discourteous salespeople. At last inspection the housekeeping was deplorable—dirty aisles, merchandise in disarray, and poorly stocked displays that were covered with dust.

The present department managers are local people who began as salespersons and were promoted to their present jobs. They know one another well and often socialize on weekends at each other's homes or on trips to the beach. The previous store manager usually communicated with them through George Perry, Christine's assistant manager, who is also a member of the firm's management training program.

Yesterday morning Christine had her first general meeting with her department managers. She emphasized how pleased she was to be in charge of their store, expressed her pleasure at working with them, and mentioned that she looked forward to making some positive changes that would benefit everyone.

Afterward, one of the older department managers remarked, "We're really going to miss old Bob, the top boss before you. He was a fine person to work for. We hardly heard from him at all, and things ran as smoothly as silk on the selling floor—just ask anyone! We're sort of a big happy family down there, and we hope you'll take that into account in these changes you referred to. Welcome aboard!''

Christine wondered exactly what he meant and how the department managers would react when she began making the changes required to correct the problems she had been told to fix by higher management.

Case Questions

1 Suggest how Christine should begin to correct the problems that exist in her store.
2 Recommend steps to gain the support of the informal organization in making any changes.
3 How might the remark, "You have to break some eggs to make an omelet" apply to Christine's situation?
4 How do you feel George Perry should fit into Christine's plan of action?

NOTES

1. O. Jeff Harris, Jr., *How to Manage People at Work—A Short Course for Professionals* (New York: John Wiley and Sons, 1976), p. 14.
2. Harold Stieglitz, "Optimizing Span of Control," *Management Record* (September 1962): 25–29.
3. Lawrence L. Steinmetz, *Human Relations: People and Work* (New York: Harper and Row, 1979), pp. 189–191.
4. Gordon L. Lippitt, "Organizational Climate and Individual Growth," *Personnel Administrator* (September–October 1960): 485–487.
5. "Child Care Grows As A Benefit," *Business Week,* 21 December 1981, p. 60.

SUGGESTED READINGS

Hicks, Herbert G., and Gullett, C. Ray. *The Management of Organizations.* New York: McGraw-Hill, 1976.

Kast, Fremont E., and Rosenzweig, James E. *Organization and Management: A Systems Approach.* New York: McGraw-Hill, 1974.

Katz, Daniel, and Kahn, Robert. *The Social Psychology of Organizations.* New York: John Wiley and Sons, 1966.

Peter, Laurence J., and Hull, Raymond. *The Peter Principle: Why Things Always Go Wrong.* New York: William Morrow, 1969.

Schein, Edgar. *Organizational Psychology.* Englewood Cliffs, N.J.: Prentice-Hall, 1970.

3

Improving Work Group Relations

When you complete your study of this chapter, you should be able to:

1 Describe the stages of group development from beginning to maturity,

2 Discuss the variables affecting group behavior: status, roles, norms, conformity, and cohesiveness,

3 Increase cohesiveness in a work group, and

4 Identify the effective characteristics of a work group.

OPENING CASE

Bill Sullivan recently was hired as a summer employee at Landscape Therapy, Inc. He and his three co-workers travel from house to house each day doing yard work for the firm's regular customers.

Bill's co-workers are a closely knit group. Red, who has most seniority, is a quiet, methodical person who acts as the informal foreman for the owner. He relays special instructions about each job and is the only one permitted to drive the truck from one job to the next. Johnny, a high school dropout and avid hot rodder, lives at home and appears to spend most of his money on his high-performance car. Sonny, like Red, is married and is a close friend of Johnny's. Both work nights in the same service station after their regular job with the landscape company. The three of them ride to work together and often attend weekend motorcycle races together, too. Unlike these three, Bill views the work as temporary. He hopes to earn enough money to pay his tuition when he returns to state university next September.

The three regulars, as they call themselves, have an informal code: part-time or summer employees are expected to use the worst equipment. Bill, unaware of this, took whatever came off the truck when they unloaded at a new job. At the beginning of the third day Sonny informed him of "the way we do things here."

"I don't think that's completely fair," said Bill. "I'll take whatever's next off the truck, but I'm not going to work with the worst junk for the next three months, day in and day out. Besides, you guys make more money than I do because you've been here longer and have gotten raises. I'm not going to stand back and wait while you take the best running stuff, you can say what you like."

"Well, we're the full-timers," Johnny replied angrily, "and we see things differently. This is how things have always been between us and the rest. Who do you think you are to come in here for three months and rearrange things?"

Close Encounters of the Group Kind

Do you remember the movie, "Close Encounters of the Third Kind?" "We are not alone" was the cryptic statement in the movie ads. This chapter is not going to deal with intergalactic beings, but the idea behind "Close Encounters" is also true on the job. We are not alone. Throughout life we constantly work with other people. If we are successful in relating to others, especially those we work with, chances are good we'll succeed on the job. To add to our knowledge and understanding of our co-workers let's look first at the small group.

What Is a Small Group?

Can you define "small group?"

Many definitions exist for small groups, and there are similarities in all the explanations. A small group can be explained in terms of its size, its members' views, the thinking style of its members, the needs and motivations of group members, the members' goals, the group structure, the members' interdependence, or the give-and-take between group members. For our purposes, a **small group** is two or more people (no more than twenty) interacting with one another face to face.

small group

Group Membership

Do you know how many groups you belong to? The average person belongs to many groups (large and small) at any given time: family; educational, religious, and work groups; civic and social clubs; committees; and teams.

Many researchers have evaluated the groups to which people belong, the need for them, and people's role in them. In fact, the small group is frequently studied. Businesses and industries, for instance, are interested in improving the productivity of groups. Educators are interested in studying the classroom as a social group. Government and military are equally interested in small-group activity. And groups, are of course, part of human relations.

Group Formation

Why are there so many groups?

Group memberships raise another interesting question: Why are people members of certain groups and not others? Do they join because of family or peer pressure? a desire to be known and seen? a fear of loneliness? Do the groups do anything for them? Why are groups so important? Research suggests most people choose their groups because the members share a belief or act much as they already act. That is, groups satisfy certain behavioral needs.

Group Development

There are four main steps of group development.

1. *Task-orientation.* People try to identify the job that is to be done. They are interested in getting to know one another, feeling comfortable with

one another, and discovering acceptable interpersonal behaviors.

2. *Confrontation.* Intragroup conflict arises over leadership, power, and influence. During this time group members may become hostile toward one another, express their individuality, and resist group structure. Confrontation may occur, in part, because of inability to decide on a goal. Even though members may desire closeness, there is often considerable goal ambiguity and anxiety during the first two stages. As problems arise, conflict and projection of blame become evident. At this point mutual support is often sought.

3. *Cohesion.* Compromise and harmony are sought. Task conflicts are avoided. People begin to accept each other and the job. They become close, an entity. An open exchange of information begins. They try to effect compromises between factions to preserve at least the illusion of unity. They begin to work in a personal, intimate, and supportive climate.

4. *Reassessment.* This establishes the work group as a problem-solving instrument. Solutions to the task begin to emerge. Members gain insight and find new directions for self-growth. A degree of maturity is evident. The dropping of personal defenses encourages each to take responsibility for his or her own problems and for what happens.

Group Functions

Groups provide companionship, share information, solve problems, and provide therapy. They may even set norms or acceptable performance standards for the members. For example, certain groups offer (1) self-help (Alcoholics Anonymous, Weight Watchers), (2) business contacts (Lion's Club, Kiwanis Club, Exchange Club), (3) hobbies (bridge clubs, model train buffs, antique car enthusiasts), (4) a sense of belonging (fraternities, sororities, Hell's Angels). The most basic group functions seem to be achieving goals, satisfying psychological needs, encouraging meaningful interactions, and maintaining or strengthening the group. Those who divorce themselves from active group participation often display unhealthy personality traits and become a threat to themselves or society at large.

What do groups do?

Achieving Goals

Groups provide assistance in accomplishing tasks, solving problems, and achieving group goals. Also, they aid the learning of problem-solving procedures. They reward those who achieve goals and who live up to the group's expectations. For example, Weight Watchers rewards by applause those who lose pounds each week. Those who stay sixteen weeks receive a cookbook and those who reach goal receive a gold pin with a chip in it for each ten pounds lost.

—————————— Satisfying Psychological Needs ——————————

Groups also satisfy many psychological needs. For example, a family can provide a sense of uniqueness in the universe for its members. Groups also provide friendship, support, and love. Sports groups are a safe outlet for competitive drives or use of physical skills not used elsewhere. Groups offer verbal encouragement for ideas, technical assistance on some problem, or reinforcement of self-image, value systems, and beliefs. They provide a means of coping with opposing viewpoints. And they advance knowledge in areas of interest, such as hobbies or studies.

—————————— Encouraging Meaningful Interactions ——————————

Meaningful interaction occurs through face-to-face communication, as group members learn of their effect on others. One of the communication areas for meaningful interaction is the business meeting. However, management experts estimate that half of all time in meetings is wasted. If that estimate is accurate, you should try to make interactions in your groups meaningful. For example, come to the meeting ready to discuss the issues, not to waste time on unimportant peripheral considerations.

—————————— Maintaining or Strengthening the Group ——————————

Effective groups like to keep their membership intact. Members enjoy one another and find strength in unity. In fact, many groups attempt to preserve themselves when they encounter a threat to their existence. Behaviors that symbolize this maintenance tendency are keeping interpersonal relations pleasant, arbitrating disagreements, providing encouragement, stimulating self-direction, and increasing interdependence.

—————————— Group Behavior ——————————

What causes people to behave the way they do in groups?

The preceding four functions suggest that no work group grows unless each member is influenced by others. People change as a result of their participation. For example, the manager of a group of clerical employees in one aerospace firm was told his work group would be observed by industrial engineers for a week to determine their productivity. Several workers would be laid off if the group did not seem to have enough to do. Forewarned by their supervisor, the workers united in self-preservation to look busy. They called each other on the phone, covered their desks with superfluous paperwork, and otherwise created the impression to an uninformed observer that they were inundated with work. After the study was complete, the industrial engineers reported the group was overworked and suggested that at least three additional employees be hired.

You can expect to change as your group matures. Some of your behaviors, and perhaps your values, will be altered. Five factors affecting membership behavior are status, roles, norms, conformity, and cohesiveness.

Status

Status is the degree to which a person possesses certain socially approved attributes, valued roles, or influence. Most businesses have their own status hierarchies, for example, blue-collar versus white-collar. Status may be given to or earned by a person. Most work groups assign their highest status levels. However, workers develop their own informal status hierarchies, which may or may not conform to those approved by the formal organization. If the authority of the two hierarchies is in conflict, the formally sanctioned status positions are often second best in the worker's eyes.

Once a status hierarchy is established, it influences the flow, content, quality, and honesty of the group's communication. For example, in work groups with a rigid hierarchical status structure, lower-status members communicate less relevant information when talking about the group's tasks. Lower-status members also tend to direct their aggression at other low-status members, even though their frustrations arise from their relationship with high-status members. There is also a reverse relationship for communication honesty (telling the truth, being completely open, and not coloring things in your favor) with low-status members and high-status members, especially when the low-status members have aspirations for promotion.

High-status persons have certain privileges, income, or power. They have freedom to act in ways others cannot. For example, supervisors may call workers to a meeting any time they please. But the workers do not have a reciprocal privilege. They need an appointment. Even among employees with the same rank, variations in prestige exist. Some people may defer to some in arguments while challenging statements of others regardless of the soundness of the respective statements. Some persons are free to criticize or play practical jokes. Some habitually start conversations with their counterparts, whereas others speak only when spoken to. These differences are recognized as the due of high-status individuals. It is their role.

status

What are some differences between low-status and high-status individuals?

Roles

A **role** is a pattern of behavior that characterizes one's place in a group. As groups mature, people tend to specialize in certain activities. Behavioral expectations are established by and for the members. First, a role is worked out by each person and the group together. Then the group is partly responsible for the way each member acts. Likewise, a person's role has powerful meaning for the development of his or her behavior in a given work group.

role

What roles may I expect to play on the job?

Roles are generally classified into three broad groupings: task roles, maintenance roles, and self-centered roles.

TASK ROLES.   Task roles are concerned with the work group's goals (e.g., solving a problem, making a decision, or completing a project). These roles facilitate and coordinate effort. They help the group select and define its objectives and work toward solutions. Task roles are the specific functions group members undertake to accomplish a task. These include such behaviors as forming ideas, thinking critically, giving suggestions, providing information, analyzing problems, evaluating alternatives, making decisions, and establishing work procedures.

MAINTENANCE ROLES.   Maintenance roles refer to the socioemotional needs of people. Whereas task roles focus on the problem-solving aspects of goal attainment, maintenance roles focus on personal relationships. These roles are designed to strengthen, regulate, and perpetuate the work group's way of doing its job. This makes it possible for work to flow smoothly, as group members refrain from inappropriate behavior (e.g., being too loud, bossy, or quiet; getting mad; or having to have one's own way on everything) that will interfere with group activity. Thus, maintenance roles are primarily concerned with communication and group climate.

SELF-CENTERED ROLES.   There also may exist certain individual, self-centered roles. These activities are not relevant either to the task or the functioning of a work group. Such behaviors may include aggression, cynicism, domination, recognition-seeking, and so forth. These behaviors are primarily self-centered instead of group-centered. The person is more interested in achieving personal goals than group goals. For example, a student may campaign intensely to become president of the student body because it adds value to a resume or a job application.

Norms

norms

What are the rules I must follow on the job?

Roles provide a foundation for studying group norms. **Norms** are standards developed by group members for themselves. They are derived from goals and regulate performance. Norms of behavior can be classified as formal written statements, unambiguous verbal statements or nonverbal behaviors, or learned expectations. People must conform to these norms if they are to remain as members. Norms, like roles, are formed and changed through interaction.

Employees' norms may have either a positive or negative effect. Industrial studies show that norms of highly cohesive work groups foster conscientiousness and high productivity. Everyone is expected to pull his or her load and does so to help the group. Other norms of less cohesive work groups, however, foster slowdowns and socializing activities which reduce productivity. Some seem to be in business for the self and not the group, or all are in collusion against management.

The likelihood a person will accept a norm as a determinant of work performance increases with the ambiguity of the situation, the necessity for goal achievement, decreased self-confidence, and goal appropriateness. For example, when employees do not know what is expected of them, they become dependent on the group's behavior norm. When they are technologically dependent on one another, they are willing to stick to the work group's norms. When certain employees have low levels of self-confidence, they are more apt to conform to group norms. Similarly, when the organization's goals mesh with the individual's goals, the individual is usually willing to stay with the work group's norms. Such actions suggest how easy it is for many people to conform to what others do or say.

Conformity

A work group pressures its members to conform to its norms and often manipulates their behavior. The idea "everybody else is doing it" is powerful pressure and is the reason most people conform to a group's desires. Do you remember ever using the "Aw-mom-everybody-else-is-doing-it" argument? In the same way, people conform to the work group's norms that have the greatest effect on them at a given time. Consider the influence fellow workers could have on the rate buster on an assembly line or the new management trainee who wears different clothing than other group members. People want to conform because deviates are often rejected or isolated. Thus, group members have four choices: conform, change the norms, remain a deviant, or leave the group. The pressure to conform is described eloquently in the following statement.

Why do so many people conform to what everyone else is doing?

The spread of bureaucratic structures requires increasing conformity. This pressure reaches its highest form where corps of specialists are developed to uncover deviations and maintain records of merit and demerit. Here executives with festering egos demand superficial obeisance, if not a clear "yes." As all covertly battle for the enlarged package of honors and rewards that come at each higher level, seeming conformity is saintly and overt individualism is madness. . . .

To deal with the world, the organization must present an inviting exterior and a promise of superior execution. Swamped in doubts, the leader must have assurance of internal loyalty when he acts. Conformity is one assurance he rewards.[1]

Not all people do conform to norms. Some people deliberately behave directly contrary to group norms. (This anticonformity is actually conformity.)

CONDITIONS FOR CONFORMITY TO NORMS.   People conform to norms if they desire to continue membership or become prominent in a group. Similarly, employees conform if the work group is cohesive, if approval is

*What are the factors
that prompt
conformity?*

expected, or if the issue is relevant. These forces toward conformity may be internal (based on intrapersonal needs) or external (caused by others). To illustrate how conformity can be induced, consider three processes that people use to structure their behavior: deviance discomfort, enforcement, and internalization.[2]

Deviance Discomfort.   Some people will change their opinions about some highly objective matter (e.g., the relative length of straight lines) in the face of pressure. Solomon Asche experimented with groups that contained one genuine subject and others who seemed to be subjects but were allies of the experimenter. These allies were told beforehand to deceive the genuine subjects by unanimously agreeing on the wrong answer in a series of visual judgments. That is, subjects were shown three straight lines, all a different length. They were instructed to vote on the longest line. For the first two trials the allies voted for the obviously correct answer, but thereafter they voted for the wrong answer. Slightly more than one-third (36.8 percent) of the genuine subjects giving judgments agreed with the false group consensus. They apparently were so uncomfortable deviating from the norm set by others that they went against their own best instincts.

The peer pressure that brings deviance discomfort may cause a tee-totaling fraternity pledge to start drinking beer. Management trainees have been known to take up sports like golf or racquetball because most superiors and peers play them.

Enforcement.   Enforcement of conformity may take the form of a negative comment, sarcasm or ridicule, monetary fines for things like lateness or swearing, or even exclusion from the group. Many groups have a sergeant at arms to enforce the rules and norms. This person may be either officially or unofficially appointed to preserve order within a group.

Internalization.   Internalization is assimilating the work group's norms. Employees will act in a certain way because the group considers it right. The group's philosophy has become their philosophy.

Conformity is essential for any group to work smoothly. However, procedural conformity should not be confused with conformity in thinking. Conformity in procedure is necessary, but unthinking conformity to majority opinion can be damaging to the group's functioning and to an individual's personality. It can destroy a work group's cohesiveness.

---------------------------------- Cohesiveness ----------------------------------

cohesiveness

Cohesiveness is the group's ability to stick together. It relates to the internal strength of a group. Cohesiveness influences almost every facet of on-the-job behavior: conformity, social influence, interaction, motivation, performance, and satisfaction. In general, cohesive groups are more democratic, cooperative, and friendly; better oriented and coordinated; more orderly; more willing to accept the ideas of others; more attentive to one another; more insightful; and more productive than noncohesive work groups. One of the trademarks of the Japanese, for example, is their cohesiveness and productiveness as a group. They approach their group as a family. Cohesiveness sometimes occurs in nonwork situations, for example, with foreign or minority students on a college campus, prisoners of war, or tourists abroad.

What role does cohesiveness play on the job?

Cohesiveness exists because of the attraction a group has for its members. The more closely a group conforms to its norms, the more cohesive it is. Members are likely to find a group attractive if (1) its goals, programs, size, and position in the community are acceptable, and (2) affiliation, recognition, security, and emotional needs are met. For example, the stars of long-running television series like "Bonanza," "Gunsmoke," and "M*A*S*H" became a cohesive family on and off the screen. The chemistry that can flow among members of a group often leads to exceptional productivity, mutual supportiveness, and a closeness that baffles outsiders.

COHESIVENESS AND PRODUCTIVITY. Cohesive groups typically are more productive. Members take the initiative and help each other. As cohesiveness increases, the group's capacity to retain members and the members' tendency to participate also increases. However, cohesiveness increases productivity only if the group has high confidence in its leader. Productivity will tend to be low if confidence is low. A highly cohesive group has the power to bring about conformity to its norms and to foster acceptance of its assignments to roles. Also, a highly cohesive group provides for its members a security which reduces anxiety and heightens self-esteem. It increases morale.

How does group cohesiveness affect productivity?

COHESIVENESS AND MORALE. Morale refers to either positive or negative feelings a group has toward itself or toward its actions. It includes confidence, cheerfulness, and discipline. (Morale will be discussed in greater detail in Chapter 9.) As such, it is tied to cohesion and effectiveness. To illustrate: groups with high cohesion tend to be noisy, full of joshing, personal byplay, disagreement, and even argument. Work meetings of less cohesive groups are sometimes quiet, polite, boring, and apathetic.

How does cohesiveness affect job morale?

In multiproduct manufacturing companies like aerospace firms, employees' group identities are often based on projects to which they are assigned (e.g., RAM, APAB, Walleye, Pershing). This practice, which has practical value from the formal organization's standpoint, also provides employees with a psychological home within the organization, a group identity that may build considerable cohesiveness. After hours, sports teams, carrying their identities off the job, too, may compete with one another.

Morale, however, is not yet fully understood. For example, the famous Hawthorne, Illinois, studies at Western Electric showed that small-group morale rose because of certain social and personal factors. The theoretical hypothesis of this research was to discover the relationship between lighting in the work place and the productivity of employees. Productivity continued to go up despite different light intensities. The conclusion suggested that human relations was more significant in productivity than had been previously realized. People reacted to the attention they were receiving from the researchers.

However, other studies have indicated no consistent relationship between morale and productivity. Because of differences such as these, current research about morale tends to deal with it not as a single subject but as it accompanies other areas, such as motivation or communication.

COHESIVENESS AND COMMUNICATION.   Cohesiveness results in a greater desire among employees to communicate. It also encourages feedback by reducing inhibitions. The more cohesive a work group is, the more productive is its communication. Members of cohesive work groups ask for information they need because they do not fear appearing ignorant. They also disagree more. The person who feels a decision is bad raises questions. In organizations with low cohesiveness, people allow the group to take unwise actions rather than disagree.

Can cohesiveness be increased in a work group?

HOW TO INCREASE COHESIVENESS IN A WORK GROUP.   Leaders can do several things to create greater cohesiveness in their work groups.[3] (*See* Exhibit 3.1.)

--- EXHIBIT 3.1 ---

- **Give the group an identity.** *Highly cohesive work groups always work out ways to confer identity on their units. They are never allowed to forget they are a part of a group that is important to them and to the entire organization. In food firms like General Foods and General Mills, cohesiveness may be based on product groups such as frozen foods, breakfast cereals, frozen desserts, or soft drinks. When there is no group identity, conflict within and among groups is much more likely.*
- **Stress teamwork and recognize good work.** *Highly cohesive groups accept this basic principle: "I don't care who gets the credit as long as we win!" They compliment, offer help, recognize each other through social invitations, praise, and point out the importance of a member's actions.*
- **Set clear, attainable group goals and give group rewards.** *Highly cohesive groups have clearly specified, understood, and attained goals. Also, their members are rewarded for outstanding work. They are provided group incentives (e.g., across-the-board salary increases, letters of commendation, plaques, dinners, or other social affairs).*
- **Treat group members as people.** *Highly cohesive groups have leaders who go out of their way to treat members of their work groups as human beings and not as cogs in an inhuman machine. Group members know one another—their hopes, fears, aspirations, hobbies, families, and so forth. Each member is made to feel part of a team. The leader knows and respects him or her as an individual.*

CONFLICT VERSUS COHESIVENESS. Conflict is always present and unavoidable. We'll study this phenomenon in more depth in Chapter 16, but several rules for dealing with conflict are listed in Exhibit 3.2.

--------------------- EXHIBIT 3.2 ---------------------

- Level with the other person. Tell him or her how you *really* feel.
- Be specific about the behavior, attitude, or value that is the issue. How can someone change if he or she cannot understand what you want changed?
- Don't assume you know what the other person is thinking or feeling.
- Take your time. Think things over.
- Don't try to handle too many issues at once. Agree to discuss one issue at a time and to postpone unrelated issues. Don't save up a number of issues and then bring them all up at once.
- Don't attack the other person's self-esteem.
- Don't make unreasonable demands. Ask for changes the person can make, and consider compromises.
- Don't be afraid to admit your errors. Permit others to admit their errors gracefully.
- Don't assume the conflict is over until you check back with the other person.[4]

--------------------- Group Size ---------------------

Group size has a significant effect on individual and group performance, organization, conformity and consensus, and member satisfaction. As the size of the group decreases, the strength of member relationships increases. However, effective groups may be either large or small. The key is *leadership* (which will be discussed in detail in Chapter 5).

What's the best size for a group?

--------------------- Large Groups ---------------------

According to most definitions, large groups are those with more than twenty members. One of the advantages of large groups is their greater variety of resources for solving problems. For example, each group member has a different set of past experiences, habits, ways of looking at things, and patterns of thinking. These can contribute to deeper insight and more ideas for possible solutions. In any large group of people, some will be practical, some dreamers of the impossible; some will think big, some small; some will be spendthrifts, some will hoard.

There are also disadvantages to large groups. Research shows larger groups tend to break into subgroups with divergent goals. Also, even though large groups have more resources, they diminish the role a member can play and the contribution each can make. Consensus becomes more difficult to reach. Even though an increase in size increases the chances of getting a competent person, it also increases the possibility of adding an incompetent person.

—————————————————— Small Groups ——————————————————

Estimates of an optimum group size for solving problems range from five to seven. For example, groups of four have been shown to be slower solving concrete problems than groups of two, but faster solving abstract problems. Consensus, interaction, and satisfaction are all higher in groups of five than in those of twelve. Accuracy of decision is better in groups of six than in those of two or three persons. And member satisfaction is greater for groups of five persons than either larger or smaller groups. In general, research concerning the relationship of group size to productivity indicates ideal productivity appears to vary inversely with size.

In groups larger than seven members, the silent ones tend to move to the fringes or to talk only to the leaders. In groups of thirteen or more, five to seven people often hold the discussion while the others watch and listen. If members are added to the small group, it will gradually form two groups or the organizational pattern will change to a large group.

Optimum group size depends on the situation. The key factors are the amount of coordination required, task complexity, and urgency of the problem. The most productive groups are the ones small enough for all members to communicate face to face. Room arrangement aids this type of interaction. For example, if a small group meets around a table or sits in a loose circle, communication is usually enhanced. Therefore, the central element of any group's effectiveness seems to be its member's interactions.

—————————————————— Effective Work Groups ——————————————————

In identifying the characteristics of small groups (definition, structural types, functions, and size) one must eventually concern oneself with effectiveness. Effectiveness is often measured in terms of the productivity and satisfaction of the group members.

—————————————— Characteristics of Effective Work Groups ——————————————

What makes a group effective?

The most productive groups are usually those which can best carry out the steps in the problem-solving process. Some other characteristics of a well-functioning, effective, creative group are listed in Exhibit 3.3.

Mature development and smooth functioning depend on answers to certain questions. For example: Can the members deal realistically with their surroundings? Do they agree about group goals? Can they understand why

---
EXHIBIT 3.3

- The atmosphere tends to be informal, comfortable, relaxed. There are no obvious tensions. People are involved and interested, with no signs of boredom.
- There is a lot of discussion in which virtually everyone participates, but it remains pertinent to the group's task. If the discussion gets off the subject, someone brings it back quickly.
- The group's objective is well understood and accepted by the members. There will have been free discussion of the objective at some point until it was formulated in such a way that the group members could commit themselves to it.
- The members listen to each other. Every idea is given a hearing. People do not appear to be afraid of putting forth a creative thought even if it seems extreme.
- The group is comfortable with disagreement. It does not suppress or override disagreements by premature action, but examines reasons carefully. The group seeks to resolve conflicts rather than to dominate the dissenter.
- Most decisions are reached by consensus: it is clear that everyone is in agreement and willing to go along.
- Criticism is frequent, frank, and relatively comfortable. There is little evidence of personal attack, either open or hidden. The criticism has a constructive flavor.
- People are free to express their feelings as well as their ideas both on the problem and on the group's operation. There is little pussyfooting. There are few hidden agendas: everyone appears to know quite well how everybody else feels about any matter under discussion.
- When action is taken, clear assignments are made and accepted.
- The chairperson does not dominate the group all the time nor does the group defer unduly to him or her. In fact, the leadership shifts from time to time, depending on the circumstances. The issue is not who controls but how to get the job done.
- The group is conscious of its own operation. Frequently it will stop to examine how well it is doing or what may be interfering with its operation.[5]

---

they do what they do? Can they learn from their experiences? Can they take in new information and respond flexibly to it?

If a group is motivated to cooperate, members will work toward a group goal. They will show more positive responses to each other, more favorable perceptions of each other and of their roles, more involvement, and greater satisfaction with the task. Similarly, the members of a cooperative group are less likely to work at cross purposes. They are more efficient and productive and better able to recall meaningful contributions as well as their own ideas.

What are the results of a cooperating group?

Improving Group Participation: Self-Disclosure

Each of us can work to improve group climate and productivity, by thinking of how we relate to other group members. For the best interaction to occur, we must both give and receive information about ourselves. We must willingly share ourselves with others.

Johari window

*What does your
personality look like?*

The process of sharing oneself with others is called self-disclosure. It is the willingness to communicate personal, private information. However, before one can share this information with someone else, one must know that information. One method of viewing self-disclosure is illustrated in Figure 3.1. This model is called the **Johari window,** named after its developers, Joseph Luft and Harry Ingham.

Think of the Johari window as a picture of the personality. The rows represent things people know about us and things we have not yet revealed. The two columns represent things we know about ourselves and things we have not yet learned. The four window panes are called the public personality, the hidden personality, the blind personality, and the unknown personality.

THE PUBLIC PERSONALITY.   Information you know about yourself and is also known to others is public information. In this area a person can both give and receive information freely. There is self-knowledge, understanding of others, and open and straightforward behavior. The person is seen as honest and trustworthy. There is no guessing about what he or she wants or is thinking. The person is willing to lay the cards on the table for all to see. For example, accurate information willingly recorded on a resume or job application profiles one's public personality.

THE HIDDEN PERSONALITY.   Information known about oneself but not known by others is hidden information. For some reason it is kept secret. If asked to divulge certain data, the person might or might not, depending on the immediate benefits. We often want to know what everyone else thinks or where they stand on a particular issue before committing ourselves. Assuming that they learn more that way, some people prefer to listen. Some are afraid of involvement with others. Some may be keeping certain information private in order to manipulate someone else.

FIGURE 3.1
The Johari Window

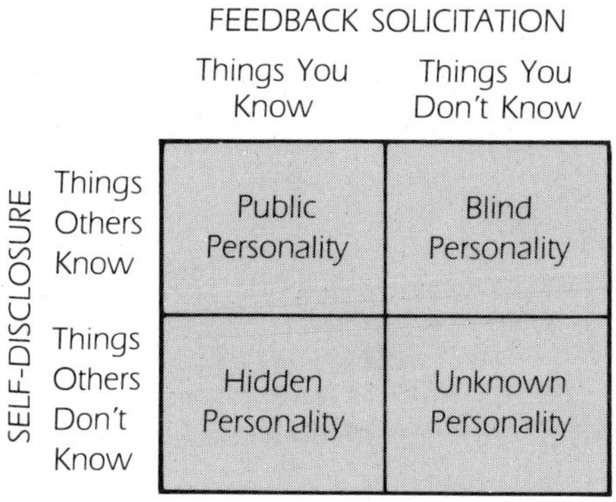

FEEDBACK SOLICITATION

For example, someone may work hard to obtain a promotion to savor the status and power the job brings or to be able to retaliate against certain former co-workers. Informed sources assert there was a drastic contrast between the hidden and public personalities of politician Richard Nixon and celebrities like the late Elvis Presley and Errol Flynn. What one saw in public may have been quite different from the way they were in private.

THE BLIND PERSONALITY.   Information known by others but not by one-self constitutes a blind spot. Such information could be very upsetting because the person may not get the reactions he or she expects. It can also be very upsetting to others when a person doesn't recognize the effect he or she has on them. Such people may bully their way into certain things, always insist on having their way, refuse to listen objectively, or want to give the orders. They never recognize these actions as negative features of leadership, but others do. They don't ask how they can improve, and others don't tell them. An example of blind personality might be the supervisor who behaves like Attila the Hun, ordering everyone to do this or that with little concern for human relations. Conquering the foe (employees) seems to be the major objective.

THE UNKNOWN PERSONALITY.   Information that neither the person nor anyone else knows is unconscious information. It represents a refusal to self-disclose and to solicit information from others. Someone might prefer to be in the dark about unexplored knowledge and abilities or feel he or she does have talent but has no idea what it could be. An example might be someone like Grandma Moses who never knew she could paint until late in life, or an actor like John Houseman who never acted until late in life. Both were unknowns who became famous.

A person's Johari window could look like any of the illustrations in Figure 3.2. It might change from one to the other depending on the situation. For example, on your first job after graduation, as you go through the first few days of on-the-job training, your unknown personality may be quite large. As you begin to learn more, your hidden personality may take over as you begin to ask questions about job operations. When you reach that point of confidence in how to do the job, you may be tempted to show

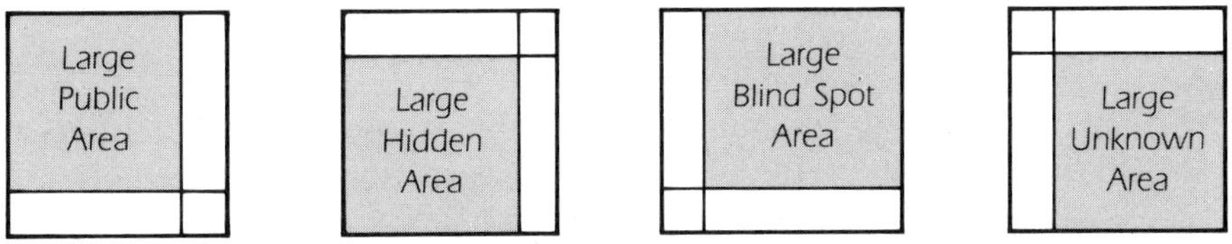

FIGURE 3.2
Johari Window
Possibilities

*How can I improve
my group
participation?*

everyone else how it should be done. Your blind personality begins to grow. Finally, when you reach the point of conscious competence, as you learn more about yourself and how to work with others, your public personality may be quite large. This is a worthy goal.

Therefore, we have two basic goals in improving group participation. First, we need to move hidden information into the public area, to self-disclose. However, not everyone is willing to share information. Some are willing only to pretend they are self-disclosing. To see this more clearly, visualize someone locked inside a prison, someone urged intrinsically to go out to others and yet afraid to do so.

The man in prison—and he is Everyman—has been there for years, although ironically the grated iron doors are not locked. He can go out of his prison, but in his long detention he has learned to fear the possible dangers that he might encounter. He has come to feel some sort of safety and protection behind the walls of his prison, where he is a voluntary captive. The darkness of his prison even shields him from a clear view of himself, and he is not sure what he would look like in broad daylight. Above all, he is not sure how the world, which he sees from behind his bars, and the people whom he sees moving about in that world, would receive him. He is fragmented by an almost desperate need for that world and for those people, and, at the same time, by an almost desperate fear of the risks of rejection he would be taking if he ended his isolation.[6]

This dilemma is faced by all of us at one time or another. Thus, there seem to be five levels of communication on which people relate to one another. (*See* Exhibit 3.4.) Each successive, descending level represents less willingness to communicate our selves to others.

─────────────────────── EXHIBIT 3.4 ───────────────────────

- **Level 1—peak communication**—*deep and authentic friendship, absolute openness and honesty, complete emotional and personal communication, perfect and mutual empathy.*
- **Level 2—our feelings**—*gut-level ideas, judgments, and convictions and our emotional, honest reactions to those ideas, judgments, and convictions.*
- **Level 3—our ideas and judgments**—*ideas and judgments revealed under strict censorship, attempting to be what pleases listeners.*
- **Level 4—reporting the facts about others**—*reports about what so-and-so has said or done; no personal, self-revelatory commentary on these facts.*
- **Level 5—cliche conversation**—*no communication except by accident, superficial and conventional, no sharing of persons at all, talk in cliches (e.g., "How are you?" "Just fine, thank you.").*[7]

Reaching level 1, peak communication, is not necessarily simple. To reveal oneself openly and honestly takes a great deal of courage.

---------------------- Feedback Solicitation ----------------------

The second goal in improving group participation is to move blind information into the public area by feedback solicitation. To do so, we need to ask questions about how we affect others. We will need to play the role of interviewer more often, to practice effective listening skills. For example, we must actively solicit feedback from those with whom we work.

CONCLUSION

By practicing both skills—self-disclosure and feedback solicitation—we gain more self-knowledge. The more self-knowledge we have, the better we can understand who we are. As the hidden and blind spot areas shrink in size, so will the unknown. We gain insight into the self and others. We grow and mature. As we understand the self, we can understand others better. As we open up to others, they too will self-disclose. This sharing and this understanding others are what human relations in small groups is all about. And the better we understand group membership, formation, development, functions, behavior, and size, the more effective our work groups will be.

KEY TERMS

Small Group: two or more people (but no more than twenty) interacting with one another face to face

Status: the degree to which a person possesses certain socially approved attributes

Role: a pattern of behavior that characterizes one's place in a group

Norms: standards developed by group members for themselves

Cohesiveness: the ability a group has to stick together

Johari Window: a human relations model that presents a picture of one's personality

QUESTIONS

1   Reread the opening case.
    a. Which of the following needs do the regular members of the landscaping crew satisfy in their relationships, and how?
        (1) psychological,

       (2)   goal achievement, or

       (3)   maintenance.

    b.   How might the regulars react if Bill continues to ignore the norms the group has set? Suggest how he could deal with these reactions.

    c.   Relate the three kinds of roles discussed in this chapter to the relationships that exist among Red, Sonny, Johnny, and Bill.

    d.   Recommend actions the company's owner might take to increase group cohesiveness and resolve potential conflicts among the regulars and summer or part-time workers.

2   Choose one of the following groups to which you belong. Why did you join it? What satisfactions do you receive from membership?

    a.   social or service fraternity or sorority,

    b.   volunteer service organization,

    c.   student government,

    d.   political action group,

    e.   student organization (newspaper, literary magazine, or other),

    f.   intramural sports team,

    g.   study group,

    h.   informal work group, or

    i.   other.

3   Analyze a small-group activity that you participated in recently. How did it parallel or deviate from the sequence described in the group development section of this chapter?

4   Diagram the status hierarchy of the group that you selected in item (2). What determined your position in the hierarchy? Who, if anyone, holds a position superior to yours? Why?

5   Contrast task roles with maintenance roles. How do they relate to human relationships in an organization? What effect do self-centered roles have?

6   Discuss the advantages and disadvantages of conformity in each of the following groups:

    a.   squad of Army infantry,

    b.   task force assigned to develop a new company advertising slogan, and

    c.   committee to select the homecoming theme for a university.

7   How does cohesiveness affect a group's productivity, morale, and communication? How could cohesiveness be increased in at least two groups to which you belong?

8   What effect does self-disclosure have on group productivity? Provide specific reasons why people may be reluctant to disclose very much about themselves.

9   Which pane in the Johari window fits you best at the present time? What would you have to do to improve your view? Are you willing to do that? Why or why not?

10   Describe the following steps in group formation and summarize what occurs during each:

    task-orientation→confrontation→cohesion→problem solving

11   List at least three goals that you achieved within the past year through group action. Could you have reached these goals without the help of the group? Why or why not?

12 Think of a group that satisfies one or more of your psychological needs. What would you do if you suddenly found it impossible to interact with this group? Would you feel compelled to join another that provided similar satisfactions? Why or why not?

13 Discuss how at least two of the following groups can provide maintenance or strengthening to their members:
    a. employee grievance committee,
    b. union,
    c. student government organization,
    d. club for retired company employees,
    e. organization of families whose relatives were declared MIAs in the Viet Nam war,
    f. club for single persons,
    g. university alumni association, or
    h. chamber of commerce.

14 Describe the role of norms in group behavior. What are they derived from? List several situations that would make someone likely to accept a group's norms as determinants of work performance.

15 Comment on this advice given by a senior state legislator to a junior colleague: "To get along, go along."

16 How does cohesiveness relate to productivity, morale, and communication? Suggest what leaders can do to increase cohesiveness in their work groups.

17 Discuss the advantages of large groups. What will probably occur if a group becomes too large? How does size influence a group's productivity?

18 List at least five characteristics of a well-functioning, effective work group.

19 Summarize the four panes of the Johari window:
    a. public,
    b. hidden,
    c. blind spot, and
    d. unknown.
    Why may it be advantageous to enlarge your public area? What causes some of us to avoid doing so?

CASES

Mike Ulmer, a supervisor for Interlachen Industries, recently attended a management seminar that included a presentation on the Johari window. The concept impressed him deeply, and he thought at length about how well he knew himself and how well others knew him.

Case 3.1

"You know," he confided to a fellow supervisor, "I really don't have much to conceal or be embarrassed about; my life's an open book. I think my workers might find it refreshing if I were a little more open and direct with them about my feelings as a boss and as a person. That Johari idea is pretty intriguing. We could all benefit from it!"

Mike made a concentrated effort to give his personality a facelift. During coffee breaks with employees, he freely aired his views on topics such as abortion, homosexuality, and top management decisions that applied to their plant. He asked their advice on a problem with his fifteen-year-old daughter (she was caught smoking marijuana) and discussed the benefits he had received from psychotherapy after his divorce.

Not long ago Mike noticed that two of his workers appeared to invent something to do whenever he joined the group in the coffee lounge during break time. Agreeing with everything he says but volunteering very few opinions of their own, three others treated him with a blend of patronage and suspicion. He overheard several of them having a private discussion that unmistakably focused on him. There were remarks like, "Mike's really gotten *weird,* man!" and "Ask him anything about himself and he'll tell you—complete with details. I think he's gone off the deep end!"

Although Mike felt more relieved because he started disclosing his feelings instead of bottling them up, he's now concerned that he has overstepped the boundary separating supervisors from their employees and that he has upset the group's equilibrium.

Case Questions

1 If you had had the opportunity to talk with Mike before he started his self-disclosure campaign, what advice would you have offered?
2 What risks do managers encounter when they decide to enlarge their public personalities with employees? with peers? with superiors?
3 How does the motto, "Engage brain before putting mouth in motion," apply to this case?
4 What standards would you apply when deciding how much of yourself to make public and how much to keep hidden?
5 What future action would you suggest to Mike?

Case 3.2

Yamasuki Motor Company of Japan recently built an automobile manufacturing plant in Cleveland, Ohio. Shortly after it opened, the United Auto Workers union began attempts to organize the assembly-line workers. Prounion workers started wearing to work caps, buttons, and patches with UAW insignia.

Soon afterward management passed a policy on dress requiring workers to wear plain white coveralls without exposed buttons, buckles, or other objects that could scratch the paint on the cars. Workers were told that a uniform appearance would also foster esprit de corps and a sense of unity and identity among workers, thus leading to a better-quality product.

Yesterday, George Dow, a worker acting as spokesperson for the others, requested a conference with the plant manager.

"We can go on strike, union or not, if you're going to make us look like clones," he stormed. "That's undignified. We're individuals, and we should have the right to dress as we please! Besides, we think you really just want to frustrate the union's organizing efforts."

"That's not the idea at all," countered plant manager Yoshi Sigura. "We've explained that we feel the practice will contribute to product quality and employee identification. It has nothing to do with being antiunion or trying to destroy your individuality!"

1 Discuss what group-formation goals management might have. What might be those of the workers? Do the two coincide? If not, suggest how management could try to reconcile them so both groups move toward the same goals for the same reasons.

2 How might plant management deal with this issue to minimize conflict and build the cohesiveness it desires?

3 Discuss the possible public, hidden, and blind personalities that each party in this case may have.

4 What measures would you suggest to improve understanding and disclosure between management and the workers?

NOTES

1. Melville Dalton, *Men Who Manage* (New York: Wiley-Hamilton, 1959), pp. 182–184.

2. Orlando Behling and Chester Schriesheim, *Organizational Behavior—Theory, Research, and Application* (Boston: Allyn and Bacon, 1976), pp. 150–155.

3. Adapted from Ernest G. Bormann et al., *Interpersonal Communication in the Modern Organization* (Englewood Cliffs, N.J.: Prentice-Hall, 1969).

4. Robert J. Doolittle, *Orientations to Communication and Conflict* (Chicago: SRA, 1976), pp. 23–25.

5. Douglas McGregor, *The Human Side of Enterprise* (New York: McGraw-Hill, 1960), pp. 232–235.

6. John Powell, *Why Am I Afraid to Tell You Who I Am?* (Allen, Texas: Argus Communications, 1969), pp. 50–51.

7. Ibid., pp. 54–64.

SUGGESTED READINGS

Asch, Solomon. "Effects of Group Pressures Upon the Modification and Distortion of Judgments," in Guetzkow, Harold S., *Groups, Leadership, and Men—Research in Human Relations.* Pittsburgh: Carnegie Press, Carnegie Institute of Technology, 1951.

Cartwright, Dorwin, and Zander, Alvin. *Group Dynamics—Research and Theory.* Evanston, Ill.: Row, Peterson, 1953.

Luft, Joseph. *Group Process: An Introduction to Group Dynamics.* Palo Alto, Calif.: National Press, 1963.

Mayo, Elton. *The Human Problems of an Industrial Civilization.* New York: Macmillan, 1933.

Rosenfeld, Laurence B. *Human Interaction in the Small Group Setting.* Columbus, Ohio: Merrill, 1973.

2

Essential Skills for Managing Human Relations

4

Managing Time

When you complete your study of this chapter, you should be able to:

1 Analyze how you spend your time,
2 Budget the activities of your work day,
3 Identify personal and professional time wasters, and
4 Control major time wasters.

—————————————— OPENING CASE ——————————————

At 6:00 A.M. Monday, Jana Cannon was awakened by her alarm clock. Because she had not gotten to bed until 1:00 A.M., she stole another fifteen minutes of rest. By 7:30 A.M., Jana was on the road to work at Unisource Incorporated, where she was assistant personnel director. Suddenly she remembered she had been asked to attend an emergency personnel conference that included her boss and several higher managers. They were going to review a new policy and procedure for hiring workers. Glancing at her watch and realizing the meeting had already started, she edged her Omni to sixty-five miles per hour. Shortly afterward she lost fifteen minutes waiting for a state trooper to write her a speeding ticket.

Upset about the way the morning was going, Jana rushed into the meeting thirty minutes late, offering her apologies. Her boss, the president, and the vice-president grunted in disapproval. After listening carefully to pick up the thread of their conversation, Jana's boss asked, "What's your response to this proposal? I asked you to read it over during the weekend."

"Oh, my gosh," Jana thought, "the proposal is at the bottom of my briefcase. I forgot all about it." Looking thoughtful she said aloud, "It seems basically sound, but I need more time to compare it with some of the case incidents we've had within the last year. I should have that done by Wednesday afternoon." She was relieved when no one pressed her further.

By 8:45 the meeting was over and Jana was back at her desk. The telephone rang, and when she answered it she knew something was wrong. Jack Swartz was calling to complain about the new person hired last week. "He didn't show up for work this morning," growled Jack. "Did he call in?" asked Jana. "No, and I need him badly. We've got six trucks coming in today that'll need unloading. See what you can do to locate him, huh?" "Okay, let me see if I can reach him at home," answered Jana. "His number's here somewhere. I'll call you."

Making a mental note, Jana headed for the receptionist's desk. On her way she stopped to congratulate several office workers who won the city industrial trophy in last week's bowling tournament. As the group broke up, Sam Merrill, a production foreman, asked Jana if he could get another clerical worker to replace the one retiring this month. Jana said she'd check the budget allocation and call him that afternoon. The receptionist interrupted saying, "There's a call for you from Bert McMillan on line three."

"We're having trouble getting all the materials ready for the first day of next week's training program," Bert said. "Can you stay late one day this week and help collate the notebooks?" "Sure," said Jana, "let me call you this afternoon and see which day is best for me. Right now though I think it's probably Wednesday.''

Returning to her office, Jana reviewed several disciplinary action reports from Emma Deils, a supervisor, then called Emma in to discuss them. They went over each one to make the necessary decisions concerning the employees. Jana's phone interrupted their discussion three times. It seemed that today everyone had a problem.

As Emma was leaving the office, Bryan Reston, the word processing supervisor, stopped in with several purchase requests that needed Jana's signature. While signing the forms, Jana asked Bryan, a boating enthusiast like herself, about his weekend. After they had both shared their weekends on the lake, it was 11:30. Bryan went back to the word processing center, and Jana answered another telephone call.

John Howard, the plant manager, wanted to know if she'd have lunch with him today in the executive dining room. He had some new ideas about expansion and how to handle shift work. Jana said she'd meet him in fifteen to twenty minutes. As she hung up the phone, she suddenly remembered Jack Swartz's absentee employee, Sam Merrill's request for budget figures, and Bert McMillan's request for late work. "Well, I haven't got time to take care of those things now," she thought. "I'll have to do them right after lunch."

I Haven't Got the Time

Time is a most precious and limited resource. Every manager knows that improved use of time results in greater productivity, higher performance, and better relationships. But who has the time to organize their time? One of the manager's most trying problems in organizational life is time management. Certainly it is one of Jana's major problems. Trying to finish up items left over from yesterday, to accomplish today's job, and to plan tomorrow's activities creates much pressure. The time problem is ever present. And by trying to solve their own time problems, many managers compound the organization's time problems. By improperly accepting and scheduling new assignments, they affect those around them. The organization misses deadlines and breaks promises.

What is the most precious and limited resource?

In Part 2, several managerial skills will be introduced. These skills are essential to productive human relations. They provide the means for dealing with the problems in Part 3.

The first skill is time management. This is discussed first because control of time allows a person to give adequate time to co-workers (and their problems). A person who cannot control work time will not be productive on the job. Time is life; a person who wastes time, wastes his or her life.

What is the profile of a manager who does not manage time well?

The typical profile of a manager who does not manage his or her time productively is someone who constantly is on the phone, has people in the office, forgets appointments and deadlines, takes work home, spends time socializing, and so forth. These time traps can be avoided by someone who starts scheduling and organizing time now. Set deadlines, work toward them, and reward yourself when you achieve goals. Control interruptions.

Understanding the Time Problem

What are some requirements of time management?

Time is unique in that it is limited, cannot be accumulated, and is unceasing. Everyone is a time consumer; therein lies part of the problem. Most collegiate management courses or management development programs teach people how to deal with money, material, and people—not how to manage the work day. But unless managers learn how to manage time, they will never be able to handle money, material, and people productively. Therefore, **time management** requires a desire to get more done, a willingness to plan, and a disciplined self to practice time-management techniques. It calls for changes in habits and attitudes. This is readily apparent in the opening case. Jana must decide where she needs to improve her time use and whether she is willing to spend the effort needed to improve.

time management

What is your attitude toward time? Many people feel time is against them, an enemy constantly sabotaging good results. Perhaps you've found yourself running out of time on some class project recently. Or maybe you've wished you had more time to visit with a new acquaintance.

Attitudes Toward Time

Why do some people find time management difficult?

People's attitudes toward themselves and others influence how much they expect of themselves and how much time and effort they will put into getting things done. Time management is primarily a matter of self-discipline; that is why many people find time management so difficult. Unable or unwilling to control the self—thoughts, habits, actions—they can't control their time. Instead they end up killing time, and, in one sense, committing suicide. Someone has suggested it is easier for most people to adjust to the adversity of failure than to take the time to adjust to the sacrifices leading to success. That is, we never have the time to do a job right, but somehow we always have the time to do it over. Time is not the enemy; we are.

Time Myths

time myths

People hold and practice myths about time that produce only frustration. **Time myths** are nothing more than false ideas of how people structure their time.

People hold many myths about time management, but the following ones are some of the more prevalent. See if you are guilty of any of these, then rid yourself of such erroneous thinking. Think how you normally react to your time use, others' time use, and the possible conflicts of time schedules.

What are some myths about time?

I HAVEN'T GOT THE TIME.   "I don't have time for that." Have you ever made that statement? What did you really mean? If your best friend asked you to do something for him or her, would you make the time to do it? Most people who make this statement mean that what they've been asked to do is not important enough for them to get involved. There are higher priorities needing their effort. If the request was sufficiently rewarding, they would find the time to do it. So the next time you're tempted to exclaim, "I haven't got the time," stop and ask youself why. You'll discover the time if you really want to do what is asked of you.

YOU HAVE TO DO IT YOURSELF IF YOU WANT IT DONE RIGHT.   Many people seem to think they are the only ones able to perform certain chores. In a few rare jobs this may be true. But mainly this attitude results from an overinflated ego. Few of us are indispensable. Perhaps the reasons we think this are, first, we are insecure in our job and don't want anyone else to know how to do it, or, second, we are so ill-organized we don't have the time to train someone else. The cures are to *organize* and to *delegate*. It is true you can do some jobs faster yourself. But it is also true many others can do the job just as well as you. By delegating, you are free to spend newly available time planning other activities better.

I WORK BETTER UNDER PRESSURE.   Those who claim to work better under pressure are often justifying proscrastination. Perhaps they are hoping that if they wait until the last minute to perform the task, they can rationalize a second-rate performance. But what will they do if the project ends up taking more time than they thought? Or, what if something goes wrong with the project? Pressure produces stress, and stress is destructive to your mind and body (as you will learn in Chapter 16). Do it early, and save worry.

Do people really work better under pressure?

THE HARDER I WORK THE MORE I GET DONE.   Many people seem to confuse activity with productivity. The two are not related, however. Those who are the most active are not necessarily the ones getting the most done. Just because you sweat a lot does not mean you produce a lot. Hard work is a virtue, but you can accomplish the same amount in less time by setting goals and meeting them. Busyness should not be a basis for rewards in organizations; accomplishment should be. Results seldom equal the amount of time spent on an activity.

I Am Most Effective When I Am Most Efficient.   Efficiency and effectiveness are not the same thing, as you learned in Chapter 2. Efficiency refers to capability and productivity. It is measured by comparing production with the costs of energy, time, and money. Effectiveness is equipping someone for active service. It is the accomplishment of a decided or desired response. For example, you are taking college courses now to improve your effectiveness in present or future jobs. It is possible to be efficient, however, without being effective and vice-versa. Efficiency demonstrates power or skill in producing results. This is why effectiveness must precede efficiency.

─────────────────── Self-Analysis ───────────────────

time analysis

In some areas of time use you are probably quite productive. In others, you are less productive. We can improve our overall use of time by learning **time analysis,** a technique for learning how to use time effectively.

How can I improve my use of time?

Learn Where Your Time Goes.   For most people, work is as necessary as eating. Yet many feel they work too hard. There is always more to do, it seems, than they can get done. Research shows, however, that many busy people could get their jobs done better, as well as more quickly, easily, and productively, if they paid more attention to where their time goes. For example, people are working too hard who fall into the traps listed in Exhibit 4.1.

─────────────────── EXHIBIT 4.1 ───────────────────

- They are not working at the kind of job they do best.
- They are working to satisfy an unwanted goal established by someone else, rather than by themselves.
- They feel subdued by their job.
- They spend time and energy on work that they would normally devote to human relationships.
- They spend all their working time doing routine work and never get to the interesting, creative, meaningful, and *rewarding* work.
- They feel guilty when they are *not* working.
- They are doing a job for which they are not qualified by ability, experience, and training.
- They never let problems take care of themselves.
- They have no say in what they do in their work, or how they do it.
- They are trying to do a job alone that could be done better by a team—or they are trying to do a job by a team that could be done better alone.
- They don't think of the work they do as being of service to someone else.
- They have work that sends their blood pressure soaring, or tightens up their stomach muscles, or gives them headaches, or keeps them awake nights, or causes them to drink too much, or gives them other symptoms of stress.
- They produce more wealth and security than they need and have time to spend.
- They haven't found a way to increase their productivity in the last thirty days.[1]

Work can become healthy, creative, enjoyable, and more productive if it is under control. Do you manage your time, or does it manage you? The keys to effective time management are thinking and planning ahead. To do that, analyze how you presently spend your day. Become conscious of what you're doing moment by moment and decide what you want from your time. You cannot manage your time if you don't know what's going on within and around you. Thus, keep a record for a week or two showing exactly how you have used your days. Such a record is provided in Figure 4.1. Write down everything you do and how long it takes. Then appraise each day and decide whether you spent your time wisely or whether you wasted it.

Will daily time analysis help?

Date		Time Wisely Spent	Time Wasted
Time	Activity		
6:00			
6:30			
7:00			
7:30			
8:00			
8:30			
9:00			
9:30			
10:00			
10:30			
11:00			
11:30			
12:00			
12:30			
1:00			
1:30			
2:00			
2:30			
3:00			
3:30			

FIGURE 4.1
Time Analysis Sheet

FIGURE 4.1 cont.

Time	Activity	Time Wisely Spent	Time Wasted
4:00			
4:30			
5:00			
5:30			
6:00			
6:30			
7:00			
7:30			
8:00			
8:30			
9:00			
9:30			
10:00			
10:30			
11:00			
11:30			
12:00			

Date _____

Sometimes we must make the most of *minutes* as well as hours. One noted humor columnist, a harried homemaker with several children, began her writing career by putting a portable typewriter on her kitchen table. She rapped out ideas and impressions whenever she had a spare moment, because it was virtually impossible for her to set aside a generous block of time under her circumstances. Making every moment count may let the busiest of us make small advances toward great accomplishments over time.

Some questions for appraising time use are:

• On which items am I spending too much time? too little time?
• Am I doing something that does not need to be done, or that could be done by someone else?
• On which activities can I make the most important time savings?
• Are any of my activities interfering with the time of others?
• Could I combine several activities for simultaneous accomplishment?

These questions can help to identify how much time you have for working on tasks. Large chunks of time should be available for big projects. It is also a good idea to have a hideout where you can work in total solitude. One chief executive officer has a secret office in his headquarters reserved for this purpose. It's furnished with a desk, chair, phone, writing materials, and dictating equipment, but no one aside from family members knows the telephone number.

Unless we can measure how our time is spent, we may never be able to coordinate it. One-quarter of the working day, if consolidated in large time units, is usually enough time to get the important things done. But three-quarters of the working day are useless if that time is only available as fifteen minutes here or thirty minutes there. After listing your activities for two weeks (in Figure 4.1) you'll have a clear picture of what blocks your effective time use. Then you can start to remedy the situation by budgeting your time.

BUDGET YOUR TIME. After analyzing our time, we can begin better planning. Time, like money, can be budgeted. Figure 4.2 provides a typical schedule for achieving a balance between what must be done and the time available for doing it. This form of budgeting simply involves writing down the things to do and how long they should take. Columns also are provided for ranking activities in the order of priority and for checking them off as completed.

How do we budget our time?

Such a list should be made for each day, although the same format could be used for monthly or quarterly planning as well. It can be done at the beginning or the end of the day and updated. Decide which items must be done first, which ones can wait, and which ones can be delegated. The key is to *do the most important things first.* Thus, you may break your list into units of three to five items, those most important, next most important, and least important (A, B, C, etc.). You could then code the items in each unit (A-1, A-2, A-3 for the top three items; B-1, B-2, B-3 for the next top three items, etc.). This would immediately identify the best way to use time at any given moment to complete high priority items. A color code (e.g., using red for high priority items) or a simple numbering system (1 for most important, 2 for next most important, etc.) may be useful. Whatever method you choose, concentrate on the tasks which will yield the greatest results.

Management consultant and advertising executive Ivy Lee once recommended that Charles Schwab, president of Bethlehem Steel, develop a priority list each day and work through it until each item was completed. Lee asked Schwab to try the system and send him a check for whatever Schwab thought it was worth. Several weeks later Lee received a check for $25,000.

If you are not accustomed to using a "To-Do List," try not to be too ambitious. It is possible to list so many items for one day that even two

FIGURE 4.2
Time Budget Form

List of Things to Do:

Date _____

Priority	Activity	Time Allotment	Accomplished
_____	_____	_____	_____
_____	_____	_____	_____
_____	_____	_____	_____
_____	_____	_____	_____
_____	_____	_____	_____
_____	_____	_____	_____
_____	_____	_____	_____
_____	_____	_____	_____
_____	_____	_____	_____
_____	_____	_____	_____
_____	_____	_____	_____
_____	_____	_____	_____
_____	_____	_____	_____
_____	_____	_____	_____
_____	_____	_____	_____
_____	_____	_____	_____
_____	_____	_____	_____
_____	_____	_____	_____
_____	_____	_____	_____

people could not do them all. Frustration and discouragement result from having more things to do than you can possibly finish. The key is to do first things first.

How will a priority list of things to do help me?

As you finish each task, check it off. This provides a psychological lift as you see how much you've been able to do today. And, if your supervisor wants to know what you've been doing, you'll have a ready reference. (Therefore, you may want to keep a month's supply of "To-Do List" accomplishments in a file or a notebook.) Unfinished tasks are transferred to tomorrow's list. Then you must get yesterday's business out of the way quickly in order to get to today's needs. Some people have an ongoing list rather than a daily list; this works best when each task may take many hours.

Using the "Time Analysis Sheet" and the "Time Budget Form" will help you to recognize quickly which items need immediate attention and which should be handled by someone else. After three months of following these programs, you should be saving at least two hours a day on the job—time you can spend in better planning and in organizing those who work for you.

IDENTIFY AND MANAGE YOUR TIME WASTERS.   Management has been called a series of interruptions interrupted by interruptions. These interruptions come from four primary sources: supervisors, employees, peers, and self. Without self-control, one cannot control the three other sources.

Who causes time-wasting interruptions?

Do you know what your biggest time wasters are? A **time waster** is any activity that causes you to use your time ineffectively. Respond to the questionnaire in Figure 4.3 before reading further.

time waster

If you have now identified your main time wasters, see how your list compares to some well-known time wasters in Exhibit 4.2. The four lists in this exhibit overlap, which suggests, perhaps, that some time wasters are universal. A discussion of these follows.

The Telephone.   Most people think of the telephone as a time saver, not a time waster. Certainly business could not function without such direct communication. It is vital. However, problems arise over frequency and length of calls. The average American business person spends about a year of her or his life on the telephone. Why should an important business executive always be available to the telephone? Having a secretary screen or hold incoming calls until a certain time of day is one solution. Or, a message recorder can avoid phone tieups and interruptions. The Bell System's Dimension phone system permits calls to be forwarded to another number automatically on the second or third ring.

How much time does the average person spend on the telephone?

Managers also could set times for making and receiving telephone calls. Or they could purchase a three-minute egg timer or time glass so socializing over the phone can be kept to a minimum. Everyone likes to hear her- or himself talk, but too much talk equals wasted time. Prepare for important calls by jotting down notes of what you want to say in advance, and be concise.

Meetings and Committees.   Complaints about meetings are widespread. Most companies have too many. The average business person spends a day a week in meetings, and most waste at least 50 percent of this time. For example, retailer Dayton-Hudson Corporation became so concerned with time lost in meetings that management formed a special task force to address

How much time do business people spend in meetings?

FIGURE 4.3
Leading Time
Wasters

Instructions: Check off your top ten time wasters from the list below and then rank them in order of priority. Number 10 is your most important time waster; 9, your next most important time waster, and so forth.

Time Waster	Top 10 (✓)	Ranking 1–10
Attempting too much		
Commuting		
Confused authority and responsibility		
Daydreaming		
Delays and missed deadlines		
Failure to plan and organize		
Family demands		
Handling mail		
Hobbies		
Inability to say no		
Indecision		
Inefficient, unclear information		
Lack of self-discipline		
Meetings		
Paperwork (reports, forms, records, etc.)		
Poor room or office layout		
Procrastination		
Reading		
Routine work		
Shifting priorities		
Socializing		
Special requests		
Stacked desk		
Telephone		
Television		

EXHIBIT 4.2

Some Well-Known Time Wasters

Of Managers[a]	Of Chairmen/women of Boards and Presidents[b]	Of Accountants[c]	Administrative Assistants[d]
Telephone interruptions	Telephone	Firefighting	Inability to say no
Drop-in visitors	Mail	Shifting priorities	Procrastination
Meetings	Meetings	Telephone	Attempting to do too much
Crisis management	Public relations	Procrastination	Lack of organization
Lack of objectives, priorities, and daily plans	Paperwork	Inadequate staff	Lack of clarity about agreements
Cluttered desk/personal disorganization	Commuting	Doing it myself	Failure to establish clear meaningful goals
Ineffective delegation	Business lunches	Drop-in visitors	Misplaced items
Attempting too much at once	Civic duties	Inability to say no	Failure to listen
Lack of clear communication	Incompetent employees	Involvement in routine detail	Routine task overdone
Inadequate, inaccurate, delayed information	Family demands	Socializing	Messy desk
Indecision and procrastination	Coping with government regulations	Attempting too much	Drop-in visitors
Confused responsibility and authority	Rumor mill	Meetings	Telephone
Inability to say no	Drop-in visitors		Supervisor
Leaving tasks unfinished	Bottlenecks		Unclear job description
Lack of self-discipline			Organizational red tape
			Getting coffee
			Too much work
			Correcting typing errors on duplicate copies
			Unnecessary company reports and memos
			Excessive meetings

[a] R. Alec Mackenzie, *New Time Management Methods for You and Your Staff* (Chicago: Dartnell Corp., 1975), p. 75.
[b] "The Top Ten Time-Wasters," *Fortune*, 6 November 1978, p. 76.
[c] Based on a two-year study (by the author) of participants in the National Association of Accountants' Continuing Education Program, Time Management, 1978–1980.
[d] Robert D. Rutherford, *Administrative Time Power* (Austin, Texas: Learning Concepts, 1978), p. 70.

the problem. As a result, the firm's chief executive officer eliminated most breakfast meetings and the time spent in the weekly top management meeting was pared two-and-one-half hours.[2]

Why are there so many meetings? to provide an audience for someone, to socialize, to escape from being productive, to pass the buck, and to fool people into believing that they are participating in important decisions.[3] Someone has even said that a committee is a group of unfits, appointed by the unwilling, to do the unnecessary.

One way to gauge the cost of a meeting is to use an Econometer, a Danish invention, which can be programmed with the salaries of the meeting's members and set to calculate the running cost of the gathering as time marches on. Another obvious solution to meetings is to have fewer meetings. However, many groups are slow to stop meeting because they can provide needed communication and coordination. Therefore, the rules listed in Exhibit 4.3 should contribute to both time and cost savings in meetings.

--------------------------------- EXHIBIT 4.3 ---------------------------------

- Don't have a meeting unless it is absolutely necessary.
- Invite only those people who should attend.
- Send an agenda to each person.
- Start on time, and keep on schedule.
- Stick to the subject; avoid needless discussion or controversy.
- Control participants who talk too much.
- Set a time limit for the meeting.

Some managers resort to timers that ring after an executive has had the floor for a certain number of minutes. Others have removed chairs, coffee, ashtrays, and other conveniences from the meeting room so participants cannot be too comfortably entrenched. A precise agenda with estimated time for each item may also help.

All committees that have accomplished their purposes should be discontinued. Also, every permanent committee should be evaluated yearly to see if it is useful and should be continued.

What can you do about people who stop by to visit, but do not have an appointment?

Drop-in Visitors.   Unannounced visitors from within and without an organization comprise a serious problem. Some people seem to prowl the halls looking for someone to interrupt with an "Excuse me, are you busy?" Then they proceed to visit anyway. Some of the solutions for drop-in visitors are: don't invite them to sit down; stand by the door; establish office hours; train secretaries to screen all visitors; and establish a framework before conversation begins. It is not always wise to discourage all drop-ins, however, since they do encourage communication and good human relations. The secret is to control the length of conversations.

One manager established a prearranged interruption code with her secretary to get rid of unexpected visitors or those who overstayed their welcome. She would press a button that lit up a light attached to the secretary's telephone, and three minutes later the secretary would announce, "It's time to make that long-distance call." This allowed the manager to excuse her guest gracefully.

Because people tend to respond to eye contact, some authorities suggest that you place your desk where you won't be seen by those who walk past your office. Some time-conscious managers position their desks so potential visitors must walk through the office door and make a hairpin turn to see if they are in.

Failure to Plan and Organize.   Goal setting helps people work faster and more productively. Managers need a game plan; otherwise, they will allocate time on a first-come, first-served basis. Yet many never set objectives or make overall plans. They have no perspective that allows them to decide which tasks are important and which should be ignored. Not only do they not have yearly or five-year plans, but they do not have plans for the next hour or day. Thus, they make the mistake of dealing with problems, not opportunities. The obvious solution is to start a to-do list (as in Figure 4.2) and work on first things first. Schedule high-priority items and impose deadlines. The more time you spend in planning, the less time you'll spend working. However, be flexible. About one-fourth of your day should be unscheduled to allow for unexpected interruptions. Another suggestion is to delegate all tasks too mundane for your attention. For example, a plant manager shouldn't be the one to run the flag up the flagpole each morning, no matter how patriotic it makes him or her feel.

How do I decide which task to work on?

In setting goals one should remember the 80/20 rule (or Pareto principle) about priorities. Simply stated, this rule says 80 percent of the value of the activities is concentrated in 20 percent of the activities. That is, you can be 80 percent productive if you achieve 20 percent of your goals. Again, though, the key is to concentrate on first things first.

Failure to Delegate.   Giving others jobs to do that neither you nor anyone else wants to do isn't delegation; it's assigning. Delegation is difficult for those who believe if you want something done right you must do it yourself. Surveys of top executives show that one-half of them are reluctant to delegate total projects; they believe their magic touch has to be placed on every job. Yet an excellent way to save time is to assign work to others who can complete the task. Proper delegation frees you from many routine matters. It allows you to train and develop others and build trusting relationships. Delegate.

Why are managers reluctant to delegate assignments to others?

How can I control the constant flow of paper?

Paperwork. The incessant flow of reports, forms, records, and correspondence never ceases. In fact, many managers view themselves as paper shufflers. However, there are ways to save time and to do less paperwork.

1. *Read faster.* Try to increase your reading speed. Look for key ideas and concepts rather than striving for entertainment. You might even wish to enroll in a reading improvement class.

2. *Decide what must be read.* The average business person spends about three months out of each twelve reading. Much of this time is spent reading things that should be ignored. Less than 5 percent of available literature produces over 50 percent of the information you need to do your job. Therefore, identify and use the information-rich sources in your career area and cut all unproductive reading matter.

3. *Do casual paperwork during your ''wasted time.''* Reading and scanning reports or organizing materials for a speech can be done while you watch television, wait in an airport, fly, or commute to or from work. Jobs that don't demand intense concentration can be done conveniently amid distractions.

4. *Handle each sheet of paper once.* Don't get into the habit of shuffling papers. Deal with the problem or request when you receive it.

5. *Delegate reading to subordinates.* They can then report important findings. Of course, this will increase meeting times. But one bank president finds this approach to work quite effectively. Each week he delegates certain reading material to his vice-presidents and then follows up on what they have learned from the readings.

6. *When in doubt, throw it out.* Perhaps this is the best advice.

Firefighting/Crisis Management. Crisis prevention is a worthy management goal. However, unexpected problems always arise and demand attention. Sometimes managers create crises by failing to plan and anticipate, by overplanning, by procrastinating, or by treating all problems as crises. It is more important to prevent new fires than to continually have to put out old ones. That is, prevention is preferable to correction, proaction to reaction.

Can anything be done about ambiguous data?

Inefficient, Unclear Information. Many times it is difficult to know what information is needed by whom. Sometimes the information is readily available; only it is not provided to those who'd benefit from it. On other occasions information is provided that is neither requested nor needed. Therefore, information processing requires criteria to discriminate among necessary, nice-to-know, or throw-away information. Hardheaded thinking is a must here because of the mountains of data that computers can produce with the touch of a button.

The biggest problem managers have is a failure to provide clear communications and to listen to what is provided. For example, people tend to lose half of what they hear immediately after hearing it. This necessitates time-consuming repetition. On the one hand, unclear and ambiguous information causes people to fill in the gaps with their own ideas—ideas that may be right or wrong. On the other hand, failure to listen creates unknown gaps. Either way, the receiver of the information will lose unless he or she asks questions.

Handling Mail.   Many managers like to handle their own mail so they will always know what's happening. Many go so far as to read everything, including junk mail. Some spend as much time as a day a week reading or handling mail. One solution to this time waster is to toss all third- and fourth-class mail into the nearest receptacle and arrange first-class mail for a specific reading time. Another is to clarify what your secretary may handle without your involvement. For example, telephone calls, mail, and letters with common themes can be processed according to a standard procedure; you deal only with the exceptions.

Is there a solution for all the mail I receive?

When you reply to mail, there are three rules to follow: (1) *Use dictating equipment or dictate to a secretary.* You can talk faster than you can write. (2) *Handle a sheet of paper only once.* Read it and respond. Don't get caught shuffling papers. A common mistake is to read a letter or report and decide to respond at a later date, and then when that later date arrives, to go through the whole process again. (3) If a short, fast answer is called for, *write answers on the original letter, photocopy, and mail.* Brevity and speed are preferable to length and delay.

Cluttered Desk.   We often think that the higher the stack of papers, the more important people are. Usually, however, people with cluttered desks are merely unorganized. There are reasons for cluttered desks: ego, fear of forgetting, procrastination, indecision, or poor scheduling. The remedy is to keep your desk clear of anything unrelated to the project on which you are presently working and to put no items on your desk until you're ready for them. Clutter tends to hinder concentration and to create tension and frustration. Clearing the desk, or at least organizing it, gets the day off to a good start.

Procrastination.   Finally, to control most time wasters that we have looked at, one must first conquer procrastination. That is, one must put an end to excuses for putting off. Some excuses are laziness, overwork, lack of time to consider a matter thoroughly. However, chronic procrastination may be caused by fear of failure, insecurity, depression, hostility, or compulsiveness. Although putting off a decision until tomorrow can sometimes be the wisest course of action, procrastination often results from indecision. That is why self-discipline is so important for effective time managers. They must *act* rather than procrastinate, do things they know must be done before they do things they want to do. They must develop willpower to control time.

What causes people to put things off until tomorrow?

Action is the key to conquering procrastination. First, sit down and get started on anything you've been postponing. Second, give yourself a designated time limit in which to finish, and stay with the job until you're through. Third, reward yourself when you've accomplished the task. For example, buy yourself a donut and cup of coffee.

--------------- Rewards of Successful Time Management ---------------

What can I expect in return for learning to control my time?

After all is said and done, it's up to you to manage your own time so it will do you the most good. You must *control* the time wasters. Getting rid of unnecessary activities increases productivity and leads to higher quality of time. These increases mean an upsurge in output and a release from the restraints of clock or calendar. Working on key tasks leaves time for thinking creatively and preparing for the future.

A statewide survey of lawyers by the Missouri Bar Association disclosed that lawyers who kept records of how they spent their time earned roughly twice as much as those who did not. An American Management Association survey of sales departments in 180 firms engaged in various lines of business showed that their outstanding salespeople were those who planned and organized their time and effort most effectively.

Other rewards include spending fewer hours working, being less frustrated, and having more time for people management (human relations). Managers who organize their time can give proper attention to training and development, make use of people's talents and abilities, and listen to their special ideas. This is the essence of productive time management: spending more time on people problems.

--------------- The Effective Time Manager ---------------

You have been asked to learn where your time goes, to adopt a time-budgeting plan, to identify your time wasters, and to apply controls to these time wasters. These steps are challenging, but their rewards are worth the effort. They can save at least an hour a day on the job—an hour that will benefit your organization. However, it is possible to manage oneself into a situation that's potentially dangerous to mental health. If time *mis*management becomes chronic enough, the frustration of too much stress on the job can cause a nervous breakdown or *burnout*.

It doesn't take a superhuman to stop the wasting of time. It does help, however, to have certain traits.

―――――――――――――――――― Helpful Traits ――――――――――――――――――

The manager who uses time wisely differs significantly from the manager who wastes time. For example, celebrated automobile salesperson Joe Girard, who for seven straight years sold more new Chevrolets than any other salesperson in the United States, did so through careful time management. He budgeted twenty minutes for each prospect (by setting a timer), and if he hadn't closed the sale within that time he moved on to another.[4] Other productive time managers, like Joe, possess certain characteristics.[5]

What are some helpful traits of effective time managers?

- *A good memory, a good filing system, or both.* They recall information when they need it, know the relative importance of each task, and know what needs to be done next. They use checklists and files when necessary. For example, create a bring-up file for items that will need your future attention. File these items chronologically by future date, and check the file daily for things that have come due for action. (Note, however, that some studies show 80 percent of everything filed is never referred to again).
- *Flexibility.* They are aware of the ever-changing environment and adjust their behavior to fit the situation.
- *Self-confidence.* They set priorities and stick to them. They steadfastly pursue the course planned without being distracted by trivia and conflicting demands.
- *Ability to maintain harmonious relationships with others.* This reduces time spent in friction, argument, and hostility.
- *Frankness in dealing with people.* They do not waste time getting to the important issues. They are direct.
- *Physical vigor.* They can work longer and more productively when necessary.

A manager may be called on to counsel employees about effective time use. The effective time manager can do this successfully.

―――――――――――――――――― Harmful Traits ――――――――――――――――――

Some traits interfere with productive time use. For example, nonproductive time managers usually possess the following characteristics.[6]

What are some harmful traits?

- *The need to make excuses, or explain past failures.* They only waste time by engaging in these activities.
- *Indecisiveness.* They then procrastinate and shift inefficiently from one task to another.
- *Perfectionism.* They work on projects long after reaching the point of diminishing returns.
- *Negative emotions.* Hostility, frustration, and worry interfere with clear thinking and good judgment and divert energy that would be better spent in getting things done.

- *Excessive tenseness.* Their thought processes and accomplishments are interrupted by excessive tension. Undue physical and mental fatigue shorten their time for productive work.
- *Insecurity, subservience, and undue defensiveness.* They waste time trying to impress others and building up their egos rather than trying to get the job done.

Thus, the best time managers are adept at planning, organizing, directing, controlling, communicating, and making decisions. The proof is in the results they produce.

CONCLUSION

In the final analysis, you have but two choices: *work harder or be smarter.* Continue to race the clock, or organize your time. Work longer hours or learn to do the same amount of work in less time. Strive for efficiency or contend for effectiveness. Which do you prefer? Time can be your ally, the moment you learn to organize it.

KEY TERMS

Time Management: the practice of time-saving techniques.
Time Myths: false ideas people hold about their time use.
Time Analysis: technique for learning how to use time effectively.
Time Waster: activity resulting in the ineffective use of time.

QUESTIONS

1 Reread the opening case.
   a. Recommend how Jana could manage her time more wisely by delegating authority.
   b. How would you evaluate her use of the telephone?
   c. What should she do to better prepare herself for the following day?
   d. What evidence do you see that others may be pirating Jana's time unjustifiably? How should she deal with such people?
   e. What benefits would you emphasize if you made the above suggestions to her as her time management consultant?
2 List at least four symptoms of a manager who manages time poorly. What makes time a unique resource?

3 Explode the following myths about time:
   "I haven't got the time."
   "If you want something done right, do it yourself."
   "I work better under pressure."
   "The harder I work, the more I get done."
   "I'm most effective when I'm most efficient."

4 Use the "Time Analysis Sheet" for one week, then write a one-page paper summarizing at least four ways in which you could improve the use of your time substantially.

5 List at least five symptoms of someone who is working too hard.

6 Suggest three questions you could ask yourself to determine if you are using your time wisely or wastefully. How can a time analysis sheet help you to determine if you are getting the most benefit from your working hours?

7 Discuss the value and construction of a time budget with priorities.

8 Conduct a time-wasting study with the other students in your class and compare your findings with those in Exhibit 4.5.

9 List the five biggest time wasters that detract from your studying time. What specific things can you do to reduce or eliminate each?

10 Consider the relationship of effective time management to academic success. Do you believe that successful students in rigorous academic fields owe their success more to efficient use of study time or to some inborn trait or gift such as a high IQ? Why or why not?

11 Pick a job, course assignment, or task with which you are most likely to procrastinate. Why is this so? How would you benefit by conquering this tendency? Do you care enough to do so? Why or why not?

12 Describe how at least one of the following persons can work smarter, not harder:
   a.   auto salesperson,
   b.   salesperson for industrial-strength cleansers,
   c.   window washer in office building,
   d.   auto mechanic,
   e.   chef, or
   f.   delivery truck driver for vending machine company.

13 In what ways can the telephone be a time thief? How can we use it to save time or at least to control the time it takes away from us?

14 List at least three rules that can save time and money with meetings. What are some of the more popular reasons for holding meetings?

15 Recommend actions that can discourage drop-in visitors. How would you discourage the person who habitually drops by for a chat every day?

16 How does the Pareto principle apply to setting priorities and managing time?

17 Relate the practice of delegation to effective time management. In what ways can subordinates benefit from delegation?

18 Summarize some rules of thumb for dealing with paperwork. How has computer and word processing equipment contributed to the paper explosion that managers have observed?

19 Discuss how these traits or characteristics can be valuable in managing time:
   a.   a sound memory and a sound filing system,
   b.   flexibility,
   c.   compatible relationships with others,

    d. self-confidence,

    e. frankness in dealing with people, and

    f. sound physical condition.

20 How can the following characteristics be counterproductive in managing time?

    a. explaining past failures,

    b. indecision,

    c. obsession with perfection,

    d. negative emotions,

    e. excessive tension, and

    f. insecurity and defensiveness.

CASES

TIME ANALYSIS LOG

Case 4.1

John Maule, Shipping Department Manager   July 25, 1983

A.M.

6:00–7:00   Put coffee on; bathroom chores; arranged briefcase with items to take to office; chose outfit to wear to work; fed cat; filled and ran dishwasher.

7:00–8:00   Left house; clocked different route to work (0.3 miles longer than usual route).

8:00–9:00   Emptied briefcase; checked schedule for day; assembled materials for 9:00 meeting; met with Owens to examine last night's orders packed; discussed Owens's plans for vacation.

9:00–10:00   Attended weekly meeting with plant manager; reviewed damaged shipment reports submitted by customers; discussed possible causes of damage.

10:00–11:00   Drafted performance goals for next six months; returned calls received late yesterday afternoon; met with Greg Ballard in his office to discuss Wilkins order; dictated memo to packers to mark it special handling.

11:00–noon   Sorted and read first-class mail; dictated replies as necessary; examined other mail as identified by secretary; drafted standard reply to customer inquiries on shipping charges and to job applicants rejected for lack of experience.

P.M.

Noon–1:00   Lunch and conference with sales representatives of Towson Scale Company and Porta-Pack prefabricated shipping containers. Filed notes and literature on these products for reference before next month's budget meeting.

1:00–2:00   Annual performance evaluation conference with Pete Walker, employee; scheduled meeting (same topic) with George Sellers for next week.

2:00–3:00   Interviewed two applicants for new shipping clerk's job; returned call of Ralph Holman, student, asking for information on traffic management term paper (referred to library).

3:00–4:00   Met with Gene Shackleton about grievance on sex discrimination (he was passed over for loading dock foreman's job); described procedure for taking grievance to higher level; made notes on this conference for future reference (Gwen Andrews promoted due to superior performance and qualifications; decision justified).

4:00–5:00   Sorted phone messages received after 3:30 into priorities, to be returned tomorrow; filled briefcase with reports to read tonight.

Case Questions

1   What specific actions indicate that John Maule is applying good time management principles? How will he benefit?
2   Do you find evidence that he could improve his approach to managing time? If so, how?

Case 4.2

Jerry Townsend, a college freshman, had a five-page research paper due at 1:30 P.M. on Friday. He started outlining the paper Monday night at the library. However, he met some friends there who wanted to go drink beer. Recalling the three classes he'd attended that day and the long semester ahead, Jerry decided to have one last fling and went along.

On Tuesday night his girlfriend called long distance and talked until 8:30 P.M. Believing that the evening was already shot, he played poker with the guys next door. On Wednesday night he returned to outlining his paper but was interrupted by three drop-in visitors, trips to the coffee pot and bathroom, and work breaks during which he tried to solve Rubik's cube. Frustrated, he went to bed resolving to finish his outline early the next morning. His alarm clock did not go off, which left Thursday night to write the paper.

He got sick at lunch Thursday afternoon and spent three hours at the campus infirmary. Feeling rotten, he went to bed at 6:00. He skipped all classes Friday morning to work on his paper, but by 1:30 he still did not have it typed. He asked the professor for an extension until Monday, explaining his dilemma.

Case Questions

1   Describe a time when, like Jerry, you missed completing an assignment because of various time constraints. Now read the case from the professor's standpoint. Would you grant him an extension? Why or why not?
2   Analyze Jerry's time management tendencies. How could he have changed his week's activities to have written the paper on time?
3   Do people tend to manage their time more effectively as they grow older? Why or why not?

-------------------------------- NOTES --------------------------------

1.   Richard R. Connarroe, "You're Working too Hard!" *American Way* (December 1976): 32.
2.   Laurel Sorenson, "Time Wasted by Meetings Irks Business," *The Wall Street Journal,* 24 September 1980, p. 33.
3.   Michael LeBoeuf, *Working Smart* (New York: McGraw-Hill, 1979), pp. 128–131.
4.   "Joe," *Newsweek,* 2 July 1973.
5.   Charles C. Gibbons, "Time: You Can Make a Friend of a Foe," *Supervisory Management* (March 1972): 11.
6.   Ibid.

—————————————— SUGGESTED READINGS ——————————————

Carlisle, Arthur Elliott. "MacGregor," *Organizational Dynamics* (Summer 1976): 50–62.

Lakein, Alan. *How to Get Control of Your Time and Your Life.* New York: Wyden Books, 1973.

Mackensie, R. Alec. *The Time Trap.* New York: McGraw-Hill, 1975.

Oncken, William, Jr., and Wass, Donald L. "Management Time: Who's Got the Monkey?" *Harvard Business Review* (November–December 1974): 75–80.

5

Leading Others

When you complete your study of this chapter, you should be able to:

1   Explain how one can develop leadership skills,
2   Describe how leadership emerges within work groups,
3   Discuss leadership traits, styles, and situations, and
4   Function as a leader through communication, results attainment, priority establishment, empathy, and group maintenance.

Bob Waller was recently promoted to supervisor at America's Fantasy, a 5000-acre amusement complex containing rides, shops, hotels, and restaurants. Promoted as a self-contained vacation extravaganza, the complex employs more than 20,000 people. Bob supervises fifteen workers who operate the Screamin' Demon, a roller coaster ride reported to be the most thrilling one in the nation. In the past, guests have demanded a refund of the park admission fee if the Screamin' Demon was closed down.

The ride has malfunctioned at least once every two days in the past four weeks. Some problems have been a loose track, oil on the braking system, burned out wheel bearings, and a short-circuit in the master control panel. Guests have become very angry each time a problem occurs, and in one case they nearly started a riot.

Last week Bob discovered that most of the malfunctions have probably been sabotage. A friend who worked in another part of the park quit and on his last day shared some surprising news with Bob.

"Most of the people who work on that ride couldn't stand Mel Gerber, the guy before you. He came on like a drill sergeant, looked out only for himself, and never communicated anything up or down. Rumor has it that your people caused breakdowns just to hassle him. I think you ought to know, though, that they've turned it into a game taking turns to see who can dream up the most original problem. According to scuttlebutt, they're going to keep it up as revenge against the whole system, no matter how they feel about you. Trouble is, one of their cute tricks is going to backfire sooner or later and somebody's going to get *killed* on that thing! You're the boss now, and I hope you can straighten the mess out. Good luck!"

Leadership

What is leadership?   Before *Star Wars* the people who came from space always demanded, in the first words they uttered, "Take me to your leader." In some respects these are very important words. We are always interested in who the leader is, and we often decide to join a group (or not) because of its leader.

Leadership is an important aspect of human activity. In any problem-solving situation, leaders play a key role. They model the behavior expected of followers. Although leaders can be found in any social arena—government, business, industry, and education—what leadership is remains elusive.

Leadership definitions involve key functions such as achieving a proper balance between completing the task and maintaining a spirit of teamwork and harmony. Thus, **leadership** might be thought of as influence directed toward others in a given situation in order to obtain a specific goal. Leadership is a dynamic relationship between leaders and followers and affects a work group's activities toward goal setting and achievement. However, leadership is not management, even though the two terms are often used interchangeably. Leadership is only one aspect of management. It deals directly with people, whereas management may be nonbehavioral and not deal directly with people. In any study of leadership we must consider not only the leader but also the followers and the situation. All groups define their concept of leadership and influence their leaders. In addition, leaders define their concept of leadership and thereby influence the choice of leadership techniques. This is why leadership skills don't happen strictly by accident. They must be developed.

leadership

Leadership Development

There are several ways to learn to lead others. Some have learned to lead through trial and error. However, the necessary skills may be learned more systematically, in one of three ways. (1) One can enroll in a formal educational program such as a college or a university and take a course in human relations, business administration, management, or liberal arts. (2) One can enroll in any of the hundreds of leadership development programs, camps, or retreats offered yearly to educate people in current human relations and managerial concepts. (3) One can read regularly from *Business Week, Fortune, Harvard Business Review, Personnel Journal,* the *Wall Street Journal,* or similar publications. Many major publishing houses have separate divisions to publish books in various career fields.

What are the necessary skills for developing leadership?

Of course, any of these options will not by themselves make someone into a leader. Leadership development requires a combination of effort and experience. It is aided significantly by a conscious desire to improve leadership effectiveness and by daily opportunities to try to do so.

However one decides to gain leadership knowledge, the most important factor in leadership growth is willingness to grow. In your job search, look for an organization that encourages personal growth and advancement. As you mature within a growth-producing climate, your natural leadership abilities will emerge.

Leadership Emergence

Leadership emergence occurs as leaders achieve status gradually by demonstrating superior abilities or behaviors. This takes place in two stages. In the first stage during group interaction some group members do not take part, and others seem uninformed or unskilled. A few members, however, stand out. They often are very active and loud, and take strong, definite

leadership emergence
How does a leader emerge within a group?

stands. Naturally this does not always hold true. A person who speaks seldom and quietly, but makes better sense (or appeals most strongly to the group's norms), may win the informal election that soon follows.

In the second stage there is intense competition for top billing among the active members. One or two members may gain the support of others, until eventually only one candidate for leader remains. There is, in a sense, an informal election of a leader. As this leader appears, the status levels of the other group members fall quickly into place.

This process of emergence may occur in either a formal or informal organization. A formal organization, as you will recall from Chapter 2, relates to the company's organization chart, showing the chain of command within the organization. An informal organization departs from formal tasks and hierarchy and creates its own channels of communication and dependence. Both types of organizations are vital and have their own leaders.

Approaches to Leadership

There are many ways to study leadership—some rather exotic, some more realistic. For example, one early method of predicting leadership ability was *phrenology,* the study of the exterior contours of the skull. Another method was *graphology,* the study of a person's handwriting. Some people looked to *astrology* for leadership clues. Although these methods are interesting, they hold little valuable information about productive leadership. However, there are approaches that are more concerned with some of the basic aspects of leadership: traits, styles, situations, power, and functions. These are the approaches we will look at in this chapter.

Leadership Traits

Which traits of leadership are most crucial?

Early leadership researchers summarized leaders' qualities and assumed these traits were innate. Leadership effectiveness could be explained by noting potential ability and personality characteristics of a leader and other group members. Think about the many leaders who have influenced United States and world history. Each of the following possessed some trait that influenced the masses: John F. Kennedy, Helen Keller, Billy Graham, Martin Luther King, Golda Meir, Winston Churchill, Adolph Hitler.

Exhibit 5.1 lists some common characteristics of leadership. However, not all successful leaders appear to possess all these traits. Think about the current student body president or fraternity or sorority presidents at your school. Which traits do they exhibit?

The three most crucial traits of leadership seem to be maturity, inner motivation, and people-centered attitudes.

EXHIBIT 5.1

A Sample List of Leadership Traits

- ability
- alertness
- cheerfulness
- common sense
- communication skills
- consideration
- courage
- courtesy
- creativity
- critical thinking ability
- decision-making skills
- dependability
- empathy
- enthusiasm
- faith
- flexibility
- foresight
- human relations attitude
- imagination
- influence
- initiative
- inner motivation and achievement drive
- intelligence
- judgment
- justice
- loyalty
- manner
- optimism
- originality
- perceived occupational level
- perseverance
- personality
- responsibility
- scholarship
- self-confidence
- self-control
- social maturity and breadth
- socioeconomic status
- tact
- versatility

MATURITY.   Leaders are emotionally stable and mature. They tend to have a broad range of interests and activities. They also have healthy self-concepts, are self-assured, and respect others. They can convey ideas, and understand and motivate others. They are neither defeated by failure nor overjoyed with victory.

INNER MOTIVATION.   Leaders are motivated to keep accomplishing. They enjoy responsibility and strive for intrinsic (internal) rather than extrinsic (external) rewards. These two distinctions refer to whether a reward is valued for itself (intrinsic) or is seen as a means of acquiring some other value (extrinsic). Money, policy, and security could be considered extrinsic motives; achievement, recognition, and growth could be considered intrinsic motives.

Seeing their work group move smoothly and productively toward their goal in turn motivates the leader to do more for the group. Leaders work for success and set an example of hard work. They don't have to be complimented, praised, and rewarded at every turn to stay motivated. As they reach one goal, they aspire to a new goal. One success becomes a challenge to greater success.

PEOPLE-CENTERED ATTITUDES.   Leaders recognize the worth and dignity of their followers and realize they can lead only as long as followers cooperate. They strive to understand human relations and to respect others.

They understand their own feelings and motivations and accept others'. They perceive their employees in positive, favorable ways rather than negative and suspicious ways. No thought is given to manipulating others to further selfish ends. A person-centered manager sets and follows ethical standards which govern the moral tone of the department and organization.

―――――――――――――――― Inadequacies of the Trait Theory ――――――――――――――――

Why do most people reject the trait theory of leadership?

Not everyone agrees with the trait approach to leadership. Since the 1950s most people have tended to believe leadership does not originate in inborn traits, since no one trait is consistently linked with leadership.

Trait studies do not discriminate between those qualities which facilitate ascent to leadership and those which enable it to be maintained; also, they do not distinguish between a good and a bad leader. Most do not establish whether, and which, leadership qualities exist before or after leadership is assumed. What a person needs to gain leadership in one group may be quite different from what he or she needs to maintain that leadership. Finally, no researcher has found the components of personality that lead to success, since it is so elusive. The study of a leader's personality in terms of traits involves debatable assumptions.

The *why* of leadership apparently resides in the contribution a person makes to the group and not in any one personality trait or even in a constellation of related traits. Thus, many researchers have looked to leadership *styles* as a better way to understand the nature of leadership.

―――――――――――――――――――― Leadership Styles ――――――――――――――――――――

What are the basic styles of leadership?

Those interested in leadership styles have been mainly concerned with autocratic and democratic behaviors. According to this approach, leadership behaviors range from leader-centered to group-centered. For example, at one extreme the leader decides and announces the decision to the group. At the other extreme the group sets the limits and decides. The leader is just another member of the group. In order along a continuum between these two extremes are:

- Leaders who announce their decisions and sell the group on the decision.
- Leaders who announce their ideas and invite reactions and comments before making the decision. However, they retain power on whether to use the comments.
- Leaders who present the issue but do not present their idea on it. Instead, they invite ideas and options from others. Based on these options, leaders make the decisions.
- Leaders who present the group with several options and allow them to choose among the given options.
- Leaders who state limits outside which the group cannot go, but permit the group to decide within those limits.[1]

The democratic (group-centered) leadership approach is usually preferred over the autocratic (leader-centered) approach. However, it is not always the most productive style. Therefore, leaders can vary their behaviors, depending on the situation.

A third leadership style is *laissez-faire*. This style is a permissive, hands-off policy, which implies a leader leads without leading. Because it is hard to describe, it has been discarded by many experts as a leadership style. Therefore, we will be primarily concerned with the autocratic (authoritarian)–democratic (participative) continuum. To determine where your leadership style falls in this continuum, stop reading and respond to the questionnaire in Figure 5.1.

Instructions: The following are various types of behavior which leaders may engage in regarding their followers. Read each item carefully and then put a check mark in one of the columns to indicate what you *would do* as the leader. Avoid indicating what you *should do*.

If I were the leader, I would:	Make a Great Effort to Do This	Tend to Do This	Tend to Avoid Doing This	Make a Great Effort to Avoid This
1. Closely supervise my employees to get better work from them.	_____	_____	_____	_____
2. Set the goals and objectives for my employees and sell them on the merits of my plans.	_____	_____	_____	_____
3. Set up controls to assure my employees are getting the job done.	_____	_____	_____	_____
4. Make sure my employees' work is planned for them.	_____	_____	_____	_____

FIGURE 5.1
Leadership Attitudes

FIGURE 5.1 cont.

If I were the leader, I would:	Make a Great Effort to Do This	Tend to Do This	Tend to Avoid Doing This	Make a Great Effort to Avoid This
5. Encourage my employees to set their own goals and objectives.	_____	_____	_____	_____
6. Check with my employees daily to see if they need any help.	_____	_____	_____	_____
7. Step in as soon as reports indicate my employees' output is slipping.	_____	_____	_____	_____
8. Push my employees to meet schedules if necessary	_____	_____	_____	_____
9. Have frequent meetings with my employees to keep in touch with what is going on.	_____	_____	_____	_____
10. Allow my employees to make important decisions.	_____	_____	_____	_____
	1	2	3	4
Totals:	_____ +	_____ +	_____ +	_____ = _____

What was your total score? If it was within the 10–20 range, you have a tendency toward autocratic leadership; 30–40, toward democratic leadership. If your score fell somewhere between 21 and 29, we probably do not have enough information to make a clear-cut distinction between autocratic-participative tendencies. However, this does not mean you are the laissez-faire, permissive type. The closer your score is to one of the preset distinctions, though, the more likely you are to prefer that style of leadership.

AUTOCRATIC LEADERSHIP. **Autocratic leadership** is a leadership style that emphasizes an authoritarian approach to management. Autocratic (or authoritarian) leaders are often seen as behaving with a minimum of group participation, and as giving orders and overemphasizing the group's tasks. They decide on the goals to be reached, set all policy, structure all tasks, and motivate the group (usually extrinsically) to accept these decisions. Also, they tend to be personal in their criticism, to praise people's actions, and to remain aloof from group participation. Thus, the value of autocratic leadership is questionable. Employees remain dependent and ego-centered. Little improvement is made in making decisions, cooperating, and learning. Progress in understanding others is limited. However, it is preferable to democratic leadership in *some* situations.

Theory X.   Autocratic leadership has been called traditional leadership. It is based on a set of management assumptions about employees that are labeled **Theory X.** These assumptions are as follows:

- The average person inherently dislikes work and will avoid it when possible.
- Most people must be coerced, controlled, directed, and threatened with punishment to get them to achieve organizational objectives.
- The average person prefers to be directed, wishes to avoid responsibility, has relatively little ambition, and desires security above all things.[2]

As you might suspect, people react differently to the Theory X approach. Some feel restricted and may react violently to this type of leader. Others enjoy the security provided by such a structure. Still others react very passively. Many reactions to a particular leadership style are, of course, based on stereotypes. For example, the autocratic leader is often seen as a ruthless dictator and the democratic leader as a compromiser. These ideas are hardly exclusive definitions. Employees' reactions, in all likelihood, will depend on their needs and the type of problem to be solved. However, we can safely say as long as Theory X assumptions exist in management philosophy, human potential and productivity will be stifled.

To illustrate the autocratic, Theory X approach to management, consider the following. A *Fortune* magazine article on autocratic managers presented these remarks by employees and by some of the managers themselves.[3]

autocratic leadership

What are the characteristics of an autocratic leader?

Theory X

Although successful, they were declared to be highly autocratic chief executives. *See* Exhibit 5.2.

———————————————— EXHIBIT 5.2 ————————————————

Employee Comments About Autocratic Leadership
- "Bright, very tough on people, likes to make decisions solo. Used to dress down peers as well as subordinates."
- "You either love him or you hate him."
- "You haven't achieved any standing if you haven't experienced his wrath."
- "Most glaring trait is his lack of feeling for people."
- "Thinks nothing of putting in eighteen hours, seven days a week. Always a hard driver and impatient."
- "Everyone has to be a superperformer. If you're insecure, don't work for him."
- "Demolishes anyone who blows smoke at him."
- "Creates aura of power and wealth and reminds people it all flows from him. They won't go to the bathroom without his permission."

Manager Comments About Autocratic Leadership
- "I like running a winning ball club ... that calls for total commitment.... If you consider that a sacrifice, you are in the wrong company."
- "I am very demanding ... won't tolerate laziness ... If you aren't prepared to bust your ass, you had better find another job."
- "I'm intense in everything I do and I expect that others will be too."
- "I don't know what my management style is.... Ask my superiors if they think I'm tough."
- "You not only let someone who has not been obeying you go, you do it publicly so everyone knows that breaking the rules brings immediate punishment.... We got rid of a bunch for the good of the rest."
- "Professionals never have a problem with me."

---

democratic leadership

What are the characteristics of a democratic leader?

DEMOCRATIC LEADERSHIP.   **Democratic** (or participative) **leadership** is a group-centered approach to leadership. The authority for leadership lies within the work group, and the group must maintain control over the leader. The leader is to facilitate communication, act as a resource person, and aid in employee development. This group-centered, participative approach allows for the most interaction and the attainment of common goals in problem solving. For example, democratic leaders clarify members' interests and goals, select problems of mutual concern, and focus thinking on the problem. They develop cooperation, respect the group members' evaluative abilities, aid in the visualization of alternatives, and assume members can make the proper decisions.

Theory Y.   Democratic leaders share a philosophy about each person's worth and potential. They believe in the value of group participation, a permissive group climate, and shared leadership. In contrast with Theory X, the participative attitude about work was labeled **Theory Y**. This more modern approach to leadership suggests the following assumptions:

- The expenditure of physical and mental effort in work is as natural as play or rest. (The average person does not inherently dislike work.)
- People will exercise self-direction and self-control toward objectives to which they are committed. (External control and the threat of punishment are not the only means to get people to achieve objectives.)
- Commitment to objectives is a function of the rewards associated with their achievement.
- The average person learns under proper conditions not only to accept, but also to seek responsibility.
- The capacity to use imagination, ingenuity, and creativity to solve organizational problems is widely distributed in the population.
- The intellectual potential of the average person is only partially utilized.[4]

Theory Y appears to be the more positive approach to leadership and usually results not only in higher morale but also in higher productivity. The leader is much more objective in praise or criticism and tries to be a regular member of the group without doing too much of the people's work. All policies are a matter of group discussion and decision. The leader encourages and assists.

Success and Democratic Leadership. A study of 16,000 higher managers strengthens the premise that a democratic, Theory-Y-oriented leader can achieve sound success. The 13 percent who were outstanding performers balanced concern for profits with a concern for people, asked for advice from employees, and were good listeners. Those categorized as moderately successful were concerned only with production and ignored input from employees. Marginal managers in the group were preoccupied with job security, lacked confidence in employees' performance, and preferred to consult policy manuals rather than either their supervisors or employees.

How are success and democratic leadership related?

Teleometrics International, the research firm conducting the survey, believes that the attitudes and philosophy of the high achievers can be ingrained in beginning managers by teaching them positive views toward their jobs and their employees.[5]

WHICH LEADERSHIP STYLE IS BEST? By now you may be ready to ask a question often asked about leadership styles: Which is best? This question has been asked for centuries; the answer is that there is no one best style. Groups working on different tasks require different kinds of leaders. Some employees need and respond to an authoritarian leader; others, to a participative leader. On the one hand, a benevolent autocracy may be the best way to lead, because centralized authority is efficient and easy for managers to exercise.[6] However, this autocratic style is tempered with some

Is there one best style of leadership?

concern for human relations. On the other hand, the best way to lead may be an approach that integrates a high concern for people with a high concern for production. The leader's major responsibility is to attain effective production and high morale through the participation and involvement of people in a team effort.

Opinions vary on how a manager can lead most productively, but Theory Y has had a tremendous effect on management and motivation theory. However, Theory Y is an opinion, not fact; therefore, it may not classify as a leadership style. Some evidence indicates it is erroneous to teach Theory Y conclusions today—that a more realistic approach is needed.

Leadership Situations

What are the situations on which leadership depends?

situational leadership

Studies of small groups in educational, military, and business settings suggest that the leadership style should depend on the situation. Some situations involve personality traits, interest levels, motivation, nature of task, physical setting, group size, power of leader, and human relationships.

Situational (or contingency) **leadership** is a leadership style that matches the manager to the incident, that is, it reveals what type of person would be most appropriate to lead in a given situation. The three primary factors determining an effective, influential leadership style include power of the leader, nature of the task, and human relationships. Since we have discussed the last two factors, we will now look at power.

Leadership Power

The concept of power is central to human relations study, because all group functioning implies a power structure. Every work group has high-status people who influence behavior. Power is similar to status and is multifaceted. "Power corrupts, and absolute power corrupts absolutely" and "He who has the gold, rules" are sayings often heard in discussions of power. However:

The instinct for power is basic to men and women—as Nietzsche observed, "Wherever I found the living, there I found the will to power"—but it is usually thought of as one of mankind's less attractive characteristics, along with violence and aggression, with which it is often confused. Most people do not like to admit that they want power, which is why they never get it, and those who do have power go to endless lengths to mask the fact. Some politicians, like the late Lyndon B. Johnson, openly relish the trappings of power, but the contemporary American style of power is to pretend that one has none. To confess that one *has* power is to make oneself responsible for using it, and safety lies in an artfully contrived pose of impotence, behind which one can do exactly as one pleases.[7]

What kinds of power are available to leaders?

One power scheme distinguishes five kinds of power—referent, legitimate, expert, reward, and coercive.[8]

REFERENT POWER.   Power given to a leader because the work group accepts the person's influence is referent power. The group responds voluntarily to this person's requests out of admiration. They place power in this person to make the right decisions about behavior standards or production problems. For example, imagine a small-town jury composed of laborers, retail store clerks, and the head teller at the local bank. Because of the latter's high profile in the community and the fact that he is outspoken and the best dressed, the other jurors fall silent when he speaks, they apologize when he interrupts their remarks with his own. The group reaches a unanimous verdict on the case by rubber-stamping the bank teller's judgment and agreeing with his opinion on every point.

LEGITIMATE POWER VERSUS EXPERT POWER.   Legitimate power involves an authority relationship whereby leaders have the right to make certain decisions because of their position. These leaders are authorized to make judgments by law, a higher level of the organization, or the work group. The recipients of their influence view such sanctions as legitimate.

Supervisors receive legitimate power through their job descriptions and formal places in the organizational hierarchy. However, their formal or official power may be broadened considerably if they earn referent power from employees as well as expert power.

As work groups mature, someone usually becomes competent in a given area. That is, a leader emerges because others see him or her as someone with superior ability. Because of this person's specialized knowledge, information, or skills, the other employees look to him or her as an expert.

Although a football quarterback may gain legitimate power when the coach says, "You're it!" he must demonstrate ability in the job to have expert power: teammates must see that he reads defenses and calls plays accurately. He then becomes a leader in fact as well as in name. Such was the case with Joe Montana, who led the San Francisco 49ers to a 1982 Superbowl victory.

If the best sales people are promoted to sales managers, they hold legitimate and expert power. They can call on previous field experience to lead and motivate employees, who come to view their managers' records as standards to be pursued.

REWARD POWER.   An individual's ability to obtain desired responses by offering payoffs is reward power. The rewards may be raises, promotions, a pat on the back, gold stars, or A's. Payoffs are usually determined by position. But this type of power is useful only if others value the rewards offered. For example, the power to determine a course grade has aspects of both reward *and* coercion if students see A's and F's as rewards and penalties, respectively.

COERCIVE POWER.   Coercive power results from the belief that failure to follow directions will result in punishment. Thus, while some employees increase productivity to gain a higher salary (respond to reward power), some may also increase productivity to escape being fired (respond to coercion). Coercive power produces fear and often provides no way to escape what the leader desires.

Which of the power sources helps build a positive work climate?

Of the five power sources, referent and expert power are thought to best support a positive work climate. However, any of the five power sources can get the job done. For example, a mechanic in an auto service center was promoted to service manager, a position of legitimate power from which he supervised the other mechanics.[9] Shortly afterward, top management decided to keep the business open until 9 P.M. The new manager, applying democratic and Theory Y leadership, asked for volunteers to work evenings, but his employees, led by one vocal individual, refused. Although it caused him personal anguish, he invoked his legitimate power and fired the informal leader of the insurrection, warning he'd do the same with the others if necessary. "It was his career or my career," he remarked. Fortunately for all concerned, the other mechanics agreed to work an evening schedule as did the remorseful leader, who requested and received his old job back.

─────────────── Leadership Functions ───────────────

What are the tasks a leader performs?

Having seen what leadership entails, we can deal with what a leader does. If people are taught the characteristics and tasks of a leader and how to perform these tasks, they may become leaders.

For example, a work group's activities relate to task accomplishment. They may be stressing goals, focusing attention on production, and reviewing work quality. Or, these activities may be solving problems, making decisions, and completing projects. Such activities are called task roles. They facilitate and coordinate effort. Task roles are the functions a group undertakes to do a job.

In addition to the task roles of the work group, we may deduce five primary leadership activities workers look for on their jobs and expect from their supervisors: (1) the ability to communicate, (2) a results orientation, (3) the ability to set priorities, (4) an empathetic attitude, and (5) a supportive attitude.

THE ABILITY TO COMMUNICATE.   Workers want clear instructions about how to do a job. They want explanations in understandable terms about the goals and the procedures designed to accomplish these goals. Good communication is one of the keys to sound organizational practice and to successful on-the-job relationships. Unfortunately, many managers cannot give clear, complete, and accurate information. Leaders should not only be concerned with sending messages, but also recognize how vital communication is for a decision maker. Provide clear, accurate facts and figures so others can effectively complete an assignment.

RESULTS ORIENTATION.   Most workers and leaders want to be measured by what they do, not by who they are. There is reason to believe managers who stick closely to job performance expectations not only get better results but also maintain higher levels of morale and production. This expectation is closely tied to communication.

THE ABILITY TO SET PRIORITIES.   One of the most frequently mentioned problems in time management workshops is crisis management or firefighting. This results from the inability or refusal to set priorities. For example, often both a worker and a supervisor will set priorities and then find they conflict. The worker will then do one thing, but the supervisor will think that the worker should do something else. Who wins? The supervisor does, and then the worker is often frustrated, dissatisfied, and unhappy. A leader must stress things that are important so everyone will know what needs to be done and when.

AN EMPATHETIC ATTITUDE.   Empathy is placing yourself in someone else's position, seeing the world from another's vantage point. Being empathetic allows leaders to project themselves into their employees' personalities. Empathy does not mean, however, that a manager accepts an employee's views or is dominated or brainwashed by that person. Nevertheless, empathetic managers remain accessible while holding onto their own beliefs, standards, and expectations. As one employee remarked of his manager, "She may not agree, but she listens, understands, and tries to help if possible—and that makes me feel better."

Empathetic leaders are viewed as approachable, interested, and understanding. They can predict how certain information affects employees, whether it will be understood, accepted, rejected, or ignored. Learn to be sensitive to others, to what they say and what they mean.

A SUPPORTIVE ATTITUDE.   Finally, employees want a manager who will focus on personal relationships. They want someone who will strengthen, regulate, and perpetuate the group's way of doing things. They want a leader with whom they can interact, a person to establish a climate for growth. They want to work for someone they know will back them up, someone who will provide a supportive and helpful environment.

—————————————————— CONCLUSION ——————————————————

One of the primary goals of leadership is to smooth the paths of human interaction. That's why organizations need leaders who are trained in human relations. Many people are probably willing to take the lead, but unless they possess the human relations skills necessary for leadership, they may do more damage than good. Qualities making a sound leader under one set of circumstances (for example, devising a marketing campaign for a new underarm deodorant) may be worthless under a different set of circumstances (for example, skippering a yacht through the edge of a hurricane en route from Miami to St. Thomas).

Good leaders are always needed, leaders who can be productive. Faithful practice of leadership functions, coupled with the background knowledge that has been presented in this chapter, will assist you in leading others.

—————————————————— KEY TERMS ——————————————————

Leadership: influence directed toward others in a given situation in order to obtain a specific goal.

Leadership Emergence: the gradual achievement of status within a work group as one demonstrates superior abilities or behaviors.

Autocratic Leadership: a leadership style that emphasizes an authoritarian approach to management with little or no group participation.

Theory X: a set of management assumptions about employees, based on autocratic leadership.

Democratic Leadership: a group-centered approach to leadership.

Theory Y: a set of management assumptions about employees, based on participative leadership.

Situational Leadership: a leadership style that matches the manager to the incident.

—————————————————— QUESTIONS ——————————————————

1   Reread the opening case.
   a.   Outline the specific actions you would recommend to Bob Waller in light of his friend's remarks.

b. Do you feel that he should relay the friend's information to higher management? Why or why not?

c. Assume that Bob did what you recommended in (a), but breakdowns occurred as often as before. What would you suggest he do next? Why?

d. Assume that you are the vice president of human resources for this firm. What would you do to prevent this kind of problem from happening again?

2 Jot down several preconceived notions about a leader's dress, body build, and general bearing and attitude. Now list at least two leaders you have known who lacked at least one of those qualities. What have you clarified about leadership fact and fallacy? How should you apply it to your future human relationships?

3 Contrast the concept of leadership with the broader one of management. Must effective leaders be effective managers? Why or why not?

4 Describe several things you can do to prepare yourself to lead others. How important is your personal attitude or desire to become a more effective leader?

5 Identify the leader of a group to which you belong. What traits or characteristics helped this person rise to leadership? How did this person's leadership emergence pattern parallel that which was discussed in this chapter? Did it differ? How?

6 Referring to the leader in item (5), what are the top five traits that distinguish that person from the followers in your group? Do you believe he or she attempts to cultivate and enhance those traits? Why or why not?

7 List at least three examples of local or national personalities (in addition to those in the chapter) who are or were considered especially effective leaders. What qualities or characteristics account for their prominence? How could you use them as models to improve your own success with leading others?

8 If a leader indeed possesses more intelligence than persons in the group he or she leads, why is it important not to flaunt that fact over the members? Would you say such a person is manipulating the rest in a negative sense? Why or why not?

9 Consider the personal objectives you plan to accomplish or have reached in your career. What kinds of intrinsic (internal) rewards motivate(d) you to work toward them?

10 Respond to the following observation: "You could diagram my intrinsic rewards as a spiral or a ladder, but never as a circle."

11 Why are trait studies an inadequate way to identify effective leaders? What bearing does the nature of the group and its expectations have on the suitability of one who ultimately earns the leader's role?

12 Review the leadership continuum on page 98. Summarize the style or approach that a leader would display at each of its seven points.

13 Tell which of the three major leadership styles would work best when leading each of the following persons or groups, and why:

a. traveling salespeople,

b. production workers being trained to run a new machine,

c. research scientists,

d. golf course greenskeepers,

e. law enforcement SWAT team,

f. patient recovering from knee surgery,

g. employees who volunteered to work during a weekend taking inventory,

    h. advertising copywriters,
    i. furniture movers,
    j. public relations managers,
    k. long-range planning managers, and
    l. counter employees in a fast-food restaurant.

14 Relate autocratic leadership to the Theory X assumptions discussed in the chapter. Present at least three hypothetical work situations that may require an autocratic (Theory X) approach.

15 Relate democratic leadership to the Theory Y assumptions discussed in the chapter. Present at least three hypothetical work situations that may require a democratic (Theory Y) approach.

16 Present at least three hypothetical work situations that may require a leader to switch from an autocratic to a laissez-faire leadership style.

17 Defend the use of a benevolent autocracy approach. How is this compatible with Theory Y?

18 "My boss never leads me the way I'd like to be led." How can the speaker benefit from this situation if he or she becomes a supervisor? What could this person's supervisor learn from the remark?

19 Apply the concept of power to the desire for promotion. What causes many persons with considerable power to deemphasize or camouflage it?

20 Distinguish among the following kinds of power:
    a. referent,
    b. legitimate,
    c. expert,
    d. reward, and
    e. coercive.

21 Would you agree that legitimate power must usually be coupled with at least one of the other kinds if a manager is going to be effective? Why or why not?

22 Describe each of the following sequential task roles or functions a group performs and the activities that occur within each:
    a. forming ideas,
    b. thinking critically, and
    c. establishing procedure.

23 Summarize each of the following leadership qualities or activities that workers expect from their supervisors. State why they are significant in a supervisor-employee relationship:
    a. communication ability,
    b. results orientation,
    c. ability to set priorities,
    d. empathy, and
    e. supportiveness.

24 Why do employee contacts, interviews, and counseling play significant roles in a manager's success with group members?

—————————————— CASES ——————————————

MEMO

MULTILINE INSURANCE COMPANY

To: All employees, claims processing section

From: R. G. Wilson, manager, claims processing section

Re: Excessive and unauthorized break time

Most of you are extending the official ten-minute morning and afternoon break by at least ten minutes. This practice must stop immediately. Doubling the work break adds twenty minutes per day of unauthorized time off the job (one hour every three working days). In a year of 239 working days this amounts to nearly two weeks (80 hours) worth of paid break time. In effect, you're getting nearly two weeks extra paid vacation every year taken in ten-minute increments. I hope you will remedy this situation without more stringent action on my part.

MEMO

MULTILINE INSURANCE COMPANY

To: All employees, accounting department

From: P. J. Owens, manager, accounting department

Re: Lengthy coffee breaks

I'd like to share a concern with you about coffee breaks. Some employees in our company have abused the privilege, and that cuts down on the working time all of us have to do our jobs. Let's be more conscious of this problem and work together to eliminate it promptly. Thank you.

MEMO

MULTILINE INSURANCE COMPANY

TO: All employees, public relations department

From: Lance Vogel, manager

Re: Breaks

Some of us are reportedly taking breaks that last longer than the specified time. Please comply with the ten-minute break limit.

1 Characterize the above managers' leadership styles from the tone of their memos.
2 Which memo would you respond to most positively, and why?
3 Judging from the tone of the memo, what kind of action is each manager most likely to take if the situation doesn't change?
4 Do you believe top management should have issued a uniformly worded memo to all employees instead of leaving the matter up to the individual managers? Why or why not?

Case 5.2   Top management at Deltech Industries, one of the largest firms in the computer industry, is concerned with the pace at which new products are being marketed. The rate of new product development has slowed considerably during the past two years, and earnings have declined more than 50 percent within the last twelve months.

Last week a confidential major decision was made: everyone except workers paid hourly will be asked to work a fifty-hour week with no pay increase. The program, which is intended to accelerate the rate of new product development, will apply to roughly one-third of the company's 18,000-member work force. Management feels the action is necessary for the firm to recover its former position as industry leader.

The employees will not welcome an unpaid 25 percent increase in their work week, regardless of management's right to declare it. And if these workers don't understand and believe in the potential benefit of this action, it may cause more problems than it is intended to solve.

Case Questions

1   Prepare an announcement to the affected workers to justify the decision and to report the expected benefits.
2   Summarize the employee reactions that management should anticipate.
3   Do you believe it's appropriate to involve the employees in deciding exactly how the fifty-hour work week is to be achieved?
4   Propose how the 25 percent longer week could be accomplished (you may use weekends and days of more than eight working hours). Be specific in your suggestions.

--------------------------- NOTES ---------------------------

1. Robert Tannenbaum, Irving R. Weschler, and Fred Massarik, *Leadership and Organization: A Behavioral Science Approach* (New York: McGraw-Hill, 1961), pp. 69–71.
2. Douglas McGregor, *The Human Side of Enterprise* (New York: McGraw-Hill, 1960), pp. 33–34.
3. Hugh D. Menzies, "The Ten Toughest Bosses," *Fortune* (21 April 1980): 62.
4. McGregor, *The Human Side*, pp. 33–34.
5. *The Wall Street Journal*, 22 August 1978, p. 1.
6. Robert N. McMurry, "Keys to Benevolent Autocracy," *Harvard Business Review* (January-February 1958): 82–90.
7. Korda, Michael, *Power! How to Get It, How to Use It* (New York: Ballantine Books, 1976), p. 7.
8. J. R. P. French, Jr., and B. Raven, "The Bases of Social Power," in Dorwin Cartwright and Alvin Zander (eds.), *Studies in Social Power* (Ann Arbor: University of Michigan Press, 1959), pp. 150–167.
9. Bernard Wysocki, Jr., "Manager's Journal," *The Wall Street Journal*, 9 July 1979, p. 16.

——— SUGGESTED READINGS ———

Blake, Robert, and Mouton, Jane F. *The Managerial Grid.* Houston, Tex.: Gulf Publishing, 1964.

Fiedler, Fred E. *A Theory of Leadership Effectiveness.* New York: McGraw-Hill, 1967.

Jay, A. *Management and Machiavelli.* New York: Holt, Rinehart and Winston, 1967.

Lewin, Kurt, and Lippitt, Ronald. "An Experimental Approach to the Study of Autocracy and Democracy: A Preliminary Note," *Sociometry* (1938): 292–300.

Likert, Rensis. *The Human Organization.* New York: McGraw-Hill, 1976.

White, Ralph, and Lippit, Ronald. "Leader Behavior and Member Reaction in Three 'Social Climates,'" in Cartwright, Dorwin and Zander, Alvin, eds., *Group Dynamics—Research and Theory.* Evanston, Ill.: Row, Peterson, 1953.

6

Communicating with Others

When you complete your study of this chapter, you should be able to:

1 List and discuss the goals of communication,

2 Discuss the nature of communication as it relates to flows, patterns, interactions, and feedback,

3 Recognize and overcome the major barriers to communication,

4 Compare the roles of nonverbal and verbal communication, and

5 Discuss the importance of quality circles to communicative interaction.

OPENING CASE

Kim Westbrook, a freshman at South Pernales Junior College, works as a sales clerk at a local department store. She planned to attend the homecoming football game, but she had to ask her boss for the day off.

Shortly after arriving at work, she said to her boss, "Mr. Ventura, I'd like to have next Saturday off, if it's OK." Mr. Ventura responded, "Sure, Kim, if you have something serious to do. I'll have to get one of the other sales clerks to work in your place." "It's serious to me," Kim answered, "so you don't mind?" Ventura shrugged his shoulders and returned to his work.

The Monday after homecoming, Mr. Ventura called Kim into his office and said, "Kim, you young people are all alike. I let you off last Saturday because you said you had something serious to do. Yesterday I learned you went to a football game. Do you call *that* serious? I think you'd better find a job someplace else. Anyone who lies about one thing will lie about other things as well. You've lost your credibility with me."

"Do you mean I'm fired, just like that?" answered Kim. "I was a member of the homecoming queen's court; that *was* serious."

"Either you're kidding or your priorities are out of order," answered Ventura as he stood and motioned toward the door.

That's Not What I Said

Have you ever been involved in a situation where communication failed? How did you feel? Was it your fault or theirs? Can you remember having told someone how to do something, but they did it wrong. You said, "But that's not what I said to do." And they replied, "Yes, it is!" What causes such misunderstandings?

What does communication involve?

No working group can exist very long without communication. Workers fulfill their roles and responsibilities by speaking and listening to each other's verbal and nonverbal expressions. Communication involves the intentions of the speaker and the impressions received by the hearer. However, it is one of the least understood processes of interpersonal relationships. In a day as advanced as ours, we should be able to solve the problems of talking to one another. The truth is, communication becomes more complex all the time. Everyone talks about communication, but not all people communicate successfully. Some people think they communicate, but their listeners don't think so. Some parents, for example, think they are communicating with their children, but their children see it as preaching. Some supervisors think they are giving clear instructions, but the employees hear muddy directives. Communication is more complex than many think. Notice some common situations.

- A six-year-old boy recently said to a friend, "You wait until I grow up and become President. Then you'll be sorry." What did he mean?
- A father (holding a tent spike) said to his son (holding a hammer), "When I nod my head, hit it." What did the father mean?
- A welfare recipient wrote her local office inquiring about payment. She stated, "I can't get sick pay. I have six children. Can you tell me why?" What did she mean?

Not everyone communicates meaning in talking—or at least not the intended meaning. That is why people say things like "That's not what I said!" Many researchers conclude communication may be the biggest problem in human relationships. As the old saw goes: "I know you believe you understand what you think I said. However, I'm not sure you realize that what you heard is not what I meant." Part of our problem stems from our inability to describe such a perplexing concept. What is communication?

The Importance of Communication

As a simple interaction, communication involves one person transmitting information about something to another person or vice versa. However, although sending and receiving are essential, they do not adequately describe the importance of interpersonal communication.

Communication is the essence of all relationships. It is the focal point for business managers, is central to control and survival, and is essential for all employees. If there is one activity that is foundational for all planning, organizing, directing, and controlling, it is communication. Without productive communication, decisions cannot be made or implemented; achievement is impossible. If we had to pick just one area of human relations to concentrate on, it would probably be communication. Therefore, communication skills—oral, written, and nonverbal—should be improved. Communication allows the accomplishment of objectives.

A Definition

What is communication?

communication

There are many definitions of communication and many disciplines that claim communication as their own invention. Because of this, the word means many things to many people. For the purposes of this chapter, **communication** is the sending and receiving of messages, the sharing of ideas and attitudes. Ideas stress an *intrapersonal* view of communication. Messages emphasize the *interpersonal* side of communication. Attitudes overlap intra- and interpersonal communication and suggest the importance of *nonverbal communication.* If communication is to be productive, it must result in understanding between sender and receiver. For example, teachers are productive communicators when their students learn; business people are productive communicators when their customers buy.

Through communication people process information, test ideas, exchange opinions, and achieve consensus on decisions. Through communication they develop interpersonal relationships and form subgroups from a large number of individuals. Communication is *the* organizing element on the job.

Communication Goals

For communication to be productive the people involved must see some reason for interaction.

What are the goals of communication?

The most obvious communication goal is to be heard. There are, however, other goals that precede and succeed this vital goal. They are to:

1. *Gain the attention of the receiver.* The sender wants the other person to listen to what he or she says. For example, if you were a manager speaking to your work group and you did not have their attention, you might as well have talked to a wall, because the results would be about the same.

2. *Achieve understanding, once the receiver's attention is gained.* A manager, for example, would want to present ideas or messages in a manner acceptable to the needs and levels of the employees. Management would want to make sure the employees structured its ideas in their minds the same way management had originally framed them, because communication is basically a process of exchanging meanings. If similarity in restructuring concepts is inadequate, misunderstandings will occur. However, in many verbal exchanges (e.g., a disciplinary conference) a receiver who is not actively trying to understand and respond to your message bears some responsibility for the failure.

To achieve understanding the sender and receiver must perceive the purpose of the communicative encounter, recognize whether the purpose is being achieved, and help one another in order to achieve the purpose. Otherwise, there is no real need to communicate. For example, if Kim Westbrook had made sure she and Mr. Ventura were talking to one another, not past one another, they might have achieved understanding. Neither emphasized what they meant by important, and so both missed their purpose.

3. *Get acceptance of one's ideas.* Although acceptance of one's opinions and beliefs is not essential to getting others to do what one wishes, it is helpful for the long-run life of the group. For example, workers are more likely to reach high levels of productivity and maintain satisfying relationships if they believe in their leader and in what they are doing.

4. *Gain productive action.* Not only do senders want others to listen to them, understand what they say, and accept their ideas, they also want others to do what they suggest. Action is one way to check communication results. It is, in fact, the main criterion for speaking or writing. For example, as a manager, if you asked someone in your work group to do one thing and she or he did something else, the results would not meet your expectations. You obtained action, but it was unproductive action.

5. *Strive to maintain good relationships with others.* Friends seldom have the problem of understanding one another that enemies do. For example, as a manager, if you develop satisfying relationships with others, they are more likely to listen to what you say and to respond as you desire.

The Nature of Communication

How well do you communicate?

It is impossible to discuss communication without relating it to the work situation. Thus, we will now explore communication according to flows, networks, interactions, and feedback in organizations. But before we get too far into the subject, let's measure your personal verbal communication habits. Respond to the quiz in Figure 6.1 before reading further.

FIGURE 6.1
Verbal
Communication Quiz

	Almost Always	Usually	Sometimes	Seldom	Almost Never
1. Do your words come out the way you want them to in conversation?	___	___	___	___	___
2. Do others have a tendency to put words in your mouth?	___	___	___	___	___
3. Do you deliberately try to conceal your faults from others?	___	___	___	___	___

FIGURE 6.1 cont.

	Almost Always	Usually	Sometimes	Seldom	Almost Never
4. Do you help others to understand you by telling what you think, feel, and believe?	____	____	____	____	____
5. Do you confide in people?	____	____	____	____	____
6. Do you have a tendency to change the subject when your feelings enter into a discussion?	____	____	____	____	____
7. Do you admit you are wrong when you know you are wrong about something?	____	____	____	____	____
8. Do you try to force your ideas and opinions on others?	____	____	____	____	____
9. Do you make sarcastic remarks about others or their work?	____	____	____	____	____

FIGURE 6.1 cont.

		Almost Always	Usually	Sometimes	Seldom	Almost Never
10.	Do you correct people in front of others?	____	____	____	____	____
11.	Do you argue for the privilege of doing things your way?	____	____	____	____	____
12.	Do you lose your temper and quarrel with fellow workers?	____	____	____	____	____
13.	Do you shout at others across the work area when you become angry?	____	____	____	____	____
14.	Do you use profane language when you get into an argument?	____	____	____	____	____
15.	Do you discuss personal problems with your co-workers?	____	____	____	____	____
16.	Do you criticize your fellow workers, your supervisor, or the organization?	____	____	____	____	____

FIGURE 6.1 cont.

	Almost Always	Usually	Sometimes	Seldom	Almost Never
17. Do you become grouchy at times?	____	____	____	____	____
18. Are you ever hostile when you talk to your supervisor?	____	____	____	____	____
19. Do your communications achieve their purpose?	____	____	____	____	____
20. Do your communications develop friendly, satisfying relationships with others?	____	____	____	____	____
	5 pts.	4 pts.	3 pts.	2 pts.	1 pt.
Totals:	____ +	____ +	____ +	____ +	____ = ____

All phases of interaction, whether interaction takes place in a two-person dyad or in a large group, depend on communication. But how do your communications work? Your total scores on the quiz in Figure 6.1 will give you an idea of your communication profile. A score of 50–70 is average. If your score is below average, you might want to reexamine the test to see where you need the most work. And, with that in mind, you can then read on to see how communication works within business, that is, how it flows and what networks exist.

────────────────── Communication Flows ──────────────────

Communication is often described as information flowing vertically or horizontally, for example, upward, downward, or laterally. Contrast is made, also, between one-way and two-way flows. One of the most important advantages of two-way communication is its role in decision making. People who have to carry out a proposal have an opportunity to react to it and

What are the advantages of two-way and one-way communication?

contribute to the decision. There are also advantages to one-way communication, however. For example:

- *Speed* is accomplished more readily with one-way communication. However, one-way messages have a lower probability of acceptance than two-way messages.
- *Appearance* of one-way messages is more impressive than that of two-way messages because directives appear businesslike and official.
- *Covering up of mistakes* is easier with one-way communication; senders will not have to hear someone imply or say there is an easier or better way to say what was said.
- *Protection of one's power* is more readily accomplished with one-way communication than with two-way. In one-way communication, when mistakes occur, the sender can blame the receiver for failure to listen. In two-way communication, the sender shares the blame.
- *Simplification of managerial life* is better accomplished with one-way communication than with two-way. When communication is two-way, people must deal with others' feelings, attitudes, and perceptions. They must also deal more directly with people.
- *Planfulness, orderliness, and systemization* characterize one-way communication. Two-way communication is not as neat because it is difficult to predict what embarrassing questions will be asked when questions are solicited.[1]

However, we can surmise that two-way communication is more valid since it allows for more accurate transmission of information.

vertical communication

What does downward communication entail?

VERTICAL COMMUNICATION.   **Vertical communication** involves messages that flow up and down the organizational hierarchy. Downward communication is the most frequent communication flow in business. It involves directives, policies, procedures, instructions, goals, or objectives. For example, the leader tells others what to do or passes on information they need to perform a job. However, downward communication is a one-way process. "I told you what to do; now do it." It can also be a stifling process in which people feel they have no say about how things are done.

Pitney Bowes, Inc., spends more than $800,000 per year communicating with employees through jobholder meetings, sessions in which lower-level workers interrogate top executives in a no-holds-barred atmosphere. Texas Instruments, Gulf Oil, and subsidiaries of Westinghouse Electric employ closed-circuit videotapes to convey information to workers. Bethlehem Steel writes separate employee newsletters for each of its twenty-three plants. The volume of AT&T's in-house employee communication doubled in five years.[2]

Some types of downward communication are identifiable, as was just noted. If these types of communication are unclear, employees will not respond in the way managers wish. If these types are limited, people may give only minimal compliance. For example, how might you feel as an employee involved in the following downward communication situation?

A Republic Airlines, Inc., public relations manager issued a news release reporting that fiscal year profits reached $13.1 million. However, this obscured the fact that profits declined 47 percent from the previous year and the company lost $2.7 million in the quarter preceding the announcement.[3]

Upward communication involves workers relaying information to their superiors. This type of message flow provides feedback. Therefore, it is two-way and, as a general rule, improves morale. People feel as though they have a voice in how things are done. They are listened to. Upward communication benefits both the company and the individual.

What does upward communication do for a manager?

Both upward and downward communication are related to formal organizations. Lines connect the various units within the hierarchy. Systems of responsibility and explicit delegations of duties are clearly drawn. Exact statements of the nature, content, and direction of communication are provided. Because of this high formality, some companies try to establish more informal atmospheres.

William M. Agee, dynamic president and chief executive officer of Bendix Corporation, shattered tradition by moving the firm's board room table to another room and replacing it with comfortable arm chairs surrounding a $30,000 Oriental rug. Calling the table a security blanket that was brown, drab, and looked like a surfboard, Agee believed it inhibited rather than encouraged communication and a relaxed atmosphere among Bendix board members. Although the directors themselves, who were uninformed of the change until they entered the board room, had varying degrees of difficulty adjusting to Agee's new arrangements, he was pleased with their reactions.[4]

HORIZONTAL COMMUNICATION. **Horizontal communication** should be the strongest flow of information in work groups because it allows for message exchange among people on the same level of authority. It is particularly prevalent at the lower levels and leads to better understanding among workers than vertical communication does. Good horizontal communication typically deals with task coordination, problem solving, information sharing, and conflict resolution.

horizontal communication

What are the advantages of horizontal communication?

Horizontal communication atmospheres provide a good opportunity to banish certain communication barriers. For example, after they bought control of the troubled Bulova Watch Company, Loews Corporation executives determined that a major source of Bulova's problems was inadequate horizontal communication among its top managers. One individual was described as "an autocratic manager who always knew more than his staff because he didn't communicate;" another reportedly "couldn't communicate with his own people and he just couldn't integrate the company."

To resolve the situation, Loews executives retired several key Bulova managers against their will and filled the vacancies with managers who eliminated the horizontal communications vacuum among such areas as finance, production, and marketing.[5]

grapevine

THE GRAPEVINE. Vertical or horizontal communication is usually considered formal communication because it follows the chain of command on most organizational charts. The system of communication that does not follow the chain of command and therefore has no official sanction is referred to as the **grapevine.** It creates an informal organization that departs from formal tasks and hierarchy and creates its own channels of communication and dependence. (The grapevine is discussed as part of the informal organization in Chapter 2.)

The grapevine is fast and selective, and it has company-wide influence. It is doubtful it could ever be destroyed. Hence, if managers understand how the grapevine works (i.e., who passes on information), they can influence and use the grapevine network by supplying accurate data.

─────────────── Communication Networks ───────────────

Every group develops its own unique structure and pattern of communication. These patterns connect the sender and receivers into a functioning social organization and are called **networks.** They show us who talks to whom. For example, Figure 6.2 illustrates a common small-group interaction system.

networks

What is a communication network?

Although every person in this figure is shown talking to and receiving feedback from every other person, communication flows are seldom that balanced. Some individuals participate more than others. For example, it would be possible for *A, B,* and *C* to do all the talking; *D* and *E,* all the listening. Productive communication, however, seeks to minimize discrepancies of power, control, and influence among group members. Thus, another goal of communication is to enhance the group's work life.

One factor affecting communication networks is group size. For example, the time available per member for communication during a group meeting decreases as the size of the group increases. Group members have fewer chances to speak in groups of twelve than of five. In addition, feelings of threat and inhibition increase with group size. Similarly, discussion diminishes as group size increases; the distribution of participation also varies. As group size increases, fewer people participate in the group. The gap between the

FIGURE 6.2
Small-Group
Communication
Network

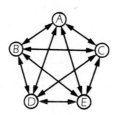

participator and the other group members tends to grow proportionately greater as size increases.

Often the communication network is preset; at other times the pattern arises during interaction. Figure 6.3 contains some geometric diagrams of communication networks and shows how persons are linked together as members of a work group. Other combinations are possible, however. These networks allow us to visualize who talks to whom, about what, and in what sequence.

What are some common network patterns?

The *circle* network shows the ability of A to communicate with B and C. B can talk to D; C to E; D to E; but E is strictly a receiver. E does not pass messages on to someone else. A has the greatest opportunity to communicate; however, it is basically a one-way system.

The *chain* network is similar to a gossip activity. A tells B who tells C, who tells D, who tells E. But, again, E's only function is to receive data from others. The chain is a serial process and is also one-way.

The *wheel* network resembles an autocratic system; it too is one-way. A sends messages to B, C, D, and E, all of whom are only receivers. They do not have the opportunity to interact with one another or to relay messages to someone else.

The *Y* network allows A to send messages to B, B to C, and C to D and E. However, D and E do not transmit. And, as in the other networks, the Y is essentially a one-way communication program.

Centralized patterns such as the wheel and chain networks are usually better than decentralized networks like the circle. For simple problem solving, for example, centralized patterns are accurate; but if the problem is complex, decentralized networks are more accurate. Morale and worker satisfaction are higher in decentralized networks. Thus, centralized patterns are superior in accomplishing tasks, and decentralized networks are superior in fostering group cohesiveness and interaction.

───────────── Communication Interactions ─────────────

Any person's behavior affects those in the group. If you choose not to be an active member and participate by actively communicating, you may influence

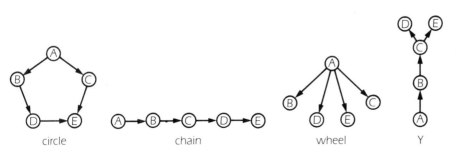

FIGURE 6.3
Some Common
Communication
Patterns

circle   chain   wheel   Y

others to remain uninvolved. If you don't better yourself, why should they? If, on the other hand, your behavior can influence others to participate actively, you can improve group interaction. A thoughtful, well-timed question could lead the group in a positive direction. So could soothing over a sensitive area where potential disruption could develop into nonconstructive conflict.

What are some styles of communication interaction?

Two styles of interaction that can influence a group either positively or negatively are those of the *peacemaker* and the *democratic* group member. A peacemaker gets a consensus and keeps people together. A democratic group member tries to include everyone in a discussion. By learning to be sensitive to the participation and interaction level of a work group, you can make large contributions to the group by spotting potential trouble areas. For example, interaction skills of group members vary. If you wish to have high communication skill, you must learn to emphasize brevity, objectivity, and listening.

How does one become known for having high communication skill?

BREVITY.   Have you ever listened to someone who always seemed to talk for at least thirty minutes and could say more about nothing than anyone else? One participant's contributions to any meeting should not be too lengthy or complicated. Other members may have difficulty understanding his or her position, or they may stop listening altogether when that person starts talking.

OBJECTIVITY.   Sometimes, a person's biased vision of a situation blinds him or her. Are you that way about certain subjects? Group participants should strive to be objective toward all ideas contributed by others. They should reserve decisions until all the group has had a chance to interact for a while. Discussion should not be an arena for public debate, promotion, or competition. A closed mind works against the good that a group can accomplish.

LISTENING.   Have you ever talked to someone you knew wasn't listening to you? How did you feel? Group members should listen to one another as much as (if not more than) they desire to be heard. One way is to let your body language tell the others you are aware of them and are interested in their thoughts. You can nod your head knowingly, or use brief encouragements like "I see," "That's a good idea," "I'm glad you said that," or "Uh, huh." The quality of listening to others is very important in the life of a work group. More will be said about this concept in Chapter 7, but begin now to show you respect everyone's right to participate in the group's work and discussion.

─────────────────────── Cohesive Patterns ───────────────────────

cohesiveness

Cohesiveness is the ability of a group to work and stay together. As a group develops a higher level of cohesion, it communicates more because members are open, supportive, and trusting. Highly cohesive groups interact more; consequently, group members feel pressure to interact and communicate. For example, a meeting in which a manager wants participation may be quiet in spite of members' desire to talk, until an atmosphere of acceptance and trust develops. Likewise, in the classroom, students are often reluctant to say much the first few days, as though they are mentally testing the water before plunging in.

How does cohesiveness aid group development?

Feedback

In all communications, feedback determines levels of understanding. If feedback is discouraged, a work group's vitality and problem-solving ability will suffer. The terms *interaction* and *communication* are often used synonymously. Group interaction is the communicative feedback provided by and for the members. Therefore, **feedback** refers to the responses each person makes to others. For example, one individual asks a question and someone feeds back an answer to that question, comments, or enlarges on another's suggestion. Each group member then influences and is influenced by others.

How does feedback assist groups and their leaders?

feedback

There are two basic types of feedback: positive and negative. Positive feedback reinforces and stimulates; negative feedback counteracts and neutralizes. Groups use both types to regulate their progress toward consensus decisions. For example, members tend to reinforce others' acceptable behavior but punish deviant behavior.

For feedback to be useful, it must be helpful. That is why feedback needs to be very specific. If recipients of feedback are to be helped, they need to understand what is said, be willing and able to accept it, and be able to do something about it. Trust must exist between senders and receivers before a message is accepted.

Barriers to Communication

Communication at work is important. Knowing the nature of communication, we can say that people's productivity cannot be improved without improving their communication knowledges and skills. The manager's objectives are to search for and use communication skills that will improve understanding. Unfortunately, many problems arise along the way.

What is a communication barrier?

Communication difficulties result from real or imagined problems. Therefore, a communication **barrier** is anything that blocks message flow so that a receiver does not get the intended message. For example, something was interfering with the communication between Kim Westbrook and Mr. Ventura in the opening case. Something caused a breakdown in understanding. When such breakdowns occur between a sender and a receiver, nonproductive communication is the cause. New and better communication must correct

barrier

the problem. However, correction usually occurs only after the problem is recognized.

──────────────── Recognizing Barriers ────────────────

Nonproductive communication may occur because people do not want to communicate, they do not provide feedback, they fail to listen, or they try to show off their knowledge. Becoming aware of potential communication barriers is the starting point in coping with breakdowns. Some common communication problems are allness, bypassing, ambiguity, and status.

How does allness interfere with communication success?

ALLNESS.   Allness is a tendency people have to believe that whatever they say about a particular subject is all that there is to say about that subject. Allness occurs when, failing to remain objective and openminded:

- People are unaware they are abstracting (i.e., selecting, condensing, and deducting). They assume they have covered the subject completely.
- People select different details from a given situation (unaware they are doing so) and assume they know everything.
- People evaluate a group on the unconscious assumption that their experience with one or a few members would be the same with all of a group.
- People close their minds to new or different ideas.[6]

Allness is a common affliction among most of us, but particularly among advertisers. For example, the following advertising slogans take full advantage of allness:

> "When you say Budweiser, you've said it all."
> "Nothing else is a Volkswagen."
> "If it's Borden, it's got to be good."
> "Nothing beats a great pair of L'Eggs."
> "Nothing runs like a Deere."

Any time people are dogmatic, rigid, or deaf to new ideas, they are suffering from the disease of allness. The cure for such mistakes is to remember many particulars are left out of everything you say, hear, read, or write. There is always more information than what is presented. There is always an et cetera.

When does bypassing occur?

BYPASSING.   Bypassing is the tendency of individuals to not recognize that one word can have different meanings. For example, have you seen the sign over a combination restaurant and service station that says, "Eat here and get gas"? Or the sign outside a university cafeteria that says, "Shoes are required to eat inside"? Bypassing also occurs when people do not recognize that different words can have the same meanings. For example, when people refer to death, they use a whole gamut of words—passed on, sleeping until judgment day, ceased to be, et cetera.

If you assume a speaker is using words the same way you would if you were talking, you can expect misunderstandings to occur. Whenever people project their meanings into someone else's words, a communication breakdown is likely. The cure for bypassing and projecting meanings is to look to people for meanings instead of to words and to be sensitive to the way words are currently used. Meanings are in people, not in words.

AMBIGUITY. Ambiguity, like bypassing, results from different word *How does ambiguity* meanings in a given context. For example, what did the manager mean *contribute to* when she wrote a recommendation for a former employee and said, "I know *misunderstanding?* this person very well and can't recommend him too highly"? Or what about the young child whose mother asked her to say grace at the noon meal? She answered, "I don't know what to say." "Just say what Mommy says," replied the mother. Bowing her head she prayed, "Dear God, why did we ever invite these people to lunch?"

Learn to spot statements that can have several types of meaning, and ask the speaker to clarify, paraphrase, or confirm; ask for specific, concrete examples. *See* Exhibit 6.1.

—————————— EXHIBIT 6.1 ——————————

Words Used Versus Meanings Intended

Business Term	Translation
Expedite	To compound confusion with commotion.
Consultant	An ordinary person carrying a briefcase who is more than fifty miles from home.
Implement the program	Hire more people and expand the department.
Meeting	A mass mulling of master minds.
Conference	A gathering that substitutes conversation for the dreariness of labor and the loneliness of thought.
Reliable source	The person you just met.
Informed source	The person who told the person you just met.
Unimpeachable source	The person who started the rumor originally.
Clarify	Fill in the background with so many details that the foreground goes underground.
We are making a survey	We need more time to think of an answer.
Let's meet and discuss	Come down to my office; I'm lonesome.
Orientation	Look busy until we find something for you to do.
Seasoned applicant	A fraternity brother.
Promising young executive	Son of a fraternity brother.
Coordinator	An executive with a desk between two expediters.
Surge in demand	Six orders received in the same mail.
For your approval	We're passing the buck.

What determines status?

STATUS.   Communication problems also result from an involvement of different people's egos, status relationships, or positions in the work group. Status can be measured by job titles, office placements, windows, desk sizes, parking spaces, and so forth. The two major status determinants are probably the nature of people's work and the size of their paychecks, however. Dissatisfaction arises when one person or group perceives another as out of line. Communication problems often arise, and the status ladder must be realigned to reduce the perceived inconsistencies.

――――――――――――――― Coping with Barriers ―――――――――――――――

How may one cope with communication barriers?

Good communication is at best a difficult process. Even though there are many barriers to communication, the situation is not hopeless, however. In fact, almost any serious effort to improve communication will have beneficial results. One of the best ways to start improving communication is to become aware of communication problems. The normal result of any communication is a partial misunderstanding. Thus decisions must be made as to how large a margin of difference in understanding can be tolerated.

Four specific ways to cope with the barriers and thereby improve communication between management and staff are to recognize the receiver's frame of reference, to use feedback, to reinforce words with actions, and to **quality circle** use quality circles as an intervention technique. A **quality circle** is a meeting of a small group of workers to identify, analyze, and provide solutions to problems in their work area. It is usually made up of a group of people who work together to produce part of a product or a service. A typical quality circle has five to ten members and conducts its meetings during work hours. Its purpose is to propose answers to management for quality control problems.

A number of organizations have employed quality circles—Northrop, Phillips Petroleum, Corning Glass, and National Micrographic. They have found that quality circles work because participation is voluntary and the members learn teamwork techniques. As long as management is supportive and committed to good human relations, members can solve problems.

J. F. Beardsley and Associates of San Jose, California, provide the following examples of benefits available in firms through quality circles:

- Critical delays caused by interorganizational conflicts were reduced. Meetings were initiated to establish priorities and communication procedures. Savings: $204,000.
- Time lost from conflicting job instructions was reduced. By rewriting the instructions, conflicts were eliminated and operations were simplified. Savings: $364,000.[7]

One key to quality circles is that they are results-oriented. People are there to seek ways to accomplish the original goal. Instead of wanting to know whose fault it is and assigning blame, they want a solution. When a communication breakdown occurs, solutions can be found through participative interaction.

Nonverbal Communication

Within the last two decades interest has developed in nonverbal communication research. Nonverbal communication has much to do with the way we perceive and respond to others. Since our ability to communicate goes far beyond our ability to speak, understanding the nature of nonverbal communication will provide us with another technique for achieving understanding among people. It is yet another principle of improving human relationships. Success depends, in part, on sensitivity to the feelings of others and on competence, sincerity, trustworthiness, and interest. All of these nonverbals must be consistent with the words expressed. The more known about nonverbal communication, the better communication will be. And, the better the communication, the more productive the human relations.

What does nonverbal communication tell us?

The conclusion of nonverbal communication research suggests we are constantly communicating information about ourselves. Tone and inflection of our voices, facial expressions, body positions, and gestures speak very clearly. These nonverbals significantly affect our sending and receiving of messages. The specific signals that alert us as to what to send or how to receive are cues.

Cues

Nonverbal cues are signals that do not require a person's concentrated efforts. These cues may be intentional or unintentional. The expressions of feelings, emotions, and attitudes are nonverbal and can rarely be concealed from others. Messages frequently consist of intentions that are logically inconsistent with the verbally professed statements. If persons are having difficulty communicating their thoughts and feelings by verbal symbols, they will communicate by means of nonverbal symbols (e.g., body language). Two concepts are especially pertinent. First, we cannot not communicate. Nonverbal cues go out constantly. Second, if our words say one thing and our nonverbals signal something else, people will pay more attention to the nonverbals.

nonverbal cues

Do people pay more attention to the verbal or the nonverbal communications?

Evidence exists showing only 7 percent of a message is transmitted by words; 93 percent of a message is nonverbal—tone of voice, facial expressions, and body motion.[8] It is no wonder people pay more attention to what we do. When people become aware of the nonverbal ways of reacting to situations, they can help one another understand what others are experiencing and under what circumstances. In fact, one of the more interesting areas of study in the nonverbal communication field is how nonverbals support the verbals. For example, the cues Richard Nixon sent during televised speeches, in retrospect, were rather accurate.

Thus, through nonverbal communication we can discover when to communicate and what to say, as well as when to listen. This statement is still often true: "What you are speaks so loudly I can't hear what you say." With that in mind, look at some areas of nonverbal communication providing cues.

--------------------------------- Body Motions ---------------------------------

What are some common areas of study in kinesics (body motion)?

The study of body motions (kinesics) concerns five primary areas: the face, gestures, posture, body shape, and physical appearance. Each of these areas provokes certain actions from other people and may assist or impede productive communications.

THE FACE.   The face is the most visible indicant of our emotions and feelings. With over 100 possible expressions, the face accurately reflects our feelings toward others and provides feedback on others' comments.

Perhaps the part of the face most likely to yield information is the eyes. When communicating with others, or when establishing or maintaining relationships, increase eye contact.

GESTURES.   Gestures can express one message or an entire language. Although the hands are most prominent, the whole body can send a message. Successful salespeople confirm that prospects send nonverbal messages of acceptance or rejection by folding or unfolding their arms, leaning forward or reclining in their chairs, and crossing or uncrossing their legs. Gestures can be large, expansive, assertive, and outgoing, or they can be limited, self-protective, and close to the body. But, as with mimes, every movement has a message.

POSTURE.   Posture also provides us with information. The way we sit, stand, walk, or lie down expresses feelings, interest, involvement, or tension. For example, body language as well as physical barriers can be used to get rid of time-wasting office guests (discussed in Chapter 4). A manager may rise and remain standing when someone enters his or her office (making the visitor reluctant to sit). Holding a pen or pencil at the ready implies someone is about to write something important and is eager to get on with it. A raised eyebrow sometimes signals irritation and an intent to get back to the business at hand.

Posture tells whether one wishes to include or exclude other people in one's thoughts or conversations, whether one is open or closed to certain ideas. It tells whether one is warm toward certain people, whether one likes or dislikes certain ideas, whether one can become emotionally involved. It also says something about one's role and status in certain groups.

BODY SHAPE.   There are three general body types: ectomorph (frail, thin, and tall), endomorph (fat, round, and short), and mesomorph (muscular, athletic, and tall). Most people stereotype each physique. For example, ectomorphs are tense, suspicious of others, nervous, pessimistic, and quiet. Endomorphs are talkative, old-fashioned, sympathetic, weak, dependent, and trusting. Some researchers contend endomorphs encounter negative prejudice in job interviews and promotional decisions. And, in fact, a number of endomorphs are going to court and charging employers with job bias. Furthermore, ectomorphs are often portrayed unfairly as uncool wimps or nerds like Terry the Toad in the film *American Graffiti*.

Mesomorphs are stereotyped as handsome, adventurous, mature, and self-reliant. For example, you need only to look at the models used in advertising to appreciate this stereotype. Probably at least 90 percent are mesomorphs. Consider, for example, the individuals promoting cigarettes, beer, sports cars, and men's cologne.

Of course, anyone can exhibit characteristics of all three groups. So try not to let societal attitudes affect the way you relate to each of these types of people.

PHYSICAL APPEARANCE.   Physical attractiveness is also a factor in nonverbal communication. Body color, smell, hair length, and clothing influence the quality and quantity of communication that occurs among people. Based solely on physical appearance, many people will make decisions regarding dating, courtship, and marriage, not to mention hiring and firing. For example, it is believed many managers put people through testing programs during interviews to weed out weak candidates, and then they hire the tallest person.

Space

Spatial relationships (proxemics) also affect the quality and quantity of communication among people. Distances between people in daily interactions or arrangement of furniture in houses and offices may enhance or stifle understanding. Personal space varies among nationalities. Native Americans, who tend to talk at arms' length, mark off a generous amount of personal space in which to operate. However, members of certain other nationalities customarily interact within inches of each other.

How does space speak to us?

Space is often referred to as territory, which assumes certain ownership rights of an area without any legal basis. Examples of territory might include a certain chair in a classroom, a certain parking space, a certain easy chair at home, a certain pew at church, and so forth. Any invader of territory is apt to be treated with suspicion.

Territory can be employed to convey an aura of power (as when the judge announces, "You may approach the bench."). Some higher managers' offices may be viewed almost as shrines by easily impressed employees. For example, a large aerospace firm held an open house one night so employees' families could tour the facilities. The two highest managers' offices were open in the executive suite. Velvet ropes barred the doorways, and an officious secretary told gaping onlookers which office belonged to whom.

Time

Although time is culturally defined, being on time, ahead of time, or behind time communicates certain things in our society. Deadlines are a way of life, and we view skeptically anyone who doesn't wear a watch or who doesn't place the same emphasis we do on the clock. Those who are always late are disrespectful, we think; they have little interest in us. The language of time is very eloquent. It can create auras of hostility or warmth.

Voice

Vocal qualities such as pitch, articulation, resonance, and tempo produce certain responses from others. Vocal characteristics such as laughing, crying, whispering, yawning, and sighing also provoke certain actions, even when no conscious attempt was made to manipulate the voice. Thus, voice may be the most important element in certain aspects of persuasion.

Silence

Another large area of nonverbal communication is silence. Therefore, it is helpful to know how to deal with silence in a work group. What happens, for example, when no one talks to us? Silence may have one or a combination of meanings. It might represent either fear or anger. In either case, silence retards our ability to relate to others.

CONCLUSION

A number of communication principles can be violated at any communicative encounter. People may not know what to say. They may blindly state their requests without reaching understanding, thereby forcing their ideas on others. Or they may unintentionally sabotage their message with certain nonverbals. Communication, at best, is difficult, but it is the key to productive human relationships in business. Therefore, we all can benefit from the American

Management Association's "Ten Commandments of Good Communication." These rules will help all of us overcome some of the verbal and nonverbal problems discussed in this chapter.

1 Seek to clarify your ideas before communicating.
2 Examine the true purpose of each communication.
3 Consider the total physical and human setting whenever you communicate.
4 Consult with others, where appropriate, in planning communications.
5 Be mindful, while you communicate, of the overtones as well as the basic content of your message.
6 Take the opportunity, when it arises, to convey something of help or value to the receiver.
7 Follow up your communication.
8 Communicate for tomorrow as well as today.
9 Be sure your actions support your communications.
10 Seek not only to be understood but to understand—be a good listener.

KEY TERMS

Communication: the sending and receiving of messages, ideas, and attitudes.
Vertical Communication: messages that flow up and down the organizational hierarchy.
Horizontal Communication: information that flows laterally throughout the organization.
Grapevine: communication that does not follow the chain of command and has no official sanction.
Networks: systems of communication lines connecting senders and receivers into a group.
Cohesiveness: the ability of a group to work and stay together.
Feedback: responses each person makes to others.
Barrier: anything that blocks message flow so a receiver does not get the intended message.
Quality Circle: meeting of workers to identify, analyze, and solve problems in their work area.
Nonverbal Cues: automatic, unintentional signals that do not require a person's concentrated efforts.

QUESTIONS

1 Reread the opening case.
   a. Identify the communication barriers that appeared in this case.

b.   If you were Kim Westbrook, what would you say to Mr. Ventura (assuming you cannot afford to lose your job)?

c.   What would you suggest to each person in this case to help them improve their person-to-person communication effectiveness?

2   How does intrapersonal communication influence interpersonal communication? Could it be said that all communication is intrapersonal? Why or why not?

3   List and discuss at least four advantages of one-way communication.

4   Diagram and describe four common patterns of communication. Which are usually better where speed and accuracy are concerned? Which may be preferred if complex problems are involved? Why?

5   "You can never communicate everything you know about a subject." Do you agree or disagree with that viewpoint? Why?

6   Discuss the responsibility of the receiver in a two-way communication. What can he or she do to confirm understanding and contribute to its success?

7   List and discuss at least four requirements for communication.

8   How would you gain the attention of the following receivers?

Your Role	Intended Receiver(s)
Football coach	Players in locker room ten minutes before game with arch rival team
Ardent admirer	Attractive person of opposite sex who just sat down adjacent to you in the cafeteria
Supervisor	Employee whose performance has not reached an acceptable level after six months on the job
Union organizer	Nonunion workers walking through the gates at a manufacturing plant
Grandchild	Hard-of-hearing grandparent
Salesperson	Shopper inspecting a riding lawn mower

9   Pick one of the communication barriers discussed in the chapter and write a two-page case study of how you have personally experienced it. Provide the consequences of your behavior, and tell what you could have done to overcome the barrier.

10   Contrast verbal and nonverbal communication. How are the two related? How can one sabotage the other? Give an example of a time when someone told you one thing and you knew that person meant something else.

11   Recommend at least four actions managers may take to improve the flow of upward communication from workers to higher management. Suggest four things managers can do to improve the flow of downward communication.

12   Discuss the importance of horizontal communication among the following groups:

a.   vice presidents of manufacturing, marketing, finance, and human resources;

b.   supervisors in the various departments of a manufacturing plant, from assembly through shipping; and

  c. operators at seven consecutive work stations along a moving auto assembly line.

13 Consider the operation of the grapevine in a previous or present employer's organization. Comment on the accuracy of the information transmitted. What was management's attitude toward the grapevine, in your opinion? What needs did it fulfill among the workers? Was its presence and influence generally positive or negative? Why?

14 Under which of the following circumstances would it be best for management to use or not use the grapevine as a secondary communication medium, and why?

  a. Increasing foreign competition may make it necessary to close one of the firm's five manufacturing plants.

  b. The president of the company is thinking about retiring in ten months.

  c. The year-end bonus will be 25 percent less than last year's because of declining sales.

  d. Higher management has decided to develop a food processor to add to the present line of small appliances.

  e. The vice president of planning has announced his engagement to his secretary.

  f. Division managers, who formerly received free use of a company car, will be charged ten cents per mile for personal mileage beginning January 1.

  g. The sales meeting will be held either in Detroit or in Hawaii next year.

  h. Top management has decided to ban alcoholic beverages at this year's Christmas party.

CASES

Case 6.1

1 "Mary, if you don't start shaping up you're going to get yourself fired."
2 "I'll need this report typed and mailed promptly."
3 "We're expecting great things from you, Miss Cryle."
4 "Drop everything and come in here!"
5 "We're going to have an important meeting this afternoon, and I don't want it to be interrupted."
6 "Did we discuss anything important in class last Monday?"
7 "I hear a funny whirring sound under the hood whenever I stop at a traffic light."
8 "You college kids—you're all alike!"
9 "The recital was outstanding. I've never heard a ten-year-old girl play piano like that before."
10 "If things work out, you'll be eligible for your first pay increase after six months on the job."
11 "I'm sorry, but we don't have any openings that fit your qualifications at this time."
12 "You're doing one heck of a job, Smedley."
13 "Whose bright idea was this, anyway?"
14 "Thanks anyway, but I don't want to work overtime, boss."

Apply the communication barriers discussed in this chapter to the remarks listed above. Describe the misunderstandings that could result. Rewrite each comment to convey the message that you believe the speaker intended to send; invent any details that may be needed.

Case 6.2

To: Val Thomas, Vice President of Finance, Fulcrum Industries

From: E. P. Payne, President

Subject: Ad hoc committee to create an employee suggestion program.

As you know from my prior memoranda, this committee will address a top-priority concern of our company. I estimate its work will take a minimum of one year, at the end of which time its proposed program and plan for implementation will go before the board of directors for their approval.

I invite you to serve as chairperson of the committee, and I would like to have your acceptance in writing within the next several days.

Val Thomas read the above memo with grave concern, because she was burdened with several major projects as part of her regular work.

"This is the *last* thing I need," she complained to herself. "If I take on that extra load, I'll end up in psychological counseling or hospitalized with nervous exhaustion. I've got so many irons in the fire that I'm working ten hours a day and five on weekends as it is. But, I don't know of anyone who has rejected Payne's little requests and stayed off his hit list. I've got to avoid chairing that committee, though—it's either him or me!"

Case Questions

1 How might Val use the grapevine to help her develop a way to stay off Payne's committee without jeopardizing her career?
2 Draft a memo from Val to Payne that declines his invitation diplomatically but effectively.
3 What suggestions would you offer Payne about the way he apparently makes special committee assignments?

——————————————— NOTES ———————————————

1. Harold Leavitt, *Managerial Psychology* (Chicago: University of Chicago Press, 1964), pp. 116–120.
2. *The Wall Street Journal,* 18 April 1976, p. 1.
3. "Flying in the Face of Stark Reality," *The Wall Street Journal,* 21 May 1981, p. 29.
4. "Board Room Table Banished at Bendix for Being A Barrier," *The Wall Street Journal,* 7 March 1978, p. 19.
5. "After the Explosion in Bulova's Executive Suite," *Business Week,* 4 June 1979, p. 108.
6. William V. Haney, *Communication and Organizational Behavior: Text and Cases* (Homewood, Ill.: Irwin, 1976), pp. 303–311.

7. Debra L. Haskell, "Emerging from the Fog of Uncertainty," *Modern Office Procedures* (March 1981): 53.
8. Albert Mehrabian, "Communication without Words," *Psychology Today* (September 1968): 53–55.

SUGGESTED READINGS

Berlo, David K. *The Process of Communication.* New York: Holt, Rinehart and Winston, 1960.

Kelley, Harold H. "Communication in Experimentally Created Hierarchies," *Human Relations* (1951): 39–56.

Knapp, Mark. *Nonverbal Communication in Human Interaction.* New York: Holt, Rinehart and Winston, 1972.

Lewis, Phillip V. *Organizational Communication—The Essence of Effective Management,* 2nd ed. Columbus, Ohio: Grid Publishing, 1980.

7

Listening, Interviewing, and Conferring

When you complete your study of this chapter, you should be able to:

1 State the purposes, skills, and principles of listening,
2 Use the types of interviews, basic questions, and potential barriers,
3 Understand an interviewer's role and responsibility, and
4 Listen productively in an interview, conference, or committee.

---------- OPENING CASE ----------

Henry Burton recently started a luxury yacht charter service in the U.S. Virgin Islands. His company rents fully crewed sixty-foot sailboats to affluent customers who want a first-class tour of the Caribbean. Henry is interviewing applicants to be permanent captains on each of his four boats. These individuals must be highly competent sailors as well as polished, gracious hosts to those who charter the boats. The success of Henry's business hinges largely on the way his captains carry out their duties to the boats and to the guests who pay several thousand dollars for a week-long cruise.

This morning Henry had scheduled a 9:00 A.M. interview with thirty-four-year-old Alex Case. Alex knocked on the door at 9:00 sharp, and Henry stood to greet him.

"Good morning, Alex," he said. "Did you have any trouble finding my office?" "Not a bit," Alex answered. "I got up a little earlier than usual in case I got stuck in traffic, but everything worked out fine." Henry motioned Alex to a chair and sat down behind his desk.

"You know, Alex, I'm looking for several permanent skippers to get this business off and running, but they've got to be willing to be captains, hosts, counselors, and everything else within reason so that every charter gets its money's worth. As wealthy people who are used to first-class treatment, they'll expect a lot from each captain and crew. How do you feel about taking on a permanent job that demands more than just sailing?"

"It sounds like what I have in mind," answered Alex. "On my last job, in the Bahamas, I sailed for a first-class charter outfit. I know about most French and German wines, and after we drop anchor I can prepare the best herbed Cornish game hen you've ever tasted. I get along well with any kind of people, whether they're millionaires or harbor rats. In fact, several charters offered me jobs skippering their private boats in the states, but I don't want to leave the Caribbean. And when it comes to knowing my way around these islands, well. . . ."

"Sounds fine," Henry interrupted. "It's important for my captains to deal with different kinds of people effectively, under varied circumstances. You're saying that you do that well?" "Yes!" Alex responded, "and the pay and benefits your secretary outlined to me the day I applied sound adequate, as far as I'm concerned."

"Of course, there are other aspects to this job, too," Henry continued. "You'll be responsible for sailing a boat worth more than $500,000. Do you have your captain's license?" "Yes," Alex answered. "Have you ever been at fault for a collision in a harbor or at sea, or lost or seriously damaged a boat under your command?"

"Safety is so basic to a person like myself that it hardly seems worth spending our time talking about it," Alex replied. "Let's talk sailing."

"According to your application, you're familiar with weather in this part of the world. How would you react if you were several hundred miles from the nearest land, heading into a major tropical storm that's building to hurricane force?" Henry asked.

"Well, just let me say that there's no bad sailing weather—just incompetent sailors. I've sailed several boats through squalls above sixty miles per hour, and I've ridden out three hurricanes. Never lost a ship," Alex assured him.

"I see," Henry reflected. "And are you up on the latest electronic navigation equipment?" "Oh, sure! No problem," Alex replied.

"Aside from the sailing and hosting parts of this work, there are also the less pleasant ones—planning the menu for each charter, stocking the boat with food, putting it in first-class condition after a charter leaves, and keeping all the records my accountant requires for sound cost controls. That includes a budget for each charter covering food, drinks, fuel, and docking fees at any ports. You'll have to keep detailed reports on everything you spend. Of course, you can delegate some of that to the mate that you hire, but you'll still be responsible."

"Wow, I hate red tape," Alex muttered. "Sailing means freedom to me; I'd hate to be turned into an ocean-going clerk!" "Tell me a little more about your feelings on records," asked Henry.

"Well, in my last job I had to write out everything in a diary-like notebook. It took forever, and I'd always leave some stuff out unintentionally."

"It sounds like you could have produced a better system if somebody had asked you," Henry observed. "Certainly," Alex responded. "Nobody ever did, though."

"How would you feel about working with my accountant to design a set of on-board financial records that would let you summarize the financial details of each charter as effectively and efficiently as possible?" "That would be *great*!" Alex exclaimed. "Lead me to him!"

"As you know, I'm looking for captains who will stay with me for an extended period of time—reliable people. I don't want high turnover. Does that mesh with your plans over the long haul?" asked Henry. "Just you and me, baby!" Alex said with a grin.

"I've got several other applicants to talk with before I make my final decisions," Henry answered. "However, I'll contact you one way or the other within ten days."

"Sounds good to me," Alex replied. "I'll be waiting!"

Nobody Listens

Very few communication tools rival effective listening. In fact, if more people were aware of the need for effective listening, we could probably double our knowledge and success. Unfortunately, many seem to have trouble paying attention to others. Do you? Research indicates most people experience a 75 percent loss of information within forty-eight hours. And what's worse, as ideas are communicated from one person to another, they are distorted by 80 percent. Based on these figures, we might question a person's memory. However, it is difficult to remember what wasn't heard in the first place. Perhaps that's why many people seem to invent stories to pass on. Or why you can't ever remember the name of that person you were just introduced to five minutes ago.

How well do you listen?

Most people seem to be aware they don't listen well. A recent study asked people to rate their listening skills. Eighty-five percent of the people rated themselves as average listeners or less. Fewer than 5 percent rated themselves as superior or excellent. To excel in human relations you must become an effective listener, someone who can project an image of interest to others. A supervisor who can project this image is a motivator. Employees are usually more committed to a supervisor who is interested in their ideas and in them personally. Most people want to be heard; and if you show a willingness to listen to their ideas, they will reciprocate.

That's why you are being asked again to stop reading and respond to a quiz—Figure 7.1. You may continue reading after you have answered the questionnaire.

Questions 1, 3, 6, 7, 8, 10, 11, 12, 18, 19, and 20 should be answered *yes*. If you were unable to do so, you will want to study the section in this chapter on how to improve your listening skills. Listening to others is so important. Everything a person says or does tells you something about that person. People want to be heard, and if you listen attentively to them, they will in turn listen to you. As Benjamin Franklin said,

The great secret of succeeding in conversation is to admire little, to hear much; always to distrust your own reason, and sometimes that of our friends, never to pretend to wit, but to make that of others appear as much as possibly we can; to hearken to what is said, and to answer to the purpose.[1]

Active Listening

Effective listening requires practice. **Active listening** relates to hearing, understanding, and responding as the message sender intended. As you study and practice the guidelines set forth in this chapter, start playing the role of an *active* listener, not a passive hearer. Become someone who hears and

active listening

FIGURE 7.1
Listening Quiz

	Yes	No	Sometimes
1. In conversation, do you let other people finish talking before reacting to what they say?	_____	_____	_____
2. Do you find yourself not paying attention (e.g., daydreaming) while in conversation with others?	_____	_____	_____
3. Do you ever try to listen for meaning when someone is talking?	_____	_____	_____
4. In a discussion is it difficult for you to see things from the other person's point of view?	_____	_____	_____
5. Do you pretend you are listening to others when actually you are not?	_____	_____	_____
6. When you are asked a question that is not clear, do you ask the person to explain what she or he means?	_____	_____	_____
7. Are you able to concentrate on a subject whether or not you are interested in it?	_____	_____	_____
8. Can you keep an open mind and avoid emotional involvement until you've heard the complete story?	_____	_____	_____
9. Do you often think of other things, unrelated to the subject, when a person is speaking?	_____	_____	_____
10. Do you consciously try to note both verbal and nonverbal clues in a conversation?	_____	_____	_____
11. Do you listen for both content and feeling?	_____	_____	_____
12. Are you sensitive to the feelings of others?	_____	_____	_____
13. Do you ever label a conversation uninteresting before you really know in which direction the speaker is headed?	_____	_____	_____
14. Do you criticize a speaker's delivery or mannerisms?	_____	_____	_____
15. Do you try to outline everything the speaker says?	_____	_____	_____

	Yes	No	Sometimes	FIGURE 7.1 cont.
16. Do you allow interferences to distract you from what the speaker is saying?	_____	_____	_____	
17. Do you avoid listening to difficult material?	_____	_____	_____	
18. Are you able to listen between the lines for what a speaker is saying?	_____	_____	_____	
19. Do you check on what your listeners have heard even if they don't ask questions?	_____	_____	_____	
20. Do you remain open and objective about everything you hear?	_____	_____	_____	

reacts to the needs stated. If you practice the art of listening, you will be sought after as a trusted employee and as a friend.

---------------------------- Purposes of Listening ----------------------------

Research estimates indicate people spend 40 to 50 percent of their time listening. Yet, their listening efficiency is only about 25 percent. Because our listening skills are so obviously below our capacity, we might wonder why people do so much talking if so many details will be forgotten. In fact, we could also ask why we listen. There are several reasons for listening:

How much time do you spend listening to others?

- to share thoughts, feelings, and sensations of others and thereby to learn more about people;
- to test the mental acuity of others, to bring into focus ideas dormant in others' minds, or to act as a sounding board for others' ideas;
- to conform to or submit to others' wishes and desires;
- to respond to the emotional feelings of others;
- to receive and learn new information;
- to change people's attitudes, values, and philosophies; and
- to improve productivity on the job.

All these reasons can be grouped under five major types of listening: instructional, creative, critical, analytical, and appreciative.

Why do you listen?

INSTRUCTIONAL LISTENING.   People listen for facts, directions, and specific details. They absorb new information and assimilate it into their total knowledge system for later use. The purpose of instructional listening is to receive new information so it can be used later. Instructional listening applies to new employee orientation programs or meetings called to inform workers of new policies or procedures.

CREATIVE LISTENING. People listen to gain new ideas and to learn new methods of problem solving. This type of listening is more comprehensive than instructional listening; besides attempting to gain new information, one must also understand what it can do. A salesperson would probably use creative listening for a lecture on new techniques of closing a sale or a new promotional campaign or an orientation of a new product.

CRITICAL LISTENING. People listen to evaluate the validity and usefulness of someone's ideas and judgments. They also listen to determine if the speaker distorts information. The purpose of this type of listening is sound reasoning. Such listening does not mean challenging the credibility of everything you hear. It does mean weighing the speaker's main points. Critical listening would be used by a purchasing agent listening to a salesperson or a company recruiter interviewing university seniors.

──────────────────────── EXHIBIT 7.1 ────────────────────────

Joe Engressia, blind since birth, may have found more fulfillment through listening than many sighted persons. When he was four years old, Joe dissected a telephone piece by piece and learned what each part did by calling the telephone company or talking to an electronics technician. His finely honed sense of hearing allowed him to identify the various buzzes and clicks that route calls and signal problems on the line. By the time he was eight years old, he was working as a volunteer for the telephone company in Ft. Lauderdale, Florida, identifying circuitry problems by listening to telltale sounds.

After moving to Colorado, his unusual ability to troubleshoot phone problems with his ears attracted the attention of a vice president of Mountain Bell in Denver, who paid Joe for his exceptional audio talent. "I dial around and listen," he explains, and after isolating a problem he suggests ways that the telephone company can correct it.

"I learned electronics over the phone. I also learned how to type over the phone. I got a lot of my education in a whole bunch of different things over the phone. Through the telephone, I [discovered] a universe that was closed and locked to me."

Source: "The Sounds of Evidence," *The Search For Solutions*, p. 14. Courtesy of Phillips Petroleum Company.

ANALYTICAL LISTENING. People listen to discern others' purposes, to discriminate between lines of argument, or to weigh evidence. The purposes of this type of listening are understanding and remembering and recall and application. Some of the common areas where analytical listening takes place are discussion groups, problem-solving sessions, and think-tanks.

APPRECIATIVE LISTENING. People listen for pleasure, entertainment, escape, and relaxation. They listen to any sound or series of sounds which are pleasurable. The purpose of this type of listening is enjoyment. To some people the purr of a properly adjusted motor is pleasurable. To other people, it's the purr of a pet cat, the songs of birds, the wind in the trees, or the roar of the surf.

Listening Skills

Our knowledge about listening has largely been shaped by research in the 1940s. However, the classifications of listening skills developed then are still applicable. These listening skills may be separated into two areas: receptive and reflective skills.

What are the basic listening skills?

RECEPTIVE SKILLS.   Receptive skills are primarily associated with listening accuracy. They include the ability to (1) keep related details in mind, (2) observe a single detail, (3) remember a series of details, and (4) follow oral directions. One student with poor receptive skills took a team-taught biological science course. She recorded one professor's words in blue ink and his colleague's remarks in red. Despite her meticulous color-coded notes—the most unusual approach that either professor had ever seen—she did poorly because she was unable to discern the meaning and appreciate the context of the words.

REFLECTIVE SKILLS.   Reflective skills are related to contemplation and mental consideration. Usually a conclusion is reached after much thought. Specifically, these skills include the ability to (1) use contextual clues, (2) recognize organizational elements, (3) select main ideas as opposed to subordinate ideas and details, (4) recognize the relationships between main ideas and subordinate ideas supporting them, and (5) draw justifiable inferences.

Improving Our Listening

Although the purposes, types, and skills of listening are essential to understanding, getting others to listen to what you have to say is a real challenge. For example, the 1977 airline disaster in Tenerife, Canary Islands, which cost 586 lives, $100 million in airplanes, and $500 million in lawsuits, apparently resulted when flight crew members heard but did not listen to radio instructions. The MGM Grand Hotel fire in 1980 was a similar incident. Many people on lower levels of the hotel were warned of the fire but did not respond.

People often pretend to pay attention when they aren't really listening. They may give eye contact, smile, and nod their heads knowingly, but their minds are on another subject. Others listen to every word until you use terminology that causes them to become so involved that they lose contact

Why don't other people listen to me?

with what you're actually saying. They become emotionally deaf. Other people let their egos get in the way. They think only about what concerns them. They're not interested in a statement unless there is something in it to enhance their status. Others are just lazy. They don't want to take the time or expend the energy to listen. What can be done to help people improve their listening?

---------------------- Two Effective Listening Tools ----------------------

What are the essential tools of good listening?

Two simple tools can be used to improve communication skills immediately. They also demonstrate that a person is listening. They are confirmation and clarification. With these two basic skills and a lot of practice you can become an effective and efficient listener. In addition, listening well is a human relations skill that can be used to solve problems (as we shall see in Part III).

CONFIRMATION.   To maintain good human relationships with co-workers, one must understand the messages they send. It is possible to hear but not actually receive a transmitted message. Confirming what was said helps one to understand exactly what was said and why. It is especially helpful to someone who disagrees with the message or is being asked to become committed to a particular program. Whenever there is doubt about what is being sent or meant one should confirm the message.

Do not assume you understand. Make sure you know what was said and why before you take action. After all, if you don't have time to get it right the first time, when will you have time to do it over? Confirm the message so you and the speaker will know you understand.

CLARIFICATION.   When you don't understand a message or are not certain about a speaker's motives, ask for clarification. For example, "I don't believe I understand what you're saying. Tell me more." Or, "Why do you think that?" Or, simply, "Oh?" Those supervisors who make sure they understand what their workers mean have better motivated and committed workers than those who do not listen.

---------------------- Obstacles to Effective Listening ----------------------

What are the major hindrances to effective listening?

Besides using the two listening tools, it is also important to recognize and avoid listening obstacles. There are many obstacles to effective listening, but most can be found among the following five major hindrances for an interviewer which are: intolerance, impulsivity, anticipation, indolence, and suggestibility.[2]

INTOLERANCE.   One's background can be a source of noise for an interviewer and can reduce listening acuity. Noise is any interference (physical or mental) hindering accurate receipt of a message. A person's speech patterns, physical appearance, dress, or mannerisms may make it difficult to concentrate because attention is often devoted to mental criticism of the interviewee. For example, in the days before television, one presidential candidate prejudiced radio listeners by pronouncing the word *radio* with a short *a*. This odd pronunciation grated on the ears of listeners and, analysts contend, they registered their intolerance by defeating him at the ballot box. Likewise, a sociology professor persistently pronounced the word *subject* as *subbick*. This greatly annoyed his students because it was a word he used scores of times during each lecture.

Such speech patterns can cause a person's message to be distorted, influenced by stereotypes or received incompletely. One survey that explored the prejudicial effect of ethnic and rural speech patterns on hiring, promotion, and termination decisions asked a group of personnel managers to listen to four taped conversations between job applicants and an interviewer.[3] Two of the applicants spoke standard English, one spoke with a rural accent, and one spoke nonstandard or black English. The managers were significantly prejudiced against the individuals with pronounced ethnic and rural speech characteristics.

IMPULSIVITY. Some talkers seem unable to wait for a listener to respond to a question. Moments of silence seem eternities, and so speakers answer their own questions, suggest appropriate answers, or change the subject. Unable to tolerate silence, talkers monopolize the conversation. Listeners are unable to present their case completely.

Impulsive American business executives have met confusion when negotiating with their Japanese counterparts. To Japanese managers, silence implies respect and serious consideration for the speaker's proposal. However, the American making the presentation may feel compelled to keep the ball rolling conversationally with a steady stream of words when the Japanese managers fall silent.

ANTICIPATION. The result of intolerance and impulsivity is often anticipation of what someone will say. Such anticipation reduces one's ability to hear what is really being said and one's ability to gain true information. Consider the young military officer attending a general briefing who tuned out the proceedings and took a mental vacation. When asked a direct question by the colonel in charge of the meeting, he stuttered momentarily, trying to summon his thoughts. A fellow officer behind him whispered, ''Tell him three tractor trailers and two Jeeps.'' The flustered officer parroted this reply, and the entire group burst into laughter. ''Lieutenant,'' asked the colonel, ''how in the world do you intend to bring security leaks under control with *that* stuff?''

INDOLENCE.   Ineffective listening is often nothing more than mental laziness. If someone dwells too long on a subject that is abstract, complicated, or difficult, listeners may become bored or distracted. They must exert effort to display a keen interest in the subject matter.

SUGGESTIBILITY.   Certain emotional or ambiguous words suggest ideas or provoke feelings. Unless speakers clarify those words, listeners can be misled easily. For example, an improperly reported remark by John Lennon of the Beatles that the group was more popular than Jesus made headlines around the globe and brought them volumes of hate mail. However, the remark was distorted and taken out of context. Lennon spoke with regret and meant the comment as an indictment against society's values—not as an egotistical boast. Ask for concrete examples when you confront words that interfere with your objectivity.

——————————————— Prescriptions for Better Listening ———————————————

How can I improve my listening ability?

Many opportunities arise every day to listen and respond, to question, and to clarify thoughts you don't understand. What can you do to be a better listener? One suggestion is to take 51 percent of the responsibility for the success of your communications. The following six suggestions also should help: concentrate, work at listening, keep an open mind, take advantage of thought speed, listen for total meaning, and be sensitive.

CONCENTRATE.   The first mandate is to concentrate, that is, to force your attention, to focus on the subject. To learn how to give undivided attention to what a speaker says, one must learn to control the environmental conditions. That is, one must not yield to distractions. Neither tolerate nor create interferences. Conduct the interview in a distraction-free, quiet, and comfortable location. If interruptions still occur, don't allow them to upset you. Take them in stride and return your attention to the speaker.

WORK AT LISTENING.   An interviewer should not pretend to pay attention, but should try to develop a sincere interest in the ideas being communicated. He or she should seek a purpose in every listening situation. It is also wise to learn to adjust to various listening situations and to different speaking rates. In short, one should work at listening and get actively involved with what is happening. An active listener can aid the speaker by creating a nonthreatening climate. Be neither critical, evaluative, nor moralizing. Instead, develop an atmosphere of equality, understanding, acceptance, and warmth.

KEEP AN OPEN MIND.   An open attitude is important. One can become emotionally deaf by submitting to certain words, but it is possible to learn to temper one's enthusiasm by not getting overstimulated about certain subjects. Avoiding arguments and avoiding criticizing a speaker's delivery before the idea has been fully developed will also help to maintain emotional stability in an interview.

TAKE ADVANTAGE OF THOUGHT SPEED.   We all can think much faster than the average person speaks, as much as six times as fast. We can use that speed difference to make mental summaries and to increase our attention span. We can also review what we are hearing and seeing. We can focus on the nonverbal as well as the verbal by noticing all cues. Use thought speed for productive listening, not daydreaming.

LISTEN FOR TOTAL MEANING.   Listen for total meaning. Both the content and the tone of a message are important. Both are necessary for understanding what a speaker means. Several skills are important to total meaning, for example, listening for main ideas as well as facts, identifying supportive elements, and analyzing the communication's basic elements. It also helps to find a natural link between the questions you ask and the responses you receive. The primary objective of listening is to listen in depth. Learn to respond to the feeling or attitude underlying the message, and try to become involved with the speaker's message and actions.

BE SENSITIVE.   Fact-sensitive listening assists human relationships. When tone is more important than content, the listener should respond sensitively to the feelings of the person communicating. Sensitivity can be thought of as the ability to predict what others will feel, say, or do about you, them, and others. Sensitivity to the needs of others creates a supportive work climate. It allows one to detect and cope with communication barriers. Thus it also gives the communicators greater satisfaction.

———————— Three Opportunities for Listening ————————

With these six skills in mind, we will turn to three areas in which a lot of listening is required: interviews, conferences, and committees. Each has its own effect on organizational relationships.

Where will I spend most of my listening time on the job?

———————————— Interviews ————————————

Interviewing is one of the manager's keys to good human relations, perhaps the best key currently available. Therefore, interviewing is a communicative skill you should learn and practice. Skillful listeners can get more information from a willing, knowledgeable person in a few minutes of talk than from

interviewing

several hours of reading or other research. **Interviewing** is the giving and getting of information. It should be a friendly, informal exchange of information between two people about a subject they both want or need to explore.

However, productive interviewing is an art. To develop it one must first be a good listener. In addition, one should understand the different types of interviews, the interviewer's role and responsibility, potential barriers and biases, basic question types, and inadequate answers to questions.

What are the basic kinds of interviews?

TYPES OF INTERVIEWS.   There are three basic interviews, all of which are useful in gathering information: directive, nondirective, and stress. In a directive interview interviewers decide what questions to ask, what to try to accomplish, and what sequence to follow. A fairly rigid structure is followed. In a nondirective interview interviewees openly express their thoughts and ideas. Although interviewers have a plan, they are flexible and guide the interviewee by judicious use of open-ended questions. In a stress interview the interviewer tests interviewees to see how they react under pressure. The interviewees' statements and beliefs are challenged to see how they handle themselves in stressful situations. This style of interviewing is still used by some companies, although it is not as popular as it was during the 1960s.

In addition, interviews may be classified according to purpose. Each type helps in building good human relations in organizations if used properly. Six of the most common interviews are shown in Exhibit 7.2.

There is some overlap among these types of interviews. One set of circumstances may require several types at various stages of the conversation. In each type, the interviewer is responsible for the direction and results of the interview.

What does an interviewer do?

INTERVIEWER'S ROLE AND RESPONSIBILITY.   Before an interviewer can gain the information desired, he or she will need to have a goal, to gather sufficient background information about the interviewee and the situation, to outline some key questions to ask, and to develop a proposal for discussion. Yet, interviewers must remain flexible. They must secure enough information on which to make a decision. To do so, they must be a combination of objective researcher, goodwill ambassador of their organization, and critical listener. They must apply all they know about the psychology of human behavior. They must be aware of themselves and their effect on others. They must also recognize potential interpersonal barriers in the interview process.

What are the barriers an interviewer faces?

POTENTIAL BARRIERS.   Although communication barriers have already been discussed, the interview presents specific opportunities for unwanted distortion. These must be recognized and dealt with. There are three distorting influences in an interview: background and psychological biases, behavioral barriers, and language barriers.[4]

EXHIBIT 7.2

1 **Information-giving interview**—supplying or explaining facts, or instructing someone about opinions, policies, methods, and so forth. Examples of information-giving interviews are employee(s) orientation, a public tour through a manufacturing plant, or a flight attendant informing passengers of safety precautions and airline rules before take-off.

2 **Information-getting interview**—seeking information and advice, obtaining beliefs, attitudes, feelings, or other data from someone. An information-getting interview would be used by newspaper reporters, bank lending officers, and insurance agents taking applications for health or life insurance.

3 **Appraisal interview**—evaluating someone's performance and behavior and providing guidelines for future performance. An example would be the yearly work performance/program reviews most organizations conduct with their personnel. (The appraisal interview will be studied in detail in Chapter 15.)

4 **Counseling interview**—focusing on someone's personal problems as they affect working relationships. A counseling interview may be appropriate for college guidance counselors and supervisors assisting subordinates in resolving problems of performance or attitude. (The counseling interview will be discussed in Chapter 10.)

5 **Employment interview**—finding the right person for the right job. The employment interview synthesizes the information-getting and information-giving interviews. (The employment interview will be discussed in Chapter 18.)

6 **Problem-solving interview**—seeking solutions. A problem-solving interview may be used by an auto mechanic who asks a customer to carefully describe the sounds or other symptoms that accompany an intermittent mechanical problem. A supervisor may use this type of interview when talking to workers about the possible cause of rejected or damaged parts on a production line.

Background and Psychological Biases.   Background barriers include age, sex, religion, income, and education. It encompasses the fixed set of attitudes, personality characteristics, values, motives, goals, and needs instilled in each of us at a very early age. Psychological barriers primarily concern a person's willingness to share information. Thus, an interviewer must learn how to see the world through others' eyes.

Behavioral Barriers.   A person's behavior may have either positive or negative effects. The interviewer will want to maximize the positive and minimize the negative. Specific behavioral facts include (1) *physical communication*—eye contact, facial expressions, and mannerisms; (2) *vocal communication*—voice pleasantness, audibility, articulation, projecting interest through the voice, and speech speed; (3) *listening and feedback behavior*—the willingness and sensitivity of an interviewer to respond to an interviewee's cues.[5]

Language Barriers.   Interviewer and interviewee must have a common language. Questions must be worded to fit the interviewee's frame of reference.

Talking over or under another's level will result in an inadequate gathering of information. A person's language competence, experience, and psychological accessibility or inaccessibility to information must be considered.

BASIC QUESTION TYPES.   Properly handled, the interview can be a key to unlock a treasure chest of information. An improperly handled interview will net nothing. Therefore, interviewers must recognize the significance of their role and know the potential barriers and biases in the interview. They need to know the basic types of questions—open, closed, mirror, probing, and leading—and how they are used.

Open Questions.   Open questions call for a response of more than a few words. One type is the open-ended question, an extremely vague and general type of question that only specifies a topic or asks the respondent to talk about something. A second type is the direct question, which identifies or limits the topic and asks for a more specific reply. Both types seek a lengthy response. Some examples of open questions would be: Why did you go to college? What caused you to pick marketing as a major field of study? Why do you want to work for our company? What's causing such a high turnover of workers on the third shift? What do you find most appealing about this project?

Closed Questions.   Questions that seek briefer, more specific responses are called closed questions. Generally they can be answered in one or two words, such as *yes* or *no* or *I don't know.* Closed questions would be: Are you in good health? Are you willing to relocate? Can you start work two weeks from Thursday? Do you know why the paint department workers want to form a union?

Mirror Questions.   Mirror questions are used to encourage the interviewee to expand on an incomplete response. Often they are restatements of what the interviewee has just said. Examples of mirror questions would be: So you believe majoring in accounting was a good decision? You're planning to leave Monday instead of Tuesday so you'll have an extra day in that city? You're sure the plane won't leave for another half hour?

Probing Questions.   The probe intends to direct the respondent's thinking to further explain what has been said. It is a follow-up question to a superficial or incomplete response. It allows for a deeper investigation into the reasons for an attitude or belief, or allows the interviewee to expand with more information. It seeks further communication and allows the interviewer to control the interaction by directing the respondent to the content objective of the interview. Examples of probing questions or remarks would be: Describe the specific factors that . . . Tell me more about . . . Draw this into sharper focus for me. Help me understand exactly how . . . Tell me your thoughts on . . . What sacrifices are you willing to make to . . . ?

Leading Questions.   Leading questions direct the interviewee to give a specific answer by suggesting what an interviewer expects to hear. If used incorrectly or for the wrong reason, the leading question can produce invalid or unreliable responses. One type of leading question is the loaded question, which may trigger high emotional responses because of its connotations. Some examples of leading questions would be: Did you work hard at that job? Can you work well under pressure? Are you able to meet deadlines? Do you work well with others? What's more important to you—the money or the job?

An effective interviewer must become familiar with and be able to recognize the types of questions that may be used. Good interviewers also recognize inadequate answers.

INADEQUATE ANSWERS TO QUESTIONS.   Familiarity with the basic types of questions and skill in their use should enable interviewers to get the information sought. However, occasionally the answers received will be inadequate. Interviewers who are not actively listening may not recognize an inadequate response. In order to recognize inadequate answers one must learn to spot too much detail, irrelevant information, or false information in an answer. Recognizing these, one can then probe more deeply or move the interviewee in a better direction. To accomplish objectives, though, one must listen actively.

Conferences

A second place to practice active listening skills is at group meetings or **conferences.** One of the most frequent complaints of supervisors and managers, though, is "There are just too many meetings around here." To make it worse, most of these managers claim almost 50 percent of the meeting time is wasted. Many managers spend from one to three hours per day in some kind of meeting, so that is quite a bit of wasted time. However, since group meetings and conferences are an essential part of a manager's day we need to know how to achieve positive results.

conferences

How can a business conference achieve its intended purpose?

HOLD A CONFERENCE ONLY IF NECESSARY.   Conferring with others is sometimes necessary, but make sure it will be productive. There's no sense in meeting on Wednesdays just because it is Wednesday. State a purpose for the conference and then meet to accomplish the objective. Minimize wasted time by sticking to the subject.

DON'T INVITE EVERYONE.   Productive conferences require planning and time and the right people. Only those who are directly involved should be invited to a meeting. For example, some of the attendees should be able to stimulate thinking, know what is going on in the organization, and aid decision making. You may wish to handpick the people to come to your conferences.

What are the various leadership styles used in business conferences?

USE PROPER LEADERSHIP STYLE.   The need for proper leadership styles was discussed in Chapter 6. In leading a meeting, one needs to be flexible and adapt one's leadership style to that meeting. For example, five types of meetings have been identified, each requiring a different leadership style.[6]

1. Meetings for *information giving* require an autocratic leader because of the necessity to give and explain orders without receiving feedback. An information-giving meeting would be held to explain reasons for closing a plant or laying off employees or to outline a company's current financial condition to stockholders.

2. Meetings for *information collecting* call for shared leadership because of the amount of participation required and group stimulation that results. An information-collecting meeting would be held between a sales manager and salespeople to discuss competitors' strategies in various parts of the country.

3. Meetings for *decision making* call for shared leadership because each member's idea is important to the final decision. A decision-making meeting would be called to determine what to name a new product; to develop a plan to add a new product to the existing product line; or, to decide how to respond to a Federal Trade Commission challenge to a company's advertising claims.

4. Meetings for *decision selling* require a combination leadership style. The leader must be autocratic regarding the decision, but share leadership when carrying out the decision. A decision-selling meeting would be held to convince grocery checkers that the newly devised checkout procedure, although initially slower, will help them work more efficiently once they've learned it. It would also be an appropriate meeting to justify management's decision to operate all retail stores in the chain from 12:00 noon to 5:00 P.M. on Sundays instead of remaining closed all day.

5. Meetings for *problem solving* call for shared leadership to use all available resources. A problem-solving meeting would be held to solicit employees' suggestions for reducing personnel costs by $500,000 per year; for reducing quality assurance rejects from 8 percent to 5 percent; or, for improving the effectiveness of new employee orientation or reducing absenteeism on the first day of hunting season.

Whatever the purpose of the meeting, the leadership style should be adapted accordingly. Meet the needs of the attendees.

Committees

The **committee** is probably the most frequently used small group. It allows for the exchange of ideas, generates information, makes decisions, and recommends action. Therefore, it is an important managerial tool. However, the committee has been much maligned as an expensive time waster. Other criticisms center on the quality of decisions made in committees. It is often said that the camel is the result of a committee that got together to plan a horse. Committees also are famous for passing the buck.

committee

How are committees used and abused?

Organizations seem to have two choices: (1) don't have any committees, or (2) learn how to meet more productively. Since the first suggestion probably will never occur, let's deal with the second one. If a committee is absolutely necessary, committee members should have both the knowledge and interest to serve, should contribute to the purpose of the committee, and should receive, in advance, a specific agenda. In addition, the committee's decisions and recommendations should be shared with management for action. Committee group meetings can be an effective communication tool if used properly. Group cohesiveness and positive results can be the outcome; human relationships can be enhanced.

CONCLUSION

Being a skilled listener and interviewer requires practice in active listening. This chapter has concentrated on the skills needed to become an effective listener. The basic techniques mentioned in this chapter—confirmation, clarification, concentration, objectivity, and sensitivity—will help managers to become skillful listeners. Work at listening, control the thought speed, and listen for total meaning. Whereas many supervisors manage with the mouth (by talking too much), they can manage more productively with the ear (by listening). The things they hear will help them make better decisions.

KEY TERMS

Active Listening: hearing, understanding, and responding as the message sender intended.

Interviewing: the giving and getting of information between two people about a subject they both want or need to explore.

Conferences: group business meetings.

Committee: a small group that allows for the exchange of ideas, generates information, makes decisions, and recommends action to management.

----------------------------------- QUESTIONS -----------------------------------

1 Reread the opening case.
   a. Identify the specific types of questions Henry Burton used in this interview. What clues led you to classify them as you did?
   b. What kinds of inadequate answers did Alex give? Why do you feel they were inadequate?
   c. List any additional questions, if any, that Henry should have asked. Why do you feel they are necessary?
   d. Assuming Alex was the only person who applied for a skipper's job, tell what Henry should do next in reaching a hiring decision? Why?
2 Describe at least three situations in which you became an inattentive listener. What factors made you inattentive in each situation? What can you do to overcome them and to improve your attentiveness in future situations of that type?
3 List and give a personal example of each of the five purposes of listening. Which purpose do you use most often? Why?
4 List the most likely purpose for listening for the following persons and suggest how they may improve their attention:
   a. politician,
   b. management trainee,
   c. telephone operator,
   d. member of debating team,
   e. person attending a seminar on "How to become a more innovative thinker,"
   f. fisherman listening to weather forecast,
   g. owner of new stereo,
   h. student in freshman orientation program at university, and
   i. potential new car buyer listening to salesperson.
5 Contrast receptive with reflective listening skills. Which courses have you taken that required you to place heavy emphasis on receptive skills? On reflective ones? Why should a successful listener possess both types of skills?
6 Differentiate between the listening tools of confirmation and clarification. Do you feel one is more important than the other? Why or why not?
7 Give an example of a situation in which each of the following interviews would be appropriate:
   a. information giving,
   b. information getting,
   c. appraisal,
   d. counseling,
   e. employment, and
   f. problem-solving.

Why is it important for an interviewer to clearly establish the type of interview to be used before the conversation begins?

8   Define in your own words the three potential distorting influences or barriers to a successful interview. How does each of these compare with the communication barriers that you learned about in Chapter 6?

9   Describe at least one specific incident in dealing with friends, family members, or other students that involved each of the following listening obstacles:
   a.   intolerance,
   b.   impulsivity,
   c.   anticipation,
   d.   indolence, and
   e.   suggestibility.
   How was each incident affected by the listening obstacle? What could you have done to ensure a more effective and successful result in each case?

10   List at least four items in the six-point prescription for successful listening. What changes can you make to follow each more successfully? What problems can you foresee if you *don't* change?

—————————————— CASES ——————————————

Janice Koberg is vice president of sales at Kregel and Sons, Inc., a manufacturer of   Case 7.1
telephone answering machines. For the past several months, she has monitored the progress of a new model (the KS 130) through the research and development department. Customers have been clamoring for an answering machine with its price and features, but no company has yet marketed one—although Kregel's nearest competitor is expected to do so within one year.

Today, Janice scheduled a meeting with George Etzioni, vice president of research and development, to discuss the KS 130's status in the testing lab and the date by which it should be cleared for mass production. She believes that if George had accelerated the testing schedule on the machine and reduced the number of tests performed it would have been released for production three months ago.

"Jan," George began, "You're going to have to be patient with us a little while longer. I'm not convinced the speaker system will hold up through the guarantee period. We discovered last week during one crucial test that the speaker produces a ragged sound and the components in the motor may fail under certain conditions that could occur in actual use. It's just one of those things! We need more time. We don't want the company's reputation to suffer by bringing this out prematurely and having to make a lot of field repairs or, worse yet, issue a mass recall. Don't you agree?"

"George, we can't sell patience!" exclaimed Janice. "We're in business to *sell* products, not just invent them! You guys have been messing around with that thing for over a year! I've promised my salespeople that we'd be first on the market with this model, but you've disappointed all of us by stretching out the testing time. You've run three months past the original schedule on the KS 130 right now."

"If you had as much pride in this outfit as I do, you'd be *glad* I'm taking plenty of time to wring out this new model in the lab," George countered. "Our whole reputation could be lost on one lousy model, and reputations can't be built overnight. This is going to be our biggest seller, and it's got to be designed, tested, and made right!"

"You've cost our salespeople commissions on a machine that should be on the store shelves instead of the testing bench right now," Jan answered. "Potential customers and our company's stockholders are the losers, too."

"You ivory tower salespeople are all alike," George shot back. "You do market research, identify a model that we should make, and 'poof' it's built. You have no appreciation for the role of research and development. We're the people who safeguard the reputation of this company, and don't you forget it!"

"Ah, yes," Janice responded, "but if it weren't for us 'ivory tower salespeople' pounding the bricks every day nothing would be sold, no money would come in, and you lab rats wouldn't have jobs where you can sit around contemplating your navels instead of supporting the people on the firing line."

George stood up, sneering. "And if we did things your way, our salespeople would be run out of every store they call on because they'd be selling lousy products. I'm not going to argue in circles. I'll clear the product for mass production when I'm sure it's reliable, and not before." He walked out and slammed the door.

Case Questions

1 What kinds of listening should each person in this case have applied more effectively? How might their discussion have benefited?
2 Suggest some specific questions that each should have asked to better clarify and understand the other's position on the central issue in this case.
3 If you were Janice Koberg, what steps would you take at this point to mend fences, assuming it's necessary for her to have a reasonably compatible working relationship with George Etzioni.

Case 7.2

When his eyes adjusted to the dim lights in the room, he found a seat, ordered a drink, and casually surveyed those seated nearby. He recognized her face immediately, and she flashed him that old familiar smile.

"You're as pretty as a picture," he said.

"Some things never change," she answered coyly, "even though it's been a long time. You're looking great," she observed. "Still up to your old tricks?"

"Oh, yes," he answered, "always hustling a buck."

"Where?"

"Wall Street. All the smart money's into it; it's as American as apple pie. And you?"

"I'm a Philadelphia lawyer," she answered. "It's like having a license to steal."

"You're kidding!" he retorted. "Man, that's heavy stuff! Gosh," he reflected, "we had a good thing going, but we've changed a lot since the good old days. You were a wild and crazy person!"

"I'll drink to that," she answered, glancing at her watch. "Unfortunately, time marches on."

"Let's have one more for old time's sake," he suggested.

"Sorry—gotta run," she said wistfully, "but call me; we'll have lunch."

"You can bet on it," he smiled. "Have a nice day."

1 Discuss the amount of information exchanged in the above encounter.
2 Relate this case to the Johari window concept in Chapter 3. Which view did each person show the other? Do you believe another was desirable? Why or why not?
3 Suggest at least four questions that each person could have asked the other to elicit more information than was provided.

NOTES

1. Robert S. Byer, "An Interview with Benjamin Franklin," *Flying Colors* 5 (1979): 23.
2. Felix M. Lopez, *Personnel Interviewing* (New York: McGraw-Hill, 1965), pp. 55–58.
3. Larry M. Blair and Hugh S. Conner, "Black and Rural Accents Found to Lessen Job Opportunities," *Monthly Labor Review* (May 1978): 35.
4. John Makay, *Explorations in Speech Communication* (Columbus, Ohio: Merrill, 1973), pp. 94–99.
5. Ibid.
6. "Stop Misusing Your Management Meetings," *Modern Manufacturing* (April 1969).

SUGGESTED READINGS

Barbara, Dominick A. *The Art of Listening.* Springfield, Ill.: Charles C Thomas, 1974.

Nichols, Ralph G., and Stevens, Leonard A. *Are You Listening?* New York: McGraw-Hill, 1957.

Rogers, Carl R., and Farson, Richard E. *Active Listening.* Chicago: University of Chicago Industrial Relations Center, 1975.

Stano, Michael, and Reinsch, N. L., Jr. *Communication in Interviews.* Englewood Cliffs, N.J.: Prentice-Hall, 1982.

8

Making Decisions

LEARNING OBJECTIVES

When you complete your study of this chapter, you should be able to:

1 Recognize the variables affecting decision making,
2 Follow a five-step problem-solving model for making decisions,
3 List the advantages and disadvantages of group problem solving,
4 Overcome the problems of groupthink, and
5 Be familiar with electronic decision-making approaches.

—————————————— OPENING CASE ——————————————

Phil Brook, a young civil engineer supervisor, works for Local Land Management Associates. He joined the firm one year ago and became supervisor of a twelve-person crew of surveyors after completing a six-month training program. One of the crew members, John Francis, has been with LLMA for twenty-three years. He told Phil on his first day as supervisor that he didn't appreciate having a "young upstart still wet behind the ears for a boss." John has been antagonistic and somewhat insubordinate toward Phil ever since.

Phil has made several attempts to develop a satisfactory working relationship with John, but nothing he has tried seems to work. He requested John's advice on several technical surveying problems, but John's standard reply was, "You've been to college—you figure it out!" He asked John to serve as the leader of a four-person client relations committee, but John refused. Hoping he would enjoy talking about some of the bigger projects he'd worked on, he even tried to get John to share his past experience on several large surveying jobs with the rest of the crew, but John said with a sneer, "Thanks—but no thanks!"

Within the past three weeks, John has become openly contemptuous toward Phil. Several days ago, when asked to carry some surveying equipment across a drainage ditch, John laughed, slapped Phil on the back, and said (winking to the others), "That looks like a job that only a big shot like you can handle. Jump in, kid!" Caught by surprise and uncertain how to respond, Phil decided to be a good sport and carry the stuff across himself. Unfortunately, the other members of the crew picked up on John's tactic, and now they've started to balk at Phil's directions and treat him in a casual, offhand manner.

Phil is concerned that his crew and ultimately his job may disintegrate if the problem is not soon resolved. However, he's not certain what is making John so antagonistic, and he's skeptical that he can ever build a satisfactory relationship with someone who uses every opportunity to be sarcastic, patronizing, or contemptuous.

—————————————— Heads I Win, Tails You Lose ——————————————

Do you remember how you made decisions when you were much younger? You probably flipped a coin. One of the beauties of this system was that if it did not come out the way you thought it should, you could always go for the best three out of four or five out of seven. Although some supervisors still follow similar unsound practices in their problem analysis, you can see a few faults in this decision-making system.

Planning, organizing, directing, and controlling are central to leadership and, thereby, to decision making. Problem solving pervades all management functions because every task requires a decision. Therefore, it plays a key role in the creation and maintenance of productive human relationships. These two terms, decision making and problem solving, will be used interchangeably in this chapter.

Work groups contain a large reservoir of problem-solving potential; they are a good source of high quality ideas. To use this potential, however, one must develop skill. To be productive problem solvers, members of a work group must seek an answer to a shared problem and offer information freely that leads to a solution. Human relations are enhanced when group members achieve simultaneous satisfaction of individual and organizational goals.

The Decision Process

What is decision making?

Decision making is natural. You've already spent a great part of your life deciding between alternatives. Should you go to college or go to work, or both? Should you major in accounting, management, or liberal arts? Your decisions provide insight into your behavior, values, attitudes, and personality. For example, if you decide to go to the movies instead of studying for an exam or completing a research project, what does that decision say about you? It is important to understand decision making and why it is crucial to management success. For our purposes, **decision making** is choosing among alternative courses of action. The way you solve problems affects what happens not only to you but also to those people with whom you work and socialize.

decision making

Decision Variables

What are the significant factors relating to the decision-making process?

During decision making, groups focus their attention and efforts on discussing the ideas proposed by their members. The problem may be insufficient production, high employee turnover, or boredom on the job. Ideas are the catalyst for interaction and lead toward consensus. Seven significant variables regarding the decision process are: the nature of task requirements, type of conflict, role structure, sex distribution, openness of communication channels, homogeneity of group members, and group climate.[1] Each of these factors should be studied as a social phenomenon influencing group decision. Each affects the relationships of group members.

THE NATURE OF TASK REQUIREMENTS.   The quality of a work group's performance decreases as the complexity of a task increases. The reason is that as a task becomes more complex the group has less time to work together on the ramifications of the task. That is why communication is so important to the problem-solving process. When the task is difficult, group performance is helped by open communication, the uninhibited expression of agreement (satisfaction) and disagreement (dissatisfaction).

Space shuttle flights, as an example, require thousands of people to complete tasks successfully. No individual understands all the facets of such a complex, interrelated, and highly technical undertaking. Computers are employed to cross-check one another and run through systems tests automatically in a programmed sequence.

TYPE OF CONFLICT.   The type of problem a work group deals with can produce conflict among the members. Most groups at some time are in conflict about something (e.g., roles, goals, rewards, skills, etc.). If the conflict is intense, consensus is difficult to achieve. Using available facts can reduce conflict and produce consensus. The emphasis must be on problem solving. The conflicting groups can present their views to each other and work through their differences. Time and commitment are essential requirements for conflict resolution.

ROLE STRUCTURE.   One significant aspect of role structure, as it relates to problem solving, is the power distribution within a group. For example, extreme specialization of tasks seems to affect consensus negatively; moderate specialization seems positively related. Also, a person's position in the group affects decisions. That is, a group is more likely to accept suggestions from a higher-status person and to ignore a lower-status person.

Groups may erroneously attribute the capacity for effective and innovative thinking to those of high formal status—something that may have grievous consequences.

The Edsel, for example, was named by a committee whose members reportedly deferred to the ranking executive, who favored the name. More appealing names such as Pacer, Ranger, and Citation became model names. Although many other factors contributed to the car's demise in the marketplace, observers feel the name was no advantage because it sounded odd and had no positive associations for consumers.

SEX DISTRIBUTION.   There are several differences between the ways males and females interact in a work group. Males are sometimes more hostile, dominating, and unreasonable than females. Also, males can be more rough in manner, language, and sentiments than females. Obviously, these communicative qualities of hostility, domination, unreasonableness, and roughness have negative affects on productive problem solving and human relations. Thus, one might wonder why so many groups with decision-making power are male.

OPENNESS OF COMMUNICATION CHANNELS.   The existing communication pattern of an organization affects the decision-making process. For example, an open communication channel affects production and satisfaction among workers. If management motivates, there is more of a chance for friendly, open, effective communication. Also, higher levels of morale generally exist within sharing communication climates. Openness, honesty, trust, and continual communication pays off in lower turnover and in increased credibility of management and its channels of communication. Management needs to let employees know what is going on because communication and decision making are inseparable in practice.

HOMOGENEITY OF GROUP MEMBERS.   Depending on the type of problem that must be solved, people who have similar personal attributes (i.e., a homogeneous group) may or may not be more productive than those who are dissimilar (i.e., a heterogeneous group). For example, homogeneous groups tend to be most productive on simple tasks that require considerable cooperation. Heterogeneous groups tend to be more productive when different opinions and capabilities and creativity are required.

An effective homogeneous group might be a team of computer programmers trying to debug a newly written program or several mechanics trying to isolate the problem in a malfunctioning automatic transmission. An effective heterogeneous group might be a committee that is composed of artists, copywriters, designers, production personnel, and an individual familiar with the Fair Packaging and Labeling Act that meets to create an appealing new package for a product.

GROUP CLIMATE.   Cooperation aids open discussion and decisions. There is a feeling that "we are in this together." People can pull together rather than push apart. Cohesiveness is crucial to this cooperative climate. When such a group climate is missing, we may find things like the following happening: workers at a General Motors Chevrolet truck plant threatened to walk off the job when they discovered, concealed in the kneehole of a supervisor's desk, a control box that was wired into the assembly line to increase its pace.[2] The box was reportedly installed by lower-level supervisors in response to higher management's pressure for increased production. The company agreed to pay the workers involved for the trucks they produced that would not have been made if the line had run at the speed prescribed in the union contract. The settlement approached $750,000.

Obviously, group and organizational climate cannot be improved directly by managerial orders. Supervisors cannot just assume that group climate will improve and human relations problems will get better given enough time. They must act to improve or to maintain group climate. Two requirements for a manager who wants to produce a good human relations climate are: (1) to know what employees need and want, and (2) to be a good listener by developing effective vertical and horizontal communication lines.

Everyone is responsible for human relations. You can assist in establishing a productive human relations environment, because your knowledge and attitudes influence others. Your decision, or acceptance of others' decisions, affects the group. But it may not be satisfactory to the group.

-------------------------- Problem-Solving Model --------------------------

Several models leading to productive decisions have been proposed over the years. Most formats include defining the problem, analyzing the problem, establishing criteria for a solution, proposing possible solutions, evaluating possible solutions, selecting a solution, and plotting a course of action.

Is there a typical problem-solving format for making decisions?

DEFINE THE PROBLEM.   Have you ever solved a problem only to discover it wasn't the real problem? Someone has said a problem well defined is half solved, and the problem represents the basis of managerial action. A problem is any deviation between what should be and what is. Thus, the first step in analyzing a problem is to focus directly on the problem area. Rejects on a production line, for example, may be caused by worker sabotage, substandard material, ineffective training, improperly adjusted machines, miscalibrated quality assurance instruments, or a combination of these things. Such a multitude of potential causes makes problem identification very challenging. That means the problem solver must gather enough facts to build a reasonable definition.

ANALYZE THE PROBLEM.   Once the problem is clear, a work group may begin analyzing it. Three specific steps are involved in problem analysis.[3] (1) Compare what exists with what is desired. Determine the scope of the problem, identify impelling and constraining forces, and analyze problem intensity. (2) Set a goal that is specific enough for members to know when it has been achieved. This may be accomplished by obtaining relevant information, interpreting statements purported to be factual, determining the degree of acceptance of others' statements, and evaluating information sources. (3) Overcome certain common pitfalls in group problem analysis (e.g., too early emphasis on possible solutions, lack of specific information, the assumption that truth will emerge during discussion, and confusion between disagreement and dislike).

GENERATE POSSIBLE SOLUTIONS.   For every problem, there are several possible solutions. Some may be better or more feasible than others. There are always constraints in decision making. However, you are most likely to find the best solution if you generate many possible ones. For example, a small grocery store, after trying a number of ways to increase fruit juice sales, increased its grape juice sales dramatically by posting a sign near a stack of bottled juice that read, "Caution! If you mix this product with a small amount of yeast and sugar and let it stand in a warm, dark place for several days, it may turn into wine!"

The only criterion for suggested solutions should be that they could meet your objectives. Force yourself to see more than two options. And, at this stage, do not stop to evaluate. Simply look for ways to get from where you are to where you'd like to be. That is really what a decision is—a choice of action from two or more alternatives.

EVALUATE SOLUTIONS.   After the possible solutions have been generated, they must be tested. Evaluation may include testing by personal experience, expert opinion, current surveys of existing data, or planned scientific research. Whatever the method chosen, all advantages and disadvantages of the options must be explored. A company that's attempting to increase sales might examine its pricing structure, advertising campaign, sales training, distribution system, and marketing channels and alter several of these factors. If some standard has not been developed, criteria to meet the group's needs must be established. Evaluation is also important after the decision is made, in order to judge its effect on the work group.

MAKE THE DECISION.   Once all possible solutions have been reviewed and evaluated, an option can be selected and a decision can be made to intervene, modify, or rectify. Reaching a final decision may include several strategies, all of which involve some form of authority, voting, or consensus. Some evidence suggests people do not like making decisions. Indecision is more comfortable; they therefore procrastinate. They let others decide and allow themselves to be swayed by chance.

Decisions often are painful because they involve risk. But risk is what decisions are all about. Mistakes in decision making are seldom final and devastating. Often they are effective teachers. In seeking a suitable material for his light bulb's filament, Thomas Edison tried at least 6000 vegetable growths, 1600 minerals, monkey's hair, and even the hair from a moustache until he finally hit upon the answer—a carbon-impregnated cotton thread that had been baked in a furnace.

Once the decision has been made, the solution is ready to be implemented. At this point, the work group should take steps to achieve the agreed-on solution. Leadership plays a significant role. Even after the decision has been implemented, however, its effectiveness should be evaluated and it should be modified if necessary. For example, in 1981 Anheuser-Busch test-marketed and later dropped its Root 66 brand of root beer. It is better to admit failure and cut your losses than to compound a bad decision with blind determination to make it work.

PITFALLS TO AVOID.   You can see from the above model that decision making is serious business that requires a systematic approach. It also has pitfalls into which a decision maker may fall. There are six such traps.[4]

What are some mistakes a decision maker should avoid?

1. *Failure to identify the real problem.* Don't get caught up dealing with symptoms of a problem. Symptoms can't be solved. Problems produce symptoms, not the other way around. Deal with the real problem.
2. *Failure to identify who owns the problem.* You can't solve others' problems for them. You can help, but the owner is responsible.
3. *Failure to identify all the alternatives.* There are always plenty of choices available if you will take the time to look for them.
4. *Failure to create a visible plan.* It is difficult to remember what you can't see. Therefore, create a written plan for implementation. Identify and get agreement on who will do what, how, and when.
5. *Failure to monitor the implementation.* Check on the plan by contacting the key people involved. Anticipate and prevent instead of redoing.
6. *Failure to use a catalyst.* Catalysts are ones who see that the problem-solving process is carried out. They have been trained in decision making, and they work to minimize process time and to maximize the end time.

The preceding steps in making decisions and avoiding pitfalls can be applied individually or in groups. Often, problem solving is best done in groups.

Group Problem Solving

Group leaders may have to decide whether they should make a decision alone or involve a group. This alone is a crucial decision. The first decision will affect alternative acceptance and implementation. Thus, **group problem solving** is essentially the decision-making process within a work group.

group problem solving

Approaches to Group Problem Solving

The role of any work group depends on the leader's view of how involved the group should be. (*See* Exhibit 5.2.) Group problem solving has one great merit: it boosts group morale. This is participation at its best. A lesser benefit may be the learning of objectivity and acceptance through personal involvement with and contributions to the solution. Problem-solving meetings provide an ideal forum for an exchange of information across departmental lines. Some common approaches to group decision making are: brainstorming, committees, juries, nominal grouping, and the delphi technique.

What are some common approaches to group problem solving?

BRAINSTORMING.   Once a problem has been identified and analyzed, a technique often used to generate a quantity of ideas is brainstorming. Its primary goal is to produce imaginative alternative approaches to a specific problem. Group members are freed from inhibition, self-criticism, and criticism of others. No judging or criticism of any type is permitted. People can state ideas as quickly as they occur.

There are four general rules for brainstorming.[5]

1   *Criticism is ruled out.* Adverse judgment of ideas must be withheld until later.
2   *Free-wheeling is welcomed.* The wilder the idea the better; it is easier to tame down than to think up.
3   *Quantity is wanted.* The greater the number of ideas, the more likely a winner.
4   *Combination and improvement are sought.*

People are encouraged not only to contribute ideas but also to suggest how others' ideas can be turned into better ideas. Or they may see how two or more ideas can be joined into still another idea. Brainstorming can be applied to almost any problem a working group faces, if there is a wide range of possible solutions.

COMMITTEES.   Committees are temporary task groups, as we discussed in Chapter 6. They are appointed to work on a project in addition to their regular duties. Once they finish the project, they give their solutions and recommendations to top management. Unfortunately, the committee's work is not highly regarded. No doubt many committees waste time, but at certain times committees are useful.

Judging that no one person is qualified to weigh all the facets of a companywide decision, Phillips Petroleum Company, as an example, has expressed a preference for committees in top management's decision making. Deciding on a new plant site, for instance, would require input from persons knowledgeable in real estate, transportation, taxation, people-power planning, marketing, and finance. Such a group would apply its combined judgment and individual expertise to recommend a site with the greatest advantages and fewest drawbacks.

To show the faith other organizations place in committees, one survey of 1200 respondents revealed 64 percent of firms with fewer than 250 employees used committees; firms with 250–1000 employees, 82 percent; 1001–10,000 employees, 93 percent; over 10,000, 94 percent.[6] Committees are clearly an important management tool, despite the criticisms of cost and wasted time. They are an important form of group interaction that can and should be made more productive because they are going to endure in organizational life. They are particularly suited to projects not requiring or justifying a permanent task force.

JURIES.   Another approach to group problem solving (very similar to the committee) is the use of the jury. Juries consist of twelve or fewer people invited to participate in a problem-solving situation. They are informed of what the problem is and are encouraged to bring any needed information about the problem. There are seven steps in the jury technique.[7]

1   The group leader presents the problem and background information to the group.
2   Each person is given the opportunity to relate to the group what she or he knows about the problem.
3   Members of the jury are allowed to ask open-ended questions of each person after his or her statements about the problem.
4   The problem is then redefined if necessary.
5   The group is broken into small work groups of two to three members to develop workable solutions.
6   The efforts of the small work groups are consolidated into an overall definition of the problem and the plan of action to be implemented.
7   Each person then assumes certain responsibilities and reports on progress at the next group meeting.

The real value of juries, as with committees, depends on how well the leader functions. It is the leader who determines how human relationships are formed. Juries, like the two preceding problem-solving approaches—brainstorming and committees—are based on interacting groups. There are two techniques that make use of group input without interaction: nominal grouping and the Delphi technique.

NOMINAL GROUPING.   The **nominal group technique (NGT)** asks group members to generate ideas by silently jotting down their thoughts about a specific question. There is no verbal interaction among the members. Six steps comprise the NGT process.[8]

nominal group technique

What is the NGT?

1. All groups are asked to respond to a question by writing their views on 3" × 5" cards. There is to be absolutely no verbal interaction among group members during this phase. Although the time allowed may vary, twenty minutes is generally satisfactory.

2. At the conclusion of this listing phase, each group is asked to select one member to serve as the recorder.

3. Using large sheets of paper (newsprint is good) and a magic marker, each recorder asks for members of the group to read off one solution from his or her list. If anyone else has the same solution, a checkmark is placed by the item. The process continues, one item at a time, on a round-robin basis until all solutions are recorded on newsprint. The process is structured to discourage discussion of each item until all items are recorded.

4. After the list is completed, discussion is allowed to synthesize, clarify, or add items.

5. Next, group members are again given 3″ × 5″ cards and asked to vote for the five solutions they think are most significant and should receive highest priority.

6. After the votes are tallied, each group reports its top five items on each list to the group as a whole. These data are then classified, and the results are presented to top management so the organization can proceed to develop strategies and action plans that will build on strengths and overcome the problem areas.

Because of the lack of interaction, groups can focus on the major issues without getting sidetracked by those who talk too much or by unnecessary evaluation of early problem variables. Therefore, the NGT may be more effective for identifying problems than the more traditional small-group techniques.

DELPHI TECHNIQUE.   Similar to nominal grouping, the Delphi technique collects and tabulates people's opinions without discussion and debate. However, the people involved (the panel) are generally unaware of who else is participating. Therefore, personality differences that might get in the way of gathering feedback are avoided. There are six steps in collecting data again.

1   Individuals independently fill out a series of questionnaires concerning problems or issues.
2   Questionnaires are collected and tabulated, and factual feedback of results is provided for the panel members.
3   If more information about the problems or issues is needed by individuals, such data are furnished.
4   Individuals fill out another round of questionnaires and receive feedback.
5   The process is repeated until there seems to be significant agreement among the panel members.
6   A final report is written that presents the results from the questionnaire process.

The Delphi technique may be used to get a consensus of experts on the direction of such things as: energy costs and consumption by the year 2000; emergence of third world nations; development of alternate energy sources; use of lasers in national defense and in surgery; use of robots on assembly lines; and other long-term predictions.

Although the Delphi technique involves a great deal of time, most managers are willing to sacrifice the time to obtain better solutions to problems or issues. The Delphi technique, like nominal grouping, is a noninteraction approach to problem solving. It eliminates committee activity and avoids many debates and compromise situations inherent in most interacting groups. Its greatest use is in forecasting the future of the group or organization.

---------------------- Advantages of Group Problem Solving ----------------------

These approaches and techniques give group problem solving several advantages. Some of the advantages are: better decisions, comprehension and acceptance, increased commitment, and higher morale.

Are there any advantages to group problem solving?

BETTER DECISIONS. Because group decision making involves total interaction, the quality of decisions is generally higher than those made by an individual. Groups usually do better on manual tasks than intellectual problems, however. A group tends to lose superiority in accuracy and efficiency if no division of labor is required, if problems of control are too great, or if the group develops low standards of productivity.

COMPREHENSION AND ACCEPTANCE. Group members normally experience greater comprehension and acceptance of decisions when they have participated in the decision making. For example, a retail store manager was concerned because three of his four full-time salespeople requested the same week in August for their vacation. Only two of the salespeople could go during that week. Therefore, the manager had to decide who would have to reschedule vacation plans. The manager could have made the decision, but he might readily create hostility between the unlucky salesperson and himself. Instead, he asked the three salespeople to work out a suitable arrangement. Each had the opportunity to discuss their points with the others. All the salespeople accepted the decision.

INCREASED COMMITMENT. Participation in problem solving increases acceptance. Therefore, participating members are more committed to the decision than nonparticipants. Productive decisions are commitments to action and results. To gain commitment, all who have to do something to make the decision a productive one should participate in the discussions. Also, action commitments must be built into the decision at the beginning, to match each person's talents.

HIGHER MORALE. Closely tied to comprehension, acceptance, and commitment is morale. Morale is desire to work toward a goal. It represents one's satisfaction not only with the group but also with the major aspects of the work situation. Participating members generally have higher morale than nonparticipants.

---------------------- Disadvantages of Group Problem Solving ----------------------

Although there are many advantages to group decision making, there are also disadvantages. The most crucial disadvantages are time, cost, social pressure, hidden agendas, and groupthink.

Are there any disadvantages to group problem solving?

TIME. The expenditure of time is a big barrier to group problem solving. Occasionally there is not enough time to deal effectively with a problem. When this occurs, goals may not be clearly stated or agreed on, discussion may not be completed, and conclusions may not be reached.

COST. There is no way to accurately estimate the cost of group problem solving. It has been said that committees "keep minutes and waste hours." The cost in people-hours can be staggering. However, a poor decision may cost more in the long run than a correct one. Some companies use a meeting cost computer at their conferences. It keeps a running total of a meeting's cost by multiplying the participants' salaries per minute by the number of minutes the meeting has run. This technique emphasizes the cost of meetings.

SOCIAL PRESSURE. Most people try to be accepted by others. This desire tends to silence disagreement and favors conformity. We discussed this phenomenon in Chapter 2.

HIDDEN AGENDAS. Any time a group meets, it has an agenda, its official reason for meeting. In addition, some members have private (hidden) agenda items that represent a need they wish the group to fulfill. The hidden agenda is unlabeled but manifests itself during group interaction. For example, two group members may not agree on a decision because they both want to win the argument to establish their leadership over the group. Content of the argument is irrelevant; they will argue and disagree over any issue. They are not interested in solving the problem so much as in winning their desired role in the group.

groupthink

When is groupthink a problem with group problem solving?

GROUPTHINK. Groupthink occurs when people are so concerned with consensus they overlook realistic appraisals of action. **Groupthink** is a drive for consensus at any cost. It results when mental efficiency is at its lowest, when group members fail to test reality, and when high moral standards deteriorate. The Watergate conspiracy during Richard Nixon's administration reflected the effects of groupthink.

Products of Poor Decision-Making Practice. There are six major defects in decision making that contribute to groupthink and thereby to failures in solving problems adequately.[9] These problems can occur in any group.

1   The group discussions are limited to a few alternative courses of action (often only two) without a survey of the full range of alternatives.
2   The group fails to reexamine the course of action that it initially preferred and that may have contained possible risks and drawbacks.

3   The members neglect courses of action initially evaluated as unsatisfactory by the majority of the group.

4   Members make little or no attempt to obtain information from experts who can supply sound estimates of losses and gains to be expected from alternative courses of action.

5   Selective bias is shown in the way the group reacts to factual information and relevant judgments from experts, the mass media, and outside critics.

6   The members spend little time deliberating about how the chosen policy might be hindered by bureaucratic inertia, sabotaged by political opponents, or temporarily derailed by common accidents.

Recommendations for Preventing Groupthink.   Although groupthink is prevalent, there are ways to combat it. Remedies for groupthink can be summarized accordingly:[10]

How can you prevent groupthink?

•   The leader should assign the role of critical evaluator to each member and encourage the group to give high priority to airing objections and doubts.

•   A leader, when making a group assignment, should be impartial instead of stating preferences and expectations at the onset. This allows the members the opportunity to develop an atmosphere of open inquiry and to explore impartially a wide range of alternatives.

•   The organization to which the group members belong should routinely follow the administrative practice of setting up several independent planning and evaluation groups to work on the same policy question, with each group carrying out its deliberations under a different leader.

•   Throughout the period when the feasibility and effectiveness of policy alternatives are being surveyed, the group should from time to time form two or more subgroups to meet separately under different chairpersons and then come together to hammer out differences.

•   Group members should periodically discuss their deliberations with trusted associates in their own unit of the organization and report their associates' reactions.

•   One or more experts or qualified colleagues within the organization who are not core group members should be invited to each meeting on a staggered basis and should be encouraged to challenge the views of the core members.

•   At every meeting devoted to evaluating alternatives, at least one group member should be assigned the role of devil's advocate.

•   Whenever an issue involves relations with a rival group, a sizable block of time (perhaps an entire session) should be spent surveying all warning signals from the rivals and constructing alternative scenarios of the rivals' intentions.

- After reaching a preliminary consensus about what seems to be the best alternative, the decision-making group should hold a second chance meeting at which every member is expected to express as vividly as possible all residual doubts and to rethink the entire issue before making a definite choice.

These prescriptions are important because as a group develops cohesivenes its members tend to share an illusion of invulnerability, rationalize to discount negative feedback, and believe unquestioningly in the group's morality. Also, group members apply direct pressure to any person who momentarily expresses doubts. The victims of groupthink appoint themselves as guardians of the leader and fellow members, and keep out adverse information.

Technological Approaches to Decision Making

What are some of the technological approaches to decision making?

Although the thrust of this book is human relations and the effects of managerial skills on relationships, there are also important nonhuman techniques of problem solving. Since the 1950s computers and technological innovations have contributed significantly to managerial decision making. Ready access to information and rapid communication have reduced the need for gathering and analyzing data. In fact, advances in the power of minicomputers, communications satellites, and new data-handling devices have totally transformed our world. Many decisions, therefore, have become quantitative and programmable. However, the primary goal of any computerized management information system is to provide managers with the necessary data for making intelligent decisions. The computer does not make decisions; people do that. Three techniques for using nonhuman decision-making tools are discussed below: breakeven analysis, the decision tree, and management information systems.

Breakeven Analysis

Breakeven analysis is used to determine whether additional units of a particular product should be produced. That is, it is a way to compare costs and revenues to find the breakeven point. For example, will the costs involved generate increased or decreased profits? If a profit is clearly visible, then a decision can be made to increase production. If profit seems likely to decline, a decision can be made to remain at the present level or drop back in production. This technique is primarily used to determine if production should occur at all within a given cost structure and competitive situation. If cost and sales estimates are accurate, profit is a certainty beyond the breakeven point that this technique establishes.

---------------- The Decision Tree ----------------

A **decision tree** is a graphic display of a series of decisions, each decision depending on the preceding decision. It shows each option or strategy as the branch of a tree, with anticipated outcomes for comparison of each alternative branch. Probabilities play a crucial role in decision trees. An example is provided in Figure 8.1.

decision tree

What does a tree have to do with decisions?

    At each of the points, *A* to *G,* a decision is made with two alternatives. For example, at the beginning decision point (*A*), you have two choices. If you take the *A–B* route, two other decisions are possible (*B–D* or *B–E*). A similar situation exists with the *A–C* route. If uncertainty surrounds any step, however, uncertainty may continue to be piled on top of uncertainty.

---------------- Management Information Systems ----------------

Management information systems (MIS) represent part of an organization's formal communication system. They are integrated systems of data gathering, transmission, processing, storage, and retrieval that link the entire organization. The key words are *data, information,* and *intelligence.* Data represent facts cataloged by some retrieval scheme. Information is problem-related and represents the necessary data for satisfying a requirement or understanding a situation. Intelligence results from analyzed information and provides a decision maker with a preferred course of action. For example, computers scratched one space shuttle launch despite the feelings of NASA officials that everything was go because the computers detected adverse launch conditions and were programmed to respond by putting the flight on hold. The computer's response was the preferred course. Thus, MIS may be differentiated by the objectives a system intends to satisfy. The hierarchy, from lowest level, and most frequently used, is as follows:

management information systems

What is an MIS?

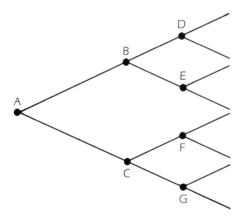

FIGURE 8.1
Decision Tree

- *Clerical system*—to substitute computer processes for manual record keeping (e.g., payroll, customer billing, dividend calculations).
- *Information system*—to supply information (not data) that is oriented toward management decision making.
- *Information-decision system*—to go beyond the simple provision of information to the decision maker and to assist the way in which the decision is reached. Decision-making tools are integrated into or superimposed on the information system.
- *Interactive system*—to develop cybernated (people-machine) information-decision systems in which the manager and the information system are coupled in a problem-solving network.
- *Programmed system*—to have the system rather than human decision makers make the decision. The manager is removed from the system completely.[11]

What is the goal of MIS?

The goal of MIS, as with all other information-gathering techniques, is to provide reliable data for effective managerial decisions. Thus, planning and control are two major areas benefitting from MIS. For example, Hartford National Bank and Trust Company, working in conjunction with General Electric Information Services Company (GEISCO), created a programmed decision-making system called Teller Management System.[12] A computer predicts traffic flow and the types of transactions to anticipate at each branch and determines how many full- and part-time tellers will be needed to handle the workload. This system, which has saved branch managers a great deal of guesswork, can also be used to reproduce the results of proposed changes before they are made and evaluate their effectiveness against current practices.

CONCLUSION

Work groups are a good source for high quality ideas. However, a leader must understand the techniques involved in group problem solving to tap the reservoir of knowledge in the group. This chapter has provided that information. Practicing good decision-making skills allows one to handle intergroup conflict when it arises and improve people relationships and productivity.

KEY TERMS

Decision Making: choosing among alternative courses of action.
Group Problem Solving: making decisions in a work group.
Nominal Group Technique: a method of generating ideas by silently jotting down thoughts about a specific incident.

Groupthink: a group's drive to reach consensus on a decision without making a realistic appraisal of action.

Decision Tree: a graphic display of a series of decisions, each of which depends on the preceding decision.

Management Information Systems: integrated communication systems of data gathering, transmission, processing, storage, and retrieval that link the entire organization.

QUESTIONS

1   Reread the opening case.
   a. In your opinion, which three of the seven decision variables are most significant in this case? Why?
   b. What could Phil Brook do to obtain a clear definition of the problem? Why do you propose that?
   c. Develop your own definition of the problem for discussion purposes based on information in the case, and recommend the decision-making strategy Phil could use.
   d. Under the circumstances, what decision-making pitfalls should Phil make a special effort to avoid?
2   Summarize each of the following decision variables:
   a. nature of task requirements,
   b. type of conflict,
   c. role structure,
   d. sex distribution,
   e. openness of communication channels,
   f. homogeneity of group members, and
   g. group climate.
   How can an understanding of these variables improve the decisions you reach in your personal life and in your work? What difficulties might you encounter if you *don't* take them into account?
3   List at least four of the six pitfalls into which decision makers may fall. Which of these have you encountered recently? What was the result? If you could repeat the experience, how would you approach the decision differently?
4   Diagram the problem-solving model. What must you be concerned with at each phase? Relate this model to your responses in (2) and (3), and discuss how they relate to and affect the model's various phases.
5   Why should group leaders attempt to involve group members in the decision-making process? What benefits will accrue to the leader? to the followers? to the group as a whole? Discuss the potential undesirable consequences of not seeking participation in decision making.
6. Differentiate among the following verbal techniques of decision making:
   a. brainstorming,
   b. committees, and
   c. juries.

In your opinion, which would best be used in each of the following circumstances, and why?

  a. selecting a new retail store location,
  b. choosing the theme for a new advertising campaign,
  c. evaluating a group of management trainees after their first six months on the job,
  d. choosing a price for a new product,
  e. reducing the amount of scrap from three tons to one ton per month,
  f. picking the site for this year's annual sales meeting, and
  g. anticipating how competitors will improve their products for the upcoming model year.

7. List at least three situations or kinds of decisions in which the nominal group technique or the Delphi technique might be used successfully.

8   Suggest at least two ways to minimize wasted time in group problem solving. Respond to the remark, "Time is wasted only if you allow it to be."

9   Consider the phenomenon of a hidden agenda. Do you believe it's possible to prevent group members from having them? Why or why not? Recall family, social, or other group exchanges in which you had your own hidden agenda. Did the group's action result in your fulfilling the items on it? If not, what did you do in response?

10 List at least three decision-making defects that contribute to groupthink and recommend at least four remedies to combat it.

11 Recall a personal or work situation in which you experienced groupthink. What was the result? Might it have been a more successful decision if groupthink had been prevented? Why or why not?

12 Describe breakeven analysis and decision trees and provide examples of decisions in which each would be useful.

13 Comment on the following remark: "Decisions should be reached by a combination of human and nonhuman approaches. To use one or the other exclusively will probably lead to problems in itself."

14 How would you describe the goal of an organization's management information system? Why should it be considered essential to the organization's overall success?

CASES

Case 8.1

Last semester a group of fraternity men threw a pie in a professor's face. They were masked at the time, so the professor could not identify them. However, one of the students in the class was seen snickering about the incident and had given the OK sign to the fraternity members who ran quickly out of the room. He was questioned and revealed the name of the fraternity but not the ones who threw the pie.

A group of professors from the same department as the professor hit with the pie complained to the dean of their school. The dean in turn talked to the director of student services and demanded the fraternity be kicked off campus. Other faculty across campus learned of the incident and brought pressure on the administration to take appropriate action. Many students were sympathetic toward the professors' cause. The director of student services met with the fraternity leaders about the problem. They refused to reveal the names of the perpetrators. In fact, they had taken a secret oath not to reveal the names of the ones involved. The director then informed them of the ultimate consequences of their behavior if something was not done soon to rectify the situation.

Case Questions

1 Summarize the decision variables affecting the fraternity members and those which may influence the director of student services.
2 What verbal or nonverbal decision-making technique would you recommend to resolve the issue? Why?
3 Describe the possible hidden agenda items of (a) the fraternity members, (b) concerned faculty members, and (c) the targeted professor if everyone meets to resolve the problem as a group.

Case 8.2

An executive of a drug company and a staff scientist were discussing a proposed drug. The scientist had requested permission to present his negative findings about the drug at the next board meeting. The executive rejected the request.

At the board meeting the chairperson opened the meeting with optimistic remarks about the company's past growth and high dividends. The marketing manager followed with hopeful predictions of a good investment and high return on the newly developed weight-reducing drug. Several members of the group asked questions about competition, government clearances, and safety. All questions were confidently answered or overridden with comments about "inconclusive data," "quacks," "cranks," and "those FDA guys." When the lawyer, however, suggested the company ought to test its product further, protests broke out from other members. They said things like "risks are necessary," "it's a prescription-only drug," "the company has the finest reputation in the field." The lawyer was chided for being dissident and became silent. Then one member firmly insisted, "Let's go with it. We don't have anything to worry about." On that confident prediction, with no further questions, the group made a unanimous decision to market the drug.[13]

Case Questions

1 What hidden agenda items may the board members have? top management? the scientist who asked to speak to the board?
2 What type of decision-making technique would you suggest to this firm in deciding whether to place a new drug on the market or to hold it for further testing and modification? Why?
3 What evidence of groupthink do you see in the above case? Do you agree with the decision-making techniques they used? Why or why not?
4 What could be done in this firm to prevent faulty problem-solving practices and leadership bias?

NOTES

1. Dennis S. Gouran, *Discussion: The Process of Group Decision Making* (New York: Harper and Row, 1974), pp. 55–59.

2. "GM Settlement Averts Strike Over Speedup," *The Wall Street Journal,* 30 January, 1979, p. 12.

3. Larsen, Carl, "Forms of Analysis and Small Group Problem Solving," *Speech Monographs* 36(1969): 452–455.

4. Bledsoe, John L., "When Solving Your Own Problems, Here Are Six Pitfalls to Avoid," *Training HRD* (May 1977): 86.

5. Bobby R. Patton and Kim Griffin, *Problem-Solving Group Interaction* (New York: Harper and Row, 1973), pp. 141–160.

6. Rollie Tillman, Jr., "Problems in Review: Committees on Trial," *Harvard Business Review* 38(May–June 1960): 6–12, 162–172.

7. Donald W. Devine, "The Jury Technique: Will the Real Problem Please Stand Up," *Personnel* (September–October 1976): 27–28.

8. Richard C. Huseman et al., *Interpersonal Communication in Organizations—A Perceptual Approach* (Boston: Holbrook Press, 1976), p. 146.

9. Irvin L. Janis, *Victims of Groupthink—A Psychological Study of Foreign-Policy Decisions and Fiascos* (Boston: Houghton Mifflin, 1972), pp. 207–224.

10. Ibid.

11. Dickson, G. W., "Management Information Decision Systems," *Business Horizons* (December 1968): 18–22.

12. "A Computer Modeling Case History," *Administrative Management* (September 1981): 44.

13. Adapted from "Group Dynamics: 'Groupthink'," CRM Educational Films, 1975.

SUGGESTED READINGS

Argyris, Chris. "Interpersonal Barriers to Decision Making," *Harvard Business Review* (March–April 1966): 84–97.

Hall, Jay. "Decisions, Decisions, Decisions," *Psychology Today* (November 1971): 51–54, 86–88.

"Managerial Decision Making," *Organizational Dynamics* (1975).

Simon, Herbert A. *The New Science of Management Decisions.* Englewood Cliffs, N.J.: Prentice-Hall, 1977.

9

Motivation and Morale

When you complete your study of this chapter, you should be able to:

1 Apply the theories of motivation and morale to a job,
2 Recognize the basic motivation patterns of organizations,
3 Understand the motivational needs of both employees and supervisors, and
4 Design specific techniques for keeping motivation and morale levels high.

—————————————— OPENING CASE ——————————————

Rocky Breckenridge's father owns a small home-remodeling company in Eastland, Texas. Rocky worked for his father throughout high school and now works for him on weekends while attending college. He enjoys the work and plans to own and operate a similar business (if not this one) after graduation.

Rocky has become concerned about one of his father's employees, Joe Bristol, who is a master carpenter and the company's general foreman. Rocky often finds Joe loafing on the job. However, instead of being embarrassed, Joe merely smiles cordially and says, "Hiya, boss!"

Rocky has wanted to fire him for several months, but his father has told him to ignore the problem, that it will correct itself before long. Behind the scenes, however, Rocky knows this employee has offended four of their best customers within the last month with his rudeness. Because most of their work comes through word-of-mouth, Joe Bristol has probably cost the company several profitable jobs, but Rocky's father is unaware of this situation.

Today Rocky met with his father and outlined the circumstances to him. However, he presented several alternatives to firing Joe based on information he recently learned about motivation in his business administration courses. He believes it's worthwhile to salvage an experienced individual like Joe if possible.

"I don't know, son," his father replied, scratching his head. "Your ideas sound good, but I'm not sure any of that stuff is practical for a small outfit like ours. Sure, your professors see them work in big outfits like AT&T, but those companies have got the resources and people to *make* things work! What proof do you have that these theories have ever been applied successfully in an eight-employee outfit like ours? People don't like to be experimented with. Maybe we'd just better let things work themselves out."

———————————— It's a Good Theory, but It Doesn't Work ————————————

Now that we've completed our study of the skills necessary for managing human relationships, we are ready to look at some human relationship challenges. The first challenge is motivation. We are beginning with motivation and morale because to handle all of the other challenges in Part III a manager or supervisor must first deal with how to motivate employees and keep them motivated.

Vast amounts of information have been written about motivation. Theories have been proposed and their corollaries applied. However, their application sometimes yields either negative or neutral results. Many management practitioners are then quick to point out that the theory is good, but it's irrelevant or not workable. However, the fault may be in poor application. The intent of this chapter is to take a look at motivation and how to translate conceptual knowledge into practice effectively. Motivation is evidenced—in absenteeism, turnover, grievances, quality, and output—and it can be measured. Anyone who aspires to management must learn about motivation, and how to control it.

A Definition

There are two ways to view motivation. The traditional way is to define motivation as a process of directing (stimulating or actuating) people to action in order to accomplish a desired goal. Based on this definition, motivation is a function supervisors perform to get their employees to achieve goals and objectives. The second viewpoint looks at individual motivation. Such motivation represents an unsatisfied need that creates a state of tension (disequilibrium), causing the individual to move in a goal-directed pattern toward need satisfaction and equilibrium. The goal of behavior then is to reduce tension by achieving a goal that will satisfy that need. Both approaches to the study of motivation are valid and will be pursued in this chapter. But, to develop a good, applicable theory we need a workable definition. For our purposes, **motivation** is either an internal or an external drive that directs a person toward need satisfaction or a goal.

How should one study the subject of motivation?

motivation

The Carrot and the Stick

Before we look at these approaches in detail and their accompanying theories, however, let's look at a method that seeks to encompass both approaches. This method deals with rewards and punishments. Most human motivational systems are, in fact, based on the belief that people can be led to expend energy in a desired direction if they are offered the proper reward or are threatened with punishment. Most organizations are based on that premise. For example, in business the reward system might include promotions, salary increases, and prestige. The punishment system would include no promotions, no raises, and nonrecognition.

The reward-punishment system is intrinsically sound. However, it fails to consider the multiplicity of responses possible in people. Many of the human relations problems in business may be due to narrow definitions of rewards and punishments. If so, future motivational theory must seek to make jobs so challenging and exciting they become their own reward.

Motivational Patterns

A manager or supervisor, or a potential one, needs to be familiar with the possible motivational patterns in an organization. The six motivational patterns that seem most relevant will be described in this section.[1] These patterns are rule compliance, instrumental system rewards, instrumental individual rewards, intrinsic satisfactions from role performance, internalization of organizational goals and values, and involvement in primary-group relationships. As you study these patterns, keep in mind the idea that people behave the way they do (i.e., are motivated) because they learned to do so. Motivation theory and learning theory go hand in hand.

Rule Compliance

Why do people conform to organizational rules?

People conform for several reasons (some of which were discussed in Chapter 2), but one reason most pertinent to understanding organizational behavior is a generalized acceptance of the rules of the game. When employees enter a company, for example, they accept that membership in the company means complying with certain rules—both formal, company rules and informal, peer-group rules—if they want to remain with that company. Through socialization we develop a readiness to play almost any role according to the established norms in the systems to which we belong.

One large corporation's employment application contains the following agreement on rule compliance:

I voluntarily give the company the right to confidentially investigate my personal and employment history, agree to cooperate in such investigation and release from all liability or responsibility all persons, corporations, or organizations furnishing such information.

As a condition of employment I consent to taking the pre-employment physical examination. I also agree to take future physical examinations as required by the company. I agree that the entire contents of this application as well as any investigation connected therein will be for the sole use of the company and treated confidentially.

If employed, I further agree to comply with all company rules, policies and procedures including those pertaining to patent/invention matters, conflict of interest, health, safety and security.

I further understand that any false answers, omissions, or statements made in this application or any supplement thereto or in connection with the above named investigation will be sufficient grounds for immediate dismissal.

Instrumental System Rewards

Are there any rewards for working within the organizational system?

Membership in certain organizations brings rewards and benefits. These rewards also apply to all employees in a given classification. They are called instrumental because they provide incentives for entering and remaining in the system. Thus they are instruments for creating need satisfaction. Some examples of instrumental system rewards are fringe benefits, recreational facilities, and working conditions.

Sears, Roebuck reportedly has an exceptional retirement program; IBM's attempts to follow a no-layoff policy fit the category of instrumental system rewards, also. Beyond a certain management level, many executives receive the unlimited free use of an automobile, eat in the executive dining room, and fly on a company plane instead of taking a commercial airline.

Instrumental Individual Rewards

Whereas system rewards apply across the board, individual rewards are attained by differential performance. Two examples of instrumental individual rewards are the piece rate in industry and the singling out of employees for honors because of their specific contributions.

How are individual rewards attained?

In 1979, International Telephone and Telegraph Corporation developed the annual Harold S. Geneen Creative Management award which Geneen termed "sort of the ITT Oscars."[2] Awards are conferred on middle managers for achieving such goals as improving departmental efficiency or putting a money-losing division back into the black once more.

The winners receive a thirty-pound statuette (a miniature marble version of an eight-foot-tall statue that stands in the lobby of company headquarters). Each Creative Management nominee also receives a check for $10,000.

Intrinsic Satisfactions from Role Performance

Intrinsic satisfaction provides for expression of skills and talents of employees. **Intrinsic** means internal to oneself. Satisfaction comes because the job is gratifying in itself. The employee finds his or her work so interesting, or so much the type of thing she or he really wants to do, that earning money is incidental to working. In some instances it would take a heavy financial inducement to shift to a job less congenial to his or her interests. A financial reward would be **extrinsic** motivation—external to oneself.

intrinsic

What is the difference between intrinsic and extrinsic motivation?

extrinsic

Internalization of Organizational Goals and Values

Some employees find their organizational behavior rewarding because they have taken the goals of the organization as their own. The employee who derives satisfaction from being a good machine worker could be equally happy working in many organizations but unhappy as a supervisor in any organization. The employee who identifies with the goals of one organization and its specific problems, potentialities, and progress wants to stay with that organization, and is willing to accept other assignments.

How does goal identification help both the organization and the individual?

What are the sources of one's social satisfactions?

The social satisfactions derived from one's primary-group relationships are an important source of gratification for employees. A primary group is one's first group—the family, the school, the job, the church, et cetera. A secondary group would be all other groups formed within one of the other structures. One of the things people miss most when they withdraw from an organization is the sharing of experiences with those group members with whom they have become identified. Supervisors must see to it that these social satisfactions become channeled for organizational objectives.

With these six motivational patterns in mind, we can now move on to the theories of motivation. Several will be discussed, but many more will be left out because of space limitations. The ones we will discuss were chosen because of their potential effect on human relationships within organizations.

────────────── Motivational Theory ──────────────

Within the last twenty-five years two specific strands of motivation theory have drawn closer together. One of these concerns the nature of the individual's needs and goals and the interrelationship among these needs and goals. The other concerns the individual's behavior and his or her goal attainment and need satisfaction. We shall look at both of these strands, as well as their supporting theories, in an attempt to learn how a supervisor or manager can motivate employees. Since motivation is concerned with behavior (i.e., the whole person), the supervisor must view motivation as being related to activities both on and off the job.

────────────── Human Needs ──────────────

needs

Where do primary and secondary needs *fit into motivational theory?*

Everyone needs something, but different people have different needs. Supervisors have certain needs, and workers have others. Sometimes these needs mesh, but often they don't. **Needs** are requirements necessary for work or social satisfaction. Everyone needs something. Do you know what it would take for you to be completely satisfied?

The primary needs of people are basic and physiological. They deal with breathing, eating, drinking, and sleeping. Secondary needs are psychological and include security, social relationships, respect, and fulfillment of potential. Such needs exist in all people in varying degrees, but it is the unsatisfied needs that motivate our actions.

MASLOW'S NEED HIERARCHY.   Many people have attempted to explain the range of needs, but Abraham Maslow's hierarchy (shown in Figure 9.1)

FIGURE 9.1
Maslow's Need
Hierarchy

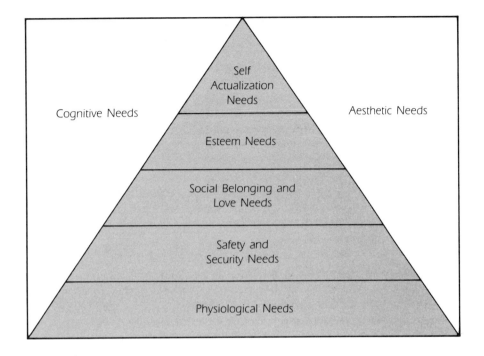

is the most representative. He placed all human needs into the following rankings: basic, safety, social, self-esteem, and self-realization.[3] The most basic needs seem to be the physiological ones—oxygen, water, food, maintenance of body temperature (i.e., clothing and shelter), sleep, and exercise. A person does not search for much else in life when these elements are not provided. When these needs are satisfied, safety demands emerge: avoidance of sources of anxiety or fear (i.e., falling, loud noises, flashing lights, bodily injury, illness, pain). Safety needs are often coupled with the security needs of an organized, orderly, predictable environment. Job security likewise fulfills a safety/security need.

What are the five most basic needs of people?

When the safety/security needs subside, social needs arise. These belongingness or love needs include friends, sweetheart or spouse, children, affectionate relations with others, or a place in a chosen group. These needs encompass both giving and receiving love. One of the strongest desires we have is to belong and to be accepted by others. This feeling of belonging is usually more than mere membership in a group, however. Belonging is acquired by participation. An individual contributes something valuable to the work group, and the group recognizes the contribution as worthwhile. Thus, you can see how a manager may enhance human relations on the job by involvement.

Once the social needs have been met, esteem needs become important; for example, high self-regard and respect for others. We all need love, support, and respect. These needs may be met by self-estimations of strength, confidence, freedom, and by others' recognition of one's status, prestige, reputation, importance, or competence. Self-concept is the most important factor in relations with others. It comes from significant others who have loved (or not loved) the person. Once esteem needs are satisfied, the need arises for self-actualization—doing what one is fitted for, fulfilling one's potential, and becoming everything one is capable of becoming. Included in this category are the needs for creative expression and contribution to worthwhile objectives.

Any or all of these needs, from the basic to the highest level, may be satisfied through some social, human contact with others. However, the underlying principle of need theory (as already stated) is that once a need is satisfied it can no longer motivate behavior. Also, these needs are not mutually exclusive. Just because a certain need is satisfied does not mean the person will never have to satisfy that need again.

Are there any problems with Maslow's hierarchy of needs?

There is a human relations problem presented to management by this hierarchy. Managers must arrange the organizational environment so workers can achieve personal goals by directing their efforts toward organizational goals. How, for example, can a supervisor create opportunities for workers to satisfy their basic needs, provide growth opportunities for workers to exercise their potential, recognize worker accomplishments, or coach workers to overcome their weaknesses? These are by no means easy questions, but they do provide us with the arena for practicing human relations on the job.

Healthy, Mature Persons. Because of potential problems within the need hierarchy, Maslow studied various groups to determine how people attain goals. He concluded that healthy, happy people demonstrate ten characteristics:

1   clearer, more efficient perceptions of reality;
2   more openness to experience;
3   increased integration, wholeness, and unity of the person;
4   increased spontaneity, expressiveness, full functioning, aliveness;
5   a real self, a firm identity, autonomy, uniqueness;
6   increased objectivity, detachment, transcendence of self;
7   recovery of creativeness;
8   ability to fuse concreteness and abstractness;
9   democratic character structure; and
10   ability to love.[4]

These characteristics of self-actualization are ideal goals for which to strive. Someone who possesses them can be invaluable to others.

How can a manager meet the needs of employees?

Unsatisfied Needs. Because satisfied needs are not motivators of behavior, they can create problems at work. Satisfied needs can produce boredom, laziness, or sloppiness. However, it is probably the unsatisfied needs that produce the largest headaches for managers. Unsatisfied needs can result in frustration, conflict, or aggression.

The management of Walt Disney World in Orlando, Florida, responded to one opinion poll of nearly 9,000 workers in a variety of ways, which included:

- improving hourly pay for more than 70 percent of hourly workers,
- making employees eligible for vacations sooner than they were under former policy,
- improving the employee pension plan and maternity benefits under the health insurance program,
- adding one more paid holiday per year,
- renovating employee break rooms and dining facilities,
- investigating the possibility of installing a day-care center for employees' children, and
- regularly informing employees of available job openings.

Managers must direct their efforts toward reducing any tensions arising from unsatisfied needs or blocked goals.

HERZBERG'S MOTIVATION-HYGIENE THEORY. Another need-based motivation theory is Frederick Herzberg's dual factor or motivation-hygiene theory. Based on data collected from 200 engineers and accountants, Herzberg and his associates postulated answers for what makes people (1) happy and satisfied with their jobs or (2) unhappy and dissatisfied with their jobs. There were two basic sets of factors with which employees were concerned:

- *Hygiene*—job context or job environment factors; for example, salary, personal life, working conditions, job security, status, company policy, administrative supervision, and interpersonal relationships.
- *Motivator*—job content factors; for example, recognition, advancement, responsibility, achievement, and the work itself.

Are there factors that dissatisfy and demotivate?

The hygiene factors are often considered negative, although they are not totally negative. They can dissatisfy and demotivate. When any of these factors falls below what employees feel is adequate, they become dissatisfied. Since hygiene factors are not motivators, supervisors must periodically replenish these needs. The motivators are positive and have the power to satisfy an employee's needs for self-fulfillment or self-actualization. To the extent these factors are present on the job, motivation occurs. Hygiene factors are necessary, but once they have been satisfied they will not lead to positive results. Only motivators will lead to superior performance.

Who needs a KITA?

KITA. One of Herzberg's corollaries to the dual-factor theory was an acronym—KITA. The initials stand for "kick in the ass" and are a caustic description of the traditional managerial approach to motivation. KITA can be either positive or negative. A supervisor can use motivation to prod or entice a worker. However, as Herzberg points out, KITA is not motivation.

Herzberg's theories have received much criticism because of their oversimplification of the relationship between motivation and job satisfaction or dissatisfaction. Available research indicates that the hygiene factor of money, for example, does indeed influence an employee's level of motivation or satisfaction. Thus, again there is a need to take into account individual experiences of a situation, individual needs. However, several of the recommendations resulting from the dual-factor theory do merit attention. The emphasis on job enrichment—making work meaningful and interesting—can positively influence employee motivation. So can the provision of more opportunities for achievement, recognition, responsibility, and advancement. The key is to consider the nature and needs of the employees.

Why is money not considered a motivator?

Monetary Rewards.   Maslow, Herzberg, and others place monetary reward low on the list of importance as a motivator of human performance, if it is placed at all. However, a belief that money does not motivate may be a self-fulfilling prophecy. Money can motivate an employee to work harder if the amount of money is high enough, or if the monetary gain is clearly contingent on performance (e.g., a commission paid on gross sales). Monetary rewards fail if they are unrelated to performance. In the past if employees pleased management, they received their regular salary. Money did not differentiate between average and excellent performance. (This is still true in many organizations.) Therefore, money had no incentive value. Under these conditions money will not motivate.

--------------------- Task Motivation and Goal Setting ---------------------

How can a manager clear an employee's path to a particular goal?

The second strand of motivation theory is based on the premise that a person's conscious goals are the primary determinants of task motivation. This theory was proposed by Edwin A. Locke and suggests that hard goals result in greater effort than easy goals and specific goals result in higher effort than no goals or more generalized goals. These propositions are generally supported by research, so long as the goals are accepted by the employees. Therefore, supervisors should be concerned with setting clear, challenging, and specific goals for employees.

path-goal theory

The relationship between tasks and goals, between people's behavior and their goal attainment/need satisfaction, is called the **path-goal theory** of motivation. The basic postulate is that a supervisor's function is to set important goals for employees and to clear their paths to those goals. Three factors are involved in affecting a path-goal instrumentality.[5]

1 *Employees must perceive that they can achieve their goals.* There must exist a supply of rewards and punishments; rewards must be distributed se-

lectively in accordance with employee needs. (Presumably, supervisors also set clear, specific paths.)

2 *Employees must see that rewards and punishments (from an abundant, sophisticated source or from a meager, simplistic one) are coming to them as a result of their specific behavior.* There must be a perceived connection between the employees' behavior and the rewards or punishments they receive.

3 *Supervisors must make judgments about which paths are high performance paths and which are low performance paths.* For most paths these judgments will be relatively unambiguous.

The path-goal approach emphasizes the supervisor's role in maximizing motivation for the achievement of goals. It provides insight as to the relationship between action and goal attainment and the relationship between job satisfaction and job performance. The next motivation theory presented will also be concerned with the relationships among satisfaction, performance, and reward.

Action Guides for Motivating Self and Others

Unless the preceding theories are applied to the human relationships within the organizational setting they remain just that—theories. Motivation is possible and employees' psychological needs can be met if a supervisor will learn and use the necessary skills. Wherever human relations are a problem, it is up to the supervisor to correct it. However, before supervisors can hope to meet the needs of employees, they must first know what level they or their employees are operating on. This is one of the keys for motivating to higher performance. In essence, people work to satisfy needs, and if managers wish to motivate workers, these needs must be satisfied.

If I know your need level, can I motivate you?

Do you know what motivates you? Stop reading for a moment and respond to the questionnaire in Figure 9.2. A nationwide study of thousands of people in retail stores, service organizations, and business and industrial firms, based on the questionnaire in Figure 9.2, yielded some interesting results. Figure 9.3 shows what supervisors said employees want and what the employees themselves said they wanted. Notice the differences. How did your rankings compare to theirs?

A comparison of the lists in Figure 9.3 indicates that what supervisors thought were most important to employees were not really all that important. And what supervisors thought were least important were considered by employees as most important. The implication is clear: when supervisors don't know what their employees want and need, their motivational attempts are likely to fail. Also, these abortive motivational attempts are a detriment to effective human relations.

FIGURE 9.2
A Motivational Quiz

From the following list of ten items, *first* rank the items in order of importance as to what would motivate you. Place a *1* after the item you think is most important, a *2* after the next most important item, et cetera. *Second,* rank what you think most employees want. *Third,* rank what you think most supervisors want. Remember, you are ranking what you think is most important to motivation.

	What I Want	What Employees Want	What Supervisors Want
1. Help on personal problems			
2. Interesting work			
3. High wages (salary)			
4. Job security			
5. Loyalty of supervisor			
6. Tactful disciplining			
7. Feedback on work well done			
8. Feeling of involvement in job			
9. Good working conditions			
10. Promotion in the company			

--------------------- Employee Needs ---------------------

What are five motivational needs of employees?

Did your top five motivational needs match the employees' needs? There are five basic needs of employees.[6]

1. *Employees have a right to know precisely and accurately what they are expected to do.* But here we run into a peculiar situation. Workers want to know what's going on, to have clear descriptions, delineations of authority and responsibility. Top management agrees workers should know. After all, employees who know what's expected are usually happier and more productive than employees who are kept in the dark. What is the problem? Why do so many employees not do what is expected of them? The top and bottom of the organization agree. Is it middle management's fault? To some extent this is true. Middle managers are often caught in the dilemma of what to do. They have policies and procedures about how much they can do in their operational areas. But they often do not know how much authority and responsibility to delegate. Thus, the employee is confused about how far to go with a particular job. The answer to the dilemma, therefore, seems to be the establishment of better job descriptions—descriptions that define the responsibilities and the authority that accompanies each.

2. *Workers like to be involved in the job to the point of designing the job and establishing goals and objectives.* Employees are not just numbers, not just

	What Employees Say They Want (Ranking)	What Supervisors Say Employees Want (Ranking)
1. Help on personal problems	3	9
2. Interesting work	6	5
3. High wages (salary)	5	1
4. Job security	4	2
5. Loyalty of supervisor	8	6
6. Tactful disciplining	10	7
7. Feedback on work well done	1	8
8. Feeling of involvement in job	2	10
9. Good working conditions	9	4
10. Promotion in the company	7	3

Source: "What Do Employees Want Most from Their Jobs?" *Personnel Journal* 47(February 1978):130.

FIGURE 9.3
What Do People Want from Their Jobs?

cogs in the machine. They have ideas about how things should be done and questions about why certain things are done. They want to be involved. Therefore, one way a manager can motivate workers is to ask them for help in setting work goals.

3. *Employees want to receive feedback on how they are doing.* Managers need to provide recognition of achievements or progress toward goals. Unfortunately, many workers do not feel they receive the recognition they deserve. As a result, their commitment to the job is marginal, and their alienation from their organizations and supervisors increases. And when the commitment and recognition level is low, workers will seek recognition elsewhere—perhaps outside the organization. To overcome such situations, managers may need to revamp their communication systems to provide feedback. They can provide motivation by evaluating results of work directly with the employee.

4. *Employees have a need to receive help from their managers and to receive guidance in improving skills.* Therefore, managers must know that most of the time spent interacting with workers deals with advising, guiding, coaching, counseling, and training. In fact, today's managers must realize they are the teacher, judge, specialist, generalist, planner, coordinator, organizer, motivator, and evaluator.

5. *Workers have a need for rewards and penalties*—rewards when they do something well and penalties when they violate expectations. The rewards may be internal or external, but the most potent ones are intrinsic.

—————————————— Motivational Plans ——————————————

Employees have needs that must be satisfied, and the supervisor is the key person in motivating these employees by satisfying their needs. However, managers need to be prepared with a plan. One motivation plan will be described below.

What are some techniques of motivation?

GENERAL TECHNIQUES OF MOTIVATION. There are eight general techniques of motivation, each with one main goal: to make the day-to-day jobs more purposeful and interesting to employees.

1. *Motivate by encouraging competition.* Correctly used, competition increases job interest and stimulates production. When an employee or group of employees competes, performance almost always improves. In competition, however, it is important to let each employee know where she or he stands and how his or her team compares with others.

2. *Motivate by change.* However, be aware that changes disturb people. Supervisors can dispel employees' fears and worries by preparing for change, making sure employees have all the facts, stressing the positive side of the change, not downgrading the method being replaced, and following up on adjustment.

3. *Motivate by promotions.* Supervisors who provide opportunities for employees to advance attract and keep high-caliber workers. They build morale, increase productivity, and make the best use of people power. However, the supervisor must promote only on the basis of qualifications and have the courage to turn down the popular but unqualified candidate.

4. *Motivate by increased responsibility.* Many employees can handle more responsibility than they presently have. Supervisors should explain that they are going to share more of the responsibility and really mean it. Give employees a constructive outlet for their latent talents and enthusiasm.

5. *Motivate by programs of recognition.* Each employee needs to feel important. Give credit, recognition, and frequent praise for jobs done well. Recognition can be shown in forms other than salary or job classification. A supervisor can (a) show confidence in employees by putting them on their own, (b) let them know they don't need as close supervision as others in that particular job, (c) encourage them to make suggestions and improve the work to which they are assigned, and (d) urge them to participate in the company suggestion plan.

6. *Motivate older employees by showing interest in their problems and help them overcome anxiety during periods of adjustment.* A supervisor may convince older workers they are as efficient and stable as younger ones, boost their self-esteem, list reasons why the company wants to retain them, and get them to talk out their job worries.

7. *Motivate new employees by getting them off to a good start on the new job.* A good start means a minimum of lost time, wasted materials, departmental

friction, production cost, and turnover. A good start will increase the new employee's self-confidence and should increase efficiency on the job.

8. *Motivate all employees by keeping the communication channels open.* Unless managers and supervisors communicate, they'll never effectively motivate their employees.[7]

SPECIFIC PROBLEM AREAS OF MOTIVATION.   Every organization has its share of problem employees. They are a nuisance and may threaten the productivity of their work group. To help you spot these problem people and their detrimental influences on human relationships, some problem employees are listed below. You may have met some of these people who are listed in Exhibit 9.1.

Who are the major problem employees I may expect to meet?

--------------------------------- EXHIBIT 9.1 ---------------------------------

- The Goldbricker—a person with an aversion to work, who sidesteps it with every trick known.
- The Wise Guy—a person with a know-it-all attitude, who argues for any reason at all, and who has a quick comeback for everything that's said.
- The Chronic Grouch—a person who's always angry at everybody, including the self, who is unhappy about everything.
- The Complainer—a person who gripes about everything and everybody, who imagines and looks for trouble.
- The Meddlesome Do-Gooder—a person who keeps busy trying to improve things and helping people, whether help is needed or not, a reformer too occupied with others' troubles to take care of his or her own work.
- The Weakling—a person who lacks self-confidence and has a fearful personality, who depends on others for instruction, and who shows no initiative.
- The Noncooperator—a person who feels superior to his or her job or co-workers, who does not cooperate willingly and freely.
- The Nonconformist—a person who always thinks of different ways to do things (not necessarily better), an individualist.
- The Dead-Ender—a person who has reached the top of his or her salary range, who has no prospects of a promotion in the near future.
- The Compulsive Talker—a person who can keep even the most inconsequential conversation going for hours and who gives long and not-to-the-point answers to short questions just to postpone going back to work.
- The Busybody—a person who is a professional meddler, who thinks he or she knows everything but is almost always wrong.
- The Buck Passer—a person who, when things go wrong, will insist she or he was never there, who passes the blame to someone else.
- The Taciturn Employee—a person who is a lounger, completely indifferent to the job, doing only what is required, passively resisting change, and rejecting all efforts to arouse enthusiasm.[8]

Such problem employees are often encouraged to quit or are fired. Properly motivated, though, they could become above-average employees.

Often the supervisor can motivate problem employees by making them feel important.

As stated earlier, the purpose of motivation is to make jobs more interesting and purposeful to employees. If the manager fails to achieve this goal, the company loses in terms of quality and quantity, efficiency and effectiveness.

HIDDEN AREAS THAT AFFECT MOTIVATION. In addition to the specific problem areas of motivation there are some other areas that are frequently overlooked. These deal primarily with absenteeism (Chapter 12), alcoholism (Chapter 13), and women workers (Chapter 14). Because there are chapters devoted to these areas, we will not discuss them at this time.

--------------------------------- Supervisor Needs ---------------------------------

How do a supervisor's needs differ from an employee's needs?

Supervisors also have certain needs at work (Figure 9.4). For example, notice the accumulated weights given to categories by over 300 first-level and second-level supervisors in one organization over a three-year period (1974–1976). You will find both similarities and differences in what supervisors say they want. Remember, each item is a potential motivator.

If we compare this with what employees want (Figure 9.3), we may notice similarities between what supervisors say they want and what supervisors think employees want. This may suggest to us a certain fallacy in employee

FIGURE 9.4
A Comparison of
Supervisors' Rankings

	What First-Line Supervisors Say They Want	What Second-Line Supervisors Say They Want
1. Help on personal problems	10	10
2. Interesting work	1	2
3. High wages (salary)	2	1
4. Job security	5	5
5. Loyalty of supervisor	7	8
6. Tactful disciplining	9	9
7. Feedback on work well done	4	4
8. Feeling of involvement in job	8	7
9. Good working conditions	6	6
10. Promotion in the company	3	3

Source: Michael J. Abbound and Homer L. Richardson, "What Do Supervisors Want from Their Jobs?" *Personnel Journal* 47(June 1978):309–310.

appraisal systems. Sometimes appraisals may tell us more about the person doing the appraisal than about the person being appraised.

The study in Figure 9.4 looked at only one organization. However, since it did deal with a fairly large number of subjects over a three-year period, the data are probably representative of supervisors in similar organizations. Therefore, it can indicate what the typical supervisor wants from his or her job. Knowing what both supervisors and employees want from a job, we can be aware not only of certain need levels of motivation but also of how to keep morale high. Motivation apparently provides the potential for morale.

Morale

Morale can be defined in many ways. In fact, both morale and motivation can have several interpretations. For our use, **morale** is a mental attitude that describes peoples' feelings about their work, their job, their organization, and their supervisor. Morale causes both individuals and groups to (1) subordinate willingly their own purposes to a common end, (2) cooperate willingly with their associates, (3) accept cheerfully reasonable discipline, and (4) give their best efforts without pressure.[9] The relationship between motivation and morale is high. Therefore, both motivation and morale relate directly to productivity.

morale

What is the difference between motivation and morale?

In addition, we can outline three specific aspects of morale that affect individuals and groups: the individual, the group, and the individual within the group on any occasion.[10]

1. *The individual.* Morale refers to a condition of physical and emotional well-being in individuals, a condition that makes it possible for them to work and live hopefully and effectively while feeling they share their group's purposes. Morale makes it possible for them to perform their tasks with energy, enthusiasm and self-discipline, because they are sustained by a conviction that in spite of obstacles and conflict, their personal and social ideals are worth pursuing.

2. *The group.* Morale refers to the conditions of a group in which there are clear and fixed group goals felt to be important and integrated with individual goals; to conditions where there is confidence in the attainment of these goals, and subordinately, confidence in the means of attainment, in the leader, associates, and finally oneself; to conditions where the group's actions are integrated and cooperative; and to conditions where aggression and hostility are expressed toward the forces frustrating the group rather than toward other individuals within the group.

3. *Individual within the group on any occasion.* When there is a task to be accomplished by the group, morale pertains to all factors that cause an

individual to energetically participate in helping the group accomplish the task at hand.

How can a manager keep motivation and morale at a high level?

Most organizations are concerned with the third aspect of morale—the individual within the group. This is why supervisors need to emphasize some specific ways to keep morale and motivation high.

Some firms have found that in-house exercise facilities reduce the average cost of health insurance claims and elevate employee morale.[11] The Federal Reserve Bank of Boston spent $25,000 to transform a storage room into a fitness center, and InterNorth, Inc., in Omaha, Nebraska, has a facility complete with an Olympic-size swimming pool and physical fitness testing equipment. Management found that workers who took part in its aerobic exercise class were absent only one-sixth as often as those who did not. Furthermore, some human resource managers discovered that the facility is a worthwhile feature to mention in employee recruiting brochures and personnel interviews.

As another example, Continental Group provides the following schedule of service awards to keep morale at high levels:

Length of Service	*Choice of Awards*
5 years	Tie tac, ribbon brooch, chrome pen, or horseshoe key ring
10 years	Tie bar, purse atomizer, French key ring, money clip, or chrome felt-tip pen
15 years	Pen knife, cuff links, brooch, or neck pendant
20 years	Leather wallet, French purse, or credit card case
25 years	Wristwatch or pocket watch
30 years	Woman's or man's gold pen-pencil set
35 years	Combined money clip, knife, and file; pocket lighter; or charm bracelet
40 years	Gold ring or barometer
45 years	Quartzmatic clock or chime clock
50 years	President's Award (a personalized gift) plus choice of tie tac with diamond or brooch witn diamond

--- CONCLUSION ---

Our needs and motivations tell a lot about who we are. They also provide information about how we respond to others. And in these response patterns we learn how we feel about people and human relationships. Although human relations is everyone's business, we must see ourselves as people who will initiate or improve relationships. Often the reason relationships are so poor is that everyone is waiting for someone else to do something. That kind of thinking creates an unhealthy climate. We must each be willing to work at human relations first. We know what we need and what motivates us. Now we can begin to help others discover themselves. Build a motivational platform for others to learn human relations skills.

KEY TERMS

Motivation: either an internal or external drive that directs a person toward satisfaction of a need or a goal.

Intrinsic: internal to oneself.

Extrinsic: external to oneself.

Needs: human requirements necessary for work or social satisfaction.

Path-Goal Theory: interrelationships between people's actions and their goal attainment and need satisfaction.

Morale: a mental attitude that describes people's feelings about their work, their job, their organization, their supervisor, and so forth.

QUESTIONS

1 Reread the opening case.
   a. What motivational actions do you think Rocky should have suggested to correct the situation with Joe Bristol?
   b. How would you respond to his father's comment on the practicality of using business-course theories in small companies?
   c. In what ways might it be more risky or difficult to apply some of this chapter's motivational theories in a large firm than in a small one?

2 Summarize the difference between motivation and morale. How are the two related? Would highly motivated persons typically have high morale? Why or why not?

3 Discuss the characteristics of each of the following motivational patterns:
   a. rule compliance,
   b. instrumental system rewards,
   c. instrumental individual rewards,
   d. intrinsic satisfactions from role performance,
   e. internalization of organizational goals and values, and
   f. involvement in primary group relationships.

4 Compare and contrast Maslow's and Herzberg's theories. How does each relate to monetary motivation?

5   Review Figure 9.3. What perceptions, priorities, or experiences cause supervisors to misunderstand what their employees want? What specific things would you do as a manager to improve your understanding of what your workers wanted from their jobs?

6   Review the eight general techniques of motivation that appear on pages 196–197.
   a.   Which may be controlled by the individual supervisor?
   b.   Which require top management support in order to succeed?
   c.   Which three would you most prefer to be exposed to in a career position, and why?
   d.   Which four have the greatest motivational value to you, and why?

7   Review Figure 9.4. What perceptions, priorities, and background or experiences cause first- and second-line supervisors to rank what they want from their jobs so closely?

8   How does the comment, "I love my job—it's the work I hate!" reflect a potential problem in blending morale with motivation? Why must managers be concerned with building both simultaneously?

9   Consider the following statement: "If managers work to keep individual morale high, group morale should follow." Do you agree with this position? Why or why not?

10   Offer at least one work-related example (actual or fictitious) in which the following would exist:
   a.   high group morale, low individual morale;
   b.   high individual morale, low group morale;
   c.   low individual and group morale; and
   d.   high individual and group morale.

11   Describe the negative morale-building actions that you encountered in a past or present supervisor. How did you respond? What caused your supervisor to take such a negative action(s)? What was the long-term result? What did you learn from the experience that could be applied to those who work for you?

12   Review the positive morale-building techniques on pages 199–200. Why do you believe some managers have difficulty applying them in daily relations with subordinates? Reflecting on a present or previous job (or a job you hope to have), which five would be most effective if applied to you, and why?

13   "Some employees bring so many personal problems to work in their heads, that it's practically impossible for me to keep their morale up. Certain circumstances are simply beyond a manager's control!" What would you say to a subordinate manager who feels that way? Justify your advice.

——————————————— CASES ———————————————

Case 9.1

Mark Gwinn is the most respected department head at Allied Industries' Greenville textiles plant. Starting as a packer after high school graduation, he rose through three levels of supervision to manage the yarn preparation department. He knows production operations thoroughly, receives outstanding performance from his subordinates, and runs a department that's a model of efficiency.

Mark's talent hasn't gone unnoticed. Higher managers are impressed with his job performance and his confident, unassuming personality. Clearly, Mark is capable of further advancement.

Allied Industries' top management training program welcomes experienced employees with performance records like Mark's as well as inexperienced college graduates. Recently the division president told plant manager Harold Brown, who is Mark's boss, to recruit him into the program.

After organizing his remarks and reviewing Mark's personnel file, Harold called him in for a conference. Harold outlined the program and emphasized higher management's favorable impression of Mark. Harold concluded with, "Would you like to come aboard? You've earned the opportunity."

"Harold," Mark answered, "I grew up in Greenville. My friends and family roots are here; it's where I plan to live the rest of my life. I'm very flattered to hear what you've just told me. Nevertheless, I'd have to pull up a lifetime's worth of stakes and move every several years if I was in that program. My wife and kids would be upset; they're native Greenville people. What's wrong with just keeping my present job until retirement? You're obviously pleased with my work."

"Absolutely," Harold replied. "But you're an exceptional guy, Mark. The company needs people of your caliber at higher levels, and there simply aren't enough to go around. I see this as a tremendous opportunity for you to step beyond Greenville and build a company-wide reputation. There will be new challenges, formal training courses and seminars, abundant recognition from higher management, and of course the pay—within five years you should double your present salary."

"Harold, I could take a couple of days to think this over, but I see no reason to delay," Mark said. "I know myself well enough to give you an answer right now. I like Greenville, I love my job, and I hope to have it for many years. The prospect of following another course—well, it's just not for me. I hope you understand."

"Of course," Harold answered. "Better to have an outstanding preparation department head than a dissatisfied top management trainee."

Case Questions

1   What instrumental system and individual rewards did Harold offer Mark?
2   Which did Mark seem to value highest, intrinsic satisfaction from his role performance or internalization of the company's goals and values?
3   How do you think higher management should treat Mark Gwinn in the future, and why?
4   Complete the following comment, using your personal experience and opinion: "A person's interest in moving up in any organization depends upon . . . "
5   Discuss the experience that helped you form the opinion you expressed in (4).

Case 9.2

Joe Sherman is a service station attendant at McCollum's garage. In addition to pumping gas and servicing cars, the business provides complete repair facilities that can, as its motto boasts, "rebuild your car from the ground up—better than new."

When owner Paul McCollum hired Joe, he assured him that he would have the chance to become a fully qualified auto mechanic, something that Joe has been interested in throughout high school. Joe would be allowed to do minor repair work but later on, Paul assured him, he would be sent to training programs and paid to take night courses in auto repair at the local vocational technical center.

Joe has worked the front for six months now. Pumping gas and doing basic auto maintenance work were things he knew very well before he started. Occasionally he has been allowed to change a fuel pump or install a set of spark plugs, but he's experienced none of the training Paul described.

Recently Paul has heard a rash of customer complaints about Joe's work. He allegedly refuses to clean windshields and to check tires for full-service customers, and his attitude fluctuates between arrogant and hostile. After watching Joe during random moments, Paul tends to believe there's some basis for the customers' complaints.

Paul realizes he has not followed through on the experience he promised Joe, but business has been especially slow lately, and there's barely enough work to keep the mechanics themselves busy back in the shop. Something must be done, however, because Paul receives at least two complaints per week about Joe's treatment of regular customers.

Case Questions

1 What general motivational techniques would you suggest that Paul attempt with Joe under the circumstances, and why?
2 What positive morale-building practices might Paul apply successfully to Joe?
3 How would you contrast Joe's needs with Paul's?

--------- NOTES ---------

1. Daniel Katz, "The Motivational Basis of Organizational Behavior," *Behavioral Science* (1964): 133–135.
2. Priscilla S. Meyer, "Lonely in the Field? Some Hot Managers Return in Triumph," *The Wall Street Journal*, 12 October 1979, p. 19.
3. Abraham H. Maslow, *Motivation and Personality* (New York: Harper and Row, 1954), pp. 35–58.
4. Abraham H. Maslow, *Toward a Psychology of Being* (New York: Van Nostrand Reinhold, 1962), p. 148.
5. Martin G. Evans, "The Effects of Supervisory Behavior on the Path-Goal Relationship," *Organizational Behavior and Human Performance* (1970): 277–298.
6. Glenn H. Harney, *Management by Objectives* (the Dartnell Corporation, 1971), pp. 68–74.
7. "Action Guide to Motivating People," (Waterford, Conn.: Bureau of Business Practice, 1970), pp. 15–51.
8. Ibid., pp. 30–41.
9. John N. Darr, "Motivation and Morale: Two Keys to Participation," *Personnel Journal* 47(June 1968): 392.
10. Morris S. Viteles, *Motivation and Morale in Industry* (New York: Norton, 1953), p. 282.
11. Robert Guenther, "Employers Try In-House Fitness Centers to Lift Morale, Cut Cost of Health Claims," *The Wall Street Journal*, 10 November 1981, p. 29.

SUGGESTED READINGS

Campbell, J. P., Dunnette, M. D., Lawler, E. E., and Weick. K. E. *Managerial Behavior, Performance, and Effectiveness.* New York: McGraw-Hill, 1970.

Fabun, Don. *On Motivation.* Encino, Calif.: Glencoe Press, 1968.

Porter, Lyman W., and Lawler, Edward E. *Managerial Attitudes and Performance.* Homewood, Ill.: Irwin, 1968.

Vroom, Victor. *Work and Motivation.* New York: Wiley, 1964.

10

Employee Counseling and Discipline

When you complete your study of this chapter, you should be able to:

1 Distinguish among discipline, coaching, and counseling,

2 Practice counseling and discipline,

3 Understand the roles employees, supervisors, and organizations play in on-the-job misconduct,

4 Recognize when an oral warning, a written warning, suspension, or dismissal is necessary, and

5 Conduct a coaching-counseling-discipline session.

OPENING CASE

Vernon Krantz is a shift foreman at Lukens Breweries. He was promoted from a brewkettle tender to supervisor of sixteen former co-workers, most of whom are longtime friends who tend the 500-gallon brewkettles. As part of their job they add ingredients in the proper quantities and at the correct time to produce beer according to the famous Lukens process.

Today Vernon saw Terry Mobley, his friend and subordinate, spitting in a brewkettle. "What are you *doing*?" yelled Vernon. "People *drink* that! What's the matter with you?"

"Aw, don't get all riled up, Vern," Terry answered. "There's 500 gallons of boiling beer in there; that'll kill any germs. You could call it one of Lukens's secret ingredients!"

"Hey, that's totally out of line," said Vernon. "Our company sells this product as a quality beer brewed with the best ingredients and care. Your friends drink it, Terry. Where's your pride?" Terry just smiled and went back to his work.

Later this afternoon, while crossing an overhead walkway, Vernon saw what was obviously a contest in progress among Terry and three other workers. They were making bets on who could spit farthest across a brewkettle.

Vernon pondered the issue back in his office. What the guys were doing hardly seemed to matter in a 500-gallon brewkettle where the heat was above the boiling point, anyway. Still, the company has a rule against employee actions that would "damage, destroy, or otherwise impair the quality of its products and/or reputation."

Vernon recalled with some embarrassment that these contests had gone on when he was a kettle tender, too. Nevertheless, as a foreman he didn't see how he could ignore what was going on. He wasn't sure higher management would back up any action he took, though, because it was hard to prove what the guys were doing.

Nobody Likes Criticism

Poor discipline is a serious problem in human relations. It contributes to low morale and reduced productivity. But many supervisors dislike having to counsel, criticize, or correct others. Some of the more common reasons why supervisors avoid criticizing others include lack of training in how to handle discipline problems, fear of losing control of the situation, or belief

How is discipline a problem at work?

they will lose a friend because of disciplinary action. Thus, few supervisors relish the idea of discipline. However, it is an unavoidable part of managerial work at any level. People violate the accepted ways of doing things. They come in late, quit early, waste time or materials, handle tools carelessly, create accident hazards, drink alcoholic beverages on the job, steal, and so on. The supervisor's job is weighted with problem workers who deviate from expected standards.

——————— Employee Counseling and Coaching ———————

constructive criticism

What is constructive criticism?

coaching counseling

What is the difference between coaching and counseling?

Someone must be willing to criticize and counsel others. And the supervisor is usually the one who must do the criticizing. The type of criticism we're speaking of is not carping, censuring, crabbing, condemning, or complaining; it is constructive criticism. Although criticism usually carries a negative connotation and produces either fear or apprehension, **constructive criticism** should be thought of as in-depth communication about a problem that must be solved. Constructive criticism thus aims at producing some kind of improvement in an employee's attitude or work performance. It is a helping relationship. Because criticism produces such negative feelings, however, we will think of it in terms of coaching and counseling.

Coaching is concerned with improving job skills and knowledge. **Counseling** deals with solving attitude or interpersonal problems. In a broad sense, both activities involve (1) the use of *managerial power* (2) to elicit *self-analysis* by the employee which (3) combines with the manager's *own* insights and knowledge (4) to produce *self-understanding* on the part of the employee, *commitment* to mutually accepted goals, and a *plan of action* for achieving them.[1] Both should lead toward organizational growth and employee development. Therefore, in this chapter both terms will be used interchangeably.

We can thus assume that counseling refers not only to formal interactions such as the yearly performance appraisal but also to daily informal interactions. These informal encounters might include giving instructions, orienting and guiding new employees, and receiving employee feedback. Managers who understand the counseling and coaching process will be better able to help employees solve problems.

For example, Drake Beam Morin, Inc., a New York-based consulting firm, offers an executive salvage service termed *midcareer counseling* for managers who are one step away from being fired.[2] Although Drake Beam Morin is primarily in the executive recruiting business, it decided to add midcareer counseling to its roster when it began meeting a number of seasoned executives who were fired for reasons that could have been eliminated with evaluation and assistance.

The company charges 10 percent of the troubled manager's annual salary ($5,000 minimum) for the service, which includes initial psychological testing and regular sessions with a psychologist and with a consultant experienced in management. Periodic meetings between the manager and supervisor to iron out work problems are another essential ingredient in the package.

Human relations difficulties with colleagues account for 80 percent of the troubled managers' problems. Other executives have jeopardized their careers because of a hot temper or insubordinate behavior. Executive burnout—the feeling that one's energy, ambition, and resourcefulness have been exhausted—also causes some problems.

Approaches to Counseling

Two of the most discussed styles of counseling—formal and informal—are known as directive and nondirective counseling. (These concepts were introduced in Chapter 7.)

How do directive and nondirective counseling differ?

Either approach will work, depending on the circumstances surrounding the need for a counseling session.

DIRECTIVE COUNSELING.   In a directive interview the counselor (or supervisor) decides what questions to ask, what to accomplish, and what sequence to follow. This approach assumes the interviewer is more capable than the interviewee in analyzing and solving problems. Hence, discussion is generally formal, methodical, and fairly rigid. Although it is fairly thorough, it may seem stilted or unduly authoritarian.

NONDIRECTIVE COUNSELING.   In a nondirective interview the counselor (or supervisor) lets the counselee (or employee) express his or her thoughts freely. Although the counselor has a plan, almost all decisions regarding what is to be accomplished and how are made by the interviewee. This technique is conducive to an informal atmosphere and a feeling of good fellowship.

Core Dimensions of Counseling

Whether you choose a directive or nondirective approach to counseling, your success will depend on four core dimensions. They are empathy, positive regard, genuineness, and concreteness.[3]

What are the factors of success in counseling?

EMPATHY.   Empathy is the ability to see the world from another person's viewpoint, to try to experience the world with the same emotions, attitudes, and reasoning as that person. Empathy can assist supervisor-subordinate relationships in several ways. For example, assume one of your employees comes to you with a request to take her vacation two months earlier than she had planned because her husband suddenly has an opportunity to visit one of his company's branch offices in Hawaii. To accede to her request would interfere with your company's busy period. There are at least two ways of handling the problem. You can deny the request or listen with empathy and let her know that you will do your best to approve the request. The second choice will help keep the working relationship open.

POSITIVE REGARD.   Positive regard is a demonstration of respect and acceptance. It involves caring for another person, treating him or her as a human being, and helping that person grow and improve. It also involves nonpossessive warmth—no unreasonable demands or conditions.

GENUINENESS.   Genuineness is honesty and consistency in one's ability to communicate valid statements of one's feelings. Most people aren't always aware of what their true feelings are. But the extent to which one understands oneself is the extent to which one can express one's inner self. The more one reveals about oneself, the more aware of self one will become. Although one's feelings may be verbalized, genuineness or sincerity is itself mainly communicated nonverbally.

CONCRETENESS.   Concreteness is directness and accuracy in communication. It avoids abstractness in talking about things. For example, instead of talking about a dog, you may talk about a full-grown, brown and white St. Bernard. Instead of talking about hating a job, you would talk about what you really hate about it. Without concreteness, one will never reach understanding and problem solution.

─────────────────────── Coaching ───────────────────────

What are some techniques of coaching?

The preceding four skills are the foundation on which to build a coaching relationship with others. Coaching is helping employees to improve job skills and knowledge. The manager helps employees overcome a specific problem by giving them advice or encouragement. Some steps for using coaching in solving people problems follow.[4] Most supervisors may be able to coach better than to counsel. Therefore, these four steps are very important.

1. *Collect information about the employee's demonstrated ability to perform the work to be assigned.* Sources of information about the employee's work can be job descriptions or position guides, work now in progress, or work already committed but not underway. Other information could be gathered from a list of assignments based on the manager's best estimate, or from business, project, and department plans.

2. *Collect information about anticipated events and other business factors affecting the employee's ability to do the assigned work.* Sources of information about the employee's relevant past performance include the manager's memory or notes on critical performance incidents (favorable or unfavorable), past

performance evaluation forms, past annotated accomplishment reports, employee self-appraisal, evaluations of former managers, personnel records, and preemployment checks.

3. *List personal experience applicable to the employee's work, other sources of know-how, possible resources to be made available, and other actions the manager might take to accomplish the employee's work.* Some of the typical factors affecting the employee's ability to do his or her work are organizational and staffing changes, salary review and budget changes, facility bottlenecks, new programs, methods or system changes, schedule and design changes, market and customer changes, competitive moves, economic shifts, and changes in laws or tax structure.

4. *Choose the performance areas to be improved and select the managerial actions most likely to pay off in improved employee performance.* Some of the typical managerial actions to help an employee improve performance are (a) clarifying work assignments, results expected, work standards and measurements, roles and relationships; (b) reviewing likely obstacles and roadblocks and ways around them, alternate ways of getting results, and progress at suitable milestone points; (c) sharing relevant personal knowledge and experience; and (d) coaching to develop needed skills. If the goal is to help the employee gain independence, maturity, and self-discipline, the manager may need to provide additional resources and incentives, pave the way through personal contacts, identify or provide sources of help, or make changes in methods, systems, and organizations.

Because coaching and counseling seek to improve both individual and organizational performance, these interviews can be seen as positive forces in human relations. Another type of interview is often viewed as negative, however—the discipline interview. Discipline often is necessary when coaching and counseling fail. It does not have to be negative, but many people do view it that way. As a government employee recently told me, "I hate it when my boss calls me or stops by my office and says, 'I'd like for you to stop by my office when you've got time.' Then I know he's going to jump on my case about something." Because of such attitudes, supervisors should hold meetings for positive feedback, too.

How are coaching and counseling viewed as a positive force?

Constructive Discipline

Discipline in its broadest sense means orderliness. On the job **discipline** means working, cooperating, and applying oneself in a responsible and orderly manner so work may be accomplished. It means employees:

- report to work regularly and on time;
- call in early when unable to report to work;

discipline

What does discipline mean?

- do the work with integrity and according to established standards and schedules;
- use time and supplies efficiently and economically;
- exercise alertness and diligence to avoid waste, errors, and accidents;
- show respect and courtesy for co-workers, supervisors, managers, and the public;
- carry out reasonable orders and job assignments;
- follow the work rules necessary for safety and efficient operation—and participate in the recommendation and implementation of new rules when conditions warrant any modification; and
- conduct themselves in a manner that helps make the unit a pleasant and productive place in which to work.[5]

Why is discipline necessary?

Discipline is necessary. No group can be productive without it. That is why the subject occupies an important section of most company manuals and training programs. Managers are expected to maintain orderly conduct and apply effective disciplinary measures. And most employees conduct themselves in a normal and reasonable manner. They conform to rules of conduct and obey reasonable orders, as long as they clearly understand what is expected of them. Thus discipline reduces itself primarily to dealing with those who resent authority, have little or no respect for the rights of others, and ignore or defy the usual rules of conduct.

Because employee discipline is such a crucial area of human relations, consider some of the basic causes of employee misconduct.

—————————————— Reasons for Employee Misconduct ——————————————

Why do people misbehave on the job?

Why do employees misbehave? And how can discipline be administered so human relationships will be improved and behavior changed? Three reasons why people misbehave on the job could be summed up in the employee, the supervisor, and the organization.

THE EMPLOYEE. Employees become discipline problems because they lack knowledge to perform assigned tasks. They don't like their job, or they resent authority, rules, regulations, or orders. Also, they may be unsuitable to the job. They may be fully aware of what is expected of them; they may even have the desire to comply with the instructions and rules; yet they may be unable to complete the assignment. Finally, employees may create discipline problems because they carry their financial and family problems to work. Thus they respond inappropriately to the work situation.

THE SUPERVISOR. Supervisors also contribute to disciplinary problems. One of the reasons is the way they manage. For example, if the supervisor is unduly negative and authoritarian, ignores the human relations part of supervision, and stresses pressure, coercion, and punishment, she or he contributes to discipline problems. Employees may react to such management techniques with sabotage, slowdown, and unnecessary waste; or, they may resort to aggressiveness or repression.

Another way supervisors contribute to disciplinary problems is by giving improper assignments or orders. Supervisors should not assign activities beyond the employee's capabilities. Jobs requiring the performance of dangerous tasks or work with unsafe tools and equipment should be avoided. Such assignments will result in improper job performance, frustration, or refusal to obey orders.

Can a supervisor improve conduct through better orders?

When the orders are important, or the manager is inexperienced in giving instructions, there are six rules to obtain action:

1. *Determine what is to be accomplished by whom.* Managers must know the state of affairs they wish changed or brought about before they give effective instructions. No one can get a clear print from a blurred negative. Managers also need to know *who* is the right person to accomplish that objective. There are times when the success of a given project depends on the skills of one particular person. When that is true, don't settle for the next best person.

2. *Be precise and clear in wording instructions.* Managers must plan the communication path to gain understanding and then encode words carefully. They also must predetermine how much information to give the employee, since too little detail opens the door for all kinds of inference-observation confusion and too much detail drags out the assignment unnecessarily. The simplest language is the best.

3. *Give a reason why.* Employees should know why they are doing a certain job, why that job is important, and what the benefits are. Busy work is never very satisfying. Thus managers need to mesh the employee's goals with the organization's objectives.

4. *Demonstrate and dramatize.* Managers often need to show the employee an example of what is to be done rather than rely solely on verbal expression. By showing an employee something or doing something so the task can be visualized, a manager can often clarify a concept that would require hours of talk. Employees enjoy, pay attention to, and remember what happens or unfolds before their eyes. A picture is still worth a thousand words.

5. *Encourage questions.* Unless managers check with the employee to find out what was heard, they will never know how well the instructions have been accepted and understood. Managers must remember communication is a two-way street. Unless they look for or initiate feedback they will learn too late their message did not get through. Just saying "Do you understand?" is not enough, however. Find out what they understand.

6. *Keep tabs on progress.* Check the order-giving results. Follow up and evaluate the results. By proper use of the questioning technique, managers can check to see if they are understood. Also, they can see how far along

employees are toward task completion. The earlier a mistake is caught the less time will be needed to redo the project.

It is important to understand these instruction-giving techniques because the most frequent contact managers have with their employees is through giving orders or directions. A climate for good human relations can be established or destroyed through this process. That is why adequate instruction is basic to good supervision and human relations.

THE ORGANIZATION. The third cause of disciplinary problems is the organization. Unsound and unnecessarily restrictive policies and regulations or improper expectations invite employee violations. Policies and regulations should be related to overall job performance. Expectations should match employees' capabilities.

─────────────── Categories of Discipline Problems ───────────────

What are the major and minor disciplinary problems at work?

Another matter to be considered when discussing discipline is the differences in the types of discipline. Some violations are more serious than others. Each case must be handled individually. Minor misconduct includes tardiness, absenteeism, failure to call in when not coming to work, and leaving work early. Major misconduct includes intoxication, stealing, fighting, deliberately creating accident hazards, insubordination, and sabotage.

The distinction between major and minor is based on the seriousness of the problem and the resulting disciplinary action. Many behaviors may result in only a verbal warning, whereas other infractions may result in immediate suspension or dismissal. Also, although certain problems may seem of major concern to the organization, they are defined as minor disciplinary problems because they do not normally justify suspension or discharge. However, these minor areas may require formal, written back-up notes if trouble persists. Supervisors should have a formal procedure to follow for minor infractions to prevent them from becoming larger problems. *See* Exhibit 10.1.

The two general categories—major and minor—might also be classified as formal and informal. The informal disciplinary measures would include oral cautions, warnings, and counseling. The formal measures include written warnings, counseling, suspension, and dismissal. The emphasis is normally on the informal or minor corrective measures. If these fail then more formal methods must be adopted. A flow chart indicating when to make these decisions is depicted in Figure 10.1.

─────────────── Difficult Questions About Discipline ───────────────

How are you at disciplining others?

You now have some feeling for what discipline is, what causes problems, and what the categories of discipline are. Before dealing with some other

---
EXHIBIT 10.1

Hooker Chemical Company has three categories of offenses: minor, major, and intolerable. Some examples are:

Minor

Leaving early or starting late
Wasting time in washroom or other areas of the plant
Unauthorized reading on the job
Failure to wear safety goggles or hard hat
Unauthorized solicitation of any kind on company property

Major

Falsifying time records
Failure or refusal to carry out prescribed orders
Abusive language toward supervision or fellow employees
Willful destruction of company property
Horseplay

Intolerable

Carrying firearms or dangerous weapons onto company property
Drinking alcohol on company premises
Immoral conduct on company property
Assault
Deliberately smoking in a no-smoking area

---

difficulties of discipline, involve yourself in an experiment. Respond to the questionnaire in Figure 10.2 as if you are a supervisor or manager.

The discipline quiz may be scored accordingly. For every yes or no answer give yourself one point. Then add up the number of yes answers and divide by 37 to get an average score. An average score below 90 percent indicates disciplinary attitudes and practices that need examining.

WHO SHOULD DISCIPLINE? The best type of discipline is self-discipline. In fact, the ultimate goal of discipline is to promote self-discipline, even though managers spend a great deal of time correcting, strengthening, molding, and perfecting. The manager who has a team of self-disciplined employees is free to plan work and to review progress without always looking out for the errant employee. To develop self-disciplined employees, the manager must be able to establish a working climate in which employees want to participate. This requires a manager to remember three things.[6]

How can a manager improve the working climate through discipline?

1. *Employees need and want productive discipline.* They like the challenge of productive discipline and respect the leader who provides it. They do not

FIGURE 10.1
Flowchart for
Deciding Who Gets
Overtime Work

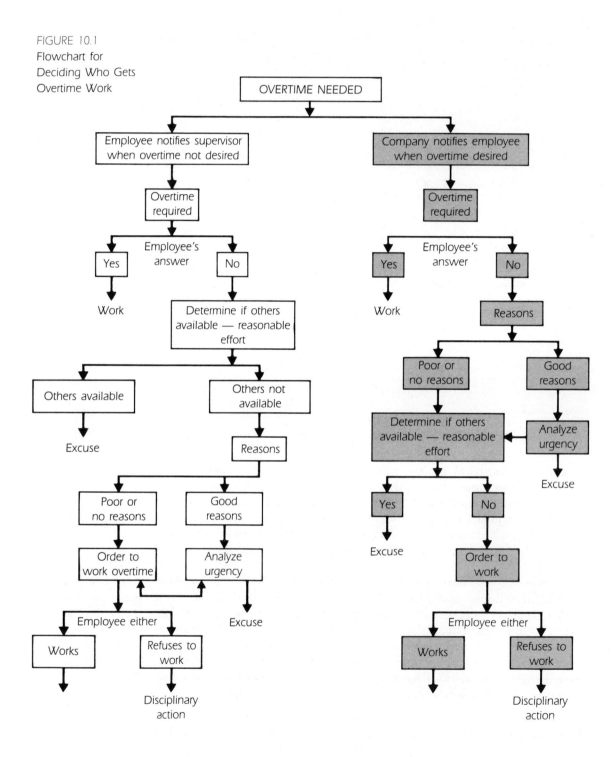

Be honest with your answers; there are no correct ones. The purpose of this quiz is to determine what you actually do.

FIGURE 10.2
A Discipline Quiz

Item	Yes	No
1. Do you give employees reasonable deadlines?		
2. Do you plan your work so it is always completed on time?		
3. Do you thoroughly understand the work of each person under you?		
4. Do you make it easy for employees to talk with you?		
5. Do you personally see to it that people in your department work under good conditions?		
6. Are you sympathetic with workers' problems?		
7. Do you always give clear and understandable instructions?		
8. Do you compliment employees when they do a job well?		
9. Are you considered even-tempered?		
10. Do you make every effort to keep grievances from arising?		
11. When complaints do arise, do you try to handle them honestly and objectively?		
12. Do you have a good worker trained to be a back-up person to yourself?		
13. Do you always reprimand in private?		
14. Do you encourage suggestions and ideas from your people?		
15. Do you avoid passing the buck on mistakes?		
16. Do you always give credit where credit is due?		
17. Are you cooperative with other supervisors and managers?		
18. Do you always set a good example?		

FIGURE 10.2 cont.

Item	Yes	No
19. Do you try to improve your ability in human relations and technical skills?	_____	_____
20. Can you take constructive criticism?	_____	_____
21. Do you keep employees posted on their progress?	_____	_____
22. Do you keep your promises?	_____	_____
23. Do you avoid jumping to conclusions?	_____	_____
24. Do you give reasons for changes or lack of changes when needed?	_____	_____
25. Do you avoid sarcasm?	_____	_____
26. Do you give employees the real facts to cut down rumors?	_____	_____
27. Do you try to remember names and faces?	_____	_____
28. If someone disagrees with you, can you usually argue the point without getting irritated?	_____	_____
29. Do you make special efforts to fully indoctrinate new employees?	_____	_____
30. Do you avoid a superior attitude?	_____	_____
31. Do you avoid favoritism?	_____	_____
32. Can you make decisions promptly?	_____	_____
33. Do you help employees work toward advancement?	_____	_____
34. Are you impartial in making assignments?	_____	_____
35. Can you accept change without getting upset?	_____	_____
36. Do you have confidence in yourself?	_____	_____
37. Are you a self-starter?	_____	_____
TOTALS	═══════	═══════

Source: Adapted from Edward B. Gale, "What a Foreman Should Know About Constructive Discipline," The Dartnell Corp., 1975, pp. 12–13.

object to reasonable orders, rules, and regulations. What they want is positive leadership. When they receive it, there is seldom a serious problem of discipline.

2. *Good discipline requires continuous, full-time leadership.* Supervisors cannot afford to be slack in *any* key area of management. But in particular, the following factors require close attention:

- *Employee selection.* Don't hire someone else's trouble. Check references and review past work history.
- *Employee orientation.* Explain the organizational rules and regulations to new employees. Don't rely solely on the employee handbook.
- *Probationary periods.* Use the probationary period (usually the first six months) to determine if the new employee can perform the work required and can behave properly on the job.
- *Performance review.* Supervisors must continually review the performance of each employee. Such reviews should not be relegated to a once-a-year evaluation.

3. *Potential disciplinary problems should be forestalled.* Supervisors who show positive leadership in administering their work groups seldom need to resort to formal disciplinary measures. When problems do arise, they are not allowed to linger, grow, or spread to other employees. An attempt is made to solve problems informally in the early stages so they do not have to reach the formal stages of grievance or arbitration. This suggests that if the supervisor is well disciplined in his or her approach to managing, then employees will demonstrate greater self-discipline.

Thus, as noted earlier, self-discipline is the best form of discipline. However, if external discipline is needed, the employee's immediate supervisor is the logical person to provide correction. The immediate supervisor is responsible for the actions of those under him or her and should know whether an employee is meeting the standards. Criticism from the immediate supervisor is usually more palatable than from someone else.

Who is responsible for a lack of discipline at work?

WHEN IS CORRECTIVE ACTION APPROPRIATE? Another difficult question concerns when managers should take disciplinary action on employee mistakes and when they should remain silent. Some supervisors take action at the first sign of a mistake, whereas others postpone action until a deliberate pattern of errors is established. The two extremes might be reconciled by agreeing to act only after the facts indicate the employee has performed unsatisfactorily and has failed to take the initiative in correcting behavior.

The basic reasons for criticizing employees are to motivate or stimulate them and to provide them with feedback about their job performance. From these reasons we might conclude discipline is effective only when it meets six criteria.

When is discipline effective?

1. *Discipline must be private.* Oral reprimands should always be given privately. Discussing an employee's behavior in front of others embarrasses the employee and causes dissension within the work group.

2. *Discipline should be prompt.* The longer the delay between a rule infraction by an employee and the supervisor's action, the greater the employee's resentment. Delay gives the employee time to rationalize his or her behavior. Immediate reprimands add credibility to the supervisor and avoid any misconception that infractions are condoned.

3. *Discipline must be impartial.* Employees are quick to spot inequities in the handling of disciplinary matters. Therefore, supervisors should take consistent disciplinary action for problems created by employees with roughly similar records. In addition, the degree of discipline must be reasonably related to the nature of the employee's offense and service record.

4. *Discipline should be nonpunitive.* The purpose of discipline is to prevent future problems, not to get revenge for employee wrongs. The focus should be on preventing the recurrence of past problems and the arising of new problems rather than on administering punishment.

5. *Discipline must be announced.* Employees have a right to know about the rules which determine acceptable job behavior. Supervisors need to give advance warning of their determination to enforce policies. Thus, supervisors must see that: (a) discipline rules are known to employees before they start their jobs, (b) rule changes are made clear before a new rule is to take effect, and (c) there is a clear statement about how serious the organization considers any category of discipline offense.

6. *Discipline must be followed.* Supervisors need to follow through with discipline. Employees need to know their behavior will be reviewed. Such knowledge tends to motivate them to avoid committing the infraction again.

What is the purpose of corrective discipline?

Briefly stated, corrective discipline attempts to invoke penalties appropriate to the error. The above guidelines are key ingredients in corrective discipline. They should assist the supervisor in maintaining productive human relations even when criticizing someone else's performance. However, managers must also recognize the need for clear policies, procedures, and rules that enable them to determine when a violation has occurred and to act according to a clear disciplinary procedure without appearing arbitrary or capricious. This also enables employees to know the boundaries of acceptable conduct. As a result they will not have to guess whether an act will subject them to disciplinary action. Such clarity makes disciplinary action easier to take and accept.

What are some key questions to ask about discipline?

WHAT ARE THE KEY FACTORS IN DISCIPLINE?   Supervisors must know when corrective discipline is required. They must consider several factors to analyze discipline problems. Not all supervisors respond identically to problems, but discipline can be fair when the following questions have been considered:

- What rule was violated or what misconduct is the employee guilty of?
- How severe is the problem or infraction?
- What is the employee's prior conduct record?
- Is the current problem part of an emerging or continuing pattern of discipline infractions? Have there been other discipline problems in the past?
- How long has the employee worked for the organization?
- Are there extenuating, mitigating, or aggravating circumstances related to the problem?
- How have similar infractions been handled in the past within the department or within the organization?

Supervisors should not rush into disciplinary problems or the decisions for actions with the misbehaving employee. They should determine the rule(s) violated, consider the above questions, get whatever advice is thought necessary, and then make a judgment as to how to administer corrective techniques.

HOW SHOULD DISCIPLINE BE ADMINISTERED? As has been mentioned several times, the first step is a problem-solving one. Before you start criticizing, know why. Find out what happened, when, and how. Then deal with the root cause of the employee's discipline problem. Exhibit 10.2 cites some examples of employee offenses and offers some disciplinary solutions to be administered. The list is by no means exhaustive. However, it is representative of industrial management practice. *How should criticism of another person be handled?*

When considering the examples of employee negligence you may not find a certain offense listed. Or you may decide a certain rule infraction does not warrant a disciplinary interview. Some supervisors might suggest a day off with pay to assess oneself as a more positive approach. Perhaps the person needs time off to decide whether she or he really wants the job, feels willing to follow organizational goals, and so forth. If discipline is necessary, however, the typical sequence to follow is oral warning, written warning, suspension, and dismissal.

Oral Warning. Oral warnings should be conducted in an informal atmosphere. Conversation should be private and confidential. The purpose is to inform the employee that misconduct has occurred and that repeating the infraction will result in further discipline. Emphasis is placed on determining if the employee understands job duties and expectations. The employee is given an opportunity to identify the error. If she or he cannot or refuses to identify the problem, the supervisor must clarify and explain the employee's job and responsibilities. The approach is constructive. The interview is directed toward solving the problem or avoiding it in the future. *What is the purpose of an oral warning?*

——————————————— EXHIBIT 10.2 ———————————————

Suggested Guidelines for Disciplinary Action

A Examples of offenses resulting in immediate discharge:

1 Intoxication or use of drugs
2 Fighting
3 Refusal to work
4 Theft
5 Willful destruction of property
6 Gross insubordination
7 Gross misconduct unbecoming an employee
8 Conviction of a felony charged by court of proper jurisdiction, provided the felony is relevant to the position
9 Falsifying time cards
10 Use of undue influence to gain or attempt to gain promotion, leave, favorable assignment or other individual benefit
11 Falsification, fraud, or omission of information in applying for a position
12 Failure to report to work without notification for a period of three days
13 Failure or inability to complete a required training program that is a part of a job assignment
14 Failure to obtain or maintain a current license or certificate required by law or organizational standards as a condition of employment
15 Any other act which endangers the safety, health or well-being of another person, or which is of sufficient magnitude that the consequences cause or act to cause disruption of work or gross discredit to the organization

B Examples of offenses resulting in first, a written warning; and second, an immediate discharge:

1 Gambling
2 Careless, negligent or improper use of property
3 Unauthorized or improper use of any type of leave
4 Failure to report to work without notification for a period of one or two days
5 Releasing confidential information without proper authority
6 Sleeping on job
7 The violation of, or failure to comply with, an executive order, or published rules and regulations of the organization

C Examples of offenses resulting in first, an oral warning; second, a written warning; and third, an immediate discharge:

1 Uncivil conduct
2 Tardiness
3 Unauthorized absence from the job
4 Failure to maintain satisfactory and harmonious working relationships with the public or other employees
5 Smoking in unauthorized areas
6 Failure to punch the time clock
7 Foul and abusive language
8 Inefficiency, incompetency or negligence in the performance of duties

Source: Rodney L. Oberle, "Administering Disciplinary Actions," *Personnel Journal* (January 1978): 30.

How does a written warning differ from an oral warning?

 Written Warning. A written warning is preceded by one or more oral warnings. It is the first formal step in the discipline process and now becomes a matter of record. It often has a greater psychological effect on employees. It offers clear evidence of managerial reprimand. Employees seem to take things more seriously if they see them in writing rather than hearing about them. Another reason to put the complaint in writing is to protect oneself as a supervisor if the employee countercomplains to a union or affirmative action board.

The written warning, or letter of reprimand, must accurately reflect the outcome of an oral interview. Figure 10.3 shows such a warning. Written warnings should include:

- a statement of the problem—facts surrounding the misconduct,
- identification of the policy or work rule violated and when,
- previous oral warnings about the problem,
- consequences of continued misconduct,
- follow-up action to be taken, and
- the employee's signature.

After the warning is written and discussed with the employee, a copy is sent to the personnel office to be included in the employee's official file. The written warning provides a record of misconduct should the employee have to be suspended or dismissed from the job.

Suspension. The third step in administering discipline is to suspend the employee for three to ten days depending on the severity or repetition of the problem. Suspension usually comes after two or three written warnings and cautions the employee to modify behavior or face possible termination. However, the disciplinary layoff period varies according to policy as does the number of written warnings that may precede a layoff or the number of suspensions preceding a discharge. Too much cajoling wastes management's time and implies a wishy-washy rather than a firm-but-fair image.

When is suspension of an employee necessary?

Since the suspended person is not paid during this time off, she or he often gets the message of what could happen if past behavior continues. Also, this situation would be difficult to explain to another employer.

Dismissal. If after two or three suspensions the employee still misbehaves, the final step is dismissal from the job. This is a severe step and involves three aspects. For the employee it means financial hardship. For the organization it means financial loss in terms of experience, recruitment, placement, and training. For the supervisor it means getting involved in an unpleasant experience that may result in loss of friends and ostracism by subordinates.

Is it sometimes necessary to dismiss employees?

There are some cases where discharge is the only correct solution. When there is just cause for termination and company policy is followed, the supervisor should terminate the working relationship rather than allow an unsatisfactory situation to continue.

CAN THERE BE DISCIPLINE WITHOUT RESENTMENT? Our final difficult question about discipline concerns correction without resentment. Is it possible

FIGURE 10.3
Written Disciplinary
Report

TO: _____   DATE: _____

The following disciplinary report was issued today and is to be entered in the official records of the employee named below:

Name _____   Dept. _____

1. (_____) Failure to comply with company/departmental regulations

2. (_____) Unreported absence

3. (_____) Unauthorized handling of materials

4. (_____) Violation of company or departmental procedures

5. (_____) Destruction of company property

6. (_____) Fighting on company premises

7. (_____) Tardiness

8. (_____) Defective and improper work

9. (_____) Carelessness

10. (_____) Insubordination

11. (_____) Under influence of drugs or alcohol

12. (_____) Failure to obey orders

13. (_____) Improper conduct

14. (_____) Leaving without permission

15. (_____) Other _____

Remarks (Set forth all facts in detail):

_____

_____

_____

_____

The above offense or offenses have been noted and are made a part of the above employee's record as of this date. (Note: Forward Directly to Personnel)

Offense No.   1   2   3   4   Recommended action:

1. _____ Warning and/or reprimand

2. _____ Disciplinary Layoff

3. _____ Discharge

_____
Signature of Supervisor

I have read this report: _____
Signature of Employee

WHITE — PERSONNEL
CANARY — EMPLOYEE
PINK — SUPERVISOR

to administer discipline so as to lessen resentment toward the supervisor or organization? Can employees be made to accept accountability for the consequences of their misconduct? Probably not. However, discipline is still an effective supervisory tool for solving employee problems and improving working relationships. Effective communication backed by reference to clear and fair policies and rules should help minimize resentment in disciplinary cases.

CONCLUSION

The manager's challenge is to promote self-discipline by strengthening, molding, or perfecting workers. The experience can be very rewarding in the long-range affairs of the organization. It can yield positive results in human relations if the supervisor will heed the suggestions in this chapter.

KEY TERMS

Constructive Criticism: in-depth communication aimed at improving an employee's attitude or work performance.
Coaching: improving employee's job skills and knowledge.
Counseling: helping employees solve attitude or interpersonal problems.
Discipline: working, cooperating, and applying oneself in a responsible and orderly manner so work may be accomplished.

QUESTIONS

1 Reread the opening case.
   a. Discuss the reasons Vernon might have for avoiding disciplinary action against Terry and the others.
   b. Which style of counseling seems best suited to this case, and why?
   c. If you were Vernon, how would you apply to this problem the four steps involved in coaching?
   d. Outline the points Vernon should emphasize during a formal disciplinary conference with Terry.
   e. What further disciplinary steps would you recommend if Vernon's original measures fail?
2 List at least four reasons why supervisors avoid criticizing subordinates. Which ones would most likely affect you, if you had to discipline a subordinate? How might you cope with them?

3 What is the difference between counseling and coaching? What is their common goal?

4 Which style of counseling (directive or nondirective) would work best in each of the following situations, and why?
   a. An employee harasses all his male co-workers who have shoulder-length hair.
   b. A once-outstanding sales representative suddenly finds herself failing to close sales.
   c. A supervisor is reluctant to accept a promotion to department manager.
   d. A small business owner's workers are about to form a union.
   e. An employee's money management habits have pushed her to the brink of bankruptcy.
   f. A small business owner is thinking about buying a minicomputer.

5 Respond to the following statement: "Either type of counseling will work, depending on the circumstances and the need for a counseling session."

6 How would you differentiate empathy from sympathy? Do you feel that the more empathetic supervisor is more easily manipulated by subordinates? Why or why not? What would you suggest to a supervisor who wants to be more empathetic but who also must guard against manipulation by workers?

7 Respond to the following comment: "Positive regard for others is something you're either born with or without. I don't believe it can be cultivated." Do you agree? Why or why not?

8 Consider several persons you have dealt with recently—salespeople, family members, friends, or others. Which seemed most genuine or sincere? What behavior or characteristics communicated that impression to you? Do you believe you would benefit by acting the same way? Why or why not?

9 Express the following remarks more concretely and supply facts or details by drawing on your imagination:

   a. "You haven't seemed very motivated for the past two weeks, Owens."
   b. "If you like your job, you'd better shape up!"
   c. "Our company is one of the leaders in the industry."
   d. "Oh, wow, is this place screwed up."
   e. "We promote from within whenever feasible."
   f. "The company has suffered some financial embarrassment in the past three years."
   g. "You'll have to perform better if you want to be in line for the department manager's job, Mary."

10 List the four steps involved in effective coaching, and summarize the actions required in each step to become a more effective coach.

11 In what ways do employees themselves make discipline necessary? How can an organization's employment procedure reduce the likelihood that problem employees will be hired?

12 List several characteristics of supervisors that make employee discipline necessary. Suggest at least four rules managers may follow to minimize the need for employee discipline that results from a supervisor's ineffective instructions.

13 What conditions or characteristics within the organization contribute to the need for disciplinary action? What three actions could managers take to minimize these conditions?

14 How would you demonstrate instructions to do the following?
    a. fill out a weekly time sheet listing hours worked,
    b. punch a time clock,
    c. sign on and off a computer terminal,
    d. evaluate a customer's credit application,
    e. conduct a performance evaluation interview, or
    f. assemble a children's swing set.
15 Referring to the items in question (14), develop at least two open-ended questions
    you could ask the employee to evaluate progress and confirm that your instructions
    were understood.
16 List at least four examples of major and minor employee misconduct. How might
    a violation's seriousness be affected by the nature of business operations (retailing
    versus manufacturing, for example), the employee's length of service, and the
    employee's interpretation of policy language.
17 Discuss the informal disciplinary measures that managers may apply to minor
    disciplinary problems and the formal measures that pertain to major breaches
    of discipline.
18 React to the following statements as they relate to disciplinary action:
    a. Make the penalty fit the crime.
    b. An ounce of prevention is worth a pound of cure.
    c. Look before you leap.
    d. Believe half of what you see and nothing of what you hear.
    e. Spare the rod and spoil the person.
    f. Dealing with the past prepares us for the future.
    g. Don't make mountains out of molehills.
    h. We have two ears and one mouth, so we should listen twice as much as
        we talk.
19 Discuss the actions taken by a supervisor at each of the following steps in the
    disciplinary process:
    a. oral warning,
    b. written warning,
    c. suspension, and
    d. dismissal.

——————————————————— CASES ———————————————————

Brenda Bratten, who has established an open-door policy for her subordinates, en-   Case 10.1
courages them to talk to her at any time about any problems that may affect their
work. Several weeks ago Frank Freidel, one of her employees, revealed that he and
his wife were undergoing a bitter and protracted divorce.

"I know this mess may affect my work," he admitted. "But you know, with
all the plans Thelma and I have made and the years we've spent together, it's
impossible for me to keep my mind on my job until this is over. I'm afraid my kids
will grow up strangers to me, and our financial matters are an accountant's nightmare.
This doesn't concern you directly, Brenda, but I wanted to tell you what I'm going
through in case you notice that I'm not behaving like my usual self."

"Of course, Frank," Brenda answered. "I've been down that road with my ex-husband, Jim. It's tough, and you have my deepest concern. You're an exceptional guy, though, and I know you'll come through it all right. Let me know how things work out."

Occasionally Frank dropped in to say a word about developments with his situation, and Brenda would usually describe what she went through on each point. As the matter wound down they were exchanging news every day.

Today Brenda heard rumors from a friend that she was considered the other woman in Frank's divorce, and that the two of them were planning to vacation in Mexico next summer. Brenda vehemently denied any role except that of sounding board and friend.

Upon returning to her office, she saw Frank standing by her door, smiling warmly. "It's finally settled," he said. "Everything. Visitation privileges, money, how to split our house and furniture, the works. I'm so glad this is all behind me so I can get on with my new life. I want to tell you that your concern and support have meant more than you know. Let me show you how much I appreciate your understanding by taking you to dinner. We've shared so much, there's no reason why we shouldn't enjoy each other's company off the job as well as on. We'll go to your favorite restaurant, and on the way home I'll show you my new apartment. It's got mirrored ceilings, a full stereo system, a fireplace, and even a bearskin rug! Besides, I mix the greatest martinis in town! What do you say?"

Brenda was almost too astonished to speak as she beheld Frank, radiating hope and confidence, his eyebrow upraised in anticipation.

Case Questions

1 At what point would you have suggested that Brenda turn the trend of events in another direction? How could she have done so?
2 Briefly outline a code of conduct for supervisors to follow when counseling workers of the opposite sex who have problems like the one in this case.
3 Under the circumstances, how should Brenda respond to Frank's offer of dinner and other amusements?
4 How would you suggest that Brenda deal with Frank in the future?

Case 10.2

Bill Drewry is an electrician with Interstate Wiring Contractors. He has twenty years seniority and is considered a master craftsman. Despite his once-outstanding work record, however, Bill's recent performance has slipped. He wired three control boxes incorrectly within the past two weeks which caused two minor fires and a major one. The latter resulted in $2,000 worth of damage.

Jack Goltz, Bill's supervisor, is concerned about this trend. Thinking back over recent conversations with Bill and Bill's co-workers and other incidents he recalls the following:

• Bill has complained of chest pains off and on for three months, but he refuses to see a doctor.
• He refuses to wear the new glasses he got recently because he thinks they make him look too old.
• Jack noticed that the floor of Bill's car was littered with beer cans yesterday.
• Bill's oldest son was hospitalized recently after being involved in a major automobile accident.

- Several electricians have complained that electrical components made by the company's new supplier have a different design, which presents greater opportunities for wiring mistakes like the ones Bill made.

Jack weighed all of this against Bill's recent mistakes, wondering what was happening in his personal life and how much bearing that had on his recent performance.

Case Questions

1 Which form of counseling would you suggest that Jack use, and why?
2 Apply the four steps of coaching to this case. What should Jack do in each step as he discusses Bill's problem with him?
3 Would you say that discipline is necessary in this case? If so, discuss how Jack should apply the six rules of discipline to Bill's situation and outline the subsequent steps that would be needed if Bill continues to make mistakes.

--- NOTES ---

1. V. R. Buzzotta, R. E. Lefton, and Mannie Sherberg, "Coaching and Counseling: How You Can Improve the Way It's Done," *Training and Development Journal* 32(November 1977): 50.
2. Roger Ricklefs, "How Bosses On the Brink Are Rescued," *The Wall Street Journal,* 28 January 1981, p. 31.
3. George L. Frunzi and Joseph R. Dunn, "Counseling Subordinates: It's Up to You," *Supervisory Management* (August 1974): 4–6.
4. Marion S. Kellogg, *What to Do About Performance Appraisal* (New York: American Management Associations, 1975), pp. 36–43.
5. Leonard J. Gordon, "Developing Self-Disciplined Employees," brochure, Superior Printing, 1978, p. 2.
6. Ibid., pp. 5–7.

--- SUGGESTED READINGS ---

DuBrin, Andrew J. *Managerial Deviance.* New York: Van Nostrand Reinhold, 1976.

Kolb, David A., et al. *Organizational Psychology: A Book of Readings.* Englewood Cliffs, N.J.: Prentice-Hall, 1971.

Lewis, Edwin C. *The Psychology of Counseling.* New York: Holt, Rinehart and Winston, 1970.

3

Challenges in Managing Human Relationships

11

Grievances and Union-Management Relations

When you complete your study of this chapter, you should be able to:

1 Discuss unionism, collective bargaining, complaints, and grievances,

2 Trace the development of the labor movement in the United States,

3 Discuss the major labor legislation influencing management-union relations,

4 Recognize the goals of unions and how these goals can conflict with management goals,

5 Discuss the chief components of collective bargaining,

6 Describe the grievance procedure, and discuss its importance to both management and union, and

7 Recognize the best ways to handle grievances.

—————————————— OPENING CASE ——————————————

Louise Thomas, an experienced switchboard operator, was pleased to get a job offer from Independent Telephone Systems, a small telephone company in the Midwest. Arriving on time for her orientation appointment, she was greeted in person by Marilyn Camp, the personnel manager.

"Welcome aboard, Louise," she said. "We're glad to have someone of your background with us. Experienced operators are hard to find in this area."

"Thank you," answered Louise. "I've been hoping you'd call. It's good to be here."

Included in the package of pre-employment paperwork that Louise had to complete was Independent's employment agreement. When Louise read it, she asked Marilyn what it was for. "It's just a standard procedure," said Marilyn. "You agree to abide by company policies, including not joining a labor union. We have all our new employees sign this when they become part of the Independent family." Louise signed the document hurriedly, glad to be through at last.

Several weeks after being hired, Louise was approached by Bill Johnson, her supervisor. The subject of unions arose again. "You've probably heard that the Communications Workers Union has been sniffing around here and talking unionization. We're confident that no union could get you a better deal than we're giving you now, but they always seem to think they can. I need a really loyal person like yourself to tell me what union baloney is being thrown around. I'd like you to attend the union meeting tonight and let me know just what went on—who is especially in favor of a union, who is lukewarm about it, that sort of stuff. We want to know who our friends are. We're going to get rid of the ungrateful ones who vote for a union. Would you summarize the meeting for me next week?"

"Well," answered Louise, "I'll see what I can do, Bill."

Later the same day, Louise was approached by co-worker Glenn Yancey, who was spearheading the union-organizing drive. "Louise, you know that it's us or them around here," Glenn said. "Management and we workers have been battling about the union for years. We're confident that it will reach a vote this time, though, and we want everybody in line. The people who are badmouthing the union and who vote against it are going to have some real trouble. You'll see an epidemic of flat tires and sugar in the gas tanks that you won't believe—all happening to the antiunion people, of course! Get my drift?" Louise smiled and nodded.

"Besides," Glenn continued, "the union's going to deal such a strong contract that only union members can be hired here—nobody else. Anyway, we're looking forward to seeing you at the union meeting tonight. Solidarity, sister!"

--------------------- Look for the Union Label ---------------------

Labor unions permeate our society. Almost every industrial concern is affected by a local, national, or international (United States and Canada) union; or it depends on some other organization that is unionized. Because unionism is so common to industrial life, supervisors need to know the implications of union-management relations. First, however, let's make a few distinctions. We are concerned in this book primarily with human relationships; that is, the relationships between managers and their employees. If an organization has a union, the supervisor must be concerned not only with human relations but also with labor relations—the relationships between management and the employees' union. A **union** is an organization of employees seeking to advance its members' interests through collective bargaining. It stands between the supervisor and the employee. In a company without a union, the supervisor bargains with upper management for improved salaries or working conditions for employees. In a unionized organization, union representatives and management representatives collectively bargain for a labor contract. The contract sets forth the terms under which employees will work for a certain company.

union

What is a union?

   Although in this chapter we will be speaking broadly of unionism, not all unions are alike. They differ in such things as history, leadership, and the organization in which they operate. Allowing for such differences, however, there are some common characteristics. One way to view this commonality is to see what a union is not. For example:

- *A union is not an idealistic organization.* It is practical, usually hard-boiled, with its eye on securing material gains for its members and, at the same time, enhancing the prestige and power of its leaders.
- *A union is not a revolutionary organization.* On the contrary, it is one of the most conservative. Unions are in the forefront fighting communism and are impatient with socialism.
- *A union is not a public-service organization.* It is primarily interested in its own members and in its own leadership. Of course, like all economic and political groups, a union may well argue that by serving its members it also serves the public. Nevertheless, it is essentially a self-interest organization. Its primary aim is to get the very best wages, hours, and working conditions for its members.
- *A union is not a democratic organization.* Virtually every union has a constitution providing for the usual democratic procedures such as secret ballots, periodic elections of officers, and regular conventions made up of delegates from the respective locals to formulate and adopt policies. However, behind this democratic facade there stands a political (and some would say, dictatorial) machine.
- *Unions are not polite, well-mannered, or even diplomatic in their dealings with corporation executives, or even with government officials.* Indeed, they usually

adopt a posture of hostility, at least publicly, as they organize pressure to obtain their objectives.[1]

With these general distinctions and definitions in mind, let's move on to a general discussion of American unionism, collective bargaining, and the grievance procedure.

Unionism in the United States

American unionism is not a recent development. It has had a long rough road to travel. From our country's beginnings workers and artisans have banded together to discuss problems of mutual concern and to devise methods of solution. From these early beginnings the present-day labor movement was forged.

The Growth of Modern Labor

What events have caused labor to grow?

The growth of labor as an organization and, finally, what we know as unionism can be viewed through four mileposts:[2]

KNIGHTS OF LABOR.   Uriah S. Stephens founded the Noble Order of the Knights of Labor in 1869. It represented a small local union of Philadelphia garment makers, but functioned in secret because of bitter feelings toward unions. The objectives of the Knights of Labor were to establish a union embracing all workers and replace a competitive society with a cooperative one. They called for an eight-hour work day, equal pay for equal work by women, abolition of convict and child labor, public ownership of utilities, and the establishment of cooperatives. Emphasis was placed on education and politics. These goals clashed with those of stronger craft unions that wanted collective bargaining procedures for higher wages and improved working conditions. When the clash between the Knights and the craft unions could not be resolved, the latter formed the American Federation of Labor.

AMERICAN FEDERATION OF LABOR (AFL).   The AFL was founded in 1886 for skilled craft workers (e.g., plumbers and carpenters) with Samuel Gompers as its head. He served as president until 1924 and emphasized collective bargaining as the means for obtaining better wages and working conditions. Following these pure and simple lines of unionism, the AFL grew in numbers. By 1920 it had 4 million members. But in 1935 there was an internal struggle over the question of whether all workers in an industry, or only those strictly on a craft or occupational basis, should be included. Compromise could not be reached. In 1938 nine unions were expelled from the AFL and formed the Congress of Industrial Organizations.

CONGRESS OF INDUSTRIAL ORGANIZATIONS (CIO). John L. Lewis was elected to head the CIO and to promote the organization of workers in mass production and organized industries (e.g., steel, automobile, and textile). The rivalry between AFL and CIO stimulated the growth of both groups.

THE AFL-CIO. In 1955 the AFL and the CIO merged into one organization with approximately 16 million members. George Meany was elected president and Walter Reuther was appointed vice president. However, the AFL-CIO marriage lasted only until 1968. The Teamsters and the United Auto Workers split from the AFL-CIO and formed the Alliance for Labor Action, but the ALA disbanded in the early 1970s after the death of Reuther.

--- Labor Legislation ---

As the labor movement grew and unions gained power, individual states began to take various stands on labor law that eventually led to the enactment of major federal labor laws. The following legislation has affected labor-management relations.

What are the major legislative acts regarding union action?

CLAYTON ANTITRUST ACT. In 1890 Congress passed the Sherman Antitrust Act to prevent monopolies. However, it was unclear whether that applied to unions. To clarify, Congress passed the Clayton Antitrust Act in 1914 to indicate unions were not subject to the Sherman Antitrust Act and to limit the use of court injunctions in labor disputes. However, the Clayton Act was interpreted by the courts to mean activities (e.g., price discrimination, interlocking directorates, etc.) of unions and actually led to increased use of injunctions.

NORRIS-LaGUARDIA ACT. In 1932 Congress passed the Norris-LaGuardia Act to restrict the issuance of court injunctions and to guarantee workers' rights to organize. This act also outlawed yellow-dog contracts— agreements signed by workers promising not to join a union while working for their employers. Such agreements were usually signed as a condition of securing a job and were one of management's bargaining methods. It was called a yellow-dog contract by union sympathizers because they said only a yellow dog (a coward) would take one of these jobs.

WAGNER ACT. In 1935 the National Labor Relations Act, or the Wagner Act, was passed to encourage collective bargaining and to protect workers' rights to unionize. This prounion legislation created the National Labor Relations Board to administer the act, to investigate cases of alleged unfair labor practice, and to conduct elections to determine if a union would be the certified representative of a particular group of employees.

THE FAIR LABOR STANDARDS ACT.   In 1938 Congress defined the forty-hour work week, required time and a half for over forty hours, and established a minimum wage. This Fair Labor Standards Act also set the stage for later federal action regarding discrimination on the basis of age, sex, race, and color.

TAFT-HARTLEY ACT.   Because the Wagner Act favored labor, unions grew in strength and management was at a disadvantage during collective bargaining. Thus Congress passed the Labor-Management Relations Act, also known as the Taft-Hartley Act, in 1947 to limit union tactics. This pro-management legislation specified unfair labor practices by unions and established procedures for settling industrial disputes. It also prohibited union practices listed in Exhibit 11.1.

--- EXHIBIT 11.1 ---

- **Unions cannot restrain or coerce employees to join unions of their own choosing or to refrain from joining the union.** This prohibits unions from threatening and harassing employees during a representation election.
- **Unions cannot discriminate against nonunion applicants.** Prior to the Taft-Hartley Act, some unions were able to secure agreements from employers that job applicants must join the union before they could be hired. This is called a closed shop security agreement. This kind of security agreement is no longer legal except in certain cases, for example, the building trades industry. The Taft-Hartley Act permits the union shop security agreement, which makes it legal to require that new employees join the union within thirty days after employment. However, it also permits state right-to-work laws—legislation prohibiting the union shop agreement.
- **Unions cannot refuse to bargain with an employer.** Some unions had become so powerful that in contract negotiations no real bargaining took place. The bargaining consisted of the union representing its demands and saying, "Agree to these demands or we'll close your organization down."
- **Unions cannot participate in certain strikes and boycotts.** A primary boycott is union pressure (e.g., strike and pickets) against an employer with whom it is negotiating a contract. A secondary boycott is economic pressure against a neutral employer so that the neutral employer will encourage the primary employer to agree to union demands. Both are illegal.
- **Unions cannot charge excessive initiation fees.** Some unions charged excessive initiation fees and dues in order to restrict the supply of personnel in an occupation. This is effective when a union has a union shop or closed shop security agreement with the employer. Deciding what initiation fees and dues are excessive is left to the secretary of the U.S. Department of Labor.
- **Unions cannot cause or attempt to cause an employer to pay for services that are not performed.** This provision was directed against featherbedding, but it failed mainly because make-work rules are not prohibited. Make-work rules refer to unnecessary tasks that are performed in order to avoid the chance of featherbedding.[3]

The Taft-Hartley Act also provided an eighty-day presidential injunction request in cases of national importance.

LANDRUM-GRIFFIN ACT. The Wagner Act protected the unions, and the Taft-Hartley Act protected management. In 1959 the Labor-Management Reporting and Disclosure Act, also known as the Landrum-Griffin Act, was passed to protect individual union members from union corruption. This act provided for a bill of rights containing standards and safeguards and for reports to be filed with the Secretary of Labor and disclosed to the union's members. It also guaranteed each union member the right to vote in union elections, to sue the union for violations of the act or for discrimination, and to receive a hearing before the union takes disciplinary action.

Since the Labor-Management Reporting and Disclosure Act, the main growth in unions has been in the public sector rather than in the crafts or industrial unions.

New Legislative Programs

Even with all the legislation passed regarding labor relations, there are pathological excesses in a minority of unions. These excesses are demonstrated by such things as corruption, infiltration by the Mafia, and abuse of office. To assist in detecting corruption a new legislative program should be established. This program should have four main objectives:

Are new legislative programs needed today regarding unionization?

1 *To ensure investigation of union funds.* The vast funds accumulating in union treasuries and in pension and welfare funds should be scrupulously investigated and safeguarded as are any insurance or bank funds.
2 *To help unions maintain their democratic framework.* Adequate checks should be set up—not against centralization, for that is inevitable, but against oppressiveness and civil rights violations.
3 *To safeguard workers and the community against unfair union practices.* A fresh study should be made in order to prevent abuses such as picketing to compel an employer to accept a union, though the employees themselves have indicated no such desire. Secondary boycotts also need a fresh examination to protect the interests of enterprises not directly involved in a labor dispute.
4 *To appoint periodically a legislative committee to bring union practices to public attention.* Perhaps even more than legislation, hearings may, in the end, be of greatest help in keeping unscrupulous people from exploiting American workers and the community.[4]

The unions' right to exist has been the result of a long struggle to accomplish certain goals and objectives. But unions need to steer toward moral goals and away from corruption. They should enhance, not stifle, human relationships.

Union Objectives

What are the
objectives of unions?

To understand unionism, it might be helpful to know why workers accept or reject unions. Most employees will join unions for greater bargaining power, to make themselves heard, or as a condition of employment. Employees may reject unions because they feel unions are socialistic, because unions are below their social status, or because they prefer to be associated with management.

Unions have three major types of objectives: political, social, and economic.[5]

POLITICAL OBJECTIVES.   Since the United States has no separate labor party, as do most Western European countries, union leaders attempt to fill this void. One way they try to speak for the labor force is through lobbying. For example, AFL-CIO's Committee on Political Education lobbies for the passage of prolabor laws and helps prolabor candidates get elected.

SOCIAL OBJECTIVES.   Local unions can serve almost as a club by allowing workers to build close friendships around a common purpose. Thus union leaders view their job as showing greater interest in members' problems. One of the ways they are doing this is by opening their doors to minorities and doing away with discrimination.

ECONOMIC OBJECTIVES.   Union leaders also seek to satisfy their members' economic needs. Specifically, they attempt to improve their members' standard of living through higher wages, shorter working hours, better working conditions, pensions, and paid vacations. They are also concerned with workers' security. For example, most contracts have a seniority provision, which specifies rights and privileges that accrue with length of service. These rights may regard layoffs, transfers, and promotions.

Sources of Union-Management Conflict

What causes conflict
between labor and
management?

Six areas of conflict can exist between labor and management. Several of these grow out of the objectives both groups are trying to accomplish. The six areas are profit, jobs, the right to manage, seniority, productivity, and inflation.[6]

PROFIT.   How should profits be distributed? Both labor and management agree that organizations should make a profit. But if profit is too high, unions often think their workers must not be getting enough pay or benefits.

JOBS.   Recent unemployment levels have made workers seek job security. The idea that an organization's goal is to provide jobs has been replaced by the idea that it must provide security. One method has been to include supplemental unemployment benefits (SUB) in labor contracts. SUB deals with short-term joblessness by requiring an employer to pay a certain amount of money into a fund for each hour an employee works. These accumulated funds are then paid to workers who are laid off.

RIGHT TO MANAGE.   "Who is in control?" is a basic question around a negotiating table. Management often sees its decision-making authority diminish. Of course, it would like to retain decision-making authority. Thus, it seeks to ward off encroachments. This becomes more difficult as unions seek to increase the scope of bargainable issues.

SENIORITY.   A seniority system disregards an individual's ability and ambition, but labor argues that any other system for deciding wages and salaries is subjective. Management resists seniority systems in favor of productivity.

PRODUCTIVITY.   Productivity is the ability to produce goods and services from labor and capital. The problem is in determining how much productivity is due to labor and how much is due to capital. For example, if workers increase output they want more pay. But management may argue that the increased output resulted from better machinery.

INFLATION.   Cost-of-living adjustments are common in labor contracts. That is, as the cost of living rises, the consumer price index rises, requiring wage hikes. These shelter the worker from inflation. However, it could be argued that cost-of-living increases are inherently inflationary because producers raise the cost of products to consumers to cover labor's pay increases. The result is a wage/price spiral. Thus, the value of cost-of-living adjustments as a shelter is short-lived.

COPING WITH THE SOURCES OF CONFLICT.   Because each of the preceding factors can cause conflict between labor and management, communication often breaks down. If communication breaks down, so do good human relations. However, through the "Delta family feeling," the management of 36,000 employees at Delta Airlines has kept the company 99 percent union-free while building team spirit that is a model for the industry. By promoting from within, paying at least as well as competitors, and avoiding layoffs, Delta management has achieved exemplary employee loyalty and productivity.

Participative management abounds. Management permitted a group of flight attendants to pick the type of uniform the company would adopt. Supervising mechanics are selected by their peers. Employees haven't struck at Delta since 1947, and the last union representation vote occurred almost three decades ago. To some union organizers Delta's curtain of sound labor-management relations seems almost impregnable.[7]

---------- Labor-Management Tactics ----------

What are some tactics management uses when labor wants to strike?

If discontent is widespread in an organization, both labor and management may react in some manner. When a peaceful settlement of differences cannot be achieved, other tactics are used. For example, labor may strike, picket, or boycott. Management may retaliate with lockouts (refusal to allow employees to return to work until they accept management's terms). Management may get a court injunction to keep the union from interfering with production. It may use layoffs to force early acceptance of an agreement. Or it may subscribe to strike insurance funds to enable it to hold out longer in case of a strike. Of course, each side blames the other for causing it to resort to these tactics.

---------- Improving Labor-Management Relations ----------

Management would like to maintain a stable relationship with a union. But managers need to remember that unions exist in many firms because management ignored sound employee relations techniques until it was too late. At this point these techniques were condensed into a quasi-legal document (the union contract). Thus some people believe management historically has brought unionization on itself.

Can labor-management relations be improved?

To improve management-union relations, management can implement policies in three areas to establish a stable industrial relations policy.[8] These areas are communication, negotiation, and administration of the collective bargaining agreement.

COMMUNICATION.   First, management should foster communication and establish an effective working relationship between the various parties concerned with the collective bargaining agreement. It should especially consider the existing relationship between

1 employees and their immediate supervisor,
2 employees and higher management,
3 supervisors and the shop steward, and
4 upper levels of management and top local union officials.

Sharing information to understand each other's legitimate problems can help create the type of work environment that encourages efficiency and effectiveness.

For example, in the early 1980s inflation caused management and labor to reach an unprecedented level of teamwork. Several major airlines including Pan American, United, Braniff, and Continental negotiated employee givebacks that included wage freezes, pay cuts of up to 10 percent for some or all workers, and changes in pilot work rules that increased productivity.[9] Ford Motor Company and Chrysler had to perform similar feats.

NEGOTIATIONS.   Negotiations that result in a contract should be handled with a constructive, forward-looking attitude within the framework of achieving management's reasonable objectives. Negotiations represent the beginning of the collective bargaining process. But grievance procedures represent the mechanism for continuing the process. Therefore, management should negotiate a solid grievance procedure that can be used to settle problems promptly.

ADMINISTRATION OF THE COLLECTIVE BARGAINING AGREEMENT.   If negotiations are handled properly, the stage will be set for management and union officials to work together to achieve a fair and effective day-to-day administration of the collective bargaining agreement. Day-to-day administration of the collective bargaining contract is concerned primarily with the grievance procedure and how grievances are handled by supervisors.

––––––––––––––––––––––––– Keeping the Unions Out –––––––––––––––––––––––––

Collective bargaining and the grievance procedure will be discussed in more detail later. First, let's deal with one last question concerning unions: Are they really needed? The answer depends, obviously, on the situation. In some companies they are needed, and in some they aren't. However, companies without unions cannot just have a policy stating unions are unnecessary. They must also have a program demonstrating that fact to employees; that is, they must have top management commitment. To make a visible commitment, the following actions can be taken:

Are unions needed?

- Establish a clear, coherent, and cogent philosophy regarding employees.
- Implement *policies* to support this philosophy.
- Review existing company policies and procedures from an employee relations viewpoint and assess new policies, before implementation, for their effect on employee relations.
- Integrate effective employee relations goals into every senior management member's objectives for the year. Accountability goes a long way towards ensuring that things get done.[10]

A company will succeed in keeping a union out if it gets the line managers involved and keeps them involved. This involves three steps.[11]

1. Set up employee relations teams to deal with potentially troublesome areas in the company and to review impending programs and changes from an employee relations viewpoint. These teams would have senior and line management representation and, in some cases, employee representation as well.

2. Institute a workable complaint-handling procedure and make sure that line supervisors realize it is not directed against them but is designed to allow ventilation of employee dissatisfaction and to solve problems. This can be accomplished by involving line management in policy formulation as well as implementation.

3. Make effective employee relations part of the stated goals for every line manager in addition to their other objectives for the year. Firms such as Eli Lilly, Gillette, Polaroid, Black & Decker, and Grumman have remained nonunion over the years by paying special attention to sound human relations practices and by providing pay and fringe benefits that are at least equal to competing firms with unionized employees.[12] At DuPont, another nonunion giant, only 5 percent of the company's 66,000 production workers have joined a national union. Although union elections have been held in various DuPont plants for nearly half a century, the national unions have won less than 6 percent of them.[13] International Business Machines boasts a track record similar to DuPont's.

The staff services support (e.g., public relations and marketing) can help create effective employee relations if the personnel department performs four tasks.[14]

1 Publicize internally the company's position on unions and employee relations through use of the house organ, employee meetings, ERISA-required literature, and a one-on-one basis during counseling sessions.
2 Communicate to both top and line management information and recommendations culled from what has been picked up from the shop floor.
3 Develop viable programs to support each level of management.
4 Act as a catalyst, buffer, hand holder, and conduit, if necessary, for both management and employees.

These three areas working together—top management, line management, and staff—are necessary to keep a union out or to work with one that is in. In either case management needs to have some knowledge of collective bargaining.

───────────── Collective Bargaining ─────────────

collective
bargaining

Collective bargaining is the process whereby representatives of management and representatives of labor (the union) meet together to bargain over and agree upon worker incomes, job security, working conditions, hours, and other terms of employment. By law, collective bargaining involves four steps: (1) recognizing the appropriate bargaining unit, (2) bargaining in good faith, (3) meeting proposals with counterproposals, and (4) incorporating the findings in a written contract.[15]

------------------------------ The Bargaining Unit ------------------------------

A company must recognize the union chosen by the workers as their bargaining agent. Management-union relationships in collective bargaining can be based on six attitudes:

How does collective bargaining help resolve labor-management conflicts?

1. *Conflict.* This is an uncompromising management attitude that is fading from the labor scene. However, it existed on a wide scale prior to World War II.

2. *An armed truce attitude.* The company representatives are well aware of the vital interests of the company and see unions as representing an opposite goal. This does not mean, however, that forcing head-on conflict is in the best interest of either group.

3. *Power bargaining.* Management's task is to increase and use its power to offset that of the union where possible. Management engaged in power bargaining can accept the union and in fact take pride in its sense of realism, which forces management to acknowledge the union's power.

4. *Accommodation.* This is a learning process in which management and union adjust to one another to minimize conflict, to conciliate whenever necessary, and to tolerate one another. Accommodation is not the same as cooperation and in no way suggests that management goes out of its way to help organized labor.

5. *Cooperation.* Management fully accepts the union as an active partner in a formal plan. This is a rare occurrence because in cooperation management supports not only the right but also the desirability of union participation in certain areas of decision making. The two groups deal jointly with personnel and production problems as they occur.

6. *Collusion.* In this form of mutual-interest monopoly, each party is unconcerned with any interest except its own. These situations are relatively rare because they are deemed illegal.[16]

Collective bargaining between management representatives and union representatives is intended to be a process of give-and-take. Interdependence is required. To assist this interdependence, both groups must negotiate in good faith.

------------------------------ Good Faith ------------------------------

Good faith means that a company sends a management representative with the authority and intent of reaching an agreement to meet with the union representatives; that it sets up reasonable conditions for bargaining; and that it will not violate a written contract once agreement has been reached. According to the National Labor Relations Board, good faith means each group is willing to compromise. To be able to compromise, both groups usually begin negotiations by exaggerating their real positions so they can

good faith

How does good faith assist negotiations?

make compromises without losing what they want. However, in order to maintain a good relationship between the two groups, each should view its work as an ongoing process. The relationship does not end when an agreement has been reached.

Proposals and Counterproposals

How do labor and management reach decisions about what is fair?

When labor and management meet to negotiate salaries and working conditions, as we have stated, both take extreme positions. Then through a series of proposals and counterproposals they eventually compromise on an acceptable medium. Figure 11.1 shows contract negotiations between management and labor during collective bargaining. The left side represents a positive negotiating zone. It shows the union's real position as being somewhere below management's real position. There is some overlap between both sides' demands.

The right side represents a negative negotiating zone. It indicates that the best offer management is willing to make is less than the smallest offer the union is willing to accept. Negotiations falling into this zone usually result in a work stoppage.

Thus, at this point some other method—mediation, arbitration, or compulsory investigation and delay—may be necessary to settle the dispute. Mediation involves the use of a third party to bring both sides to agreement.

FIGURE 11.1
Contract Negotiations and the Bargaining Zone

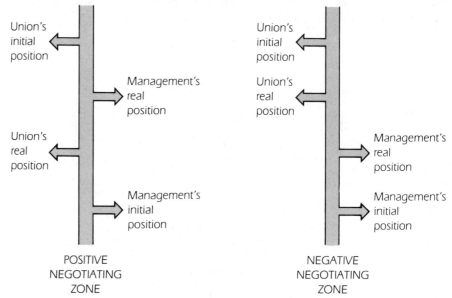

The mediator often offers proposals to bring the two groups together. In arbitration both groups submit their proposals to an individual arbitrator or a board of arbitration. Both sides agree to abide by the arbitrator's decision whether or not it is favorable to them. Finally, if a threatened strike could imperil public health or safety, it could be postponed while a third party investigates the conflict. This process is called compulsory investigation and delay.

During the initial phases of contract negotiations, in either zone, the union makes excessive demands in its proposal and management counters with a proposal that also is far removed. The goal is to reach a midpoint acceptable to both groups. Once the two groups have reached that point, their agreement is incorporated into a written contract.

The Written Contract

Many issues can be bargained over during negotiations. Some items that may find their way into the labor contract are listed in Exhibit 11.2. Items agreed on are put into a written contract, and both sides must sign the contract in good faith and indicate their willingness to abide by the decisions reached in negotiations.

One of the items in the contract is the grievance procedure. This is the procedure for administering the written contract, which includes all of the items in Exhibit 11.2.

EXHIBIT 11.2

Typical Items in a Labor Contract

1	Arbitration procedures	15 Overtime and premium pay
2	Bulletin board use	16 Pension plans
3	Conditions governing transfers	17 Practices concerning probation
4	Dates of the contract	18 Rest and lunch periods
5	Discipline and discharge rules	19 Seniority
6	Grievance procedures	20 Separation allowance
7	Hours of work	21 Shift differential
8	Incentives	22 Sick leave
9	Insurance and hospitalization	23 Union activities on company time
10	Layoff and recall procedures	24 Union dues
11	Leaves of absence	25 Union recognition
12	Management decision-making rights	26 Vacations and holidays
13	Nondiscrimination clause	27 Wages and salaries
14	Nonstrike, lockout, or boycott agreements	

---------------------------------- The Grievance Procedure ----------------------------------

What are a grievance and a grievance procedure?

Almost all labor contracts have a grievance procedure to control complaints or conflicts arising during the term of the contract. The grievance procedure interprets and clarifies the collective bargaining decision, and it provides a means of communication for dealing with on-the-job human relations problems. It is important to know the difference between a complaint and a

grievance

grievance. A **grievance** is a specific, formal employee dissatisfaction. It is usually first expressed verbally to a union representative (shop steward) or the employee's immediate supervisor. At this point it is just an expression of discontent, not a formal accusation or charge. But such complaints often become grievances if they are not settled at this stage. The unsettled complaint, real or imagined, can become a written grievance presented to a management representative or company grievance committee or the department or plant manager.

Grievances must be handled properly. If they are not, an employee's dissatisfaction can affect the entire organization and its human relationships. And at this point the personnel department, industrial relations director, and the local, national, or international representatives may be called together. If they can't solve the grievance, it's time for an arbitrator.

---------------------------- Functions of the Grievance Procedure ----------------------------

If supervisors are doing their jobs properly and if management is keeping channels of communication open, a potential grievance should never get to, and certainly not beyond, the complaint stage. For example, a group of aerospace engineers working on Saturday moved a piece of electronic test equipment fifty feet across a shop floor to plug it in. On Monday union workers noticed the box had been moved. The workers who were next in line for overtime work filed a grievance because they were not called in to move it. They were paid for the work they did not do because it was described in the labor-management contract as union work, and the engineers admitted that they had known on Friday that the equipment would have to be moved to accommodate their Saturday plans. Prior planning and open communication could have avoided a grievance.

How should a grievance procedure proceed?

To expedite the solution of potential complaints, the grievance procedure should include the following provisions.[17]

1 Each step in the grievance procedure should define time limits for presenting a grievance, rendering a decision, and taking an appeal.
2 Both management and union representatives should present their respective positions in writing, including the factual basis of the grievance and the section of the contract allegedly violated.

3 Grievances should be settled at the lowest possible level, unless broad policy issues are involved.

4 The grievance procedure should afford adequate opportunities for both management and the union to investigate the incident involved in the grievance.

5 Grievances involving discharge, suspension, or some other disciplinary action should receive priority over other grievances. To facilitate these provisions for solving problems, you should know the basic functions of the grievance procedure. These purposes are listed in Exhibit 11.3.

———————————————— EXHIBIT 11.3 ————————————————

- **To settle disputes as soon as possible and as close to the source as possible.** Although procedural delays are inevitable, time limits at each step are intended to keep things moving. The old legal axiom, "Justice delayed is justice denied," can be readily applied to the grievance procedure.

- **To formulate disputed issues early.** There is normally a requirement that grievances be in writing. This forces the aggrieved party to be specific, thereby eliminating frivolous complaints. A clear statement of the issue early in the process also tends to focus discussion and investigation.

- **To establish final authority.** The procedure in the labor agreement will delineate successive steps in the process and their limits.

- **To help monitor contractual problems.** Issues that might require further discussions can be discerned when the contract is renegotiated.

- **To serve as a channel of communication.** This channel may indicate employee morale as well as allow employee participation.

- **To indicate which supervisors are having problems.** These supervisors may need additional training, transfer, or replacement.

- **To help set a uniform labor policy.** Decisions reached in the grievance procedure will normally be implemented for any similar instances that occur. Because of this, careful review of grievances is doubly important.

- **To help management in analyzing and modifying administrative structures.** When a dysfunctional procedure has been established, the grievance procedure will point out and help eliminate these cumbersome elements.[18]

These functions of the grievance procedure can alert a supervisor to the sources of dissatisfaction and potential problems. A good supervisor will listen to what employees are saying, find the causes of the problem, and eliminate the problem before a formal grievance is filed.

——————————————— What Employees Complain About ———————————————

One of the errors managers frequently make is failing to listen carefully to what employees are saying. The art of listening (discussed in Chapter 7) is one of the most important for a supervisor. Employees often say things that

What do employees complain about?

allow a supervisor to solve a grievance while it is just a gripe. When employees are asked about their life on the job, their complaints generally fall into four categories:[19] the working environment, company policies and procedures, supervision, and management.

THE WORKING ENVIRONMENT.   About 30 percent of employee comments deal with deficiencies in the workplace. For example, employees complain about poor lighting, temperature in the work area, dirty restrooms, or lack of supplies in food-vending machines. In one nonunion manufacturing plant, shipping department employees were disgusted because water reservoirs on the gummed tape dispensers attracted maggots. The department manager told them that the glue on the back of the tape was made from animal hide, and the reservoirs had to be washed out every two or three days to prevent the problem from occurring. The workers objected to that messy, smelly job and filed a grievance with the plant manager through the open-door policy. He resolved the issue to everyone's satisfaction by ordering a switch to sealing tape not made from organic material.

COMPANY POLICIES AND PROCEDURES.   About 10 percent of employee comments focus on procedural problems. For example, employees complain about someone's trouble with the profit-sharing system, incorrect payroll deductions for instance, or alleged inequities in vacation policy administration between departments.

SUPERVISION.   Another 30 percent of employee comments involve supervision that is harsh, abusive, tyrannical, arbitrary, or inept. For example, employees complain about supervisors playing favorites, ignoring requests for help, burying themselves in paperwork, driving too hard, or using bad language.

MANAGEMENT.   About 30 percent of employee comments are directed at management. These complaints generally divide into four subcategories:

1. *Wasted resources.* Many employees worry about wasted company time, energy, and money. They react strongly when they witness or are a part of wasteful activities.

2. *Supervisory neglect.* The average hourly employee expects supervisors not only to help his or her work effort but also to be helpful to the company. Workers regard supervisory neglect as one aspect of wasted resources. Worker feelings that are favorable toward the supervisor are often reflected in lower absenteeism and turnover, less waste and spoilage, better quality, fewer accidents, and higher productivity.

3. *Managerial indifference.* Supervisors are judged by their capacity to operate their departments smoothly, and managers are judged by their capacity

to operate their companies smoothly. This ability is seen as dependent on doing the right things, today, to facilitate quality production.

4. *Equipment and maintenance.* Employees resent shoddy, ill-maintained equipment, and they complain repeatedly about equipment and the lack of preventive maintenance.[20]

Handling Grievances

If an employee complains or files a grievance, the supervisor must realize that the employee feels she or he has a legitimate complaint and deserves serious and sensitive treatment. Thus, much of a supervisor's success as a part of the management team is determined by how well she or he is able to handle grievances and eliminate the causes of conflict. A solid grievance procedure will assist the supervisor.

How should a manager handle a grievance?

Pat Foley, president of Hyatt Hotels Corporation, meets with workers at various hotels and encourages them to air their complaints in an open-door gripe session. Many problems are trivial such as those involving work uniform designs or menu offerings. However, as a session progresses, workers often reveal more substantial problems such as inadequately trained supervisors or those with irritating management styles.

After investigating each gripe, Mr. Foley writes the complainant a personal letter outlining any action that will be taken. He says, "Every time I do one of these meetings, I realize it's the little things that most often affect morale. This is a way to make the employee feel like we care."[21]

The effective grievance procedure should meet four objectives.[22]

1   The contract should contain a no-strike clause, providing all disputes involving the interpretation or application of the terms of the agreement are to be settled without strikes, lockouts, or any other interruption to normal operations.
2   The grievance procedure should provide for clearly defined, successive steps ending in arbitration. The process of making appeals should be explained explicitly so everyone understands the exact procedure for processing grievances.
3   The grievance procedure should be designed to deal with and resolve disputes that might arise under the provisions of the contract.
4   It should expedite the prompt solution of problems. In addition to a solid grievance procedure, the rules of managerial conduct listed in Exhibit 11.4 will assist the supervisor in handling grievances.

Every worker deserves a clear, open communication channel for the expression of complaints. If that channel is blocked, a small complaint may become a grievance because of worker resentment and frustration. That's why the supervisor stands at a crucial spot in the organizational hierarchy.

--------------------------------- EXHIBIT 11.4 ---------------------------------

- **Listen.** Get the employee to describe the problem. Don't interrupt; let the grievant talk the problem out without fear of retaliation.
- **Discuss the grievance.** The grievance must be understood from the employee's point of view. Do not assume the employee is wrong; grievances are often justified. Since arguments can develop during the discussion phase, try to keep the discussion calm.
- **Get input from other relevant individuals.** Most incidents involve more than one person, so supervisors should not rely on only one person's version of what is wrong. Facts should be gathered to ensure fairness to all those involved.
- **Look at the situation from the employee's point of view.** Be empathetic and objective; show that you are trying to be fair.
- **Evaluate the facts and opinions relevant to the situation.** Facts are not in dispute; opinions are judgments. Avoid snap judgments when evaluating facts and opinions.
- **Make the decision.** Try to be logical and avoid letting bias enter into the decision.

If the grievance pertains to discipline, it is important for the supervisor to consider these additional rules:

- **Distinguish between major and minor offenses.** Disciplinary action should fit the nature of the offense.
- **Distinguish between long-service employees and recent hires.** Disciplinary action which is appropriate for a new employee may be too severe for a long-time employee.
- **Except for major offenses, follow the proper disciplinary sequence:** oral warning, written warning, suspension, and discharge.
- **Impose similar penalties for similar offenses.** Be consistent.
- **Correct undesirable behavior;** do not punish the employee.
- **Communicate the decision.** When communicating the decision, remember the importance of timing. Don't act too quickly, and don't delay too long.[23]

The supervisor must learn to handle complaints and grievances so that every employee feels free to discuss problems.

------------------------------- Supervisory Training -------------------------------

How should a manager view grievances?

One way top management can assist supervisory development and improve this key link in union-management relationships is to provide training for handling complaints. Specifically, they must encourage supervisors to develop the following four attitudes towards the total grievance procedure.[24]

1. The objective of the grievance procedure is to achieve a sound and fair settlement of disputes arising in the workplace. Accordingly, it is not as important for supervisors to have a record of winning grievances as it is for them to have a record of promptly settling any problems arising within their jurisdiction so their department can continue to operate with a minimum of friction.

2. Supervisors should not see the filing of a grievance as a personal affront or as a challenge to their authority, but should see it as a tool to

help them discover and remove what may be minor problems before they develop into major issues.

3. All persons who become involved in the grievance procedure must evaluate each grievance fairly and independently to determine how it can be settled. Therefore, management representatives at each step of the grievance procedure must avoid the tendency to automatically support the decisions of earlier management representatives just to back up their subordinates. If it is necessary to overrule the decision of a subordinate in order to achieve a fair and just settlement, the decision to do so should first be discussed completely with the subordinate along with the necessity for overruling his or her decision. Only after this conversation has taken place should the reversal be announced to the union.

4. Management must stress to its supervisors and other representatives the need to take adequate time to handle and dispose of grievances, if the grievance procedure is to function properly. Busy supervisors are unlikely to take this time unless higher management encourages them to do so.

CONCLUSION

Unions fulfill a need in business. They can, however, be both a help and a detriment to management. Managers must be concerned not only with human relations but also with labor relations. Of course, there are areas of conflict (profit, jobs, right to manage, seniority, productivity, inflation), but a peaceful settlement of differences must be sought. If that cannot be achieved, collective bargaining is the next step. A contract must be negotiated. One of the areas of the contract is the grievance procedure—a method of controlling complaints or conflicts. One of the best techniques for handling complaints is listening. An available and sensitive ear can often alleviate a problem before it becomes a point of contention. Thus management must be willing to do what it can through training to enhance its people-relations skills.

KEY TERMS

Union: an organization of employees seeking to advance its members' interests through collective bargaining.

Collective Bargaining: the process whereby representatives of management and labor meet together to bargain over and agree on worker incomes, job security, working conditions, hours, and other terms of employment.

Good Faith: an intent on management's part to reach an agreement with labor, to set up reasonable conditions for bargaining, and to abide by a written contract once agreement has been met.

Grievance: a specific, formal employee dissatisfaction.

—————————————— QUESTIONS ——————————————

1 Reread the opening case.
   a. List the laws that management and labor representatives violated. What specific evidence from the case supports your answer?
   b. What legal actions could management have taken during Louise's orientation to minimize the union's appeal to workers?
   c. What would you suggest to Louise to help her reconcile her position between her supervisor and the union supporter?

2 Briefly outline the history of labor unions in America. Which movements were the most significant in your opinion?

3 List at least three ways that management can use a union to improve communication with lower-level workers.

4 Describe the philosophical differences that caused craft unions to split from the Knights of Labor and from the American Federation of Labor. How did the Congress of Industrial Organizations differ from the AFL with regard to the type of workers it organized?

5 Summarize the most significant provisions and effects of the following labor laws:
   a. Clayton Antitrust Act,
   b. Norris-LaGuardia Act,
   c. National Labor Relations (Wagner) Act,
   d. Fair Labor Standards Act,
   e. Taft-Hartley Act, and
   f. Landrum-Griffin Act.

6 What conditions have evolved within the unions themselves that call for preventive legislation? What objectives should such legislation have?

7 Summarize a union's political, social, and economic objectives. How might management in a nonunion organization help workers meet these objectives and in doing so make a union unnecessary?

8 List and summarize at least four issues that cause union-management conflict. Why is it important for all members of management to be aware of these issues?

9 What tactics may labor employ against management when grievances cannot be resolved peacefully? How might management retaliate? Which side seems to have the most effective tactic, and why?

10 "If management had been more human-relations-oriented over the years, there would be no need for unions. Management usually brings unionization on itself." Do you agree with this statement? Why or why not?

11 How would you characterize each of the following union-management relationships?
   a. conflict,
   b. armed truce,
   c. power bargaining,
   d. accommodation,
   e. cooperation, and
   f. collusion.

   Consider a unionized organization located nearby, or one that you have worked for. Which of these relationships seems to exist there? What seems to be responsible for it? Do you believe a different type of relationship would be better? Why or why not?

12 "I don't believe in beating around the bush. I'll come out with my best offer right up front, and my workers can take it or leave it. Why waste a lot of time playing games?" Do you agree with this manager's philosophy on negotiation? Why or why not? What potential problems might he or she encounter in labor negotiations?

13 Contrast the four possible methods of resolving a deadlocked labor-management dispute. Which method is most likely to succeed? Why?

14 Suggest at least ten topics that are usually included in a labor-management contract. Why should management establish policies and procedures on these topics, whether or not workers are unionized?

15 Assume you're a consultant to an organization that has no grievance procedure. What benefits would you cite for creating one? What general principles or provisions should it include?

16 Describe four major categories of employee grievances.

17 Assume you have been hired to conduct a supervisory seminar on rules of managerial conduct in processing grievances. What specific actions should you discuss? How would you stress their importance to seminar participants? What measures could you employ in the seminar to emphasize their value and the fact that they should be used regularly?

18 Describe the most productive and positive attitudes that managers should adopt toward the grievance procedure. How should they feel with regard to:
   a. "winning" a grievance,
   b. having their authority challenged by a grievance,
   c. backing up the decisions of subordinate managers, and
   d. time spent processing and resolving grievances?

CASES

Last year Hank Shapiro, shipping supervisor at Hamilton China factory, hired enthusiastic young Kenny Walker to work with Sam Johnson.[25] Sam, who is in his early sixties, has worked in the shipping department for twenty years.

Case 11.1

Most cartons of china are heavy, but Kenny didn't complain and seemed to enjoy the work. Sam was grateful for the help, but soon he started disappearing when it was time to load the heavier cartons. Kenny would load most of them, and Sam would show up a few minutes before the job was finished and ask if there was anything he could do.

Hank has heard several complaints from the home office about cups and saucers arriving at their destinations with chips and broken handles. Today he called Kenny into his office saying, "Ever since you started we've had complaints about our china arriving damaged. You've got to be more careful. This can't go on, Kenny."

"But, Mr. Shapiro," Kenny began, "I think you should know . . ."

"I don't want to hear excuses; it's results that count," Hank interrupted. "I'm not mad yet, but don't let it happen again."

Kenny continued to struggle with the heavy cartons, and Sam continued to disappear. Finally one day, as Hank was walking through the shipping department, he noticed Kenny manhandling a heavy carton onto a dolly. With bulging veins and straining muscles, he nudged the carton into position. "Remember what I told you about being careful," Hank warned. "Our damage rate hasn't improved a bit. There had better not be one chip in the contents of that box."

Kenny gulped, turned red, and threw the carton on its side, shattering three dozen teacups. Facing Hank he shouted, "You think you're so smart, don't you? Well, get off my back and look around at what's going on in this department! When was the last time you saw Sam lift anything over ten pounds? When was the last time you saw Sam at *all?*" Slamming his fist through a nearby carton, Kenny stalked out the door as Hank stared in disbelief.

Case Questions

1   How would the circumstances of this case have been different if Hamilton China had been unionized?
2   How could Kenny's complaint have become a grievance that ended in arbitration?
3   How would you criticize Shapiro's action in the first discussion involving damaged merchandise?
4   If Kenny is willing to continue working for Hamilton China, how would you suggest that Shapiro proceed from this point?

Case 11.2

Cal Hunter manages the Bithlo smelting plant for Global Metals, Inc. The company has been nonunion throughout its forty-year existence, but as the last holdout in the industry, Global has attracted considerable attention from union organizers. The American Metal Smelters Union believes that if it can unionize the workers at one Global plant, workers at the rest will follow suit within three years.

Global's management is aware that the company is a prime union target. The company's current pay scales and fringe benefits are equal to if not better than any of its unionized competitors.

A new metal smelting process involving experimental equipment had its pilot run at the Bithlo plant last year. It refines metal using fewer steps and less time than normally. However, the heat and odor generated from this process are especially noxious. Workers complain that the temperature exceeds 110 degrees and the odor, though not harmful, is a cross between rotten eggs and a stable.

A crisis arose last week when the experimental process workers practically mutinied against their supervisor. They claimed that management had not alleviated the conditions in the department since its creation except for installing a few largely ineffective ventilation fans.

Today Cal received a call from his boss, the division manager, who said the workers in the Bithlo plant's experimental department had asked an organizer from the AMSU to meet with them during the weekend and map out an organizing campaign for workers at the Bithlo plant.

"We simply don't know what to do to correct the heat and odor problems," Cal told his boss. "We installed a few fans, but we'd have to get the breeze up to hurricane force to carry all that stuff out of the building and bring the temperature down. We should have redesigned the building before we brought that new process in. There's no quick fix. Anyway, I thought we explained that we'd need time to debug the process and iron out problems. What's the matter with workers today? Don't they understand *our* problems?"

1 If you were a higher manager who realized the problems of this experimental process before it was installed, how would you have presented it to the workers in order to gain their support?

2 What can Cal do at the plant level to seek a solution that might mollify workers' feelings and buy management some time?

3 What recommendations for introducing change can you offer to managers in nonunion organizations?

NOTES
---

1. Benjamin M. Selekman, "Trade Unions—Romance and Reality," *Harvard Business Review* (September 1977): 78.

2. Raymond E. Glos, et al., *Business—Its Nature and Environment* (Cincinnati: South-Western Publishing, 1976), pp. 287–289.

3. John H. Jackson and Timothy J. Keaveny, *Successful Supervision* (Englewood Cliffs, N.J.: Prentice-Hall, 1980), pp. 343–344.

4. Selekman, "Trade Unions," p. 89.

5. John A. Reinecke and William F. Schoell, *Introduction to Business—A Contemporary View* (Boston: Allyn and Bacon, 1977), pp. 390–395.

6. Ibid., pp. 395–399.

7. Janet Guyon, "'Family Feeling' at Delta Creates Loyal Workers, Enmity of Unions," *The Wall Street Journal,* 7 July 1980, p. 13.

8. Michael J. Shershin and W. Randy Boxx, "Building Positive Union Management Relations," *Personnel Journal* (June 1975): 326–331.

9. "The Demands Airlines Are Pressing On Labor," *Business Week,* 7 December 1981, p. 37.

10. Randall Brett, "No Need for a Union Today," *The Personnel Administrator* (March 1979): 23–24.

11. Ibid., p. 24.

12. "Non-union Firms Are Productive and Happy," *American Business* (December 1981): 1.

13. "An Acid Test at DuPont," *Business Week,* 14 December 1981, p. 123.

14. Brett, "No Need," p. 24.

15. Claude S. George, Jr., *Supervision in Action* (Reston, Virginia: Reston Publishing Co., Inc., 1977), p. 182.

16. Arthur Sloane and Fred Witney, *Labor Relations* (Englewood Cliffs, N.J.: Prentice-Hall, 1972), pp. 32–37.

17. Frank Elkouri and Edna A. Elkouri, *How Arbitration Works* (New York: Bureau of National Affairs, 1973), pp. 107–108.

18. Peter A. Veglahn, "Making the Grievance Procedure Work," *Personnel Journal* (March 1977): 122–123.

19. Woodruff Imberman, "Letting the Employee Speak His Mind," *Personnel* (November–December 1976): 12–14.

20. Ibid., pp. 14–17.

21. Lawrence Rout, "Hyatt Hotels' Gripe Sessions Help Chief Maintain Communications with Workers," *The Wall Street Journal,* 16 July 1981, p. 27.
22. Shershin and Boxx, "Building Positive Relations," p. 329.
23. Jackson and Keaveny, *Successful Supervision,* pp. 356–357.
24. W. Randy Boxx and Michael J. Shershin, Jr., "The Supervisor: A Key to Improving Union-Management Relations," *Supervision* (January 1978): 4–6.
25. Adapted from J. F. Wandschneider, "Nip the Grievance in the Gripe," *Supervisory Management* (June 1973): 33–34.

SUGGESTED READINGS

Beal, Edwin, et al. *The Practice of Collective Bargaining.* Homewood, Ill.: Irwin, 1976.

Grievance Guide. New York: Bureau of National Affairs, 1978.

Kochan, Thomas A. *Collective Bargaining and Industrial Relations: From Theory to Policy and Practice.* Homewood, Ill.: Irwin, 1980.

Trotta, Maurice S. *Handling Grievances—A Guide for Management and Labor.* Bureau of National Affairs, 1976.

12

Absenteeism and Turnover

When you complete your study of this chapter, you should be able to:

1 Discuss the causes of both absenteeism and turnover,
2 Describe the types of problems created by absenteeism and turnover,
3 Calculate the costs of absenteeism and turnover,
4 Suggest ways to enrich and restructure work, and
5 Conduct an exit interview.

―――――――――― OPENING CASE ――――――――――

Jamie Kingston has been a secretary at McGill Institute for three years. During the first two years she had perfect attendance, and her secretarial skills gained the respect of everyone for whom she worked. Shirley Sorrels, manager of the secretarial pool, was confident Jamie could be promoted to office manager within five years if she followed her original work pattern.

After two years, however, Jamie's attendance became irregular. At first her excuses for being late or absent seemed valid, but she began repeating herself after several months (the same aunt died twice). There were rumors that a romance had turned sour and also that she had a drinking problem and a personality conflict with another secretary.

"Whatever is wrong must be dealt with," thought Shirley, so she called Jamie into her office to discuss her absentee record. The conversation did not go well.

"Jamie," Shirley began, "I've been very lenient with you because of your past record. But six absences in as many weeks can't be ignored. We've got to deal with this problem now, because it's contagious. Other employees may think we don't care if people show up for work. That's why I'm placing a copy of this written absentee warning in your file. If you receive two more within one year, policy requires that you be discharged." Jamie sat without comment as she was handed a copy and asked to read and sign it.

"Jamie, I want to help you resolve this attendance problem any way that I can. You have showed great potential for two straight years, and the company doesn't want to lose you. What can we talk about? Tell me what's wrong with your job, the people you work with, your home life, or whatever's made this conversation necessary. I want to help."

At this point Jamie began to cry, exclaiming, "It's none of your business why I'm absent sometimes. I've got my reasons, and I do better work than anybody when I'm here. I don't stick my nose into your problems, so don't bug me about mine."

"I want to help you, Jamie," Shirley answered, "but you're not leaving me many options."

"I can't say anything more," Jamie sobbed as she left the unsigned warning on her chair and walked through the door.

―――――――――― No-Shows at Work ――――――――――

Absenteeism is a major human relations problem for managers and supervisors. Some people, like Jamie, don't want to be helped, or at least that is the image they portray. Others are deceptive so their supervisor won't know the real reasons for tardiness, absenteeism, or leaving the job. How can a manager deal with these problems most effectively? This chapter will offer some suggestions for reducing the costs of absenteeism and turnover through job restructuring. To reduce these costs, one must understand the causes of the problems and their effects on human relations. We will discuss absenteeism first because it often predicts future turnovers.

Absenteeism

Absenteeism is the practice by an employee or group of employees of being away from work. It adds up to dollars lost in every organization. In fact, absenteeism now costs organizations $15–20 billion a year just in wages paid for days when employees are absent.[1]

absenteeism

Why is absenteeism such a problem at work?

Figures released by the Bureau of Labor Statistics show that in an average week, 2.4 million of the 56.5 million nonfarm wage and salary employees who normally worked full time were on unscheduled absence part of the week, for an average of two days. This adds up to 1.4 million absent because of illness, and 1.0 million for miscellaneous reasons. That's an increase of some 15 percent in just five years. Unscheduled leave of more than a week went up by about 10 percent in the same period.[2]

That amounts to over 100 million people-hours lost per week on the job due to absenteeism. If we multiply the hours lost by the average salary of an employee, we can see that the nationwide figure is staggering. Other significant costs are the expense of training workers to fill in for absentees, disruption of production, and a perpetual overstaffing to minimize the effect of absenteeism.

Causes of Absenteeism

Why are so many employees absent on any given workday? Of course some of these absences are legitimate, but many are not. The principal causes of absenteeism that are partly or wholly controllable by management include:

What causes absenteeism?

- absence proneness in specific job candidates and employees,
- personality problems in employees leading to personality conflicts and dissatisfaction,
- employee alcoholism and drug abuse,
- employee fatigue brought on by an excessive work pace or excessive work hours,
- lack of in-house medical and/or dental services,
- lack of company-sponsored child-care facilities,
- work-related injuries or illness,

- apparent management indifference to absenteeism—seen in vague or non-existent attendance standards, poor communication or reinforcement of attendance standards, and extremely liberal sick-leave benefits, and
- employee dissatisfaction or low morale stemming from poor supervision, unpleasant or uncomfortable working conditions, boredom, a belief the work involved is unimportant, inadequate employee training, inadequate pay or opportunities for advancement, ineffective grievance procedures, or employees' belief that they have little control over decisions affecting their work.[3]

Many causes of absenteeism could be listed, but these are representative.

Is absenteeism contagious?

Absenteeism is contagious. Thus, many employers have created wellness programs that keep workers healthy on and off the job.[4] For example, the medical director of New York Telephone Company reported annual savings of nearly $3 million from the nine preventive medicine programs created for employees. A ten-year cancer-screening campaign at Campbell Soup Company saved the company almost a quarter of a million dollars. Former NASA medical director Dr. Charles Berry contends that alcohol abuse campaigns and related health programs that reduce absenteeism save individual firms more than $2 million per year.

Should rules about absenteeism be enforced?

A few people (maybe only 5 percent) try to get away with as much as they can. Of course, this has a very negative effect on human relations in most organizations. The good employee becomes frustrated when she or he must carry the weight of the slacker. That is why it is important to have and enforce rules about absenteeism.

--- Types of Problem Absentees ---

What can be done about absenteeism? The answer depends in part on the type of employee who is causing the absenteeism. At least one study has discovered some common characteristics of high absence employees. They are typically people who were hospitalized at least once before the age of twenty-one, carry a small amount of life insurance, and have had poor health in recent years. Many high absence employees are alcoholics or other drug abusers. It is estimated that alcoholics in the American labor force account for between 6 and 10 percent of all absenteeism.

Who are the problem absentees?

Employees under thirty years of age also compose a high percentage of chronic absentees. These high absence employees are of several types: Friday/Monday absentees, the chronically ill, AWOL employees, moonlighters, and situational absentees.

FRIDAY/MONDAY ABSENTEES.   Absentees on Fridays, Mondays, and the days-after-payday are the easiest to recognize. If supervisors keep records, they can notice such a pattern. For example, a worker may have been absent fifteen work days out of a possible sixty in the past three months, and ten of these absences were on Fridays, Mondays, or the day after payday. Such an attendance record should not be tolerated. If attendance does not improve substantially, the eventual solution is termination.

CHRONICALLY ILL.   Some employees always seem to be in poor health, or think they are. Also, some employees who have been legitimately sick simply become accustomed to staying home. They never get better. Because it is hard to prove that these people are not really ill, they create delicate situations for supervisors. There are no fast or infallible solutions to this type of absentee. As a preventive measure a supervisor can make a policy of asking an employee to provide a written statement from a doctor saying the employee is not endangering his or her health by continuing to work.

AWOL EMPLOYEES.   An away-without-leave or **AWOL employee** is one who is absent from work without prior excuse. Some of these employees are able to bring in a doctor's certificate even though witnesses saw them engaged in leisure activities. They argue that the doctor told them to rest for a few days and get plenty of sunshine. In addition, there are some employees who apply for sick leave to go vacationing. Companies have been known to grant the sick leave and then discharge the employee for getting sick leave monies through fraudulent means. Proof is difficult, however.

AWOL employee

MOONLIGHTERS.   The employee who has another job (or maybe two or three) that interferes with the first job is called a **moonlighter.** Moonlighters often have trouble showing up regularly for work. They can be handled in much the same way as any other chronic absentee, by saying, "Your attendance record is unsatisfactory, and if it doesn't improve . . ." Or the supervisor may have to tell the employee to choose between the two jobs.

moonlighter

SITUATIONAL ABSENTEEISM.   Some employees are chronically absent because of a given situation. For example, an employee could have a very sick child needing attention. Another may be facing deep personal problems such as a divorce. These people did not plan to be absent, but circumstances beyond their control precipitated the absence. There could be a whole host of such short-term crises.

——————————— Costs of Absenteeism ———————————

Absenteeism is expensive. Roger Smith, a top executive at General Motors, remarked on "Face the Nation" that a lot of what we need "can be gained if people just come to work every day as they're supposed to. Absenteeism cost GM more than a billion dollars last year."[5] Three other firms reported the following absenteeism costs:[6]

How much does absenteeism cost?

Type of Business	Absenteeism Cost per Worker per Year
Auto dealer	$300
Manufacturing plant	150
Department store	110

Many of these costs are indirect or hidden. However, among the costs resulting from absenteeism are the following:

- Compensation of employees during their absence (In nearly all cases, fringe benefits are paid for during an absence and, in some instances, employees are also given their usual sick leave.),
- Training of other employees to fill in for absentees,
- Recruitment and employment of temporary help to fill in,
- Overtime pay for other workers who fill in,
- Reliance on overstaffing to minimize disruptions during absences,
- Decrease in employee efficiency,
- Disruption of production schedules and work flow, possibly even shutdown of some operations,
- Dissatisfaction among employees who must shoulder a heavier burden (This is particularly true when employees must be moved from one department to another.),
- Product spoilage,
- Lower product quality and/or increased product inspection (Employees substituting for absentees usually aren't as proficient or as experienced at the jobs in question.),
- Extra record keeping, and
- Loss of customers through failure to meet delivery dates.[7]

Can absenteeism be cured?

Overcoming these costs involves analyzing each absenteeism problem through the eyes of the individual employee. A department that has an absenteeism problem probably has general job dissatisfaction. Such problems may be cured in two ways: by alleviative cures—those approaches intended to only partly reduce absenteeism; and specific cures—those which are, for all practical purposes, intended exclusively to reduce it and its associated costs.[8] These cures involve some change in job design. However, such job restructuring is not only a response to absenteeism. It is an excellent reward for the good employee.

———————————— Alleviative Solutions to Absenteeism ————————————

Three major organizational programs and management practices offer solutions to a number of problems, including absenteeism. These problems may be individual or departmental. The practices are job enrichment, the four-day work week, and flextime. Unhappily, these three approaches yield rather indifferent results in some organizations.

JOB ENRICHMENT. **Job enrichment** is a process of analyzing job content to see if jobs can be redesigned so employees will have more interesting and challenging tasks, greater responsibility, more opportunities to experience achievement, and more timely feedback on performance. Some of the aspects of the organization on which job enrichment can have an effect are illustrated in Figure 12.1. As shown in this figure, job enrichment can have far-reaching implications for an organization.

Applying job enrichment techniques to absenteeism involves trying to make a high absence worker's job less dull, repetitive, and boring. The theory of this approach assumes the nature and scope of a job makes the difference as to whether a worker comes to work or stays home. If the job is challenging and satisfying, workers will be eager to face the work day. However, job enrichment is no panacea to absenteeism. Some workers don't want their jobs enriched. They are happy in unchanging, routine, or fragmented jobs requiring little personal adjustment. For them change equals stress (Chapter 17). In fact, an attempt to enrich some jobs (such as those in a mass-production industry) may result in higher absenteeism levels. Managers need to help employees with change and to be sensitive to it as a cause of stress. Wrong decisions about job enrichment can cause quality to deteriorate, productivity to fall, accident rates to increase, and turnover to worsen.

There is evidence, however, that in some companies job enrichment can improve quality, increase production, raise the level of job satisfaction,

job enrichment

How does job enrichment help reduce absenteeism?

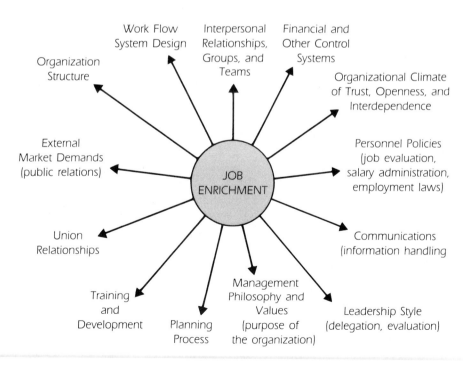

FIGURE 12.1
Job Enrichment
Impacts All Aspects
of the Organization

reduce absenteeism and turnover, and cut the size of the work force. Whether success or failure prevails depends on common sense and several basic precepts. *See* Exhibit 12.1.

EXHIBIT 12.1

- **Analyze the labor force.** To reduce the chance of involving uncooperative and unqualified personnel, conduct studies, surveys, or experiments before beginning a project to measure employee attitudes. Such documentation can also later serve as the basis for evaluating the outcome of a job enrichment project.
- **Prepare the organization.** Several things facilitate change within the organization and reduce the trauma experienced by some people as their ways of working and relating to others are modified. Commonly used techniques are the formation of work teams; introduction of management-by-objectives programs; and the sponsorship of job design seminars, sensitivity training, confrontation meetings, and other devices that reduce inertia in work environments.
- **Involve management.** Without management's belief in and commitment to the changes being made, there is little hope of success. There are two ways to actively involve managers in the change process. The first is for them to participate in a group whose jobs are being redesigned. The second is for them to be change agents in the enrichment process and to be responsible for formulating, planning, and implementing the changes to be made.
- **Set objectives.** Clear and concise objectives should be set before implementation to serve as guideposts in the day-to-day development of the project, as well as in evaluation of the outcome. If the objectives are satisfied, the project is a success.
- **Redesign work intelligently.** Be creative! Changes that will achieve behavioral objectives (such as increased job satisfaction) can be combined with performance objectives (such as increased production output). Job enrichment is an opportunity to use new methods and tools that complement the human factor. The components of successful projects, ranked from most to least used, are feedback, closure (producing a whole unit of work), quality control, self-pacing, methods control, participation, variety and team formation, increased knowledge or skill requirements, and opportunities for advancement.
- **Measure and analyze the results.** Whenever possible, control groups or pilot studies should be used. Extensive data should be collected to permit at least a pre- and postimplementation comparison of employee performance. Detailed reports should always be kept of the costs of supporting the project and the benefits that result.
- **Replicate projects.** The larger the organization, the greater the chance of finding work units that perform identical or similar functions. Take advantage of these intracompany similarities, by choosing a work unit for enrichment that exists in a similar form at other locations. Doing this will permit economies of scale because the same work design can be used over and over again. It also forewarns management of the types of problems that may occur and provides sufficient time to develop techniques for reducing undesirable consequences, or even avoiding them altogether.
- **Don't overdesign the project.** It is possible to overdesign a job and wind up spending a fortune to acquire the needed hardware. By adding variety, allowing employees to complete a whole unit of work, giving employees responsibility for controlling the methods content of their job, and letting them manage more of what they do, one

---
EXHIBIT 12.1 cont.
---

makes work more complex. Care must be taken not to make the job so difficult one person can't do it.

- **Don't underestimate the training needs.** As jobs become more complex and employees assume more responsibility, more training is needed to prepare employees adequately. Lack of training often leads to short-term problems, such as a deterioration in quality and reductions in productivity.
- **Don't panic.** If performance in certain areas begins to deteriorate, wait a reasonable length of time and continue to monitor performance. When you have sufficient information, isolate the problem and determine just how serious it is and how likely it is to disappear as the labor force adjusts to the changes made. Don't be stampeded into reacting before all the facts are in.
- **Don't underestimate the real costs.** There are five design-related costs to consider: wage/salary increases, facility change costs, inventory costs, charges for implementation, and training expenses. A complete appraisal of both benefits and costs is necessary to evaluate fairly the organization's returns from using job enrichment.
- **Don't try to con the employees.** Job enrichment requires the cooperation of everyone concerned, from top management to the lowest level employee. Don't try to deceive the people involved. You may get away with it the first time, but everyone will remember, and you will never again gain their cooperation. The best approach is to be completely straightforward.
- **Do have faith in the concept.** Since a successful job enrichment project depends on so many factors, it would be presumptuous to believe that every difficulty can be avoided. Planning, common sense, and faith in the underlying principles of job enrichment will help the progressive manager succeed.[9]

The supervisor who works at it, following the above guidelines, should be able to enrich employees' jobs and reduce absenteeism. For example, job design has reached impressive heights at the Siemens plant in Karlsruhe, West Germany.[10] Workers operate in three- to seven-person groups at work islands throughout the plant. They can trade jobs, relate to one another, and do tasks that require up to twenty minutes instead of several seconds to complete. German government officials report that more than 1000 such work humanization programs exist in both government and private industry.

In some German manufacturing plants any worker who spots a problem can stop the moving assembly line. The same feature is built into Mazda's mile-long production line in Japan.

Expanded job cycles allow assemblers to regulate their own pace by either working fast to build a few extra units (and take a generous break) or by building at a slower, steady pace. Workers can be crosstrained and substituted more freely when some are absent, and the social interaction that flows among colleagues at each island or station is a very positive factor according to German officials.

Will a four-day work week help reduce absenteeism?

FOUR-DAY WORK WEEK. Another tested approach to solving absenteeism is the four-day work week. The four-day week was an attempt to shorten the work week. It was believed workers would be more likely to show up as scheduled if they had an added day for doctor and dentist appointments, errands, and the like. Evidence suggests, however, that this approach works only in the short run. The effect seems to lessen once the novelty has gone, and absentee rates then begin to climb back to or near their previous levels. To combat this, some companies that have switched from a five-day to a four-day work week charge employees with an unexcused absence a percentage of their weekly earnings (up to 25 percent). This action may lead to some reduction in absences.

flextime

How does flextime work?

FLEXTIME. A third approach to reducing absenteeism is to give employees **flextime,** or flexibility in working hours (within certain limits). There are at least two kinds of flextime arrangements: gliding work time and individual work time. The first one requires employees to be at work for certain fixed hours (e.g., from 10:00 to 12:00 and from 2:00 to 4:00). The other working hours are a matter of personal choice, within certain confines (e.g., 7:00 to 7:00). The second type of flextime allows employees to select at the start of each month a specified work schedule in which the total number of hours varies.

A one-year government-sponsored flextime experiment involved 75,000 federal employees in various agencies.[11] After that year, the U.S. Commerce Department pronounced it to be a success and the American Federation of Government Employees reported positive feedback from most members. Claiming employees working flextime were too hard to locate when needed, the General Services Administration rejected the concept, however. The Office of Personnel Management suggested that federal agencies apply the concept at their discretion.

In many organizations where flextime has been used, absenteeism has been reduced. However, later evidence suggests the drop in the absence rate was only temporary. Flextime at Hewlett-Packard Company produced gratifying decreases in tardiness and sick leave; TRW, Inc., found that flextime is a selling point when recruiting new employees.[12] The practice seems to work best for jobs whose hours don't have to conform to traditional ones kept by outside suppliers and customers. Banks, insurance companies, government agencies, and other organizations with a large population of clerical employees may apply flextime productively.

Thus, as with the other two cures—job enrichment and the four-day work week—a lasting reduction in absenteeism is elusive. The best approach may be a combination of these and other approaches. Some of these other approaches follow.

Specific Solutions to Absenteeism

Many organizations have tried various positive and negative measures to combat absenteeism. Certain auto manufacturers have given gifts such as monogrammed glassware or trading stamps to workers who accumulated unbroken attendance records for specified lengths of time. Some employers award well pay (the opposite of sick pay) to workers who do not take sick leave.

Are there any solutions to absenteeism?

Harsher measures were employed at one paper company plant, which instituted a series of oral and written warnings and suspension as preludes to discharge. The absenteeism rate declined 63 percent over a five-year period.[13] One bank deals with the problem by sending supervisors computerized absence reports.

Such alleviative cures to absenteeism, however, often treat only the symptoms of absenteeism. Often more specific solutions are needed. Some of the specific cures are listed in Exhibit 12.2.

Although none of these solutions to absenteeism is the one cure, the ideas suggested should be of some benefit to supervisors. Absenteeism can be contagious and can affect human relations severely. The supervisor's role is to find the method(s) that works in his or her department. One final help to a supervisor in attacking the absentee problem is the checklist in Exhibit 12.3. Check the items on which you need to work and then apply the suggestions.

Turnover

Another human relations problem closely related to absenteeism is **turnover,** or separation from the job. Both absenteeism and turnover can be viewed as forms of alienation or withdrawal from an organization. In some cases excessive absenteeism will lead to turnover. Job satisfaction plays a crucial role as the mediating variable between these two. As job dissatisfaction crises increase, employee turnover rates grow. And turnover is expensive. For example, firms that calculate their turnover costs generally find that each turnover costs over $1,000. Although this figure may not seem significant, for those industries with high turnover rates, the total cost can be astronomical.

turnover

How is turnover related to absenteeism?

Despite high employee turnover and accompanying costs, many managers are unaware of the need for more effective decision making to prevent turnover. There are resolutions to the problem. Managers can reduce turnover, improve morale, and create a more satisfying working climate if they know the answers to two major questions: Why do employees leave? And, why do they stay? The answers to these questions may indicate a need for an in-depth appraisal of the organization's climate. Managers may need to start listening to what employees really want, instead of assuming they know what employees need.

--- EXHIBIT 12.2 ---

- **Develop an employee attendance policy.** Establishing a clearly worded policy statement and then periodically reminding employees about it will certainly diminish the number of absences caused by ignorance or misunderstanding of standards.
- **Help employees comply with the attendance policy.** One simple possibility is to help employees organize car pools—making a special effort to include chronic absentees. Or it may be feasible to offer interesting lunch-time programs. Some firms use a telephone answering service or device to make it easier for the employee to call in the night before she or he will be absent.
- **Check up on absentees.** Some firms check up on each employee who is absent but has not notified the company of the absence. Such personal attention may discourage some employees from being absent for frivolous reasons. On the other hand, it is an expensive approach and may arouse employee resentment toward the company.
- **Tailor the approach to the individual.** This is a particularly good practice when the absentee is not a chronic offender. For example, the employee might be given a few extra catch up tasks to reinforce the idea that absences do count.
- **Counsel chronic absentees.** The supervisor should counsel the employee that (1) his or her attendance record is becoming unsatisfactory and unacceptable, (2) this situation is not to be taken lightly because good attendance by each employee is basic to efficient operation, (3) good attendance is important to each employee in terms of his or her performance appraisal, and (4) since regular attendance is ultimately the employee's responsibility another absence will result in some specified disciplinary action.
- **Take a firm stand.** Managers should take a firm stand with out-and-out absentees. For example, management should simply refuse to approve an employee's claim for sick-leave benefits unless a doctor of the company's choice says such approval is warranted or the employee is entitled to receive them.
- **Avoid a moralistic approach.** It is important to know when drastic measures are needed and when they are not. Managers who view all absentees as moral degenerates lower employee morale. They lump together employees whose attitudes and circumstances are significantly different.
- **Use positive reinforcement.** In many firms, offering a bonus (in cash or some other form) for excellent attendance has been closely followed by appreciable declines in absenteeism.
- **Adhere to a broad-based program.** Effective programs are based on (1) a good understanding of the leading causes of absenteeism; (2) careful, ongoing analysis of the firm's and each department's actual absence records; (3) regular and clear communication of the company's attendance policy, including disciplinary procedures to be invoked against violators; (4) proper—that is, knowledgeable, impartial, and consistent—implementation of this policy by all line managers and staff assistants; and (5) imaginative use of a flexible combination of alleviative and specific cures for absenteeism.[14]

——————————— Why Do Employees Leave? ———————————

Of two people in identical jobs, one will stay (perhaps as a dissatisfied employee) and one will leave. Why? There may be several reasons. Decisions to stay or leave seem to depend on the employee's satisfaction with the job and the environmental pressures inside or outside the organization. Job satisfaction usually depends on the work itself, achievement, recognition,

Why do employees quit one job for another one?

——————————— EXHIBIT 12.3 ———————————

A Checklist on Absenteeism for Supervisors

1   Insist on prompt notification *always* when someone in your department must be absent unexpectedly.

2   Insist on prior discussion about necessary absences for personal reasons, rather than explanations *after* the stay-away. In any event, call for *real* explanations rather than imaginative stories and phony excuses.

3   What is the "Blue Monday" situation in your department? Keep a running record of absences on Monday or the day after each holiday, compared with absences on the best-attendance day (which will probably be payday!). The difference is a good indicator of phony absenteeism.

4   Avoid crises due to unexpected absences by having standard operating procedures and standard backstop procedures: who is to be kept informed of what details; who is to pinch hit for whom.

5   Be sure to give prompt notification to other departments that may be affected by delays caused by unexpected absences in your department.

6   Maintain good departmental and individual absence records. Make periodic checks to see who are the absence-proners.

7   Have heart-to-heart discussion with the ones who cause most of your absentee problems. If there are personal problems, provide counseling yourself or have someone in the personnel or medical department help.

8   Is a group meeting in your department called for? Collect some facts and figures on actual costs of absenteeism to the department and to the company, including related costs as well as direct costs, to drive home the seriousness of the problem.

9   Check your departmental record with that of other departments. Is yours out of line? Where does the basic fault lie? Turn the mirror on yourself!

10 Know your employees. Without prying, show an interest in their personal lives. Encourage after-hours discussion of problems affecting attendance and productivity.

11 Look for safety hazards in equipment and operations and for poor housekeeping that causes accidents.

12 Insist every employee report to you any injury, no matter how minor it may seem. It's your responsibility to see every injured employee gets proper first aid and/or medical treatment. This applies even to minor injuries, so as to prevent infection and possible serious aftereffects.

Source: Harvey H. Shore, "Absenteeism, Part 2: Prevention and Cure," *Supervisory Management* (October 1975): 27–30.

responsibility, growth, and advancement. Environmental pressures inside the organization include work rules, facilities, coffee breaks, benefits, wages, and the like. Environmental pressures outside the organization include job opportunities, community relations, financial obligations, family ties, and other such factors.[15]

What are some classifications of turnover?

Turnovers can be classified as voluntary or involuntary. Within these classifications, turnovers fall into four categories.[16] The first category is voluntary but uncontrollable (e.g., when an employee moves to another location not within commuting distance, decides to stay home to care for children or relatives, becomes a housekeeper, or decides to change vocations entirely or to return to school). The second is involuntary but uncontrollable (e.g., retirement, disability, and death). The third is involuntary and controllable (e.g., discharge for poor performance, for unacceptable conduct, for a pattern of attendance involving lateness or absenteeism). The fourth category is voluntary and controllable (e.g., resignation for any of a number of reasons). Employees who leave a job generally do so because they are dissatisfied somehow with the job and have few internal or external pressures to induce them to stay.

―――――――――――――――― Why Do Employees Stay? ――――――――――――

Why do employees stay on a job?

The basic reason why dissatisfied or satisfied employees remain on a job is inertia. There is no force causing them to leave. A study of 406 employees from three companies revealed the following top ten reasons for staying. The statements are worded as they appeared on the questionnaire used in the study:

1 I wouldn't want to rebuild most of the benefits that I have now if I left the company.
2 I have family responsibilities.
3 I have good personal friends here at work.
4 The company's been good to me and I don't believe in jumping from company to company.
5 I'm working to make ends meet and I don't want to take the risks in a new job.
6 I wouldn't like to look for a job on the outside.
7 I'm a little too old for starting over again.
8 I wouldn't like to start all over learning the policies of a new company.
9 I like to live in this area.
10 It is difficult to find a job.[17]

These statements suggest a real need for providing a positive work climate that will satisfy an employee's needs for self-fulfillment or self-actualization. Motivation must be linked to the job content. If it is not, dissatisfaction prevails. And dissatisfaction can lead to absenteeism, which can lead to turnover. In all three instances human relationships suffer.

Measuring Turnover Costs

As we have said, turnover is expensive for organizations. For example, there are costs of advertising the position and recruiting and selecting someone for it, of new employee orientation and training, and of lost production. Turnover costs can be divided into separation costs, replacement costs, and training costs. A total model for computing turnover costs can be represented by the following equation:[18]

How does one figure the costs of turnover?

$$\text{Employee Turnover Costs} = Sc + Rc + Tc$$
$$Sc = \text{separation costs}$$
$$Rc = \text{replacement costs}$$
$$Tc = \text{training costs}$$

Once managers know the costs, they can devise programs to combat personnel turnover.

Reducing Turnover

Guidelines for reducing turnover in an organization should include communication and encouragement. More specifically, they are keeping employees informed on organizational matters, establishing clear channels of communication between employees and management, and encouraging employee creativity and self-improvement.

How can turnover rates be reduced?

In addition, the results of numerous studies suggest four functional components to assist turnover reduction:[19]

1. *When interviewing, match applicants to the job.* Two basic questions should receive affirmative answers before the supervisor hires someone: Does the job match the person reasonably well? And, will this person be likely to stay with any job she or he takes? The person hired should be neither under- nor overqualified and should show a reasonable degree of interest in the job activities required. The best predictor of all is the person's past performance.

2. *Involve the employee in restructuring a job or a group of jobs.* Both turnover and group productivity are related to participation. The more the employee participates in job design, the higher the productivity and the lower the turnover.

3. *View employees as human beings to be treated with human dignity.* Supervisors need to avoid viewing employees in mechanistic terms such as person-hours, units of production, or units of costs. Each person has a degree

of self-respect and will respond differently to different types of treatment. Supervisors must fit their methods of managing to the needs and motivations of the individual employee.

4. *Establish an equitable and competitive wage and salary program.* Employees must believe they are receiving fair treatment in relationship to others doing the same work. Otherwise, they will become dissatisfied and turnover could eventually result. In addition, a fair, competitive program is basic in keeping turnover within acceptable limits.

Any organization can effect reductions in turnover by improving its human relations through positive action. In this chapter we emphasized the need for determining the areas of weakness in keeping people on the job. When this is done, priorities can be established for dealing with the major causes of turnover. Another technique to assist in analyzing the reasons for turnover is the separation or exit interview.

The Exit Interview

exit interview

How does an exit interview help analyze reasons for turnover?

Exit interviews can assist management in identifying and solving actual or potential personnel problems leading to turnover. Thus the real purpose of the **exit interview** is to uncover the actual reason employees quit their jobs. Yet many organizations never know why employees quit. People may say they are leaving for one reason and yet have hidden reasons as well. Many companies do not identify the real reasons why employees leave. Notice:

- The employee says, "There was a personality conflict." The concealed statement is, "The supervisor treated us like little kids. We had to ask permission to go to the rest room."
- The employee says, "I just felt like changing jobs." The concealed motive is, "My supervisor was doing some things that were unethical and I felt no one would believe me if I went to a higher level. Besides, I might go down with him if he gets caught."
- The employee says, "There's no way to get ahead here." The hidden motive is, "The last person who got promoted lied about his work experience. I couldn't trust a company that permitted this to happen."[20]

When real reasons are covered up, it is impossible to gain information that will aid in solving work-related problems leading to turnover. The manager must make every effort to get below the surface if the company is to receive any benefit from the interview.

Advantages of Exit Interviews

What can an exit interview tell a manager?

Separation interviews can provide valuable information for management personnel if they will take the time to pinpoint major problem areas. For example, an exit interview is an opportunity for the employee to discuss reasons for leaving, to explain problems encountered on the job, and to shed new light on circumstances surrounding a dismissal. It is also an opportunity for the manager to hear and address criticisms of operations, to identify difficulties and situations leading to turnover, to gain information related to retaining quality employees and to reducing employment hiring costs, and to uncover a department with low morale or other problems needing correction.

Since so much valuable information could be gathered for possible solving of personnel problems, you could wonder why many managers avoid the separation interview. One could speculate that managers don't really want to know why employees quit. Perhaps the actual reason though is they just do not want to take the time to plan for the interview.

A midwestern auto dealer observed extremely high turnover among mechanics in his repair shop. Although he was confident that this was caused by the drafty old building and outdated equipment, he asked a professor at a nearby university to confirm his analysis by giving quitters an exit interview.

When the results of the study were summarized, the owner was shocked to find that most mechanics quit because of him. Interview data revealed that his abrasive personality and hard-charging management style, not his facilities and equipment, were the culprits.

Planning the Exit Interview

Of course, some people leave because of their own psyche. Their exit has nothing to do with the company. Whatever the reason, four general factors in planning a separation interview should be considered:[21]

What are some factors that should be considered in an exit interview?

RESPONSIBILITY FOR CONDUCTING THE INTERVIEW. Face-to-face interviews between a company representative and the exiting employee are usually more productive than a written questionnaire. The personnel department is usually responsible for conducting the exit interview, but an independently conducted interview may be valuable. Since employees may want a reference from this job, they may not trust their honesty to just any company person. The affirmative action officer, equal opportunity specialist, ombudsmen, or some other staff member could be authorized to interview exiting personnel. Whether personnel or someone else handles the interview, the employee should feel that the information is shared in confidentiality. In addition, there needs to be consistency in the interviewing program.

DECISIONS ABOUT SCHEDULING PROCEDURES. The personnel department needs to know as soon as possible after an employee notifies his or her supervisor about quitting so an appointment can be made with the terminating employee. This task should not be left to the employee. Frequently, such an interview is held on the last day. However, it could be conducted at any time after the employee announces the decision to leave and before the day of termination.

DEVELOPMENT OF THE PROPER INTERVIEWING CLIMATE. Several considerations are important in setting the stage for the interview. For instance, the interview should be conducted in privacy. There should be no interruptions. The interviewer should be pleasant and nonjudgmental. An effort should be made to decrease any stress, anxiety, or apprehension during the interview.

FORMAT DESIGN FOR THE EXIT INTERVIEW. The fourth component to be considered is the interview design. What questions should be asked

---

EXHIBIT 12.4

- **Reasons for separation.** The official reason for an employee's separation from the company should be documented and filed. Underlying causes for the resignation or dismissal should be pursued.
- **Positive aspects of the job.** What did the employee like about the job? If she or he can't wait to get out the front door, the interviewer may not learn much. But if the employee had a favorable working experience, the interviewer needs to know what was pleasurable. This information may help the company evaluate strong and weak personnel practices.
- **Supervision.** The interviewer should try to determine what type of supervision—good and bad practices—the employee received. For example, were job performance instructions sufficient and consistent? Were questions answered satisfactorily? Were policies and procedures clearly defined?
- **Compensation and working conditions.** Answers to questions about salary, benefits, and working conditions can contribute to knowledge about employee satisfaction. For instance, did the employee regard the salary as appropriate for the skills, level of responsibility, and qualifications required? Were the benefits comparable to those provided by other employers? Was the work environment safe and nondisruptive?
- **Career development.** Often employees who do not have opportunities to grow and to develop their skills have a high turnover rate. The interviewer needs to learn about training, promotions, or reclassifications the employee received. What are his or her views on career development and potential within the company? A job enrichment program may be needed.
- **Complaints.** The employee should feel free to share any complaints about the company, its policies, procedures, and working conditions. Many of the problems should have been mentioned before getting to this part of the interview, but any complaint should be mentioned.
- **Suggestions.** The departing employee may very well know what is wrong and what needs to be changed. Ask him or her to suggest improvements.
- **Unresolved problems.** The exit interview is a good time for both the company and the employee to resolve any outstanding problems or disputes. When the employee leaves for good, the termination should be a clean break.
- **Additional comments.** Anything that hasn't been mentioned should be. By the end of the interview, the employee should have had time to honestly evaluate the work experience, as well as to critique the company.
- **Information for employees.** The closing comments of the interview should be made by the interviewer. The employee needs to know the company's rehire, reference, and unemployment insurance policies.[22]

FIGURE 12.2
Separation Interview
Guide

Employee's Name

Job Title   Start Date

Supervisor   Date of last

Interview Date   Performance Evaluation

Identification or
Social Security No.

Department

Termination Date

Note any promotion, training or reclassification the employee has received within previous 12 months:

Reason for separation (check appropriate column):

☐ Voluntary — Resignation
        workdays advance
        notice given

    ☐ Other job: new employer
                position
                salary

    ☐ Illness

    ☐ Return to school

    ☐ Pregnancy

    ☐ Relocation of family

    ☐ Retirement (Voluntary)

    ☐ Other — specify

☐ Involuntary — Dismissal

    ☐ Excessive absenteeism/tardiness

    ☐ Alcohol/drugs

    ☐ Theft/dishonesty

    ☐ Misconduct

    ☐ Insubordination

    ☐ Retirement (Mandatory)

    ☐ Reduction in Force

    ☐ Other — specify

Explain Circumstances:

SEPARATION CHECKLIST:

☐ Property check completed

☐ Final check issued

☐ Eligibility for rehire:

    ☐ Eligible, employee notified

    ☐ Ineligible, employee notified
        Reasons:

☐ Appeal rights and procedures
    explained, if applicable

☐ Resignation memo or dis-
    missal notice filed

☐ Separation completed:

    Date   Initials

1. Employee's reason(s) for resignation. If dismissal, what are the
   employee's perceptions of reason for discharge?

2. What did you like about working with our company?

3. Comment on the supervision
   you received.
   a. Were you given sufficient and
      consistent instructions on
      how to perform your job?
   b. Were your questions an-
      swered satisfactorily?
   c. Were general policies and proce-
      dures defined clearly for you?

4. Were you satisfied with the
   following:
   a. salary
   b. benefits
   c. working conditions

5. How were your chances for
   training and promotions, as
   you saw them?

6. What types of problems or
   complaints have you had
   about working here?

7. Would you consider returning
   to work here?

8. Additional comments.

9. Information for employees:
   a. rehire
   b. references
   c. insurance coverage

Interviewer's Comments:

Date:

Interviewer's Signature:

Source: Laura Garrison and Jacqueline Ferguson, "Separation Interview," Personnel Journal (September 1977): 442.

to obtain the employee's real reason(s) for leaving the company? Several of these questions should relate to general job factors and personal attitudes. For example, if you are the interviewer, you need to uncover the information listed in Exhibit 12.4.

After the interview has ended, the interviewer should summarize what happened. Exit interview responses from former employees should be tabulated and remedial action should be taken as indicated. If this isn't done, an exit interview is just another procedure to be carried out. There must be follow-up within the organization based on clues gleaned from tabulated exit interview responses.

A form to assist you during and after the exit interview is given in Figure 12.2. Such a tool will help you retain present and future employees.

CONCLUSION

Both absenteeism and turnover affect human relations by undermining long-range goals and objectives. They raise the cost of operation and cut into the profit ratio. If absenteeism can be thought of as a life-draining disease, turnover is amputation. Naturally, there are solutions and cures for both problems, but the preventive techniques are only as good as the managers who use them and the employees who apply them. Ultimately, both absenteeism and turnover must be viewed as alienation in terms of job satisfaction. People normally will not stay away or leave work if the human relationships of the job are at satisfactory levels (as well as money, hours, locale, etc.). This is why management should make an effort to employ job restructuring and the exit interview. They need to know what is good and bad about their organization.

KEY TERMS

Absenteeism: the practice by an employee or group of employees of being away from work.

AWOL Employee: an employee who is absent from work without an excuse; that is, away without leave.

Moonlighter: an employee who has another job in addition to his or her regular job.

Job Enrichment: a process of analyzing job content to see if jobs can be redesigned.

Flextime: flexible working hours.

Turnover: separation from the job.

Exit Interview: a process of uncovering the reasons employees quit their jobs.

QUESTIONS

1 Reread the opening case.
   a. What could Shirley have done before this meeting to have made it more productive than it was?
   b. Review Chapter 7 on interviewing and write out at least five questions Shirley could have asked to reveal the cause of Jamie's unacceptable attendance.
   c. How could Jamie be criticized for the failure of this exchange?
   d. What would you recommend to Shirley at this point in her relationship with Jamie? Why?

2 Recall a past or present employer. What conditions in the organization caused absenteeism there? What could management have done to correct them?

3 How does the problem of absenteeism relate to the need for discipline that you learned about in Chapter 10?

4 Discuss the characteristics of the following types of absentees:
   a. Monday/Friday,
   b. chronically ill,
   c. AWOL, and
   d. moonlighters.

5 List at least five ways an organization may benefit from job enrichment. Why might workers react negatively to this practice?

6 What problems may management encounter when adopting a four-day work week? Suggest two types of jobs that may be adapted to a four-day week and two that would best be suited to a traditional work week.

7 What condition does management place on workers' freedom when applying gliding flextime? How does this differ from individual working time?

8 Summarize several specific solutions to absenteeism. Which ones seem best suited to managerial employees? To nonmanagerial workers?

9 Describe the relationship between absenteeism and turnover. How are they alike? Why is the organization's personnel selection process a key factor in keeping them under control?

10 List at least three questions that managers must answer when evaluating turnover rates.

11 Develop at least one example of each of the following categories of turnover:
   a. voluntary but uncontrollable,
   b. involuntary but usually considered uncontrollable,
   c. involuntary and controllable,
   d. voluntary but usually considered controllable.

12 Interpret the following formula for computing turnover costs:
   Turnover costs $= Sc + Rc + Tc$

13 Provide at least two examples of each cost in the above formula.

14 Recommend at least four actions you would take to reduce turnover in a work group that you were managing.

15 Briefly summarize the role that each of the following can play in reducing turnover:
   a. applicant/job compatibility,
   b. employee involvement in job restructuring,

    c. employee dignity, and

    d. compensation.

16 Assume that you have been hired to conduct a seminar on "How exit interviews can reduce turnover." What points would you emphasize on:

    a. pinpointing reasons for resignation,

    b. company policy evaluation,

    c. training adequacy,

    d. morale measurement, and

    e. supervisor/subordinate relations within each department?

17 List at least seven subject areas that should be covered in an exit interview. How can the information gained on these topics be used by management after the employee has resigned?

CASES

Case 12.1

Pete de Moll, a recent college graduate, is a systems engineer for Consolidated Aerospace in Cocoa, Florida. Consolidated holds several key government contracts for missiles, aircraft, and space exploration equipment. As Pete entered the cocktail lounge with several co-workers this afternoon, the talk turned to employment conditions peculiar to the aerospace industry. He listened intently.

"I hear things are getting critical for the Watchdog missile," remarked Mack Romig, a veteran engineer in Pete's section.

"Yeah," replied Fred Rountree, "They'll begin laying off several dozen people within the next two weeks because the contract's almost complete. Absenteeism was over 12 percent today: everyone's got the word, and they've gone out job hunting. Morale's lousy over there; they will be lucky if half their people show up for work in two weeks. Word's out that the Vindicator jet fighter contract is going to be cut back pretty soon, too. Those guys had better update their resumes."

"Isn't this a crazy business?" Mack asked, turning to Pete. "You'll have to get used to it. Most of us are 'space bums' or 'contract gypsies'; we follow the contracts, go where the money is. Most of the guys around this bar have worked together at one company or another before. Of course, none of us can expect much more than ten years work at any one place. That's not long enough to qualify for decent retirement benefits, but we go with the flow. The money's great, so we save and invest during the good times and spend during the bad. It's a way of life."

"I was pretty sure how things were before I started," Pete answered. "Still, it seems like a terrific waste of time and money, having people migrating from one company to another so much."

"Sure," agreed Ralph Masters, "and some companies like Consolidated make project-specific job assignments. You're identified with one project (or product) and you're expected to know your job on that gizmo intimately. Trouble is, when the orders are all filled or the contract's cut back, your job might be gone."

"That must make all of you feel pretty uneasy," observed Pete.

"Yes, you might say that," smiled Tim Diller. "But, we've developed a few ways to deal with that over the years."

"Oh?" asked Pete.

"Of course," Tim affirmed. "Think about it. Do you believe we engineers will reveal *all* our ideas on design and performance capabilities on a plane or a missile up front? Of course not! Oh, we'll develop a great model, very impressive. But when the government wants us to recommend improvements—and those mean *jobs*, fella—we'll just trot out some of our original ideas that we saved for a rainy day! Always bank some of your best ideas, Pete. This means job security. It's like hunting ducks. Don't use up all your ammunition on the first one that flies by."

"Sounds a little wasteful," Pete ventured. "I know you're talking about self-preservation, but somebody's got to pay for those changes that could have been included in the original product."

"Sure, kid," Mack confirmed. "That somebody is you, me, all of us around this bar. We're taxpayers. But no matter how it sounds, we're really creating work for our suppliers' employees and lots of military contracts people, too. Not to mention newcomers to the aerospace industry, young guys just out of school." He nudged Pete's elbow.

"What about company loyalty?" asked Pete. "How do you feel about the 'Consolidated Aerospace family' that I heard so much about during company orientation?"

"And did they talk about the tooth fairy, too?" Ralph asked with a smile. "There's only contract loyalty. Keep the contract going, and you've got a job. Your morale gets raised every two weeks—on payday. Company loyalty is just an item on an orientation agenda. Wait'll you've been around a few years; you'll see what we mean."

Case Questions

1 Discuss how the system as presented in this case affects:
   a. one company,
   b. the aerospace industry, and
   c. the national economy.
2 Suggest activities that individual managers may use to build morale and generate loyalty even though jobs depend on budget decisions beyond the company's control.
3 How would you propose that Consolidated Aerospace restructure itself to eliminate the project-specific philosophy that affects morale, absenteeism, and turnover so adversely? How might you sell this proposal to management?

Case 12.2

Harriet Keller is a switchboard operator for Omega Answering Service. Her company promotes itself as the last word in a prompt, accurate, and courteous telephone answering service. Its clients are mostly politicians and professionals such as CPAs, attorneys, and physicians.

The company prides itself on "second-ring service"—every caller is guaranteed an answer by the second ring or the answering service client whom they're calling gets one month's service free. In addition to this pressure, the job has its critical moments (handling emergency calls from patient to physician) and its nasty ones (dealing with foul-mouthed drunks calling their attorneys to bail them out of jail). Operators must be a blend of Mary Poppins and Attila the Hun to get through an eight-hour shift.

Omega supervisors use secret listen-ins regularly to monitor the quality of service that each operator gives. These listen-ins have been used to evaluate operator performance and in several cases to justify dismissals.

Employees object to the listen-in policy and to the strict controls on absenteeism and lateness. Workers who are late twice in a four-week period receive a written reprimand, and two consecutive absences without notification brings immediate dismissal. Perhaps the most demeaning policy of all, however, is the one on extra breaks. An operator who needs an additional break beyond the half-hour lunch period and standard fifteen-minute morning and afternoon breaks must raise a hand and be placed on a relief list, waiting as long as ten minutes for a relief operator to take over the board.

All this irritates newer employees considerably, and militant workers compare their working conditions to the galley of a slave ship. Not surprisingly, Omega has problems finding qualified answerers. Absenteeism exceeds 15 percent on Mondays and Fridays, and turnover averages 50 percent per year. Management freely admits, however, that all that's needed is someone with a pleasant, courteous, and articulate voice who can punch a button to record each caller's message for replay to the answering service client.

"If you need work, we've got work," John Andrella explained to Harriet during her employment interview. "If you want a country club atmosphere, join a country club."

Case Questions

1   Discuss the long-term effects of Omega's philosophy toward employee work policies.
2   Develop a slate of changes to present to Andrella that would combat his absenteeism and turnover.
3   Giving your imagination free rein, propose how Omega might restructure jobs to reduce absenteeism and turnover.

--------------------------------------- NOTES ---------------------------------------

1. Harvey H. Shore, "Absenteeism, Part 1: How to Analyze Causes and Effects," *Supervisory Management* (September 1975): 10.
2. "Absenteeism—Missing Employees Mean 100 Million Man-Hours Lost!" *The Better Work Supervisor* (Clemprint, 1979), p. 1.
3. Shore, "Absenteeism, Part 1," p. 11.
4. Marianna Ohe, " 'Wellness' Plans Profit Bosses," *American Business* (November 1981): 2.
5. "Fact and Comment," *Forbes,* 8 June 1981, p. 17.
6. "Absenteeism," p. 1.
7. Shore, "Absenteeism, Part 1," pp. 15–16.
8. Harvey H. Shore, "Absenteeism, Part 2: Prevention and Cure," *Supervisory Management* (October 1975): 23.
9. Antone F. Alber, "How (and How Not) to Approach Job Enrichment," *Personnel Journal* (December 1979): 837–841, 867.
10. "Moving Beyond Assembly Lines," *Business Week,* 27 July 1981, p. 87.
11. *The Wall Street Journal,* 17 November 1981, p. 1.
12. *The Wall Street Journal,* 2 December 1980, p. 1.

13. *The Wall Street Journal,* 29 August 1978, p. 1.
14. "Absenteeism," pp. 2–3.
15. Vincent S. Flowers and Charles L. Hughes, "Why Employees Stay," *Harvard Business Review* (July–August 1973): 51.
16. Ibid.
17. Flowers and Hughes, "Why Employees Stay," p. 50.
18. Howard Smith and Larry E. Watkins, "Managing Manpower Turnover Costs," *The Personnel Administrator* (April 1978).
19. George G. Gordon, "Putting the Brakes on Turnover," *Personnel Journal* (February 1974): 142–144.
20. Wanda R. Embrey et al., "Exit Interview: A Tool for Personnel Development," *The Personnel Administrator* (May 1979): 43.
21. Ibid., pp. 45–46.
22. Laura Garrison and Jacqueline Ferguson, "Separation Interviews," *Personnel Journal* (September 1977): 439–440.

SUGGESTED READINGS

Aldag, Ramon J., and Brief, Arthur P. *Task Design and Employee Motivation.* Glenview, Ill.: Scott, Foresman, 1978.

D'Aprix, Roger M. *Struggle for Identity: The Silent Revolution Against Corporate Conformity.* Homewood, Ill.: Irwin, 1972.

Hackman, J. R., and Suttle, J. L. (eds.). *Improving Life at Work.* Santa Monica, Calif.: Goodyear, 1977.

13

Alcoholism and Drug Abuse

LEARNING OBJECTIVES

When you complete your study of this chapter you should be able to:

1 Recognize the behavioral symptoms of high workers, and

2 Design a company program and policy for the treatment of problem drinkers and drug abusers.

—————————— OPENING CASE ——————————

Lynette Christy works in the marketing department of Mellacron, Inc. Her job requires that she work closely with Vic Norman, a longtime accounting department employee. Vic is responsible for gathering and summarizing sales and returns statistics for Lynette each week. She, in turn, relays them to higher marketing managers who track sales and customer returns on various products and recommend when to manufacture additional units.

During her short time in the job, Lynette has noticed that Vic's speech becomes so slurred by 3:30 in the afternoon that he's very difficult to understand.

She shared this information with veteran co-worker Brett Handley who remarked, "Yes, that's old Vic, all right. That guy has had his grief. Marital problems, personal illness, a Korean War injury, the works. We all look the other way with Vic because of his personal situation and because he's only got three years to go for retirement. Any of us could be Vic someday, and that affects how we work with him."

"Then I'm right in assuming he's got a drinking problem?" probed Lynette.

"Draw your own conclusions about that," Brett answered.

Lynette thought about the ever-present vacuum bottle of "coffee" beside Vic's desk, his frequent days out sick, his slurred late afternoon speech, and the faint odor of bourbon that always seemed to hang in the air surrounding him. "Yes," she thought, "he's a boozer."

Lynette has nothing against drinking, but Vic's problem is causing trouble for her. Several times he sent her error-filled reports that she had been held responsible for. "I can't chase down the correct information myself," her boss had stormed, "that's your job! I want this stuff right and on time— no matter what!"

Today she confided her problem with Vic's work to Brett and suggested that perhaps she should tell the head of the accounting department. "If you blow the whistle on that poor guy the gang will really have it in for you around here," Brett warned. "His life's a mess, he's nearing retirement, and you'd rat on him to his boss? Where's your compassion?"

"Compassion isn't the issue, Brett. My job is," Lynette replied. "My boss doesn't care about Vic's situation; he only wants the reports to be accurate. It's not fair that he holds me responsible for them, but he does! Now what should I do—try to do Vic's job for him, tell his boss and make a bunch of enemies, or ignore his getting bombed by 3:30 every day and let his sloppy work get *me* fired?"

"That's life," Brett answered with a shrug.

Working Under the Influence

addiction

How many alcoholics are there in the work force?

Is that life, as Brett suggested? Should Lynette turn her back on the situation? Alcohol and drug abuse within business, industry, education, and government constitute a significant management problem in the human relations area. Some drink because of job pressures or personal problems; others, to escape boredom. Alcohol and drug addiction have become major behavioral problems in our society. **Addiction** is the state of constantly giving oneself over to some habit such as drugs or alcohol. In an average company of 500 employees, 25 are alcoholics, and the company is losing $60,000 a year to absenteeism, lowered efficiency, work dodging, medical treatment, and work accidents.[1] Drug use contributes to similar problems.

Therefore, this chapter reviews alcohol and other drug abuse and examines some of the successful programs for dealing with addicts. Managers need to be aware there are a great number of people in business and industry, government, and education who are working under the influence. We will begin our study of the drug scene in business with alcoholism.

Alcoholism

alcoholism

What does alcoholism cost society?

Alcoholism is an illness resulting from uncontrolled drinking of alcoholic beverages—beer, wine, distilled spirits. It is estimated there are 10 million alcoholics in the United States. Likewise, one-tenth of the employees in business, industry, and government are alcoholics. It is clear from such figures that there is a problem in the working environment. For example, the individual alcoholic is very likely to ruin his or her life, have low self-respect, or risk losing health, happiness, safety, and longevity. For the alcoholic's family there is the chance of a loss of income and respect leading to divorce, delinquency, crime, or suicide. Three-fourths of the alcoholics are reasonably well accepted members of the community. But the alcoholic's behavior can affect at least four others, including spouse, children, supervisor, co-workers, friends, and so forth. For the economy, 10 million alcoholics represent almost a $50 billion drain in lost productivity, in motor vehicle accidents, in health, medical, and social services, and in violent crimes. The seriousness of this disease can be illustrated by figures showing that its incidence is exceeded only by cancer, heart disease, and mental illness. However, many of the costs on the job could be controlled if supervisors and managers recognized the signs of alcoholism in employees and did something about them *early.*

The Symptoms of Alcoholism

What are the causes of alcoholism?

Drunks may not be alcoholics (and vice versa). They may act abnormally, but not be addicted. No one is certain of the exact cause of alcoholism. It may be caused by a combination of elements, including (1) physical, chemical, or organic factors, (2) psychological, psychosomatic, or emotional difficulties, and (3) environmental factors.[2] A person is an alcoholic when she or he continues to drink in spite of painful and injurious results. Most people can drink socially without becoming addicted. Social drinkers and alcoholics differ in the ability to control their habit. Unfortunately, our social attitudes toward drinking make it less of a stigma; for example, we tell drunk jokes and drink as part of social ritual (closing a deal, signing a contract) or as a way to be one of the crowd. This only worsens the problem.

Persons under the influence of alcohol reveal certain signs of their intoxication or addiction. In fact, the alcoholic seems to go through three stages. The early stage may last up to ten years. At this initial stage, it is hard to tell a heavy social drinker from an alcoholic. There are several symptoms, however. For example, alcoholics may make promises to quit drinking but never keep them. They may start drinking more often to relieve tensions. Changes in personality may occur. Drinkers may become more irritable and forgetful. They may have mental blackouts. Their bodily system will increase its tolerance level for alcohol.

What are the stages of alcoholism?

The middle stage encompasses a behavioral cycle. The alcoholic drinks, feels guilty afterwards, isolates self because of discouragement, then drinks again, and so on. However, the signs of drinking are more noticeable, especially at work. The person drinks in the morning now, alone. Drinking is a daily necessity, but it doesn't make the alcoholic feel as good, regardless of the quantity that is drunk. This stage is crucial. From this point on, change and cure become almost impossible. The person will soon become obsessed with drink. That is why early intervention should be a managerial imperative.

The final, chronic stage of alcoholism on the job includes tardiness, absenteeism, loss of efficiency, lower quality and quantity of work, and loss of sense of responsibility. It is obvious now that the person cannot control drinking. There are often home and financial difficulties, problems with neighbors and police. The symptoms of alcoholism are leading to rock bottom. Drinkers then seek isolation from friends and family, distrust and avoid those who offer help, but also feel guilty. They never seem to eat and are nervous. They may be taking vitamins and tranquilizers, but these don't help. Tenseness and irritability increase. Alcohol is of prime importance, not family, job, or anyone or anything else. Health is ultimately affected by tremors, hallucinations, and weakness from malnutrition. The only choices at this point are ruin, invalidism, death, or a slow start to recovery.

Alcoholism is a progressive disease—and a complex one. Although drinking may not affect job performance in the beginning, it catches up with the individual eventually.

--------------------------------- Sobriety Is the Priority ---------------------------------

One may wonder why people drink to excess or what causes alcoholism. The answers are not entirely clear. No one starts out to be an alcoholic. We

Why do people drink to excess?

might conclude, however, that people drink to relieve tensions in meeting problems, to escape from such problems, or to substitute for their inability to cope. They fail to realize that alcohol is only a temporary help and often makes the situation worse. In fact, one of the most frustrating characteristics of problem drinkers is their inability at any stage of their illness to accept it or to realize that they are in serious trouble, despite overwhelming evidence.

sobriety

Is there a cure for alcoholism?

There is no cure for alcoholism. The only solution is **sobriety,** or abstinence. However, since alcoholics cannot control their thinking, abstinence requires a combination of physical and mental treatments. Physical treatments might include vitamins to offset poor diet, antiabuse chemicals to prevent drinking, and certain drugs to control discomfort of withdrawal. Mental treatments might include psychiatric counseling, institutional confinement, alcoholic clinics, or group therapy. Organizations such as Alcoholics Anonymous or the Veterans Administration are also excellent sources of help to the alcoholic. The goal is sobriety.

--------------------- Alcoholic Employees ---------------------

What is the supervisor's responsibility?

What can a supervisor do with alcoholic employees? Many managers would respond, "Fire them." However, in some cases this action is shortsighted and unwise. Alcoholism is a treatable disease. It can't be cured, but it can be controlled with systematic treatment. Because alcoholic workers' habits prevent them from doing their jobs efficiently and effectively, the supervisor must interfere with the employees' private life and should do so early. Alcoholism is a matter that concerns the organization.

Alcoholic employees hurt an organization through absenteeism, accidents, mistakes, and errors in judgment. For example, absenteeism of alcoholics is 2.5 times that of nonalcoholics.[3] The General Accounting Office estimates that payroll losses alone cost the government from $275 to $550 million a year.[4] Alcoholism is expensive, and managers must learn how to deal with it on the job. A cost-accounting analysis suggests a strong need for corporate programs on alcoholism.

--------------------- Company Programs for Alcoholics ---------------------

What are companies doing about the problem?

Companies save an estimated $10 in losses for every $1 they invest in an alcoholic program. Some of the companies pioneering in alcoholism-control work among their employees report 60 to 70 percent of those accepting treatment are helped.[5] Yet, as of 1977 fewer than one in one hundred of the corporations in America had any sort of alcoholic program.[6] Most of those programs are on paper only.

KEMPER ALCOHOLIC POLICY.   At Kemper Insurance Companies an attempt has been made to bridge the gap between management and the alcoholic employee. The Kemper program works in the following way:[7]

1. The personal assistance director is contacted by the supervisor when an employee begins to perform poorly, to have interpersonal problems, or to change attendance patterns. Normal management techniques have failed thus far to motivate the worker to change.

2. The supervisor discusses the problem with a counselor from the personal assistance program and completes a job performance evaluation form. This document is sent to the director and is the basis for confronting the employee.

3. Sticking to the observable facts, the supervisor discusses the problem with the employee. No accusations of alcoholism are made. For example, "I've noticed something is affecting the way you handle your job. I think I know what the problem is, but I can't help you until you *tell* me about it." The intent is to have the employee identify the problem. Then an interview with a personal assistance program staff member is recommended. The supervisor outlines the program, its benefits, and confidentiality. However, the supervisor also makes it clear that if the employee does not agree to the interview, she or he will face disciplinary action.

4. If the interview opportunity is accepted, the employee is given a diagnostic screening and is usually referred to a medical or therapeutic center for treatment. If the employee refuses the interview and job performance does not improve, disciplinary action is taken.

FIRESTONE TIRE AND RUBBER COMPANY PROGRAM.   Firestone Tire and Rubber Company reportedly saves $2 million per year with an employee assistance program composed of 50 percent alcoholics. The savings result from reduced lateness and absenteeism, greater productivity, and less sick leave. The firm claims that 80 percent of the alcoholics who take part in the program are treated successfully.[8]

Support from top management is crucial for success in such programs. Management must issue a policy statement of belief and intention, state their belief that alcoholism is an illness that can be treated successfully, and affirm their readiness to help those with drinking problems.[9] This policy must also be distributed throughout the organization. Some writers have recommended that corporations set aside 10 percent of their community action contribution funds for alcoholic education and rehabilitation. Such monies are important if alcoholism on the job is to be cured.

DUPONT'S ALCOHOLISM PROGRAM.   DuPont Company's alcoholism rehabilitation program, another outstanding industry model, was conceived in 1942, twenty-four years before the American Medical Association recognized alcoholism as a disease. The program involves a physician at the employee's job location and the company's medical division at the Wilmington, Delaware, home office.

The firm's special advisor on alcoholism, who is a recovered alcoholic and an expert on the disease, travels extensively to meet with program participants at their respective locations nationwide. This person outlines individual recovery programs and institutes follow-up procedures. The following elements contribute to the program's success:

1 Management at every level supports the idea that alcoholic workers need help and can be treated.
2 Alcoholism is recognized as a disease and is treated as one.
3 Early detection and prompt treatment are considered essential to success.
4 DuPont cooperates closely with Alcoholics Anonymous, an organization that began during the same era as DuPont's program.
5 The program utilizes well-qualified alcoholism rehabilitation hospitals and treatment centers throughout the country, where participants may relax while gaining a better understanding of their disease.

While acknowledging that no one can be forced to accept treatment, DuPont believes it can play a vital role in convincing alcoholic workers to control and combat their drinking problems voluntarily.

—————————— Benefits of Company Alcoholism Programs ——————————

What are the benefits of company-sponsored alcoholic programs?

Companies that do start alcoholism programs report many benefits to helping problem drinkers and alcoholics recover from their illness. Some are:

• retention of the majority as satisfactory employees,
• elimination of excessive costs caused by them,
• solution of complex and difficult personnel problems,
• realistic and practical extension of the company's general health services, which make available the required medical counsel about this illness,
• improved public and community attitudes created by concern for employees (and their families) and by eliminating employees' dangerous and antisocial behavior in their communities, and
• responsible participation in the community toward control of a major public health problem.

A benefit often overlooked in a company program is its role in preventing moderate drinkers from developing the dangerous drinking habits that lead to alcoholism. Such a program will also motivate some employees to undertake remedial action on their own, outside the scope of the company's program.

According to the Department of Health and Human Services, 2400 organizations have established work-oriented alcoholism programs.[10] However, the American Society of Chartered Life Underwriters reported that by early 1979 fewer than 150 companies in the private sector had developed such rehabilitation or recovery programs.[11]

Drug Addiction

Much of the preceding information on how to deal with alcoholism on the job is applicable to drug problems. After all, alcohol is a drug, although many people seem to forget this. The scope of drug problems on the job is as broad as the scope of alcoholism. It ranges from aspirin to heroin, from ethyl alcohol to barbiturates. Some companies have employees who are hooked on tranquilizers, Benzedrine, and Seconal. In other companies the coffee break has been supplanted by Dexedrine or marijuana. The result is a problem for supervisors. Coffee is legal; drugs are not. Health and performance considerations are also involved. Administrative decisions must be made regarding corrective discipline.

Drug Abuse

drug abuse

How can a manager deal with drug misuse?

Drug abuse is the improper use of drugs (including alcohol). And, in business and industry drugs are widespread. They are used by different employees for different reasons in different situations. Contrary to popular belief, however, the drug problem is not limited to blue-collar, minority workers. That is why managers interested in human relations must be as knowledgeable as possible about the signs and symptoms of drug abuse. If supervisors suspect employee drug misuse, there are eight steps they may follow.[12]

1. Inform their own supervisor and the personnel representative of the department. Then, with their agreement, proceed to (2).

2. Consult the medical department and describe the employee's behavior and symptoms.

3. Discuss with the employee his or her deficiencies in job performance, personal appearance, absences, lateness, and so on, but do not suggest suspected drug misuse. (Drug abuse should not be claimed without substantial proof. The employee has certain rights. If the supervisor is wrong, the employee has a just complaint.)

4. If proof is substantiated, refer the employee to the medical department for evaluation and counsel and inform the employee that his or her record is being made available to the physician. If the employee refuses to visit the medical department, explain that this may be grounds for dismissal.

5. After the medical interview, decide on further action through consultation with the supervisor, the personnel representative, and medical consultant. Rehabilitation should be attempted if there is likelihood of success. The physician will suggest appropriate sources of treatment in the community.

6. Explain to the employee exactly what improvement in performance and behavior is expected and determine if the employee understands that improvement is necessary to continue in the job. Supervisors should not engage in counseling or in therapeutic discussion. Because of the complex

nature of drug involvement, rehabilitation should be directed only by experts.

7. In conjunction with the medical department, maintain a close follow-up of the employee's progress. Follow-up should be undertaken whether the employee continues work or is institutionalized.

8. If rehabilitation is ineffectual or if the employee is uncooperative, resort to further disciplinary action: suspension or dismissal.

Documenting observations of and conversations with the employee are a necessity. Careful note taking will help eliminate guesswork and will provide necessary information for higher levels of supervision.

Employee Drug Abuse

Drug problems in business and industry have been relatively common for about twenty-five years. As we mentioned, people use drugs for a variety of reasons. Some of these reasons may relate to the supervisor's style of managing or his or her lack of concern for human relationships. Thus managers must learn to look at themselves to see if they are contributing to the problem.

What are some signs of drug abuse?

The supervisor who suspects an employee of drug abuse needs to be able to follow a sequence of action. But first she or he needs to be able to identify the problem. For example, some common signs of drug misuse are:

- changes in attitude (e.g., paranoia or excessive suspicion of others),
- change from normal capabilities (work habits, efficiency, etc.),
- increase in number of accidents,
- poor physical appearance, including inattention to dress, diet, and personal hygiene,
- wearing sunglasses at inappropriate times to hide dilated or constricted pupils,
- wearing long-sleeve shirts constantly to hide needle marks,
- associating with known drug users,
- having a flushed face, feeling chills, and experiencing occasional convulsions, and
- stealing small items.

Because a drug problem often manifests itself in an employee's work performance, behavior, or appearance, supervisors must be able to spot the drug user. Any or all of the signs we have listed may not be the result of drugs, however. If they are, the supervisor must take action.

There is ample reason to believe that drug abuse exists in most parts of the United States. Therefore, business and industry must immediately address the issues: worker safety, job performance, absenteeism, inventory shrinkage, influence on nonaffected workers, and drug selling. There is need for an appropriate policy regarding drugs, as there is with alcoholism.

─────────── Company Programs for Drug Misuse ───────────

Not all organizations have adopted formal policies to deal with drug addiction. Reasons for not doing so may relate to the illegality of the drugs or the stigma associated with their use. One organization dealing head-on with the issue of drug abuse in business and industry is Kemper Insurance Companies. Their policy follows:

Is business doing anything about drug abuse?

KEMPER DRUG POLICY.   In accordance with their general personnel policies and their underlying concept of regard for the employee as an individual as well as a worker, Kemper Insurance states the following:

1 We believe drug dependency is an illness and should be treated as such.
2 We believe the majority of employees who develop drug dependency can be helped to recover, and the company should offer appropriate assistance.
3 We believe the decision to seek diagnosis and accept treatment for any suspected illness is the responsibility of the employee. However, continued refusal of an employee to seek treatment when it appears that substandard performance may be caused by any illness is not tolerated. We believe that drug dependency should not be made an exception to this commonly accepted principle.
4 We believe that it is in the best interest of employees and the company that when drug dependency is present, it should be diagnosed and treated at the earliest possible stage.
5 We believe that confidential handling of the diagnosis and treatment of drug dependency is essential.[13]

The objective of this policy is to retain employees who may develop drug dependency by helping them to arrest its further advance before the condition renders them unemployable.

CONTROL DATA CORPORATION'S PROGRAM.   Control Data Corporation has developed a computer-based concerned parents/concerned partners educational program for adults who have personal or family problems stemming from alcohol or drug abuse. They are given facts on these illnesses and are told where to obtain further assistance. The company also has a twenty-four-hour-a-day Employee Advisory Resource (EAR) program to counsel workers on personal and job-related difficulties that can be traced to drug abuse, alcoholism, interpersonal relations, or marital or emotional problems.

The cooperation of all levels of management is essential for the success of such programs.

─────────────── CONCLUSION ───────────────

A great number of people in business, government, and education are chronic users of alcohol and other drugs. With one-tenth of all workers affected by alcoholism, and a similar percentage affected by drugs, American industry is suffering from tardiness, absenteeism, loss of efficiency, lower quality of work, loss of a sense of responsibility, accidents, mistakes, and errors in judgment. Management has a responsibility to do what it can to help employees affected by addiction. On-the-job programs and policies must be adopted. Statistics are in favor of helping the addict and not ignoring the problem. Understanding of the disease and how to deal with it on the job has been provided in this chapter.

--- KEY TERMS ---

Addiction: the state of constantly practicing a habit, such as giving oneself up or over to alcohol or drugs.

Alcoholism: an illness resulting from uncontrolled drinking of alcoholic beverages.

Sobriety: abstinence from the use of alcohol.

Drug Abuse: improper use of drugs (including alcohol).

--- QUESTIONS ---

1 Reread the opening case.
   a. If you were Lynette Christy, what would you do at this point?
   b. Do you believe she should involve Vic directly in the action she takes? Why or why not?
   c. What options (other than those referred to in the case) does Lynette have? What are the possible outcomes?
   d. Create a top-management policy on alcoholism that would resolve situations like the one in this case. How might it be implemented? What problems would you expect?
2 How may workers' personal as well as working lives benefit from assistance with alcohol problems?
3 Discuss at least three aspects of alcoholism that make the disease misunderstood and confusing to treat.
4 What symptoms characterize an alcoholic during the
   a. early stage,
   b. middle or crucial stage, and
   c. final or chronic stage?
5 "Sure, I have several beers on the way home from work, but drinking's never been a problem. I can take it or leave it." What advice could you offer the speaker after reading this chapter?
6 How do problem drinkers' self-images at each stage thwart efforts to assist them? Through what combination of treatments is alcoholism controlled?

7 List at least five costs associated with alcoholism.

8 Develop an argument supporting a corporate alcoholism rehabilitation program. How do personal privacy and timing affect the success of such a program?

9 Why do some employers fail to create a policy that deals with alcoholism or drug abuse?

10 Summarize at least four benefits of an alcoholism rehabilitation program. Do you believe top management involvement and support are essential to its success? Why or why not?

11 Discuss the eight steps supervisors can take when they suspect subordinates of drug abuse.

12 "Drug abuse in any organization can't be tolerated. If you ignore it, it's going to spread like the plague." Do you agree with this position? Why or why not?

13 List at least seven common signs of drug abuse. How might some be caused by activities or factors other than drug abuse? What implication does that have for supervisors?

14 Review the Kemper Drug Policy. Which items, if any, would you add, delete, or change? Provide reasons for your answers.

---------------------------------- CASES ----------------------------------

Evan Rauth, personnel director at Mercy Hospital, supervises a large staff of volunteers who work without pay. He is concerned that Pat Hannin, formerly one of his most enthusiastic, compassionate, and dedicated volunteers, is a drug abuser. Her work patterns and general character have changed recently.
Case 13.1

Pat works at a feverish pace but without a sense of order or organization. Employees in the records department where she works report that a higher than usual number of patient files and account cards are missing, probably misfiled. There have been scattered co-worker gripes about her body odor, bad breath, and personal appearance. Her wrinkled clothing and disorderly hair make her look ten years older than she is.

Pat has confided to co-workers during break periods that life lacks meaning, and last week she sounded almost suicidal. Her colleagues asked Evan to speak to her and try to find out what has caused her to behave so strangely.

1 What drug(s) may Pat be abusing, according to information in this case?
Case Questions

2 How would you advise Evan to handle his initial conference with her?

3 If Pat is cooperative and admits to a drug problem, what further steps should Evan take to help her?

Don Moody is a staff accountant for Howard Chemicals, Inc. His ten-year marriage recently ended in divorce, and he's trying to get his personal life back together again.
Case 13.2

Because entertainment is scarce in the small town where Don's located, he began driving his Corvette (a self-awarded consolation prize after his divorce) 75 miles to a large nearby city on Friday nights to party with other singles.

Last Friday night he demolished his Corvette just before reaching home. This led to charges of driving while intoxicated and a three-day hospital stay.

When Owen Martin, Don's boss, got news of the accident (supplemented with bits of small-town gossip about Don's condition when the rescue squad separated him from his car), he believed that Don had a problem. Being a concerned person, Owen decided to talk to Don.

"Don, I don't want to pry," Owen started out. "But I don't want to lose a good employee, either. I just want to let you know I'm available for support."

"Thanks, Owen, but everything's just fine," Don answered. "I had several drinks before I hit the road, and it hit me instead. I felt fine when I left the city, but I just fell asleep; booze had nothing to do with it, really. Trouble was, my blood alcohol level exceeded the legal limit when they took a sample at the hospital, so the highway patrol charged me with both careless driving and driving while intoxicated."

"That's too bad, Don," Owen agreed, "but I'm concerned for you and for the company, because you drive a company car on at least one trip per month. We might have some serious legal liabilities if you were to cause an accident on company time in a company vehicle. Your problem may be personal now, but the company *could* get dragged into it."

"Owen, I don't *have* a problem," Don said patiently. "I've been a social drinker for years; I admitted that on my employment application. So are you."

"Yes," Owen admitted, "but not in the morning, Don, and I don't have a four-martini lunch."

"Where did you hear all that?" Don asked, leaning forward in his chair.

"You know the grapevine," Owens replied. "Are you saying it's not true"?

"If there's any truth to that (and I'm not saying there is), it's not a problem. I can handle it," Don confirmed. "If I was a little indiscreet, there are good reasons, but the last thing I'd do is involve the company in any way. I can separate my personal life from my work. It's just a matter of priorities."

Case Questions

1 What stage of alcoholism does Don appear to be in? What evidence did you use to make your decision?
2 Do you believe Owen should pursue the issue of Don's drinking in this meeting or wait to see what changes result? Why?
3 How would you respond to Don's remarks about his drinking habits and his ability to prevent his job from becoming involved?
4 Considering Don's job, how might Owen involve him in organizing a company-sponsored alcoholic rehabilitation program?

NOTES

---

1. Tenday Kumbula, "Alcoholism on the Job—A Major Headache," *Los Angeles Times,* 27 July 1976.
2. Gary W. Wulf, "The Alcoholic Employee," *Personnel Journal* (August 1973): 702.
3. W. H. Weiss, "You Can't Ignore the Alcoholic," *Supervision* 39 (April 1977): 6.
4. Kevin W. Kane, "The Corporate Responsibility in the Area of Alcoholism," *Personnel Journal* (July 1975): 383.

5. Marion Sadler and James F. Horst, "Company/Union Programs for Alcoholics," *Harvard Business Review* (September–October 1972): 23.

6. Jack Weiner, *Drinking* (New York: Norton, 1977), p. 8.

7. "What to Do About the Employee with A Drinking Problem," Public Relations Department, Kemper Insurance Company, 1977, pp. 3–4.

8. John A. Prestbo, "Business of Treating Alcoholics Takes Off As Attitudes Change, Corporate Aid Grows," *The Wall Street Journal*, 19 October 1981, p. 31.

9. Sadler and Horst, "Company/Union Programs," pp. 25–26.

10. "More Firms, Unions Establish Programs to Fight Alcoholism," *The Wall Street Journal*, 18 October 1978, p. 19.

11. *The Wall Street Journal*, 6 February 1979, p. 1.

12. Carl D. Chambers and Richard D. Heckman, *Employee Drug Abuse—A Manager's Guide for Action* (Boston: Cahners Books, 1972), pp. 35–40.

13. "What About Drugs and Employees?" Public Relations Department, Kemper Insurance Company, 1977, pp. 4–5.

SUGGESTED READINGS

Cohen, Sidney. *The Drug Dilemma.* New York: McGraw-Hill, 1969.

"Detour—Alcoholism Ahead," Kemper Insurance Co., 1976.

Joint Guidelines for the Establishment of Employee Assistance Programs, Ontario Federation of Labor/Addiction Research Foundation.

Wilkinson, Rupert. *The Prevention of Drinking Problems—Alcohol Control and Cultural Influences.* New York: Oxford University Press, 1970.

14

Prejudice and Discrimination

When you complete your study of this chapter, you should be able to:

1 Distinguish between discrimination and prejudice,
2 Recognize the detrimental effects of stereotyping, and
3 Correct your own myths and barriers about women, race, age, and the handicapped.

—————— OPENING CASE ——————

It was late in the day, and Jim Nelson, personnel director for Barker Information Services, was about to interview the last applicant for his firm's management trainee program. Picking up Mary Ramirez's application, he noted that she was married and that she had written in the margin that she had two children aged seven and nine. She had held a variety of clerical and secretarial jobs before receiving her Bachelor of Science degree in business administration from state university three months ago. Jim buzzed his secretary to send Mary in, and moments later she walked through the door.

"It's nice to meet you, Mary. My name's Jim Nelson. Sit down; let's chat a while," he said.

"Thank you, Mr. Nelson," she replied. "I'm glad to be here."

"I see from your application that you're married and that you have two children. What took you so long to get around to college and get down to business, so to speak?"

"Well," Mary answered, "I worked to put my husband Ron through college first, and the children came along the way. We weren't able to get me through school until the kids were grown enough to be cared for. Then I became a full-time student, and I graduated with honors, as my application states. Ron's in Nationwide Department Stores' management development program; he's the assistant manager at the Ventura Shopping Mall store."

"I see," answered Jim. "Nationwide transfers their trainees around pretty often in that program. What would happen to your job here at Barker if your husband suddenly got transferred out of the area?"

"We don't expect that to happen," Mary assured him. "We've talked to Nationwide's training director, and the company will try to accommodate our plans to be a two-career family."

"Have you made reliable arrangements for afterschool care for your children, too?" Jim asked. "Blending family and career responsibilities is a big job in itself."

"Mr. Nelson," Mary responded, "those things don't influence my ability and qualifications for your management trainee position. I don't understand why you ask about them."

"Well, please understand things from our viewpoint," Jim replied. "We want full value for our time and training dollars. It would be a terrific loss to us if your husband got transferred out of the state or if a problem arose with child care arrangements and you had to quit. We have to consider the practicalities. I hope you'll forgive my concern."

"What else shall we talk about?" Mary asked, hoping to change the subject.

"Well," Jim responded, "there *is* the matter of family planning. I don't want to sound nosy, but are you intending to add any more little Ramirezes to the present team?"

"That's absolutely none of your business," Mary declared, shifting in her chair. "I think you'd better change to another line of questioning—one that's more on the issues of my ambition, qualifications, motivation, and desire to have this job."

"Sure, sure," Jim said pleasantly. "Let's lighten up a bit! Say, with a name like Ramirez, I'll bet you've got a file of great Mexican recipes. If you get this job, you'll have to give me one for chili!"

"Try the Betty Crocker Cookbook," Mary answered grimly. "My maiden name was O'Malley, and I grew up in Toledo, Ohio. My husband was born and raised in Tallahassee, Florida. Mister, are you for *real?*"

Prejudice and Discrimination

Are you prejudiced?

prejudice

Most of our views on other groups of people are based on what we were taught by parents or guardians. As we grew older, we were influenced by peers. The attitudes we hold because of such influences may be prejudices. **Prejudice** is any insupportable attitude toward others which prejudges them as inferior, unworthy, or unusual. Such attitudes are based on stereotypes. They often are the result of fear or ignorance and are generally negative.

discrimination

Prejudice leads to discrimination. To whatever extent we are prejudiced for or against, we will probably discriminate. **Discrimination** is the act of making distinctions among people or groups of people. Whereas prejudice is an attitude, discrimination is an action. Whereas prejudice is internal, discrimination is external. For example, prejudice for or against certain people at work causes discrimination for or against these people. However, prejudice and discrimination do not necessarily occur together. Prejudice can occur without discrimination and vice versa.

How are prejudice and discrimination related?

Discrimination exists because no person is completely free of prejudice. But discrimination has costs. Businesses lose money because of inefficient use of workers. Society loses money because of slums, crime, drug abuse, mental illness, and poor educational systems. In short, all of us lose money because of the personal costs of discrimination: discouragement, anger, hostility, withdrawal, or refusal to work. We can try to minimize prejudice by relying on facts, not stereotypes. And if we minimize tendencies toward prejudice, we will also minimize discrimination.

Discrimination and the Law

How does the law protect against discrimination?

The lack of prejudice and discrimination should contribute to improved human relationships not only in business but also in society. Unfortunately, however, federal legislation is often required to curb one group's actions against another group. One such law is the Civil Rights Act of 1964. Title

VII of this act prohibits discrimination in employment in regard to race, color, religion, sex, or national origin. In 1967 the Age Discrimination in Employment Act added age (40–65) as another discrimination factor prohibited in employment opportunities.

Title VII also established the Equal Employment Opportunity Commission (EEOC) to regulate business' employment practices. The work of the EEOC has resulted in Affirmative Action programs to achieve acceptable levels of minority representation in business. The EEOC has been able to add substance to equal opportunities in employment because the federal government will enforce compliance from unwilling employers. Since President Reagan took office there have been shifts in EEOC activities, however. His deregulation efforts are directed at EEOC as well as at other areas of government intervention in the private sector. The effect of these efforts is still to be seen.

Minorities

Who are these people being discriminated against? The most common answer is "the minorities." However, in one sense, we are all members of some minority. Some of us are tall; some are short. Some are large; others are small. We are white, black, brown, red, or yellow. We are young or old. We distinguish between men and women, rich and poor, white collar and blue collar, Protestant, Catholic, and Jew, those who are handicapped and those who are not. Thus, a **minority** is any small group of people regarded as different from a larger group of which it is a part.

Are you a member of a minority?

minority

A Woman's Place

Perhaps you've seen the printing on tee shirts, "A woman's place is in the house . . . and senate." This statement certainly does not reflect either history or tradition. The only women allowed to work outside the home, according to modern U.S. history and tradition, were those who were divorced, widowed, or who never married. And even then, they were supposed to be nurses, schoolteachers, secretaries, waitresses, or telephone operators. However, times are changing and so are women's roles in the home and in business. Economics as well as changing social preconceptions have driven many females into the work force. The two-income household has become commonplace. No longer is a woman's place just in the home. Yet many people still view women as the weaker sex, unable to perform outside familial boundaries. Many women hold the same self-defeating, inaccurate, or preconceived images of themselves as men do. What are your views about women in the workplace?

Where is a woman's place?

In this chapter, we have selected four groups who are currently receiving much notice because of minority discrimination—women, racial minorities, the aging, and the handicapped. We will begin with the group who makes up over 50 percent of our population. It hardly sounds like a minority, does it? Yet these people have been the object of much discrimination in business in recent years. We are, of course, talking about women.

Sexual Discrimination

How many women are in the labor force?

Over 50 percent of women over sixteen years of age are now in the labor market. This includes women of all ages, of every race and ethnic group, single, married, divorced, and widowed. However, 35 percent of these women hold clerical jobs; 45 percent are employed in service jobs, professional/technical jobs, or as machine operators. Another 14 percent are employed in sales or private households, as farm or nonfarm laborers, or as craft workers. Only 6 percent of the women in the total work force are managers or administrators. On the average, women earn only about six dollars for every ten dollars earned by men. Because of such figures many people feel America has been deprived of half its resources.

**sexual
discrimination**

Much of the **sexual discrimination,** or distinction between men and women, in business is rooted in parental motivation. For example, a boy with interest in science is usually encouraged to become a doctor or engineer. A girl with the same interest is often channeled into a feminine occupation such as nursing or teaching. In the past, female professional career aspirations have been met with disbelief, resistance, loss of popularity, and even ridicule. Similar prejudice can be found in academia. Female students are often not taken seriously by either male classmates or male professors. Women often must be exceptional to be taken seriously. Many women do not get academic promotions or top job appointments. The result of such prejudice in business, education, and medicine is a perpetuation of many myths about and barriers against women. The personal toll on women must be enormous.

Stereotypes, Myths, and Barriers

How do you feel about women working outside the home?

The business world contains several myths and stereotypes about women and barriers against their advancement. The myths have often been disproved by research, yet they still exist.

STEREOTYPES.   One team of researchers has found common stereotypes about men and women existing among groups differing in sex, age, marital status, and education. These stereotypes are shown in Exhibit 14.1. Notice that fewer positive traits are attributed to women than to men.

Such stereotypes influence judgments about women's employability and competency in managerial careers. For example, 300 male middle-line

---
———————————————— EXHIBIT 14.1 ————————————————

Stereotypic Characteristics of Males and Females

Males	Females
adventurous	appearance-oriented
aggressive	artistic
blunt	compassionate
competitive	dependent
confident	emotional, excitable
crude	gentle
decisive	humanitarian
dominant	neat
independent	needing security
initiatory	passive
intelligent	sensitive
logical	submissive
objective	sympathetic
rough	talkative
worldly	tender
---

managers with nine insurance companies in the United States examined 86 traits associated with managerial effectiveness. Sixty of these traits were judged more typical of males than females, including emotional stability, leadership, and desire for responsibility. Eight traits were judged more typical of females than males, including helpfulness, understanding, and awareness of others' feelings.[1]

MYTHS.   Such stereotypes of females in society have produced a number of commonly held attitudes about female workers that are either half-truths or complete myths. Some of the more prevalent myths are listed in Exhibit 14.2.

Using these myths and stereotypes, society discriminates against women. Shunning reality, business ignores the role of women in the labor force. In the face of overpowering statistics, we might wonder why these myths persist.

BARRIERS.   There seem to be three answers to why the female's road to equal status is blocked.[2] First, traditional male attitudes toward women at the professional and managerial levels continue to exist as shown in our list of myths. Second, there is a lack of clear career patterns for women who seek jobs leading to management positions. Career paths for women are usually ambiguous and unrewarded, or rewarded unequally. For every woman with a title, there are men with lesser titles and higher pay. Third, most males and females are skeptical about the performance of women managers. This attitude was also shown in our list of myths. Such male concerns reflect outmoded behavioral norms and role expectations.

What is blocking women's roads to success?

——————————————————————— EXHIBIT 14.2 ———————————————————————

- **American women just work for pin money.** Women do not work for pin money, even though some married women are somewhat less inclined to work if economics do not force them to.
- **Women would not work if economic reasons did not force them into the labor market.** Some women and some men would not work if economic reasons did not force them into the labor market.
- **Women are more concerned than men with the socioemotional aspects of their jobs.** Women are somewhat more concerned than men that their co-workers be friendly and helpful, but they attach more importance to competence than to niceness.
- **Women are more concerned than men with the hygienic aspects of their jobs (hours of work, pleasant conditions, etc.).** Women are somewhat more concerned than men with the hygienic aspects of work, but neither women nor men are particularly willing to trade challenging jobs for better working conditions.
- **Women are less concerned than men that their work allows them to be self-actualizing.** Women are not less interested in self-actualizing work than men.
- **Women are more content than men with intellectually undemanding jobs.** Women are not more satisfied with dreary jobs.
- **Women are less concerned than men with getting ahead on the job.** Women are not less interested than men in getting promotions.
- **Women do not make good managers because they are too emotional to make rational decisions.** Women can be trusted to make life and death decisions in a hospital or at home. They are equally competent to learn to make decisions regarding profit and loss in business.
- **Women are poor economic risks because they are often sick.** The facts prove differently. Studies show that age, occupation, and salary are more important influences on time lost from work.
- **Women only work until they get married or have children.** Statistics indicate over one-half of the women in the labor force and over one-third of the women in high-level positions are married. The child care issue is no myth, however. Having children does interrupt a woman's career path. There is a remarkable need in this society for well-run professional child care services.
- **Women are not committed to the world of work.** A study of turnover rates indicates 50 percent of male college recruits leave their first job within the first year, and 95 percent leave their first employer within ten years. The average age of women for turnovers, however, was in the early forties, and the average tenure in management jobs was twenty-four years.
- **Women do not have either the education or experience to be in managerial positions.** Statistics show the average female worker is as well educated as the male. However, women do meet obstacles in the working world in trying to obtain experience in and knowledge about management skills.
- **Women lack the proper motivation to achieve.** Young girls seem to maintain a consistent and fairly strong level of academic motivation. However, during early adulthood they do seem to become worried that achievement and success will destroy femininity.[3]

Again, many of these concerns are rooted in the way parents rear their girls and boys. Sex typing research suggests that even very young males are taught to reinforce traditional sex roles—perhaps because of the status and power it gives them. Women are typically taught not to think of themselves as managers. Thus, one of their handicaps is a tendency for passivity toward career planning. Women often expect to fail and then behave in ways that make failure almost inevitable. However, it must be determined whether this is because few managers expect them to perform as well as male counterparts or whether females are less interested in advancing toward higher positions. Whatever the cause, parental teaching has had its impact on both male and female attitudes toward sex typing.

Obstacles to Managerial Careers for Women

Certainly there are many barriers in the female path to equal status. In many companies we have probably moved only from the relative absence of women to tokenism. **Tokenism** refers to an individual female carrying the burden of reforming the organization. Therefore, we need to continue our examination of sex stereotypes as they affect management decisions.

tokenism

SEX STEREOTYPES AND MANAGERIAL DECISIONS.   Some experiments involving business students, bank employees, and 1500 selected subscribers to *Harvard Business Review* who were in management positions reveal different managerial evaluations and decisions depending on the employee's sex. For example:

How do male managers discriminate against women?

- *Selection, promotion, and development opportunities.* In selection, promotion, and career development decisions, managers are biased in favor of males.
- *Disciplinary actions.* If personal conduct threatens an employee's job, managers make greater efforts to retain a valuable male employee than the equally qualified female.
- *Performance appraisal.* Managers expect male employees to give top priority to their jobs when career demands and family obligations conflict. They expect female employees to sacrifice their careers to family responsibilities.[4]

These three areas of managerial decision making suggest a widespread pattern of sex discrimination in American businesses. Managers, therefore, have three major challenges.[5] First, to overcome the negative effects of sex stereotypes, managers need to become aware of the pervasive influence of stereotypes on perceptions, expectations, and actions. Second, managers need to take corrective action based on this awareness. Third, managers need to work toward the gradual elimination of stereotypes themselves.

What are some specific barriers to female careers in business?

MANAGERIAL CAREERS AND WOMEN.   The effect of obstacles and barriers to female career paths needs to be considered in light of women's self-concepts, aspirations, and career choices. Analysis of the barriers to managerial careers for women must deal with socialization patterns preparing women for sex-typed roles, unresolved home-career conflicts, a lack of role models, and minimal psychological support from superiors.

Sex Role Socialization.   The ideal American woman is characterized by the role of wife and mother. She possesses physical attractiveness, warmth, charm, sensitivity, and supportiveness. She is compliant, deferent, and socially and economically dependent on her husband. There are few choices because women are conditioned through early childhood experiences to be less exploratory and aggressive than males. They receive only minimal encouragement to become active, independent, and assertive. They are subjected to fewer achievement demands and lower expectations than males. These sex roles are reinforced in school. For example, boys typically are segregated for sports, whereas girls are directed toward the doll corner to practice house chores. Textbooks reinforce these roles by depicting women as mothers who stay home or as nurses, librarians, or clerks. Men are always heroes. In fact, in one survey of school books there were 147 career possibilities shown for boys, compared with 26 career opportunities for girls.[6]

Home-Career Conflicts.   Fulfilling such feminine roles has resulted in a costly commitment in terms of female self-concepts and career aspirations. Time conflicts and overloads of coping with job and family demands have created stress. Some women have responded to potential role conflicts and overloads by planning, scheduling, and organizing better, along with a dedication to work harder at each role. Others have found the strain too great and have experienced dissatisfaction with both roles. Still others have sought out part-time work, flexible hours, and minimum demands (e.g., no overtime, no work to take home, etc.) beyond the work day in order to balance the home and the career.

A survey conducted by Heidrick and Struggles, a leading management consulting firm, of more than 1000 large companies found that women officers increased 49 percent between 1977 and 1979. Nearly half the women involved earned more than $40,000 per year.[7]

For married career women, the spouse's support is a crucial determinant of success. If husbands are not willing to assume a larger share of the housework, meal preparation, and child-care responsibilities, they place an obstacle in the path of their wives who are seeking managerial and professional careers.

Absence of Role Models.   Observing current female managers is an excellent learning opportunity for aspiring female managers. However, there is a virtual absence of such role models. New female managers must learn by trial and error. They do not have the advantages of learning successful interpersonal styles firsthand as males do. Moreover, they did not learn basic skills of assertion or aggression in their growing up. This is one of the reasons there are now major magazines written to a market segment of women executives and entrepreneurs (e.g., *New Woman, Savvy, Ms., Working Woman,* etc.). These are rich with role models and motivational success stories.

Minimal Support from Supervisors.   Many male executives doubt that women have either the technical or interpersonal skills necessary to manage others. Therefore, they may assign female workers to more routine or demanding tasks, closely monitor a female manager's behavior, or specify in detail the procedures and strategies for handling a problem. Men's expectations of women's failure cause these men to withhold support and encouragement important to women's success on the job.

Some companies have developed admirable career-counseling departments to help all employees, especially women, to focus on long-range career goals and on the means by which to reach them. Such efforts help to eliminate the problems we have discussed. For example, AT&T's employee assessment program, conceived in 1958, was expanded to include women in the early 1970s as part of the firm's affirmative action plan. The program identified almost 2000 college-educated female workers who were considered solid candidates for midmanagement jobs. More than 90 percent of them elected to participate in developmental activities that would lead to middle management positions.[8]

———————————————— Legal Issues ————————————————

Several legal aspects of the employment of women are important to managers.

What are the legal issues?

FEDERAL LEGISLATION.   Four major pieces of federal legislation prohibiting sex discrimination in employment practices need to be examined.

1. *The Equal Pay Act of 1963.* An amendment to the 1938 Fair Labor Standards Act, the Equal Pay Act prohibits employers from discriminating on the basis of sex in the payment of wages for equal or substantially equal work. In June 1972 the equal pay provisions were extended to include executive, administrative, and professional workers not previously covered in the Equal Pay Act.

2. *Title VII of the Civil Rights Act of 1964.* Title VII (mentioned on page 300) makes it unlawful for employers to discriminate on the basis of sex, race, color, religion, or national origin. All terms, conditions, and privileges of employment are covered by this act. This act pertains to most private employers, public and private employment agencies and educational institutions, state and local governments, and labor unions.

3. *Executive Order 11246 of 1965 as amended by Executive Order 11375 of 1967.* Under these executive rulings federal contractors, subcontractors,

and employers involved in federally assisted construction projects who hold contracts of $50,000 or more and have fifty or more employees are prohibited from discrimination based on sex. Noncompliance could result in cancellation of existing contracts and disqualification from future contracts. Federal employment is placed under the same prohibitions by Executive Order 11478 of 1969.

4. *Revised Order 4.* The executive orders also call for the establishment of affirmative action programs to eliminate present and future sex discrimination. Revised Order 4 was issued in 1972 to clarify the requirements for affirmative action in the organizations covered by Executive Orders 11246 and 11375. Employers must develop written proposals covering the recruitment, selection, career development, and promotion of women. Timetables must be projected to remedy deficiencies in current practices, and detailed evaluation data must be collected to assess the effectiveness of the program. Public dissemination of affirmative action policies is now required by law.[9]

Are there questions interviewers should not ask?

LAWFUL EMPLOYMENT INTERVIEWS.   In addition, the EEOC considers the following questions in an employment interview to be unlawful, unless the interviewer is able to explain satisfactorily that these questions are not discriminatory: arrest and conviction records, garnishment (debt-related) records, credit references, marital status, child care problems, contraceptive problems, plans to have children, unwed motherhood, age, height, and weight. There are also areas in which certain questions could be considered discriminatory: education, English-language requirements, physical requirements, experience requirements, availability for weekend work, friends or relatives working for the company, and appearance. (Note: These are pre-employment restrictions. An employer may obtain some of this information after hiring.)

Racial Discrimination

Although it is now national policy to eliminate discrimination in employment on the basis of race, color, creed, sex, age, and physical handicaps, affirmative action programs have not eliminated prejudice. The area in which we first became aware of discrimination was race relationships. Racial discrimination is the act of making distinctions among people based on race or color. Discrimination awareness began with blacks, but Mexican Americans, Puerto Ricans, and people who speak English poorly also suffer from discrimination. Native Americans are probably the most disadvantaged group of all; they average almost 40 percent unemployment. Racial discrimination is still very much a problem.

---------------------------------- The Nature of the Problem ----------------------------------

Nonwhite unemployment is about twice that of whites. Nonwhites are also
more likely to work in low-status, low-paying jobs. That is, they typically
work as operatives, laborers, and private household workers. Such inequality
can waste much peoplepower. But why does this unemployment inequality
exist? There are at least six contributing factors:

*Why does racial
discrimination still
exist?*

1. *Outright discrimination.* America has a long history of racial bias,
even among those who have believed that they act in a socially responsible
way.

2. *Nonperception of discrimination.* Unconsciously many business people
feel certain jobs are not suited for nonwhites. Nonwhites are not viewed as
skilled tradespeople, salespeople, or executives. These stereotypes have persisted
even among people who consider themselves objective in their selection
policies.

3. *Poor communications.* There is often a conflict between what some
people say and what they do regarding nondiscriminatory policies. Action
suggests these policies are not to be taken seriously.

4. *Others' objections.* Some managers justify discriminatory policies on
the basis of their employees' and customers' prejudices.

5. *Hiring practices.* Some companies hire by word of mouth or prefer
people recommended by their friends. Some use a culturally biased pre-
employment test. Others have unnecessarily rigid hiring standards, such as
high school graduation for unskilled jobs.

6. *Technological change and plant location.* Technological change has
eliminated many hard, dirty jobs traditionally open to nonwhites. As jobs
became more pleasant, whites took over many of these jobs. Nonwhites
were offered declining or unstable employment opportunities.[10]

Joblessness has become a major issue among the nonwhite population,
especially among the three major nonwhite minority groups.

---------------------------------- Minorities in the World of Work ----------------------------------

Joblessness and poverty are not caused solely by racial discrimination. But
discrimination does contribute to nonwhites' limited access to the job market.
Three groups experiencing great difficulty in employment, income, and education are native Americans, the Spanish-speaking Americans, and blacks.[11]

*Who are some of the
racial minorities in
the work force?*

NATIVE AMERICANS.   The 1970 census estimated that about 795,000
native Americans live in the United States. Unemployment on reservations
averages about 40 percent in the spring and summer to 90 percent in the
winter. According to the Bureau of Indian Affairs, the average annual income

for residents of a reservation is about $1,500. Because of this potential poverty situation, native Americans are subject to serious illness and handicaps, deficient education, and a lack of marketable skills.

Spanish-Speaking Americans.   There are about 10 million Spanish-speaking Americans in the United States. This group includes Chicanos, Puerto Ricans, Cubans, and those who trace their ancestry to Central or South America. They work at low-paying jobs for the most part and have an above-average level of unemployment. Their average income is about $3,000 below that of whites.

Blacks.   There are about 23 million blacks in the United States. This figure represents 92 percent of the nonwhite population. Over 80 percent live in poverty areas. Blacks have faced shrinking employment opportunities as whites and industry have moved to the suburbs. Their average income is about $4,000 below that of whites.

A Positive Step.   All three groups are subject to discrimination. They are underemployed and disadvantaged. Although the Civil Rights Act of 1964 has gradually diminished overt forms of discrimination, substitute rules and informal customs still permit racist employment patterns to exist.

J. Walter Thompson, a leading advertising agency, sensed a need to increase minority high school students' awareness of advertising as a potential career field. The result was MAAP (Minority Advertising Awareness Program), which included a film, homework projects, and group activities that caused this target group to consider entering the advertising profession. The MAAP project opened up horizons that were previously obscured.[12]

RCA Corporation attempts to interest minority high school students in engineering careers through fifteen half-day seminars held at more than fifty high schools each year.[13]

R J Reynolds Industries has an extensive minority affairs program which has raised the percentage of minorities in the company in all job categories to 20.5 percent, well above the national average. In addition to numerous other efforts, the company makes annual contributions to the United Negro College Fund and the National Scholastic Achievement Program for scholarships for black students. It also has financed 40 four-year journalism scholarships for black students through the National Newspaper Publishers Association.

―――――――――――――― The Older Worker ――――――――――――――

Who are the older workers?

A third major area of discrimination deals with the process of aging. Age discrimination is a technique of distinguishing among people based on their age. In 1971 the National Advisory Committee for the White House Conference on Aging defined older worker as anyone aged forty and over.[14] The employment market favors workers between the ages of twenty-five and forty. Those who are under twenty-five are discriminated against, as well as those over forty. Teenagers and young adults are discriminated against because of a lack of experience. Older workers are discriminated against because they are viewed as less creative, flexible, and productive. In either case, discrimination robs the job market.

Reasons for Age Discrimination

A worker who is over forty years of age will have difficulty securing satisfying work for several reasons. Older workers are seen as costing more in fringe benefits, having fewer years left in which to work, being physically too weak to perform certain jobs, and having higher rates of absenteeism. Since these attitudes are largely erroneous, many companies are doing a disservice not only to the older worker but also to business and society by discriminating against the older worker.

Why does age discrimination exist?

Aging and the Law

The Age Discrimination in Employment Act of 1967 is designed to protect workers between the ages of forty and sixty-five. Thanks to this law, attitudes toward aging are changing. The basic provisions of this act are:

Are there any laws protecting older workers?

1 Employers of twenty-five or more people involved in interstate commerce may not refuse to hire qualified workers age forty to sixty-five.
2 Employers may not fire employees age forty to sixty-five because of age alone, or discriminate against them in terms of salary, seniority, or other job conditions.
3 Employment agencies may not refuse workers age forty to sixty-five to prospective employers or classify them on the basis of age.
4 Labor unions may not exclude those age forty to sixty-five from membership or refuse to refer them to employers simply because of their age.
5 Help wanted ads may not include age specifications.

Such legislation is apparently needed since the U.S. Department of Labor reports one firm out of every three that it investigates violates the law. Such discrimination overlooks some obvious advantages of hiring older workers.

Advantages of Hiring Older Workers

The many stereotypes about older workers have caused employers, employment agencies, and unions to discriminate against them. However, hiring the older worker is good business. Firing older workers in favor of hiring younger

Does anyone benefit from having hired older workers?

ones is not. For example, firms like United California Bank, Atlantic-Richfield Company, Twentieth Century-Fox, and several other large California employers have supported external programs operated by the United Way. These provide them with a pool of qualified, enthusiastic, and experienced elderly persons who want to pursue a second career after their initial retirement.

Travelers Insurance Company is considered a pioneer in utilizing senior citizen workers through its Retiree Job Bank.[15] Realizing that many Travelers retirees were bored and frustrated with retirement, management conceived plans to rehire them in temporary part- or full-time jobs, part-time permanent jobs, and several other work options that would get them back into the work force.

Travelers retirees can work almost twenty hours per week and still collect their full company pension. Participants feel valuable, useful, and appreciated again after discovering that retirement just wasn't for them, after all. Says one Travelers manager, "There's great potential in good retired people who want to work, and the company benefits from workers who have company background and knowledge."

The Handicapped and Disabled

handicap

Are the handicapped also discriminated against?

Our fourth major area of discrimination concerns individuals with **handicaps**— physical or mental impairment. Estimates range from 10 to 20 million people in the United States who are handicapped in some way. Accurate statistics are scarce. Tradition and prejudice about those who are disabled in some way have led to discrimination against them as poor employment risks. Yet people classified as disabled are often handicapped more by others' attitudes toward them than by the handicap itself. In reality, for many who are disabled, their handicaps may be helpful to certain jobs. For example, those who are mentally handicapped may perform much better in routine jobs than those who are not handicapped. The deaf or hard of hearing can work more efficiently in high noise areas than those whose hearing is not impaired.

Misconceptions About the Handicapped

There are still many misunderstandings about the handicapped. Perhaps you have seen people talk very loudly to someone who is blind or try to lead someone who is deaf. Some less-noticed handicaps are lisping, arthritis, and color blindness. Most people feel very uncomfortable around someone with a handicap, without ever thinking all of us are handicapped in some way. Ours just may not be noticeable to the vast majority.

Why do people mistreat the handicapped?

Other people often don't know how to relate to or act around the handicapped person. Employers have the same problem and offer all kinds of excuses for not hiring the handicapped. Some common attitudes about the handicapped are listed in Exhibit 14.3:

——————————————— EXHIBIT 14.3 ———————————————

- **They are dangerous to have around.** It simply is not true that handicapped people are dangerous to others. Studies show people with handicaps are not unsympathetic to the needs of other people. Sometimes mentally handicapped people have feelings of depression, but they are no more prone to depression or aggression than the normal population. Psychologists say most people get depressed.

- **They are offensive to look at.** Probably the greatest difficulty handicapped people have is that they make others feel uncomfortable when they are around. The usual ploy is to act as if the handicap itself does not exist or deny there is a problem. This is not useful to either party, because it distorts their relationship. If someone is missing a limb or has a crippled or atrophied limb, it does no good to act as if nothing is wrong. One doesn't have to laugh and shout about it, but one shouldn't ignore it either.

- **They are accident-prone.** Many people feel the handicapped are accident-prone. The ungainly motions of some of the handicapped trigger a fear that perhaps they are not in control of what they are doing. Studies of accident proneness seem to indicate that although it is a real phenomenon, it has little or nothing to do with physical disability.

- **They are costly.** It is sometimes argued that handicapped people are expensive to maintain on their jobs, that they need special tools and equipment with which to work, and that insurance rates and other costs will go up when a disabled or handicapped person is hired. Furthermore, it is argued that because they are accident-prone (which we have seen is not true) they will cause extra expense. For the most part, these expenses are one-time-only expenses, such as widening the doors to the washroom. It is definitely not true that handicapped people cause an increase in outgoing costs, such as insurance rates or worker's compensation insurance premium costs. Such allegations are usually made by people who don't understand or are afraid of handicapped people.

- **They are unreliable.** It is sometimes argued that handicapped or disabled employees are unreliable, that they cannot be counted on to come to work regularly or to do a full day's work when they are there. However, studies show handicapped people tend to be the most reliable workers. This may be because they have more appreciation for the fact that they have a job.

- **They make us feel sorry for ourselves.** Psychologists claim that when we see people who have physical disabilities, we feel sorry for them. But, they say, we feel sorry for them not because we are unhappy they have disabilities but because we think how we might be if we had their condition. In short, we are feeling sorry for ourselves. It is because of this twisted logic that most people are uncomfortable around handicapped or disabled people. However, this does not justify avoiding handicapped people. We should rather try to overcome this feeling.[16]

The conclusion is that hiring the handicapped is good business. The disabled do not create as difficult problems at work as other workers create. Their greatest handicap is overcoming the attitudes that other people have about them. Perhaps we all need to realize that we all have only temporarily able bodies.

──────────── Hiring the Handicapped Is Good Business ────────────

What are some benefits of hiring handicapped workers?

Hiring the handicapped can enhance human relationships because it gives this group of people an opportunity to be mainstreamed into the American economy. It gives them the opportunity to contribute (as taxpayers) and not receive (as welfare recipients). It gives them a sense of accomplishment and self-respect. In each instance, life, satisfaction, and human relations become more satisfying.

Control Data Corporation's HOMEWORK program, which was started in the late 1970s, enables physically handicapped employees to work full-time at home using computer terminals. For example, one participant is a tutor for the company's computer schools and answers questions from students in four nearby states from her home-based terminal. HOMEWORK also employs homebound Control Data workers to write computer programs and to do other work that can be done as efficiently and effectively at home as at a traditional work location.

─────────────────────── CONCLUSION ───────────────────────

Are there any guidelines for changing the way business treats these discriminated-against groups?

Society is changing. No doubt some of the preceding problems will disappear during the 1980s. Naturally, many minority members do not feel things are changing fast enough. Therefore, guidelines for change are needed. How can the world of work come to view equal opportunity as smart business and use an almost untapped resource of talent and skills? Six recommendations can facilitate the assimilation of minorities with officials, managers, and professionals.[17] First, the commitment to and mechanics of providing equal opportunity for all must be effectively communicated on a continuing basis. Because equal opportunity programs involve some departure from business and cultural traditions, as well as a supposed threat to certain employee groups, top management should announce and explain the following:

- any new or revised corporate philosophy or policies or programs concerning equality of opportunity;
- the names of the staff responsible for program implementation, and their functions, enforcement powers, and reporting relationships; and
- the short- and long-range effects these policies and programs have on *all* employees.

After the initial communication, channels should be kept open to:

- present the EEO staff with up-to-date information on problems and progress, employee or management complaints, and equal opportunity as it relates to other corporate programs (e.g., salary administration, organization design, performance appraisal);
- provide line management with the mechanics to foresee and forestall

problems, facilitate progress and still maintain profitability, and gauge employee reaction to equal opportunity policies and programs: and

- supply employees with information on how equal opportunity affects them, and what routes have been opened to them as a result of corporate commitment to equal opportunity (e.g., development programs, career paths).

Internal channels should also be provided for registering alleged discriminatory practices before they erupt into litigations or conciliations. These channels should exist throughout management. When they do not, alternatives can be utilized, such as a task force to check out complaints in branch locations.

Second, those responsible for equal opportunity programs must have sufficient authority to enforce company policy and to give credibility to corporate commitment. One of the best ways to do this is to make EEO a responsibility of a well-respected senior executive who has leverage in enforcing compliance, even with managers on the highest levels.

Third, organizations should contend immediately with any anxieties arising from the initiation of new programs or policies related to equal opportunity. If ignored, anxieties can hamper a program's implementation and lead to serious morale problems. A first step in handling, or in some cases preventing, widespread anxiety is to open up communication channels to pinpoint problem areas. Thoughtfully prepared diagnostic attitude surveys have been used successfully in this respect. Corporate-wide surveys not only help management define the problems but also reinforce company commitment to all its employees.

Fourth, efforts should be made to identify all promotable employees and to provide them with necessary counseling and development opportunities. By seeking out high-potential employees through an audit, skills inventory, or other formal method, an organization can better use its present human resources. Once a high-potential individual is identified, the employee should be counseled about realistic career aspirations and given development opportunities.

The importance of early, effective career counseling should not be overlooked, especially for women. If a woman and her employer can honestly evaluate her potential in light of her career commitment, objectives, and abilities, the employer can direct that woman toward the path that will best serve both their interests.

Although there has been some talk about special development programs aimed specifically at women, many employers note that such programs presuppose inferiorities in women. Unless special development programs are open to all who need added exposure to a discipline, these programs may take on negative connotations and promote the myth that some groups are innately less capable of functioning in the business environment than others.

Fifth, approaches should be developed to attract qualified females to the business community. To ensure a continuing supply of female officials, managers, and professionals, business organizations must take special steps to attract qualified women away from traditionally female occupations such as teaching. Efforts that can be incorporated into public, community, and educational relations programs include presenting female career-role models in advertisements, recruiting, or general information brochures; providing scholarships for individuals who would like to prepare for careers that would be of value to the business community; and prompting educational institutions to encourage women to enter traditionally male academic disciplines.

Sixth, practice job enrichment as one way to bury the dead-end job. An employer should not underuse the talent of any individual with short-term aspirations. The company may not achieve the maximum return on its investment if only minimal achievement is expected. Also, the employee may eventually decide to pursue a long-term career but may then be too far behind peers who chose earlier to make a long-term commitment.

In other words, those entry- and lower-level jobs in which female professionals are often grouped should be structured so they can lead to responsible positions. The best way to ensure this, as well as to achieve the most return for the organization's investment, is to maximize the challenge in every job.

KEY TERMS

Prejudice: any insupportable attitude toward others that prejudges them as inferior, unworthy, or unusual.

Discrimination: the act of making distinctions among people or groups of people.

Minority: a small group of people regarded as different from a larger group of which it is a part.

Sexual Discrimination: making distinctions between men and women.

Tokenism: the burden an individual female carries in trying to reform an organization's views toward hiring women.

Racial Discrimination: making distinctions among people based on their race or color.

Age Discrimination: making distinctions among workers based on their age.

Handicap: physical or mental impairment.

QUESTIONS

1 Reread the opening case.
   a. Which of Nelson's questions could be challenged on the basis of sex and ethnic prejudice?

    b. What information about Ms. Ramirez should he have ignored?

    c. How might formal training be valuable in helping managers like Nelson deal with unintentional prejudice and discrimination?

    d. If you were Mary Ramirez, what would you do after you left Nelson's office?

2 What is the difference between prejudice and discrimination? Provide at least two examples of positive and negative prejudice and the discrimination that could result from each.

3 Describe how each of the following can create negative prejudice in employment interviews:

    a. clothing (including shoes)—color, style, and general condition;

    b. hair style;

    c. glasses;

    d. general grooming;

    e. posture and body language; and

    f. speech patterns, including ethnic characteristics and accents remaining from one's native language.

How can you apply your answers to future job-hunting and interviewing activities?

4 "Prejudice, unlike discrimination, is impossible to eliminate." Do you agree with this position? Why or why not?

5 "I won't hire people of that sort, because they're always late to work and lazy after they arrive." Which portion of that remark reflects prejudice, and which indicates discrimination?

6 Discuss at least three costs of discrimination. How can they be affected by the personal motto, "The buck stops here"?

7 Differentiate between stereotypes and myths that apply to hiring women. Think of at least one woman (friend, family member, or other) who does not fit the female stereotype and to whom none of the myths apply. What can you learn from using that person as a mental model in your future dealings with women as job applicants and subordinates?

8 List three barriers to equal status for women. How were they influenced by child-rearing practices and parents' treatment of male versus female children?

9 Briefly summarize each of the following barriers to managerial careers for women:

    a. sex role socialization,

    b. home-career conflicts,

    c. absence of role models, and

    d. minimal support from supervisors.

10 Describe the key features of the following federal laws that address sex discrimination:

    a. Equal Pay Act of 1963,

    b. Title VII of the Civil Rights Act of 1964,

    c. Executive Order 11246 (1965) as amended by Executive Order 11375 (1967), and

    d. Revised Order 4.

11 List subjects that job applicants may not be asked about legally in an employment interview unless the employer can prove the questions are not discriminatory. Depending on the circumstances or the nature of the job, what kinds of questions might *not* be considered discriminatory?

12 Give at least four reasons for racial inequality in employment.

13   Consider the three minority groups discussed in this chapter. Which do you think deserves the most assistance, and why?

14   Discuss the prejudicial attitudes that older workers may encounter. What specific provisions of the 1967 Age Discrimination in Employment Act attempt to combat these attitudes?

15   Present at least a five-point argument in favor of hiring older workers. Do you feel stereotypes of the elderly are found more in the United States than in other countries? Why or why not?

16   Summarize the myths that apply to handicapped employees. How would you justify a hire-the-handicapped program?

CASES

Case 14.1

Sam McKee, a data processing department manager, has become involved with his company's program to hire the handicapped. His contact with handicapped persons has been limited until now, and he's uncertain how to deal with this new experience. During lunch today he talked about a recent development with Lloyd Sanders, a friend from another department.

"I just have trouble knowing what's right and what's not, Lloyd," Sam complained. "Take today, for example. I interviewed a guy for a keypunch operator's job, and I don't know what to decide. He's a Viet Nam veteran, confined to a wheelchair. He graduated from a top-notch keypunch operator's school and his references check out fine. Everything's great that way. But he'll have to work on the tenth floor, and I wonder what would happen if there were a fire. You're always supposed to use the stairs because the elevators go out along with the electrical system. He'd be trapped.

"Also, he'd have a battle just getting from the parking lot to the building in the morning. You take your life in your hands even if you *run* across that street. I think too about several Viet Nam veterans in the department. I wonder if his presence would bring back depressing wartime memories for them and cause morale problems.

"Reliability might be an issue as well. I need people who get to work on time and aren't sick more than a couple of days a year. I really want to help this guy; his attitude seems exceptional. But how can I be sure he'll work out once I've said, 'You're hired'?"

Case Questions

1   Using what you've learned in this chapter, criticize Sam McKee's impressions toward handicapped persons.

2   What argument would you give Sam for employing handicapped persons?

3   Using the information presented in this case, tell whether you would hire the applicant. Why or why not?

Case 14.2

Loren Yates, a former Army captain, welcomed civilian life and looked forward to building a second career after he retired from the service. He entered college immediately and earned his Bachelor of Science degree in marketing in three years by attending classes full time all year. His ambition has been dampened, however, by some interviews with hiring officials.

"I'm really getting depressed," he confided to Chuck Parton during lunch at the officers' club. "You wouldn't believe what I'm running into during job interviews. Personnel people have said stuff like:

- 'Some of our employees can't follow directions worth a darn! We need a military officer to restore some order around here!'
- 'We're skeptical that retired military people can deal diplomatically with the public.'
- 'You've had a wealth of experience in the military. What makes you want to start at the bottom of the ladder and work your way up again?'
- 'How would you feel having a boss who was half your age? It happens here.'
- 'Would you really be as dedicated and conscientious as someone without a government pension check coming in every month?'

and worst of all,

- 'Why don't you take it easy? You've earned it!'

"Darn it, I can't make these people understand that I *want* a second career. I worked hard for it, and I'd be *glad* to start at the bottom and work my way up on my own merits. Everywhere I've interviewed during the last three weeks they've looked at my age and my military status and seemed to write me off. I have at least twenty-five years of talent and performance to offer some employer! What's the matter with people? Can't they take me at face value?"

1 If you were Loren Yates, what would you emphasize during future employment interviews?
2 List some of the qualities he has that probably wouldn't be found in unseasoned college graduates.
3 What sources might he contact to get a serious employment interview?

Case Questions

NOTES

1. V. E. Schein, "The Relationship between Sex Role Stereotypes and Requisite Management Characteristics," *Journal of Applied Psychology* (1973): 95–100.
2. Charles D. Orth III and Frederick Jacobs, "Women in Management: Pattern for Change," *Harvard Business Review* (July–August 1971): 140–142.
3. The first seven myths are from J. Crowley, et al., "Seven Deadly Half-truths about Women," *Psychology Today* (March 1973): 94–96. The next six myths are from George E. Bile and Holly A. Pryatel, "Myths, Management and Women," *Personnel Journal* (October 1978): 572–576.
4. Benson Rosen and Thomas H. Jerdee, "Sex Stereotyping in the Executive Suite," *Harvard Business Review* (March–April 1974): 45–58.
5. Benson Rosen and Thomas H. Jerdee, *Becoming Aware* (Chicago: Science Research, 1976), p. 35.
6. "Sexist Tests," *Time,* 5 November 1973, p. 87.
7. *The Wall Street Journal,* 4 December 1979, p. 1.

8. David Robison, "AT&T Women Employees Making Faster Strides into Middle Management," *World of Work Report* (January 1978): 1.

9. Rosen and Jerdee, *Becoming Aware,* pp. 81–82.

10. Leonard R. Sayles and George Strauss, *Managing Human Resources* (Englewood Cliffs, N.J.: Prentice-Hall, 1977), pp. 222–223.

11. Raymond E. Glos et al., *Business—Its Nature and Environment,* 8th ed. (Cincinnati, Ohio: South-Western Publishing, 1976), pp. 261–262.

12. Robert L. Lattimer, "Developing Career Awareness Among Minority Youths: A Case Example," *Personnel Journal* (January 1981): 17.

13. "The Second Careers Program: A Case Study," *Personnel Journal* (March 1981): 180.

14. *The Wall Street Journal,* 14 April 1981, p. 1.

15. Michael Thoryn, "Rehiring the Retired," *Nation's Business* (October 1981): 71.

16. Condensed from Lawrence L. Steinmetz, *Human Relations—People and Work* (New York: Harper and Row, 1979), pp. 289–292.

17. D. F. Fretz and Joanne Hayman, "Progress for Women—Men Are Still More Equal," *Harvard Business Review* (September–October 1973): 141–142.

—————————————— SUGGESTED READINGS ——————————————

"Conducting the Lawful Employment Interview." New York: Executive Enterprises, 1974.

Henning, Margaret, and Jardim, Anne. *The Managerial Woman.* New York: Anchor Press/Doubleday, 1977.

Kanter, Rosabeth Moss. *Men and Women of the Corporation.* New York: Basic Books, 1977.

Levin, Jack, and Levin, William C. *Ageism: Prejudice and Discrimination Against the Elderly.* Belmont, Calif.: Wadsworth, 1980.

15

Performance Objectives and Appraisals

When you complete your study of this chapter, you should be able to:

1 Set objectives, develop action plans, implement MBO, and monitor performance,

2 Recognize the problems in performance appraisal and reward, and

3 Design an MBO and a performance appraisal system.

"It seems to me there should be a better way to evaluate performance," Pat Quigley complained to her husband Paul. "My boss, Ken Wilder, gave me my performance evaluation this morning:

- He rated me above average on communication because of my clear speech patterns and telephone voice.
- He rated me above average on motivation because of my enthusiastic personality.
- I got acceptable ratings on delegation because I never seemed to be overburdened with work when he asked me to attend emergency meetings and on subordinates' development because I wrote a memo urging them to use the company's tuition reimbursement plan for college courses.
- He rated me 'needs to improve' on job knowledge; it didn't seem to matter that I've only had this job six months.
- According to him, my planning, problem solving, and decision abilities are all acceptable, my time management is above average, as is my flexibility and ability to set objectives.

"The trouble is, I didn't know what he wanted to see me about until I walked into his office. I could have told him several things that probably would have raised my rating higher on a couple of areas if I'd had some warning about the conference.

"I hear so much about 'participative management' and giving workers a voice in their own jobs. Most of us who are honest, rational people could do a good job of deciding what we'd like to accomplish and of judging how well we did if upper management would just give us a chance!"

"No doubt about it," Paul agreed. "But an awful lot of companies are using the same traditional performance assessment system that your place is. There *are* newer ways that get the worker involved in the action, like you suggest. You've probably heard about MBO—management by objectives—right?" She nodded. "That's one of the most popular methods, and it provides for worker input and involvement. But it takes considerable time, commitment, and preparation to implement MBO," Paul said. "People have to understand and believe in its benefits and *want* to make it work. That can be a big order.

"Truly large companies like yours often find the present system easier to live with. Sometimes managers believe it's better to stick with a system with imperfections that are known than to try something new. Who wants to use their organization as a laboratory? If a new system backfires, you've got several thousand confused people at lower levels, and repealing a system that didn't work out makes upper management look indecisive and inept."

If You Don't Know Where You're Going, Who Knows Where You'll End Up?

For management by objectives (MBO) or any other management technique to work, there must be a detailed plan for beginning. People must be able to see where they are headed. They need clear direction. If they don't know where they're going, they are apt to end up someplace other than where they should.

Does business know where it is going?

Many managers, however, fail to provide insight for their workers about where the company is headed and what is going on. I am constantly amazed when I ask managers about their plans for the next five years. Frequently they respond like this: "Five years from now? I really don't know. I'm so busy fighting fires I haven't got time to think that far down the road." Maybe if they thought a little further down the road they wouldn't have to worry so much about crisis management.

Managing by objectives is one device—perhaps the most pervasive management idea in the last twenty-five years—to help managers manage the future. And it has the potential for getting you from where you are to where you want to be. That's what this chapter is about.

Management by Objectives

Management by objectives is a goal-oriented management philosophy and attitude that emphasizes results. It is a process wherein the manager and employee jointly define departmental goals, identify the areas of responsibility in terms of expected results, and use these measures as guides for operation.

management by objectives

As an integral part of the managerial process, MBO attempts to:

What does MBO try to accomplish?

- measure and judge performance,
- relate individual performance to organizational goals,
- clarify both the job to be done and the expectations of accomplishment,
- foster the competence and growth of the subordinate,
- enhance communications between supervisor and subordinate,
- serve as a basis for judgments about salary and promotion,
- stimulate the subordinate's motivation, and
- serve as a device for organizational control and integration.[1]

Thus, MBO can be a constructive device for productive management, if used properly.

MBO was first introduced by Peter Drucker about twenty-five years ago in a discussion of the management of managers. Today it is a widely recognized management technique. A *Conference Board* study involving 293 companies disclosed that more than half of them used MBO. This approach to performance appraisal received "the greatest vote of confidence expressed for any of the approaches."[2] MBO programs have been used in education, health care, state and local government, federal agencies, and public agencies.

Some employers prefer performance appraisal systems such as MBO because their objectivity minimizes fired employees' claims that supervisors judged them subjectively. This feature keeps potential lawsuits at a minimum. Thus, MBO is a management process that involves clear goal statements, action plans to achieve these goals, implementation, and monitoring of progress.

Setting Objectives

How does setting objectives help managers?

Setting objectives is a forward-looking process. It is a test of a manager's ability. The manager must correctly communicate the direction of the organization. Then she or he must make certain the unit contributes to that overall direction. Thus it may be helpful to think of the objective-setting process in three steps.[3] First, identify the areas of responsibility or activities considered crucial to the organization's long-range success. Second, determine performance measures for each key result area. Third, set the objectives to serve as standards for performance.

key result areas

KEY RESULT AREAS.   The manager must identify the **key result areas**—actions or responsibilities offering a high potential for improved productivity. What functions will yield the maximum benefits with a minimum expenditure of time and resources? Some of these key areas of performance and results are listed in Exhibit 15.1.

These key result areas are applicable (with only minor modifications) to any type of organization—business, industry, government, and education.

Should objectives be specific?

PERFORMANCE MEASURES.   One of the qualities of each example in the above list is specificity. For any work objective to be attained, it must be measurable. If it is not measurable, no one can determine to what level the objective has been accomplished. For example, "to increase productivity" is not measurable. It does not tell us when or how much. A measurable statement would be, "to increase productivity 5 percent during 1985." Objectives have four measurable elements: time, quantity, quality, and cost. The key is to be as specific as possible. Some appropriate performance measures are:

- *quantity* (how much)—units produced per shift, orders processed per work period, dollar volume sold, and number of new developments produced;
- *quality* (how good)—test failure rate, scrap loss, reject ratio, and meeting predetermined criteria;
- *timeliness* (how long)—on-time delivery, percentage of reports turned, and turnaround time; and

─────────────── EXHIBIT 15.1 ───────────────

- **Profitability** can be expressed in terms of profits, return on investment, earnings per share, or profit-to-sales ratios, among others. Objectives in this area may be expressed in such concrete and specific terms as "to increase return on investment to 15 percent after taxes within five years" or "to increase profits to $6 million next year."
- **Markets** may also be described in a number of ways, including share of the market, dollar or unit volume of sales, and niche in the industry. Marketing objectives might be "to increase share of market to 28 percent within three years," "to sell 200,000 units next year," or "to increase commercial sales to 85 percent and reduce military sales to 15 percent over the next two years."
- **Productivity** objectives may be expressed in terms of ratio of input to output (e.g., "to increase number of units to x amount per worker per eight-hour day"). The objectives may also be expressed in terms of cost per unit of production.
- **Product** objectives, aside from sales and profitability by product or product line, may be stated, for example, as, "to introduce a product in the middle range of our product line within two years" or "to phase out the rubber products by the end of next year."
- **Financial resource** objectives may be expressed in many different ways, depending on the company. Some may deal with capital structure, new issues of common stock, cash flow, working capital, dividend payments, and collection periods. Examples include "to decrease the collection period to twenty-six days by the end of the year," "to increase working capital to $5 million within three years," and "to reduce long-term debt to $8 million within five years."
- **Physical facilities** may be described in terms of square feet, fixed cost, units of production, and many other measurements. Objectives might be "to increase production capacity to 8 million units per month within two years" or "to increase storage capacity to 15 million barrels next year."
- **Research and innovation** objectives may be expressed in dollars as well as in other terms: "to develop an engine in the (*specify*) price range, with an emission rate of less than 10 percent, within two years at a cost not to exceed $150,000."
- **Organization** objectives include changes in structure or activities. They may be expressed in any number of ways, such as "to design and implement a matrix organizational structure within two years" or "to establish a regional office in the South by the end of the next year."
- **Human resource** objectives may be quantitatively expressed in terms of absenteeism, tardiness, number of grievances, and training, such as "to reduce absenteeism to less than 4 percent by the end of next year" or "to conduct a twenty-hour in-house management training program for 120 front-line supervisors by the end of 1975 at a cost not to exceed $200 per participant."
- **Social responsibility** objectives may be expressed in terms of types of activities, number of days of service, or financial contributions. An example might be "to hire 120 hard-core unemployables within the next two years."[4]

- *cost* (how much)—percentage of deviation from budget, dollar cost of downtime, estimated versus actual cost, and work hours needed to complete.

SET OBJECTIVES. Once the key result areas have been identified, the **objectives** may be set. These are standards against which performance is   objectives measured. You are already familiar with this process. But these principles should also be internalized:

- Objectives should be related to the needs of the business and should support organizational goals.
- Objectives should be clear, concise, and realistic.
- Objectives should be measurable and quantified whenever possible.
- Objectives should be guides to action. They should state what to achieve, not how to achieve it.
- Objectives should offer a challenge so a person can be proud when he or she achieves it.
- Objectives should consider internal and external constraints, that is, factors not subject to control by the one responsible for results.
- Objective setting is a joint undertaking. The objectives should be mutually agreed upon by the responsible person and her or his supervisor.[5]

Who should use MBO?

MBO is applicable to both the line and staff manager. Both types of managers, however, need to avoid certain errors. For example, errors that frequently occur are: objectives too high (overload) or too low (underload), objectives not measurable, cost measurement too high, too many objectives, too complex objectives, too long or too short a time period, or imbalanced emphasis.[6] Following the principles that we have listed should help avoid these errors. Having a plan to meet the objectives will also help. Remember, we must know where we're going. For unless we have a plan, our objective is just a dream. An example of objectives for a sales representative is provided in Exhibit 15.2.

Developing Action Plans

action plan

A plan converts a present condition into a future condition. An **action plan** consists of a series of activities for a manager to accomplish. For example, appraising, assigning, changing, deciding, inspecting, maintaining, organizing, scheduling, training. Such objectives and plans assist managers in achieving results. More action or accomplishment verbs that can be used in writing objectives to achieve results are listed in Exhibit 15.3.

How do we get from where we are to where we want to be?

An action plan helps managers respond readily to problems. It also aids in anticipating change to avoid slowdowns or shutdowns in production. The result is attainment of the objective. An overall model of how MBO and action plans fit together is drawn in Figure 15.1. Notice the movement from one's job activities, to the job elements, to the objectives, and finally to the action plans.

Such planning involves making assumptions, forecasting the future, and allocating resources. It is not a management function that can be delegated. Planning means looking ahead and drawing up a program of actions. It is the most basic of all management functions. But planning is not enough. Managers must also implement their plans and then conduct periodic reviews.

———————————————— EXHIBIT 15.2 ————————————————

Objectives for Sales Representative

Job Elements	Objectives
Identification of Potential for Sales of Westinghouse Products	To identify in monthly sales report 15 businesses in the tri-state area which have a potential need for Westinghouse products but are not presently Westinghouse customers.
	To identify in monthly sales strategy report present Westinghouse customers where sales volume can be increased or product line utilization can be expanded.
Preparation of Work Plans, Sales Objectives and Monthly Reports	To complete and submit a Sales Strategy Report containing trip plans and sales call objectives, due last Friday of the month for the coming month.
	To complete and submit an Annual Sales Objective Report due 12/1.
	To complete and submit a Sales Report, due 5th of each month for previous month.
Establishment of Customer Relations	To document in Monthly Sales Report formal sales presentations to (8) potential customers.
Maintenance of Customer Relations	To document in Monthly Sales Report monthly sales calls with all customers who purchased $10,000 during the previous year.
	To document in Monthly Sales Report quarterly sales calls on all customers who purchased less than $10,000 during the previous year.
	To document in Monthly Sales Report responses to customer inquiries by phone within 24 hours, at a cost not to exceed 25 work hours.
Development of Product Knowledge and Selling Skills	To complete Westinghouse Selling Skills Program (Level 2) by 7/1.
	To attend Westinghouse seminar on Electro-Mechanical Technology for Marketing Reps. by 10/1.
Attainment of Sales Quotas	To meet assigned sales quota for products X, Y, and Z by the end of the year.

———————————————— Implementing MBO ————————————————

To implement MBO in any organization, one must have upper-level management support. *Without* this support, the other management levels may not be committed to making the program work. *With* this support, one can implement MBO in one of three ways. First, it may begin at the top and then be implemented one level at a time until it filters down through the

How should MBO be implemented?

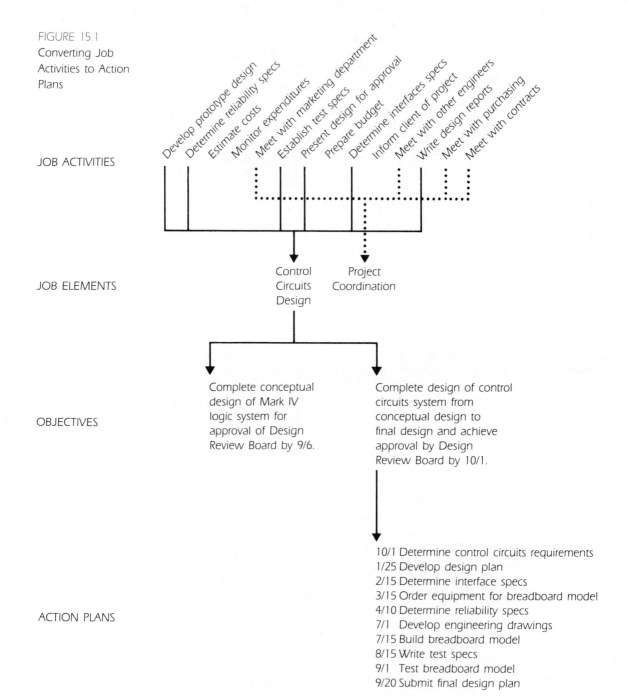

FIGURE 15.1
Converting Job
Activities to Action
Plans

--- EXHIBIT 15.3 ---

Examples of Action or Accomplishment Verbs

Advise	Find	Prepare
Assemble	Formulate	Process
Assign	Give	Program
Audit	Handle	Recommend
Check	Hire	Record
Classify	Identify	Report
Collect	Implement	Represent
Compare	Inform	Review
Compile	Install	Revise
Complete	Instruct	Schedule
Compute	Interpret	Select
Conduct	Interview	Set Up
Construct	Issue	Speak
Control	Make	Summarize
Create	Notify	Supervise
Decide	Obtain	Supply
Deliver	Operate	Terminate
Determine	Organize	Trace
Direct	Persuade	Verify
Evaluate	Plan	Write

--- EXHIBIT 15.4 ---

- How much commitment to MBO is likely from me? from higher-level management? from subordinates? from peers?
- What implementation approach or combination of approaches is best for our company?
- Who (specifically) needs to be involved at the outset if the process is to work? How can I best involve them?
- What immediate steps must I take to get the process started? by what day?
- What should be the pace of implementation? two years? five years? How much of my time and that of my key subordinates am I willing to invest initially?
- What provision must be made for initial skill training and ongoing coaching in the MBO process?
- Will there be an internal adviser or administrator? If so, who will this person be? What will be her or his roles? Will it be full- or part-time? How will I keep this job from generating only paperwork?
- Will I need outside professional assistance in my implementation efforts? If so, in what capacity? organizational survey and analysis? top management consultation? motivational presentation? tailoring of the process to our requirements? conducting in-house seminar(s)? training internal trainers/advisors/administrators? individual or small-group coaching? evaluation of related efforts? other?
- What follow-up efforts will be necessary to sustain initial enthusiasm and ensure increasing effectiveness of results?
- How and when will MBO be tied into the reward system?[7]

entire organization. Usually there is at least a six-month interval between each level. For example, during the first year the president and senior officers work with MBO. A year later the next level (major departments) starts working with MBO. The remaining levels implement it in succeeding years. This is the most common approach. Second, implementation may be limited to one department, as a pilot project. The success of this department is the basis for deciding whether MBO will be used for the rest of the organization. Third, all management levels are treated as a total unit. All implement at the same time. This may be the most difficult approach.

Regardless of the approach used, there are several key factors to consider in developing a MBO implementation plan. A manager should ask the questions listed in Exhibit 15.4 (see p. 328).

Since it is built on time-tested management principles, there are a number of ways to make MBO work. But one of the necessary ingredients is follow-up. Don't implement MBO and then leave it alone to take care of itself.

Monitoring Performance

How does a manager measure performance?

A manager who sets objectives and plans actions properly will already have the basic components of a monitoring or control system. That is, he or she will have the standards against which to measure performance. The key is to get feedback about progress. This principle is important because motivation increases as employees are informed about matters affecting their results. Thus, communication is one of the cornerstones of MBO.

For example, both manager and employee spell out the contributions for attaining the company's objectives. For setting these objectives, both manager and employee must be willing to solicit and give information. Mutual understanding and effective monitoring of performance will result only from good upward communications. They will not be attained solely by downward communications. Employees will perform with maximum productivity when they are aware of the objectives and their purposes. In addition, they must receive feedback on how well they are doing in meeting the company's goals.

This checking of progress is a daily, hourly, monthly activity. The manager who waits only until the end of a project to check its accuracy is programming the project for possible failure. Minor corrections are nearly always necessary. Remember the constant problems and corrections made on the space shuttle Columbia. And think of the constant monitoring of both capsule and astronaut performance on its voyage. Success depends on a control system. Managers must conduct periodic reviews, and that includes almost daily checking and monthly summary review.

Performance Appraisal and Review

Managers are concerned with exacting a specific type of performance from employees. Plans will be made, goals set, standards established, and employees monitored. Such monitoring will come in the form of performance reviews. For example, Figure 15.2 indicates that performance appraisal not only completes one MBO cycle, but also starts the next.

How does performance appraisal fit in with MBO?

The **performance appraisal** frequently is a private meeting between employee and supervisor to discuss the employee's past and present performance. In fact, one of the primary objectives of performance appraisal and review is to assess the parts of performance needing improvement. Therefore, the performance appraisal meets several needs. For example, employees want to know how they are doing. Most employees want their work to be satisfactory to the supervisor. Or they want to know how they can improve their performance. Supervisors need to communicate this information so the employees can plan future courses of action.

performance appraisal

Formal appraisal is rather new to many supervisors. The reason is that for ages they have ignored or violated the following human relations practices:

- People are an organization's most important resource.
- People are capable of growth toward more effective behavior, even though their basic personalities do not change.
- Performance-appraisal and managerial-development activities are central to the management process, that is, to the process of getting things done through people.
- The activities of managers can either impede or stimulate the growth of subordinates.

FIGURE 15.2
The MBO Cycle

Source: William E. Reif and Gerald Bassford, "What MBO Really Is," *Business Horizons* (June 1973): 26.

- Skills in appraising people and in developing their capabilities can be learned.[8]

However, during the 1960s and 1970s more and more organizations adopted employee performance-review plans. Management was becoming attuned to the need for reviewing performance. It attempted to respond to employees' rights to know. Yet many of these programs failed. Why?

--------------------------- Problems in Appraisal ---------------------------

Are there problems in the appraisal process?

Before managers can design an appraisal system, they need to understand some of the likely pitfalls. There are eight such problem areas: avoidance, unexpressed hostility, getting lost in the form, the hidden presence of others, mistaken impressions, combinations, trivia, and fear of failure.[9]

AVOIDANCE.   The most common problem in appraisal is avoidance. The supervisor ignores the process, refuses to discuss the appraisal form, or discusses the appraisal with only surface regard. Personnel appraisal may be avoided because of embarrassment, fear, busyness, or dislike. We typically avoid the areas in which we feel uncomfortable. However, such avoidance will not assist the employee in self- or job-development.

UNEXPRESSED HOSTILITY.   Sometimes employees go beyond disagreement and argument and become hostile. However, they don't express their hostility. Instead, they leave the appraisal interview with extremely negative feelings that will be expressed elsewhere—at home, to fellow employees, in drink, and so forth. The supervisor leaves the interview thinking everything is fine, when really there is a failure to communicate. Such a situation will arise when the supervisor dominates the interview and refuses to listen. A rule of thumb is to listen twice as much as you talk.

GETTING LOST IN THE FORM.   There are a variety of appraisal forms ranging from open-ended essay questions to a hundred or more items to be checked. If the form is ambiguous or overbearing in detail, the supervisor may become engrossed in completing the form and lose sight of the actual purpose of the interview—to appraise performance. Also, such forms may end up telling us more about the supervisor (i.e., his or her likes or dislikes) than about the worker.

THE HIDDEN PRESENCE OF OTHERS.   When appraisal forms are filed in other offices, there is always the possibility that someone else other than the supervisor will see the evaluation. This hidden presence of others places pressure on both employee and supervisor. Both become concerned about looking good—rating and being rated. After all, what will other people think of them when they look at the appraisal?

MISTAKEN IMPRESSIONS.   Sometimes an employee leaves an appraisal with a mistaken impression. Because the interview went exceptionally well, surely a raise or promotion must be in the wind, even though the supervisor never mentioned it. When the raise or promotion does not materialize, the employee becomes disappointed, frustrated, or even hostile.

COMBINATIONS.   Performance appraisal should be separated from salary review. Using the performance review to determine a salary increase destroys the purpose of an appraisal program. When both reviews are conducted at the same meeting, dollars will overshadow the need for improvement. Most people are more interested in money than in criticism, even if it is constructive criticism.

TRIVIA.   Supervisors sometimes waste time in appraisal interviews talking about day-to-day infractions and annoyances. These activities should be discussed when they occur, not annually or semiannually. When supervisors engage in trivial conversations during performance review, it is probably because they have not kept sufficient records or they do not have sufficient training to do good appraisals. The appraisal interview must concentrate on helping employees improve their performance.

FEAR OF FAILURE.   Many supervisors fear that if their workers don't look good, *they* may not look good. This problem adds pressure and stress to both supervisor and employee. It results from the hidden presence of others.

───────────────── Objectives of Appraisal ─────────────────

These appraisal problems suggest a need to know what will and won't work. There are three major objectives for appraisal.

What are the objectives of appraisal?

1. *To improve performance on the job.* The appraisal procedure should not stop at an examination of the past; it should move on to a plan for the future.

2. *To develop people.* People development can be achieved by providing the organization with people qualified to step into higher positions that open up and helping people who wish to acquire the knowledge and abilities they need to become eligible for a higher job.

3. *To provide answers to employees on how they are doing and where they are going.* These two questions are recurrent concerns of all employees.[10]

One communications company uses its appraisal system to clarify employee expectations; establish the degree to which employees are meeting objectives; develop an improvement plan that the supervisor and the subordinate understand and accept; give subordinates some personal responsibility for their development by clarifying and establishing personal goals or ambitions that they intend to reach; facilitate communication between supervisors and subordinates; and, identify employees who are qualified for promotion.

Performance Appraisals

Where does appraisal fit into the MBO cycle?

Appraisal is a crucial step in evaluating and developing employees, but it is neither the beginning nor the end. It is a middle step in a cycle that begins when employees are hired to do a specific job and ends when they leave the job. If the other steps are omitted, there is little hope for the performance appraisal interview. For example, the first step in the cycle is that the job must be defined. The employee and supervisor discuss the job description and agree on the job content and the relative importance of the employee's major and minor duties—the things she or he is paid to do and is accountable for. If a supervisor uses an MBO approach, she or he may ask employees to establish short-term goals. Thus, the supervisor's role is to help employees relate their goals and plans for the ensuing period to organizational realities.

The second step in the cycle, performance, requires the supervisor to communicate the job description to employees and to detail expectations. Goals are set for a certain period (e.g., six months). These goals become the specific actions the employee takes. (Thus, there should be mini-appraisals along the way.) At the end of the agreed-on period, evaluation is necessary. This third step, appraisal, is a comparison of performance with job expectations. Has the employee hit the targets at which she or he was aiming? In an interview, the supervisor and employee discuss what has happened and what should happen. This is step four. It culminates in a resetting of goals for the next designated period. The cycle then repeats itself.

What are some types of employees managers must appraise?

CATEGORIES OF EMPLOYEES.   During the review process managers must work with various employee groups. Employees who need to improve must be identified. One national firm provides its managers with the following checklist for appraisal interviews:

- Plan and outline your remarks and topics to be discussed with the employee.
- Anticipate reactions (especially unfavorable ones) and decide how you will respond.
- Clarify specific incidents, favorable and unfavorable, that will be used to support your appraisal of various areas that are germane to the job.
- Identify specific performance areas that should be praised and major weaknesses that require discussion.
- Propose remedial action that will help the employee resolve performance deficiencies, such as training, seminars, and other formal programs; and self-help activities—things the employee can do off the job.
- Consider the effect this and future appraisals may have on the employee's promotion and ability to handle greater responsibilities.

Generally, employees fall into four major categories.[11]

What kind of performer are you?

1. *Outstanding performers* are those who, once they understand the desired results, are constant achievers. Clarity of goals is the key factor. They are able to devise appropriate actions to get results through their own perceptions, experience, and analytical skills. They require minimum guidance and encouragement. They express a high level of job satisfaction.

2. *Satisfactory performers* are those who are able to achieve, or come quite close to, established goals. They are not outstanding performers, but they perform well enough to make valued contributions to their companies. They experience relatively high job satisfaction. With some help they are able to work out effective action plans.

3. *Below-average performers* are those whose efforts consistently miss the target. These employees may not have adequate resources, or may have a nonwork problem affecting performance. They may be unable to identify and pursue proper goals. Or they may lack insight to distinguish between effective and ineffective job behavior. They are not necessarily lacking in motivation, but they do need explicit guidance.

4. *Unsatisfactory performers* are those who (because of some combination of inability, lack of motivation, inappropriate goals, or off-the-job problems) perform well below standards. They require more help than the manager alone can provide. They may need reassignment, transfer, or counseling. Or, they may need to be fired.

The high achievers are easy to work with on a day-to-day basis. And their performance is easy to appraise and review at the end of the year. That is not true of the low achievers. But for both groups, and those between these extremes, a good performance review program can be designed.

DESIGNING A PERFORMANCE APPRAISAL PROGRAM. A performance-appraisal design needs to go beyond the one in Exhibit 15.5. But an effective program is often difficult to design. There are several essentials for a good program, however.

What is necessary for a good appraisal program?

- *Personnel appraisal should involve the chief executive.* The chief executive officer must wholeheartedly endorse the program both by words and example. When the top executive demonstrates belief in the program, it will be implemented down the line.
- *Managers must understand human behavior.* Effective managers know a great deal about human behavior. They recognize that understanding human behavior is their job and that the ability to get along with others will help them over many rough spots.
- *The emphasis must be on performance, not personality.* The manager's responsibility is to help an employee change toward more effective job performance, to provide job challenges that will motivate employees.

EXHIBIT 15.5

Guide to Supervisor Performance Appraisal Degrees

	Far Exceeds Requirements	Exceeds Job Requirements	Meets Job Requirements	Needs Some Improvement	Does Not Meet Minimum Requirements
Quality	Leaps tall buildings with a single bound	Must take running start to leap over tall buildings	Can leap over short buildings or medium buildings with no spires	Crashes into buildings when attempting to leap over them	Cannot recognize buildings, let alone leap over them
Timeliness	Is faster than a speeding bullet	Is as fast as a speeding bullet	Not quite as fast as a speeding bullet	Would you believe a slow bullet?	Wounds self with bullets when attempting to shoot gun
Initiative	Is stronger than a locomotive	Is stronger than a bull elephant	Is stronger than a bull	Shoots the bull	Smells like a bull
Adaptability	Walks on water consistently	Walks on water in emergencies	Washes with water	Drinks water	Passes water during emergencies
Communication	Talks with God	Talks with angels	Talks to himself	Argues with himself	Loses these arguments

- *Managers must involve themselves in the design and use of the performance appraisal program.* Managers who are required to review and develop their people should be involved in the conception, design, use, and evaluation of the program. Performance appraisals handled by outsiders are doomed to failure. Managerial involvement is at the heart of motivation and effective performance.
- *The manager-employee relationship must be recognized as crucial.* The manager's relationship to an employee significantly affects the way both do their jobs.
- *Motive and attitude are more important than technique and skill in an appraisal program.* Dynamism in an organization is exhibited in the way employees express enthusiasm about their jobs, about each other, and about the company. It is a sense of personal involvement. A major determinant of such a spirit of dynamism is good leadership.[12]

After Corning Glass Works overhauled its performance appraisal system, the company sent 3800 managers to a two-day seminar to prepare them to implement the program as it was intended.[13] In similar fashion, General Telephone and Electronics Corporation (GTE) employed an outside management consulting firm to show 400 managers how to apply its newly developed company-wide performance appraisal system effectively and correctly.[14]

The basic idea behind the annual performance review is: the organization should know where it is before it begins planning where it wants to go. This is why MBO offers great potential for most managers. It can improve planning, performance, and relationships. But it must be tied to some reward system resulting from appraisal. Lockheed Corporation currently gives separate performance reviews and salary reviews but may combine them in the near future because some workers overemphasize the salary review.[15]

 Effective Review Plans

In the review process, two major areas of skills are important: skills for managing people and skills for managing tasks. Plans that reflect these two types of skills are shown in Figures 15.3 and 15.4. Managers can fill out such forms for each employee and then discuss the points needing improvement. Some managers find it helpful for the employee to fill out a self-appraisal form and bring it to the meeting for comparisons and discussions. Whatever method is used, the appraisal should help to satisfy an employee's needs for group acceptance, self-esteem, and proper recognition. Also, it should support management's objectives.

What should an effective review appraisal do?

Large companies like Bell Telephone Company of Pennsylvania have the resources to develop sophisticated appraisal systems that ensure maximum objectivity—something that smaller firms cannot afford to do.[16]

FIGURE 15.3

Evaluation of People Management Skills

Name	Outstanding	Satisfactory	Below Average	Unsatisfactory
1. Communication—The ability to share thoughts and feelings; verbal and nonverbal skills; attentive listening, empathy, and interested concern.				
2. Motivation—The ability to elicit desire, enthusiasm, commitment, and productive behavior from others to accomplish specific results.				
3. Delegation—The ability to assign useful tasks to employees, including the authority to act freely and exercise necessary initiative.				
4. Development—The ability to create an atmosphere in which an employee can reach maximum potential.				
5. Appraisal—The ability to recognize the skills, strengths, weaknesses, and developmental needs of oneself or one's employees. This ability must be exercised on an ongoing basis.				
6. Counseling—The ability to listen analytically to problems and create a climate sufficiently secure to gain fresh insights into problems and their resolution.				
7. Correction—The ability to confront others and point out errors, shortcomings, and mistakes in a way others can correct them without feeling bitterness or resentment.				
8. Supervision—The ability to give employees day-to-day instruction, guidance, and discipline to the degree required for them to fulfill their duties and responsibilities; to adapt one's supervision style to the needs of the situation and individual.				
9. Coordination—The ability to group and interrelate diverse resources in the most productive and economical way for the accomplishment of objectives.				

FIGURE 15.3 cont.

	Outstanding	Satisfactory	Below Average	Unsatisfactory
10. Team Building—The ability to create an atmosphere in which different people can cooperate in the accomplishment of agreed-on goals; to develop and maintain high morale among the members.				
11. Conflict Resolution—The ability to establish a climate where differences can be openly and equitably settled to the greatest satisfaction of all involved persons.				
12. Goal Setting—The ability to set challenging but achievable goals for each person in the work group.				

FIGURE 15.4
Evaluation of Task
Management Skills

	Outstanding	Satisfactory	Below Average	Unsatisfactory
Name _____				
1. Job knowledge—The ability to know the role the job plays in the overall effectiveness of the organization and the relationships that exist relative to one's place in the organizational authority chain.				
2. Planning—The ability to establish the series of activities necessary to achieve a specific goal.				
3. Decision making—The ability to weigh all available and relevant facts, consult all fruitful sources of information and within a reasonable time determine a course of action.				
4. Objectives setting—The ability to determine the immediate and intermediate targets to be attained in order to accomplish agreed-on goals within the predetermined time schedule.				

FIGURE 15.4 cont.

	Outstanding	Satisfactory	Below Average	Unsatisfactory
5. Strategy development—The ability to develop and establish a detailed course of action to accomplish a particular newly established objective with minimal expense, risk, time, human resources, and maximum output, profit, service, and morale.				
6. Problem solving—The ability to identify the real difficulty, to draw from all possible sources of information, and to arrive at a course of action contributing to the desired goals with the least expenditure of physical, financial, or personnel resources.				
7. Projects initiation—The ability and courage to undertake activities that could prove useful or productive.				
8. Time management—The ability to use time with the greatest possible efficiency for productivity, profit, and personal satisfaction.				
9. Systems and procedures establishment—The ability to establish standardized activities to accomplish objectives.				
10. Budget maintenance—The ability to accomplish the assigned objectives within established financial limitations.				
11. Technical know-how—The ability to handle and maintain tools or equipment needed to operate one's area of responsibility effectively.				
12. Practical expertise—The ability to learn old techniques and develop new ones for safely, efficiently, quickly, and economically carrying out one's duties.				

Pennsylvania Bell's two-track rating system rates a worker on accomplishments and on factors that enabled the worker to achieve them. If the two ratings vary widely, the appraising manager must align them more closely by reconsidering evidence in both areas.

RCA Corporation's system involves a manager's peers, subordinates, supervisor, and several managers higher than the supervisor in a group or committee appraisal. This provides a three-dimensional performance picture that the company feels is more objective than alternative methods.

CONCLUSION

MBO is a demanding management system requiring highly competent managers to operate it. It offers some great opportunities for improving communication and human relations among colleagues. Participation in decision making is encouraged, as is concern for productivity. The MBO system, however, must be tied to rewards. That is why performance appraisal is so important to managers. They must review progress and plan for the future.

KEY TERMS

Management by Objectives (MBO): a management process that involves establishing goals and action plans, implementing them, and monitoring their progress.

Key Result Areas: crucial actions or responsibilities offering a high potential for improved productivity.

Objectives: standards against which performance is measured.

Action Plan: a series of activities for a manager to accomplish.

Performance Appraisal: a meeting between a manager and subordinate to discuss the employee's past and present job performance.

QUESTIONS

1   Reread the opening case.
   a.   How might Pat Quigley try to convince her company's management to adopt MBO?
   b.   Describe the specific steps to be taken and the degree of commitment required for this employer to shift from its traditional system to MBO. What problems should management anticipate?

    c. Criticize the performance appraisal system now in use in this case.

    d. How would you criticize Pat's boss's approach to performance appraisal? List at least three things he should do differently in assessing Pat's work, and state why a change is necessary.

2 List at least five goals of an MBO program. Why must the program be considered an integral part of the managerial process?

3 Summarize the relationship of each of the following words to the concept of MBO:

    a. goals,

    b. action plans,

    c. implementation,

    d. measurement, and

    e. remedial action.

4 How would you characterize the supervisor's role in MBO? Do you believe training is necessary to prepare managers to fill such a role successfully? Why or why not?

5. Construct a five-point argument for using MBO. What problems or disadvantages may be associated with this concept?

6 List at least six key result areas that employees may refer to when setting objectives and provide at least one example of a quantifiable goal for each area.

7 "Objectives set under MBO don't always have to be quantified, but they must be verifiable in an objective way." Do you agree with that opinion? If so, provide at least two examples of goals that are verifiable but not expressed in quantities.

8 Summarize how each of the following relates to objectives set under MBO:

    a. organizational needs and goals;

    b. clarity, realism, and conciseness;

    c. quantifiability;

    d. challenge;

    e. internal and external constraints; and

    f. mutual agreement.

9 Why, do you think, would some managers prefer to avoid setting goals for themselves unless formally required to do so? What personal and career difficulties might such an attitude create?

10 List at least ten action words that may be used when writing an MBO action plan. What sometimes causes these action plans to fail?

11 Defend the following comment: "Ultimately, any successful MBO program must be implemented from the top down and include all levels in the hierarchy. Scattered applications in various departments will have mediocre success at best."

12 What factors must managers consider when implementing an MBO plan? How would you describe the degree of commitment required from you? your superiors? your subordinate managers? your peer managers?

13 How often should the progress of MBO plans be monitored? Why do you think that frequency is necessary?

14 Summarize each of the nine problem areas in performance appraisal and suggest how supervisors can deal with each:

    a. avoidance,

    b. unexpressed hostility,

    c. getting lost in the form,

    d. hidden presence of others,

    e. mistaken impressions,

    f. combinations,

    g. trivia, and

    h. fear of failure.

15 Discuss the three key objectives of appraisal that were presented in the chapter. Suggest at least three secondary objectives based on your personal opinion or experience.

16 Diagram the performance appraisal cycle. What role does the job description play in its success, and why?

17 Describe the following types of employees:

    a. outstanding performers,

    b. satisfactory performers,

    c. below-average performers, and

    d. unsatisfactory performers.

18 Outline at least four essential factors that must be considered when designing a performance appraisal program.

19 Contrast Exhibit 15.3 with 15.4. How are they related? Do you feel that an individual rated highly on people management skills would receive a comparable rating on task management skills? Why or why not?

20 List at least ten attitudes or practices that can kill the success of MBO. Which three are most deadly in your opinion, and why?

CASES

A year ago Washington Gas Light Co. decided to implement MBO on a trial basis.   Case 15.1
To determine whether supervisors and managers were already using MBO, a questionnaire was mailed to each person. The results of this study follow.

1 Does your department establish goals each year for the department?

    (33) Yes

    (34) No

    (33) Don't know

2 To what extent are you aware of the specific goals established?

    ( ) To a very great extent

    ( ) To a great extent

    ( ) To a moderate extent

    (80) To a minor extent

    (20) Not at all aware

3 How much effort did your department devote to develop departmental goals and priorities?

    ( ) Great deal of effort

    ( ) Quite a bit of effort

    ( ) Moderate amount of effort

    (60) A small amount of effort

    (40) Very little effort

4   How much influence on setting goals and priorities in your department does the department head have?
    ( ) Very great influence
    (20) Great influence
    (60) Quite a bit of influence
    (20) Little influence
    ( ) Very little influence

5   How much influence on setting goals and priorities of your department do line (or staff) members have?
    ( ) Very great influence
    (20) Great influence
    (20) Quite a bit of influence
    (40) Little influence
    (20) Very little influence

6   In setting your own professional objectives, what degree of freedom do you have?
    ( ) Very high degree
    ( ) High degree
    (60) Moderate degree
    (20) Low degree
    (20) None at all

7   To what extent do you believe compatibility exists between your personal and professional objectives and departmental objectives?
    ( ) Highly compatible
    ( ) Very compatible
    (50) Slightly compatible
    (25) Low compatibility
    (25) No compatibility

8   How often are you given feedback on your progress toward departmental objectives?
    ( ) Very frequently
    ( ) Frequently
    (40) Occasionally
    (40) Very infrequently
    (20) Never

9   How did the amount of effort you put into your position last year compare to that of previous years?
    ( ) Very much greater
    ( ) Much greater
    (50) Somewhat greater
    (50) No change
    ( ) Less

10 How applicable would the management technique *management by objectives* be to your position?
    ( ) Very applicable
    ( ) Quite applicable
    (40) Fairly applicable
    ( ) Not applicable
    (60) Don't know

Case Questions

1   Analyze the results of this study. What specific changes, if any, should be made to ensure the success of an MBO program to deal with these survey results?
2   Do you believe some performance appraisal system other than MBO may be appropriate for this organization? If so, outline the nature of the system you would use and why you believe it would be preferable to MBO.
3   Drawing on your experience as a student and on your imagination, describe at least six factors to be considered in implementing MBO in this kind of organization, a utility company (as opposed to a retail chain store or a manufacturing company, for example). What problems peculiar to this kind of organization may arise?

Case 15.2

Hal Urich is a department manager for a large insurance company. As a member of middle management, he has viewed the company's MBO program with some skepticism since it was implemented.

"I'm still not sold on MBO as a feasible appraisal technique," Hal confided to Alice Olson, another department manager. "It seems that we never catch up. We set goals for one year and reach them, and the next year management expects us to go even higher. If I reduced the number of claims overpayments by 10 percent this year, my boss would want 12 percent next year. They're never satisfied!

"I have one meeting a year with my boss, and if my objectives don't suit him, I've got to raise them higher. Then, a year later, we sit down to see how well I did. If I reach them, I get a pat on the back; if I don't, I get chewed out for nonperformance."

"My situation's not quite like yours," Alice answered. "Since I am in public relations rather than claims and accounting, my objectives are harder to express in numbers. I deal with requests for company information. Every time we're mentioned in a newspaper story, we get an avalanche of mail asking for details or clarification. My boss is a problem too, though. He rates just about everyone high, because he almost never questions the goals we set. Most of us set ones we're sure we can reach, because we've got him figured out! It's not fair, though, because there are some real goof-offs and some terrific go-getters, but nobody's recognized as either. We just ride with the tide."

Case Questions

1   What would you do to move the system more closely to genuine MBO?
2   What training experiences would you suggest for getting the various managers together on the concept, implementation, monitoring, and assessment of the program?
3   Using your imagination, create at least four quantified goals for someone like Hal, who works as an accounting clerk and claims processor for an insurance company.
4   Suggest at least four verifiable (if not quantified) goals for someone with a job like Alice's.

—————————————— NOTES ——————————————

1. Harry Levinson, "Management by Whose Objectives?" *Harvard Business Review* (July–August 1970): 126.
2. Harry B. Anderson, "Formal Job Appraisals Grow More Prevalent but Get More Criticism," *The Wall Street Journal*, 23 May 1978, p. 1.
3. William E. Reif and Gerald Bassford, "What MBO Really Is," *Business Horizons* (June 1973): 26.
4. Anthony P. Raia, *Managing by Objectives* (Glenview, Ill.: Scott, Foresman, 1974), pp. 38–40.
5. Reif and Bassford, "What MBO Really Is," p. 26.
6. W. J. Reddin, *Effective Management by Objectives—The 3-D Method of MBO* (New York: McGraw-Hill, 1971), pp. 87–88.
7. George L. Morrisey, "How to Implement MBO in Your Organizational Unit," *Training and Development Journal* (April 1977): 12.
8. Howard P. Smith and Paul J. Brouwer, *Performance Appraisal and Human Development—A Practical Guide to Effective Managing* (Reading, Mass.: Addison-Wesley, 1977), p. xi.
9. Robert G. Johnson, *The Appraisal Interview Guide* (New York: American Management Association, 1979), pp. 9–14.
10. Alva F. Kindall and James Gatza, "Positive Program for Performance Appraisal," *Harvard Business Review* (November–December 1963): 156.
11. William J. Kearney, "Behaviorally Anchored Rating Scales—MBO's Missing Ingredient," *Personnel Journal* (January 1979): 20–22.
12. Smith and Brouwer, *Performance Appraisal and Human Development*, pp. 53–58.
13. "Appraising the Performance Appraisal," *Business Week*, 19 May 1980, p. 153.
14. "Training Managers to Rate Their Employees," *Business Week*, 17 March 1980, p. 178.
15. *The Wall Street Journal*, 2 March 1982, p. 1.
16. Anderson, "Appraisals Grow More Prevalent," p. 1.

————————————— SUGGESTED READINGS —————————————

Carroll, Stephen J., and Schneler, Craig Eric. *Performance Appraisal and Review Systems.* Glenview, Ill.: Scott, Foresman, 1982.

McConkey, Dale D. *How to Manage by Results*, 3rd ed. New York: American Management Associations, 1976.

Odiorne, George S. *MBO II.* Belmont, Calif.: Fearon Pitman, 1979.

16

The Stress of Change and Conflict

When you complete your study of this chapter, you should be able to:

1 Recognize the effect of stress, change, and conflict on your personal life and job behavior,

2 Explain why people resist change in their social and work lives,

3 Identify your personality as type A or B, and determine the relationship between stress and disease,

4 Contrast the relationships between stress and job performance and between stress and strain, and

5 Determine methods for measuring, reducing, and preventing stress.

OPENING CASE

Allen Beane is proud of his reputation as a self-made man. Rising through the ranks of Allied Products without the benefit of a college education, he now manages the third largest Allied plant in the southeastern United States. Success has its price in terms of pressure, though, as Allen confided to his physician, Ben Martin, during a recent office visit.

"Ben, you're about the only person I can unload my problems on in confidence," Allen chuckled. "I look forward to these meetings just so we can talk!"

"That's part of my work, too," Ben replied. "So, what's been happening down at the plant? How's your job treating you?"

"It's been rough these last few months," Allen answered. "For one thing, I've got this new management trainee that my division boss wants me to break in. The higher-ups think he's a superstar (he graduated from a prestigious Eastern college) so if he doesn't work out everyone will probably blame me. The trouble is, the guy has no background in manufacturing, doesn't relate to production concepts very well, and is catching on very, *very* slowly. I've got to cover his mistakes, watch him constantly, and hope he'll come around. Right now, though, I've been doing his job *and* mine for the past three months."

Ben Martin nodded. "What else?"

"Well, that new machine in the preparation department is a bottleneck for the whole plant. It's still screwing up the raw material, even though we've had the manufacturer's engineers in the plant for days at a time to adjust it and set it up properly. You see, if it treats the raw material with the wrong proportion of chemicals or overstretches it, the stuff doesn't run right when it goes out to the production area. That causes downtime on the production machines while the mistreated material is pulled off and thrown away. So, when that prep machine causes problems that shut down the production machines, they use less raw material than I forecast—which creates a temporary inventory surplus in my warehouse. Then the head accountant jumps all over me for overstocking inventory and also for the waste material that we have to cut out and discard—the misprocessed stuff that stopped the machines and threw our materials consumption estimates out of whack."

"Sounds like a heap of pressure," Ben observed. "I understand there is some kind of labor trouble at the plant, too. Is that right?"

"Sort of," Allen confirmed. "The workers are griping about production machines being down too much because of incorrectly prepared material (that blasted prep machine again!) and since they work on a piecework plan, downtime costs them wages. The union's been trying to crack this company for years, and it's made contact with some of our workers and said if they unionized, management would act faster to correct the problem. Top management has let it be known that the first plant manager whose workers unionize will be considered a failure. It'll be the kiss of death for my career if my workers vote the union in."

Ben Martin shook his head. "How are things at home?" he asked.

"I don't know for sure," Allen replied. "My oldest kid has been acting strangely lately—locking his door, being very secretive. His grades have slipped. I think he's fooling around with some kind of drugs, but I can't be certain. And my workweek's the same as usual. I put in about ten hours a week at home at nights and on weekends along with my fifty hours a week at the plant."

"How well are you coping?" asked Ben.

"Maybe that's part of the reason I'm here," Allen answered. "My digestion's gotten so bad I can't even tolerate mustard on a hot dog any more without suffering heartburn. There's something else, too—a few little chest pains off and on at night for the past three nights. Probably just indigestion; I'm not really worried."

The Pressure-Cooker Age

Over the last few decades there has been an increase in the uncertainty of human relationships. Every day people face situations that have no predictable outcome. They face aggression, change, and conflict. The pressure cooker is no longer just a cooking utensil. Its method has been transferred to the managerial arena. Many people feel overworked, pressured, and pushed. These feelings may be real or imagined, but they may cause physical illness and emotional misery. From the top of the organization to the bottom no one is immune to these diseases of stress.

Do you sometimes feel as if you're living in a pressure cooker?

Every historic age is characterized by certain ailments; ours is the pressure-cooker age. As we look at our era in historical perspective, we see

the Middle Ages dominated by the Great Plague and leprosy ills of the common people; the Renaissance characterized by syphilis; the Baroque Era marked by such deficiency diseases as scurvy and such luxury diseases as gout; the Romantic Period linked with tuberculosis; and the nineteenth century, with its rapid industrialization and development of the cities, general nervousness and neuroses. And now we have the twentieth century, where tension headaches, high blood pressure, and peptic ulcers keep pace with the Dow Jones average and where oscillation of the economy can be traced by the ebb and flow of tranquilizer prescriptions.[1]

Perhaps this twentieth-century psyche of the pressure cooker is best illustrated in a recent Anacin television advertisement: "I like my job and am good at it, but it sure grinds me down sometimes, and the last thing I need to take home is a headache." None of us has time for ailments; yet the frenetic pace of our lives produces stress.

Stress

stress

Stress is an internal conflict resulting from an external situation. That is, stress is a person's reaction to, or ability to handle, a certain situation. There are a great many **stress** factors triggering imbalance in our personal lives. Changes in family, occupation, personal relationships, finance, religion, health, and residence can produce stress. For example, if the divorce rate is an indicator of job stress, then data processing managers are near the head of the pack. According to *Datamation* magazine, the only professional group that gets divorced more often than data processing managers is air traffic controllers. And, as stress increases, so do ailments and disease.

Stress-Producing Events

What causes stress?

life change units

After twenty-five years of work, researchers have identified forty-three stress-producing experiences in life.[2] Each event is associated with a weighted number ranging from 11 to 100, since some changes create more stress than others. The total number of these **life change units** (LCUs) predicts a change in health. Determine your LCU score by checking the events listed in Figure 16.1 that occurred in your life within the last year. Then add up the mean values for each event. Notice that both pleasant and unpleasant life events can create stress. In fact, *all* change (whether it be positive or negative) is stressful.

FIGURE 16.1
The Stress of Living

Instructions: Check the events that occurred in your life within the last year, and then add up your life change units.

RANK	LIFE EVENT	MEAN VALUE	
1	Death of spouse	100	_____
2	Divorce	73	_____
3	Marital separation	65	_____
4	Jail term	63	_____
5	Death of close family member	63	_____
6	Personal injury or illness	53	_____
7	Marriage	50	_____
8	Discharge from job	47	_____

RANK	LIFE EVENT	MEAN VALUE	
9	Marital reconciliation	45	_____
10	Retirement	45	_____
11	Change in health of family member	44	_____
12	Pregnancy	40	_____
13	Sex difficulties	39	_____
14	Gain of new family member	39	_____
15	Business readjustment	39	_____
16	Change in financial state	38	_____
17	Death of close friend	37	_____
18	Change to different line of work	36	_____
19	Change in number of arguments with spouse	35	_____
20	Mortgage over $10,000	31	_____
21	Foreclosure of mortgage or loan	30	_____
22	Change in responsibilities of work	29	_____
23	Son or daughter leaving home	29	_____
24	Trouble with in-laws	29	_____
25	Outstanding personal achievement	28	_____
26	Spouse beginning or stopping work	26	_____
27	Beginning or ending school	26	_____
28	Change in living conditions	25	_____
29	Revision of personal habits	24	_____
30	Trouble with boss	23	_____
31	Change in work hours or conditions	20	_____
32	Change in residence	20	_____
33	Change in schools	20	_____
34	Change in recreation	20	_____
35	Change in church activities	19	_____
36	Change in social activities	18	_____
37	Mortgage or loan less than $10,000	17	_____
38	Change in sleeping habits	16	_____
39	Change in number of family get-togethers	15	_____
40	Change in eating habits	15	_____
41	Vacation	13	_____
42	Christmas	12	_____
43	Minor violations of the law	11	_____
TOTAL SCORE			=======

FIGURE 16.1 cont.

Source: Thomas H. Holmes and Richard H. Rake, "The Social Readjustment Rating Scale," *Journal of Psychosomatic Research* 11(1967): 216.

An LCU score of 150–199 points is considered a mild life crisis; there is a 37 percent chance of appreciable health change within the next twenty-four months. An LCU score of 200–299 points is considered moderate and gives a 51 percent chance of a health change. An LCU score of 300 or more points in a single year is considered severe and indicates a 79 percent chance of health change. A score below 150 points indicates a probability of no adverse physical symptoms. If your score alarms you, do something about it. Postpone any change under your control until your score settles down.

. The Life Crisis Scale does not mean the same thing for everybody. The stress-disease link is not perfect. What is one person's tension may be another person's relaxation. Depending on the amount and type of stress one encounters, one's score can indicate serious changes in health.

─────────────── Stress and Disease ───────────────

Is stress related to any diseases?

Changes in health include all changes from simple physical ailments to life-threatening diseases. Physiological and psychological stress result in irritability, anger, loss of objectivity, increase in work-related errors, apathy, fatigue, depression, loss of sex drive, panic, frustration, poor memory, lowered self-confidence, impotence, insomnia, indecisiveness, procrastination, overeating, or loss of appetite. Stress is a factor in diseases such as peptic ulcers, migraines, hypertension, rheumatoid arthritis, backaches, emphysema, ulcerative colitis, asthma, mental disease, cancer, and heart attacks.

When we are faced with stress, our body prepares for fight or flight. Oxygen consumption increases, blood pressure rises, heart rate increases, and so forth. Under normal conditions the body restores itself by making quick decisions, taking vigorous action, or defending itself against injury. Unfortunately, most twentieth-century stress is psychological. Thus, the body neither fights nor flees. Stress accumulates, and chronic high blood pressure or some other disease results.

What are some effects of stress?

TWO CASE STUDIES.   One middle manager for International Business Machines Corporation was transferred nine times during his first twenty years with the company. This peripatetic life caused adjustment problems for his children, who were always strangers in school and who didn't have the time to build enduring friendships. His daughter experienced stomach and personality problems; his son was sometimes hostile and withdrawn; his wife required extensive dental work to correct problems caused by grinding her teeth in her sleep. And the executive himself, although relishing the challenge, recognition, and satisfaction that accompanied each new job and transfer remarked, ''What's the use of succeeding at work when I've screwed up my family?''[3]

The Wall Street Journal profiled the devastating effects of failure-related stress on the former chairman and chief executive officer of a bankrupt medical products firm.[4] A successful, hard-driving overachiever all his life, this manager founded the company and saw its stock shoot from less than $1 to more than $16.00 per share. His holdings were worth more than $3 million, and he became a celebrity in his part of the state. His job was an integral part of his identity and his major reason for living.

When his company began slipping into financial difficulty, alarmed creditors demanded that this manager and one other top executive be dismissed. At the onset of this financial crisis the manager began crying at staff meetings and was hospitalized for exhaustion. At last, the final blow came: his formerly docile board of directors fired him in a highly publicized action that connected him with the firm's eventual bankruptcy.

Memories of his first year of unemployment were sketchy. Converting from an aggressive, confident extrovert to a reclusive introvert, he slept, read, and watched movies on a video recorder. He declined to talk even to his mother on the telephone and feared going out in public because some people would recognize him. His children experienced conflicts at school and at work because of his business failure, and the family relationship was constantly in turmoil as their father's moods swung between hostility and withdrawal. He openly contemplated suicide.

Gradually, he emerged from this mental and emotional snake pit, started another company, and moved along the road to recovery. He and his family agree that their lives have been permanently changed by his business and personal disintegration, but the experience has given him a different set of personal priorities and a view of life he had not considered before. No one is certain if the harrowing mental effects of his stress have been permanently resolved or if they'll arise once again—triggered, perhaps, by another business failure. Only time will tell.

STRESS AND PERSONALITY.   One way to view the relationship between stress and disease is to contrast type A and type B personalities. These behaviors relate to patterns most likely to sustain heart disease. *Is stress related to personality?*

Type A Behavior.   The type A personality is competitive, hurried, and hard driving. Type A people are persistent and compulsive. They are oriented toward autocratic leadership and high achievement. They continually race the clock to meet deadlines and frequently react to frustration with hostility and anger. They are apt to neglect all aspects of life except work. That is, they are workaholics. Type A people are constantly involved in several projects and tend to take on excessive responsibility. They live under constant stress they create themselves (e.g., by time urgency, aggressiveness, lack of properly defined goals, and thinking about two things at once).

Type B Behavior.   The opposite behavior pattern is called type B. Type B people are characterized by an easygoing, open manner and are not so preoccupied with competition and achievement. Type B persons often take more time to think about things and appear to be less compulsive and success oriented. They feel confident, secure, and relaxed without a chronic desire to beat the clock. They are seldom impatient. They can relax without guilt and work without agitation. However, individual temperaments and styles may vary.

Tendency toward type A or type B behavior can be identified by responses to the questionnaire in Figure 16.2.

FIGURE 16.2
Type A Versus Type B
Behavior

Check the appropriate blank.	Always 4 pts.	Usually 3 pts.	Seldom 2 pts.	Never 1 pt.
1 Do you have a habit of explosively accentuating various key words in your ordinary speech even when there is no real need for such accentuation?	_____	_____	_____	_____
2 Do you have a tendency to utter the last few words of your sentences far more rapidly than the opening words?	_____	_____	_____	_____
3 Do you move, walk, and eat rapidly?	_____	_____	_____	_____
4 Do you feel an impatience with the rate at which most events take place?	_____	_____	_____	_____
5 Do you strive to think of or do two or more things simultaneously?	_____	_____	_____	_____
6 Do you find it difficult to refrain from talking about or bringing the theme of any conversation around to those subjects which especially interest and intrigue you?	_____	_____	_____	_____
7 Do you pretend to listen to others but really remain preoccupied with your own thoughts?	_____	_____	_____	_____
8 Do you feel vaguely guilty when you relax and do absolutely nothing for several hours to several days?	_____	_____	_____	_____
9 Do you no longer observe the more important or interesting or lovely objects that you encounter in your environment?	_____	_____	_____	_____
10 Do you not have any time to spare to become the things worth *being* because you are so preoccupied with getting the things worth *having*?	_____	_____	_____	_____

FIGURE 16.2 cont.

Check the appropriate blank.	Always 4 pts.	Usually 3 pts.	Seldom 2 pts.	Never 1 pt.
11 Do you attempt to schedule more and more in less and less time, and in doing so make fewer and fewer allowances for unforeseen contingencies?	_____	_____	_____	_____
12 Do you find yourself compelled to "challenge," be aggressive or hostile toward others with a personality that is similar to yours?	_____	_____	_____	_____
13 Do you resort to certain characteristic gestures or nervous tics (e.g., clenching fist, banging hand on table, pounding one fist into palm of other hand, clenching jaw, grinding teeth)?	_____	_____	_____	_____
14 Do you believe that whatever success you have enjoyed has been due in part to your ability to get things done faster than others?	_____	_____	_____	_____
15 Do you find yourself committed to translating and evaluating not only your own but also the activities of others in terms of numbers?	_____	_____	_____	_____
TOTALS	= _____ +	_____ +	_____ +	_____
	_____	_____	_____	_____

Source: Adapted from Meyer Friedman and Ray H. Roseman, *Type A Behavior and Your Heart* (New York: Alfred A. Knopf, 1974), pp. 82–88.

A score from 46 to 60 indicates a chronic type A personality; 31–45, a moderate type A. Steps perhaps need to be taken to monitor and control the traditional risk factors in heart disease—blood pressure, blood fats, and smoking. These people also may need to modify behavior by slowing down and reengineering their lives. Scores ranging from 15 to 30 probably indicate type B behaviors. People with these scores harbor no free-floating hostility and feel no real need to discuss or display accomplishments or achievements. They are people who are able to operate by the calendar, not the stopwatch.

Stress in the Work Environment

Does everyone experience stress?

Stress can be defined many ways: pressure, nervousness, or tension. Everyone experiences degrees of job stress. Accountants experience a growing tension from about the middle of January until April 15. Sales clerks and many others in the retail industry experience increased stress with certain gift-giving holidays, sales quotas not met, or inventory time. Industrial workers feel the tension for meeting certain deadlines and quotas. Students experience high levels of frustration and stress at final examination time. And some men and women dread the fortieth birthday. What are the things creating stress in your work life?

One management trainee suffered from insomnia which grew worse toward the end of each month. This was caused by company policy which required him to write a monthly activity report that went to three executives beyond his supervisor. "That report's crucial to my career," he said, "because people whom I've never met read it. They get impressions of my work and form opinions about me from its contents, so the closer the deadline gets the worse I sleep at night. I have trouble assembling a solid list of accomplishments for this month and goals for the next one—and I feel each month should sound better than the last!"

A friend suggested he review back pages from his daily calendar for notes he'd jotted down that would refresh his memory on what he'd done that should be mentioned in the report. This technique (along with keeping a formal record of significant incidents, ideas, and occupational victories) gave him a better-organized body of material from which to write the report. It proved to be a remedy for his sleepless nights.

Recognizing Stress on the Job

How does one recognize stress?

Some airline pilots confess to a case of the jitters before taking the periodic physical examinations required for flight certification. Workers in all fields report symptoms of stress just before a significant performance evaluation—one that may determine their eligibility for promotion or give them feedback on their attempts to remedy a deficiency that has been mentioned at the previous evaluation.

Workers who experience a change in supervision confirm that breaking in a new supervisor can be a stressful experience for them, and also for the new supervisor.

All jobs produce anxiety and tension. Sometimes job-related stress is mild and hardly recognizable. At other times this stress is not only unpleasant but also painful. What are the symptoms of moderate and severe tension?

What are the symptoms of stress?

A decade ago the Kiplinger Newsletter identified seven recognizable symptoms of job tension:

1 Getting boiling mad at some small irritation, such as a stuck desk drawer.
2 Habitual teeth grinding or lip tightening; nervous habits like nail biting or leg swinging.
3 Gulping meals; smoking more than ever.
4 Carrying a chip on the shoulder; being suspicious of people, mistrustful of friends.
5 Getting no satisfaction from pleasant incidents; always thinking of problems.
6 Feeling trapped, inadequate, doubtful of personal ability.
7 Being chronically tired, with no great physical exertion to account for it; finding it hard to sleep.

Such reactions may arise from extraordinary workloads, too much responsibility, or conflicts in expectations of certain roles. What is mild stress for one person, however, may be traumatic for someone else. What may be productive stress for one may be unproductive for another.

What is the effect of stress on job performance?

———————————— Stress and Job Performance ————————————

Productive stress is controlled stress. It comes from accepting new tasks, taking risks, and expanding one's competencies. Unproductive stress is uncontrolled stress: a person's usual mode of behavior is insufficient for confronting a certain situation. When stress is productive, job performance will be improved. The relationship between stress and job performance is illustrated in Figure 16.3. As stress increases so does performance—up to a point. Beyond that point, stress causes decreases in performance. The problem is how to determine where any one person fits on the curve.

Because stress affects both the body and job performance, some people have a greater tolerance for stress than others. Figure 16.4 shows what happens when different people experience stress. Before experiencing significant strain (yield point), Person *C* in this figure is able to withstand more stress than persons *A* and *B*. If slightly more stress is applied at the yield point, severe change (elastic limit) in normal behavior may occur.

Do some people have a greater tolerance for stress?

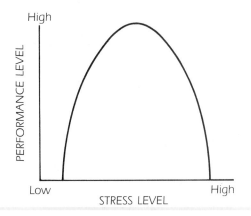

FIGURE 16.3
Relationship Between Stress and Job Performance

FIGURE 16.4
Stress/Strain
Relationships

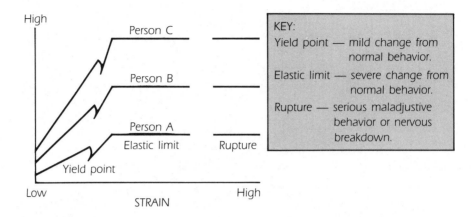

Beyond the elastic limit neither people nor materials return naturally to their normal behavior or original shape. Thus, if stress continues to intensify, breakage (rupture) can occur. Serious maladjustive behavior or a nervous breakdown is experienced, and outside intervention must take place. It is important, therefore, to identify people within the organization who are more vulnerable to stress and strain so the amount of pressure can be geared to individual tolerance. That is the way to obtain maximum performance and productivity without disruption.

A cooperage division manager for Glenmore Distilleries Company succumbed to higher management pressure for productivity by falsifying inventory tags to inflate production statistics.[5] The falsified inventory had such a material effect on earnings that the company had to restate its finances for the previous fiscal year.

Stress, Change, and Conflict

What are the origins of stress?

Stress is often a natural outgrowth of change and conflict. And because both are ever present, the potential for stress is inevitable. Managers and subordinates are constantly struggling with issues of competition, cooperation, and conformity. Executives are struggling with evaluation, correction, and discipline. These struggles are factors in the growth and development of employees, but they produce stress. Let's discuss the effects of change first.

Change

change

The essence of any kind of organizational development is planned change. **Change** is the substitution of one thing for another or an alteration that limits or restricts. Realistically the organization can't be changed unless the individual manager is changed. In many respects the individual is the most crucial member of the system. Yet the system often is easier to change than the person. To change either the individual or the system, we must alter the human and technical features which limit the organization and its employees from achieving their full potential.

A Model of the Change Process

A general overview of the process of change is presented in Exhibit 16.1. *How does change* Here change begins with the emergence of either exogenous (external) or *come about?* endogenous (internal) forces. These create a need for change in some part of the organization. The major external factors are technology, values, environmental opportunities, and constraints (economic, politicolegal, and social). The major internal factor is stress, in work activities, interactions, sentiments, and performance results.

The second step in the change model is the perception and analysis of a particular internal or external force. The third step is the development of change goals. There are five types of change goals.

1 *Strategic*—the change goals concerned with altering the relationship between the organization as a whole and its environment—for example, revised objectives, new product or customer mix, geographical expansion, a change in competitive emphasis.
2 *Technological*—the goals directly related to changes in the technology of production, task layout, plant and equipment, and other physical parts of an organization.
3 *Structural*—the change goals concerned with alterations in reporting relationships, communication or decision processes, authority relationships, and similar internal features of an organization.
4 *Behavioral*—the goals aimed at changing beliefs, values, attitudes, interpersonal relationships, group behavior, intergroup behavior, and similar human phenomena.
5 *Program*—the change goals which focus on altering the structure or features of the technical implementation plans in production, marketing, research and development, and other task areas—for example, changes in distribution channels, quality control requirements and procedures, and sales territories.[6]

The fourth step is to determine change targets, that is, the focus of all change efforts. The targets are either structural or behavioral. Structural targets include such things as formal work division and flow, information, incentives, and policies. Behavioral targets include the individuals, interpersonal relationships, group behavior, and intergroup behavior.

The fifth step involves getting the organization to implement change. Decisions are made on goals, criteria, and targets of change. At this stage those implementing change must be carefully chosen in light of the particular change target and resources available. Also, authority and responsibility of

EXHIBIT 16.1

The Organizational Change Process

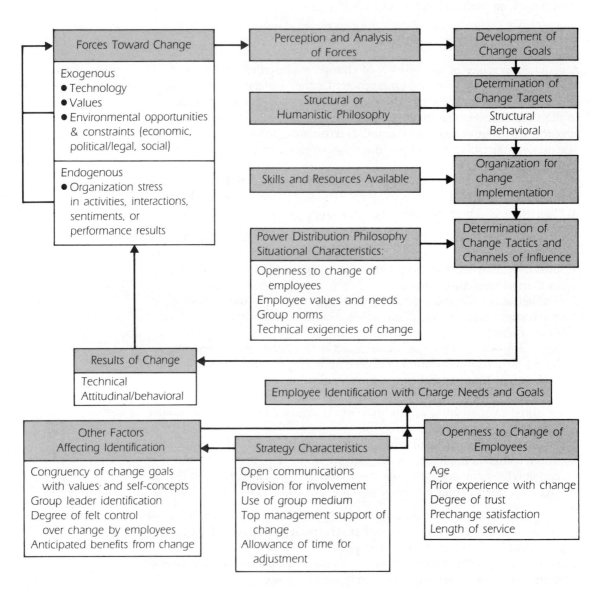

Source: Robert C. Shirley, "A Model for Analysis of Organizational Change," *MSU Business Topics* (Spring 1974): 62.

both the change agent and the client system must be explicitly defined to prevent conflict. Then, the tactics and channels of influence must be determined. Selection of the appropriate mix of change tactics and channels of influence depends on the targets of change, one's power distribution philosophy (or change tactics), and various situational characteristics. Each change situation requires close scrutiny.

The final step in the change model is evaluation of change efforts. Some indicators of success are productivity, morale, and innovative ability. Final results will depend on employee identification with change needs and goals. Some of the factors affecting identification are congruency of change goals with values and self-concepts, group leader identification, employees' feeling of control over change, and the benefits they anticipate.

―――――――――――――― Resistance to Change ――――――――――――――

Change has become a way of life. Even though it is usually initiated to improve efficiency and/or effectiveness, change can be either positive or negative. Anyone who has planned changes in an organization knows the difficulty in accurately foreseeing major problems, sees the enormous amount of time that's needed to iron them out and to get people to accept change, and experiences a lack of internal commitment, which is manifested partly by resistance by many to take initiative to help make the plan work.[7] Employees' resistance to change is often a learned response. They respond negatively in part because management expects them to respond negatively. Some common reasons for resisting change are complacency, disruption of interpersonal relationships, threat to status, fear of increased responsibilities, and economic factors.

Why do people resist change?

COMPLACENCY.   The organization is already successful and no one feels self-criticism and change are urgent. "Leave well enough alone" is the manager's motto.

DISRUPTION OF INTERPERSONAL RELATIONSHIPS.   Change sometimes means individuals who have been close associates for years are assigned to different task groups, thereby interrupting friendship bonds and common social activities. Those transferred, for example, could find themselves among new associates they may or may not like.

THREAT TO STATUS.   Realigning tasks often arouses feelings of a reduction in status among those directly affected by the change. The perceptions of those involved usually include feelings of being less highly esteemed by their subordinates and peers.

FEAR OF INCREASED RESPONSIBILITIES.   Change is sometimes resisted because people fear their own inability to handle increased work responsibilities. Because of this fear, some refuse to accept a promotion to a higher level. Of course, some managers welcome the opportunity to be measured against clear-cut standards. Poor managers, naturally, see danger in this.

ECONOMIC FACTORS.   Occasionally, resistance arises from individuals, work groups, or unions because they view change as threatening to their economic security, and hence to their physiological, safety, and esteem needs. Such fears are not entirely unfounded since technological changes have eliminated some skill levels.

People exhibit different degrees of resistance depending on the extent of the perceived threat. However, most people do not simply resist technological change. They resist potential disruption of their human relationships. That is one reason why change produces so much stress and conflict.

Conflict

conflict

What are the sources of conflict?

Conflict is a disagreement about beliefs or goals. A number of different sources produce conflict. Some of the most common are the aggressive nature of people, competition for limited resources, clashes of values and interests, role-based conflict, drives for power acquisition, poorly defined responsibilities, introduction of change, and the organizational climate.[8] To this list you can add technology and administrative allocation, labor force, and latent roles, competing pressures, and organizational posture.[9] Many potential misunderstandings result in stressful conflict. Two sources of conflict seem to stand out, however. These are communication and structure.

Communication Conflict

What causes communication conflict?

Communication conflicts often result in misunderstandings and produce stress. For example, three common sources of misunderstandings among managers and employees are semantics, lack of clarity, and too many links in the communication chain.

semantics

SEMANTICS.   Semantics, the first common source of communication conflict, is the study of word meanings and focuses on the relationship between words and their effect on people. It does not refer to dictionary definitions of words. Rather it supports the idea that meanings are in people, not in words. If you want to know what a word means as a certain person uses it, you must ask the person for the definition instead of consulting a compendium of meanings.

Supervisors should select their words carefully in stating policies, instructions, directions, or orders. People think, feel, and act according to the images they allow their nervous system to create. They react to the world according to how they symbolize it. If managers and employees can respond more sanely to one another's words and with tolerance for differences, they can reduce stress and improve work climate.

LACK OF CLARITY.   The second common source of communication conflict is ambiguity, or lack of clarity. It suggests inadequate and unclear communications. Accurate and correct information is especially necessary in the wording of instructions. The supervisor must learn to plan the best communication path to take for gaining understanding. Then she or he must encode the words carefully. The less detail given or the more ambiguous an instruction is, the more detail the employee will supply and the more stressful the job will become. Managers should never expose their employees to a barrage of words or lose them in a jargon jungle of word confusions. There is a definite advantage to being able to put things in a layperson's language.

TOO MANY LINKS IN THE COMMUNICATION CHAIN.   The third common source of communication conflict is too many links in the communication chain. The more links there are in a communication chain, and the farther the receiver is from the sender, the more chance there is for a misunderstanding. As the message travels down the chain, the message will change, details will drop out, new details will be added, some things will be made more important, and some will become less important. The message will seldom arrive at its destination in the same context it began. People's ideas, attitudes, and beliefs cause message distortion. The careless use of words or a reliance on wrong words to convey a meaning can result in a loss of understanding. And the more distorted a message becomes, the more stressful a subordinate becomes who recognizes that she or he is dealing with incomplete information.

―――――――――――――― *Reducing Communication Stress* ――――――――――――――

There are several ways to reduce communication stress. For example, to reduce stress among workers, supervisors can provide recognition on jobs well done, help employees with their work-related problems, provide adequate information on how to perform a job, explain reasons for changes in policies and procedures, or conduct annual performance reviews.

The neglect of any of these communications aids often puts employees in an ambiguous position: they won't fully understand what is expected. Most employees create enough stress for themselves and each other without supervisors creating undue work tension through unclear assignments, inadequate instructions, nonlistening attitudes, and so forth. As a supervisor, strive to be open with your employees, and keep them informed of what is happening. The human-relations climate will improve dramatically.

Structural Conflict

What causes organizational conflict?

Structure refers to the organizational factors a manager can control. These include size, clear lines of authority, responsibility, homogeneity or heterogeneity of staff, participation, goals and objectives, and reward systems. Any of these factors, and a myriad of others, can create job stress. For example, if authority, responsibility, or work methods are ambiguous, employees will not know what sort of job performance is expected. Conflict will arise because of an incompatibility of expectations. Stress will be produced.

Reducing Job Stress

Forty-five percent of United States executives work all day, and evenings and weekends; another 37 percent keep weekends free but work at night.[10] The average work day for 1200 executives who were involved in a Heidrick and Struggles survey exceeded ten hours, and 40 percent of these managers worked at least sixty hours per week.[11]

How can one reduce job stress?

   Part of the need for such daily wear-and-tear on health and performance, no doubt, can be traced to job ambiguity and conflict. What can be done about such job pressures? Ten ways to alleviate job stress are listed in Exhibit 16.2.

EXHIBIT 16.2

1   Don't overreact to crises. *Scale down emotional reactions. Anger, panic, and frustration are inappropriate.*
2   Don't take things personally. *Criticism should relate to behavior and not the individual.*
3   Don't worry about things beyond your control. *Do everything possible to remedy an unsatisfactory situation. But once it's out of your hands, there's nothing more to worry about.*
4   Learn to recognize your own tension symptoms. *Get in tune with the ways your body shows you are dipping into your emotional reserves.*
5   If possible opt for a complete change of scene. *Take a short vacation.*
6   Discover diversions on the work scene. *Go to the company library and read; do knee bends and arm exercises in the office; socialize with colleagues.*
7   Don't overorganize your uncommitted time. *Leave your schedule loose so you can go along with a spur-of-the-moment impulse that helps you do your job with flair.*
8   Rotate the "tyres of your mind." *Change the nature and pattern of your work.*
9   Tackle someone else's problem. *Help employees cope with their seemingly intractable difficulties.*
10 Give your mind a rest by putting your body to work. *Use sports, gardening, or odd jobs to take your mind off work problems.*[12]

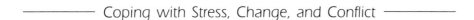

Coping with Stress, Change, and Conflict

From the preceding information you can see that stress, change, and conflict are inevitable experiences. Since all three are unavoidable, what can be done to decrease the problem of too much stress? Several possible solutions have already been suggested, and the following discussion will deal with further methods.

Methods of Reducing Stress

Because anxiety and tension are such widespread problems in corporate America, many techniques are available for coping with stress. All kinds of solutions are offered: taking short naps, listening to classical music, expressing anger, assessing your treatment of others, checking your living habits, taking minivacations. The following methods for reducing stress are some of the more frequently suggested ones.

What are some methods for reducing stress?

HEALTH EXAMINATION.   A clean bill of health from one's doctor can often relieve anxiety and help one relax. Especially in cases of chronic stress, the physician should be apprised of what's going on. Increasingly, health exams are exploring the relationship between life activities and physical disorders.

EXERCISE.   Before beginning any exercise program, one should see a physician for advice on a program to fit one's needs and abilities. Then one may begin a program to keep physically fit. The key is to pick an enjoyable activity. Try to avoid competitive sports for exercise as they often create a different kind of stress. Don't trade one stress situation for another. The point of exercise is to improve the mental outlook, not to become frustrated in trying to win.

HOLIDAYS, VACATIONS, AND HOBBIES.   Holidays, vacations, and hobbies are all important for the reduction of stress, because like exercise they take one's mind off the job. They provide a rest from mental fatigue by providing a break in routine. Vacations are a good way to get away from a stressful environment. But the office must be left behind; one must enjoy being away. Holidays are also important because we all need more than a two-week break yearly from stress attacks. Weekends should be rest periods from work when possible. A hobby or some alternative ongoing activity will involve one with something other than work.

MEDITATION AND RELAXATION.   An inexpensive technique for alleviating stress is called the relaxation response.[13] Since the risk of developing heart attacks and strokes is directly proportional to the level of blood pressure, as blood pressure goes down the risk diminishes. This lowered risk when translated into dollars saved amounts to $26.7 billion yearly (the cost of cardiovascular disease in the United States).[14] The relaxation response technique for lowering blood pressure and raising one's efficiency depends on the series of instructions listed in Exhibit 16.3.

----------------------------------- EXHIBIT 16.3 -----------------------------------

1   Sit quietly in a comfortable position.
2   Close your eyes.
3   Beginning at your feet and progressing up to your face, deeply relax all your muscles. Keep them relaxed.
4   Breathe through your nose and become aware of your breathing. As you breathe out, say the word *one* silently to yourself. Continue the pattern: breathe in . . . out, "one"; in . . . out, "one"; and so on. Breathe easily and naturally.
5   Continue for ten to twenty minutes. You may open your eyes to check the time, but do not use an alarm. When you finish, sit quietly for several minutes.
6   Do not worry about whether you are successful in achieving a deep level of relaxation. Maintain a passive attitude and permit relaxation to occur at its own pace. When distracting thoughts occur, try to ignore them by not dwelling on them and return to repeating "one." With practice, the response should come with little effort. Practice the technique once or twice daily but not within two hours after any meal, since the digestive processes seem to interfere with eliciting the relaxation response.[15]

biofeedback

BIOFEEDBACK.   **Biofeedback** is a method of using mental powers to regulate bodily systems that were once believed beyond control. It is becoming a useful tool of executives for controlling stress and hypertension and improving performance. Its primary goal is better physical health, and it has been used successfully not only by executives but also by diabetics and epileptics. In one biofeedback process a subject is connected to an electromyograph (EMG), which records muscle tension. By watching the dials and listening to the clicks of the EMG, the subject is able to tune in to what his or her body is doing. As clicks increase in speed, muscle tension (stress) is rising. By using the thought processes the subject attempts to regulate the bodily system by bringing anxieties under control. The feedback from the EMG provides information on whether the strategies are working.

Since there is no way to avoid stressful situations completely, biofeedback is one technique for reducing anxieties by concentrating on relaxation. But there are other techniques many find useful for reducing stress. For example, some people find it very relaxing just to talk.

TALK.   Sometimes it is helpful just to talk to other people about one's problems. It is important to find someone who can act as a sounding board. The person doesn't really have to offer solutions, just listen as one talks one's way to a solution. This technique is very similar to nondirective counseling. Another variation of talking is to share decision-making activities by allowing peers or subordinates to help one cope with stresses. However, some people can create more stress. So one should pick carefully the persons one talks to as a stress-reducing activity. They should be warm, friendly, and empathetic.

TAKING ACTION. Whatever technique is used to reduce stress, the key is to do something. This step may seem too simple to include, but the majority of people only talk about what they ought to do. Very few ever take the actual corrective steps. Remember that tomorrow is a dream, yesterday, a memory, and today is a fact. Act now.

Methods of Preventing Stress

The distinction between reduction and prevention of stress and conflict is probably arbitrary. In one case we are trying to deal with stress once it is part of our life. In the other case we are trying to keep from creating needless stress. Based on interviews with sixty-one executives whose lives and jobs were directly affected by traumatic events, an ideal pattern for preventing crises has been developed. Among the suggestions are the following.[16]

Can stress be prevented?

MANAGE BY ANTICIPATION. The best strategy for preventing stress is to be prepared. All plausible crises should be considered in advance, and response tactics should be prepared for each. Specific options should be devised for potential threats, risks, and opportunities.

MAKE BETTER USE OF ENVIRONMENTAL AUDITS. Survey risks and assess the possibilities of exposure if one operates within a high-risk environment. Give attention to threats and consider how to turn them into opportunities.

DEVELOP PERSONAL SKILLS. Take whatever steps are necessary to learn how better to face crises. These may include obtaining an advanced degree, training in public speaking or other communication skills, learning to work in front of a TV camera, or conducting seminars for others. Be prepared to deal with the public and still maintain favorable relationships with them.

PLAN THINGS RIGHT ALL THE TIME. Doing everything right that one is capable of doing, and in public view, is not easy. Several aids are needed. For example, one would have to be able to plan one's time (see Chapter 4). One might need to develop a management-by-objectives philosophy about how to do one's job. One would also need to recognize one's limitations as a manager, what parameters one can work within. And, one probably should have a high sense of ethical responsibility, a good moral platform for dealing with peers, subordinates, supervisors, and public.

LOOK INWARD.   The real key to stress prevention is introspection, a willingness to look inward and to tap the hidden power of one's own creativity and problem-solving abilities. An emotionally mature self-concept is helpful in both reducing and preventing stress. It also will help in solving the human relations problems that cause daily stress.

 CONCLUSION

Every day people face on-the-job pressures which produce stress. Two major sources of stress are change in work groups and conflict with others. This chapter has dealt with ways to recognize and lessen the stress on a job and methods to prevent stress. The key to handling stress, change, and conflict may be the willingness to develop a strong self-concept. Stressful situations are often in the mind's eye; what is stressful to one may not be stressful to another. A strong self-concept can help people meet most situations without falling apart from tension and pressure.

KEY TERMS

Stress: imbalance in one's personal life brought on by changes in family, occupation, personal relations, finance, religion, health, residence, and so forth.
Life Change Units: weighted numbers assigned to stressful events in one's life.
Change: the substitution of one thing for another or an alteration that limits or restricts.
Conflict: a disagreement about beliefs or goals.
Semantics: the study of word meanings.
Biofeedback: a method of using mental powers to regulate bodily systems.

QUESTIONS

1   Reread the opening case.
  a.   In your opinion, which type of conflict—communication or structural—is most responsible for Allen's stress?

    b. Recommend at least four things he could do to alleviate this stress.

    c. What techniques could he use to *prevent* stress from intruding on his life?

    d. Compute Allen Beane's approximate total on the stress of living test, Exhibit 16.1.

    e. Reflecting on Chapter 15's MBO discussion, how might Allen use the management trainee to resolve certain stress?

2 Consider your score on Exhibit 16.1 in light of this chapter's discussion. What can you do to resolve or eliminate at least one of your personal stress-producing events? Do you plan to do that? Why or why not?

3 List at least five symptoms of physiological and psychological stress. What three specific diseases may stress cause?

4 Defend the following remark: "Stress is the enemy within; you've got to learn to cope with it, because you can't escape it."

5 How would you characterize people with type A behavior? How do they react to frustration, and how do they view their jobs?

6 How would you characterize type B persons? How do they deal with frustration and view their jobs?

7 "I don't get ulcers—I *give* 'em!" Recalling this chapter's discussion, would you say the speaker has made an informed and realistic appraisal of his or her role with others? Why or why not?

8 In your opinion, which two of the following jobs may produce the greatest stress, and why?

    a. production manager,

    b. production scheduler,

    c. advertising copywriter,

    d. stockbroker, and

    e. trial lawyer.

9 Diagram the relationship between stress and job performance. Why is this a very personal relationship? Give at least one example of a situation that may generate productive stress for one individual and nonproductive or damaging stress for another.

10 In what way is each individual manager concerned with each subordinate's tolerance for stress? What may some subordinates do to conceal their individual yield points and elastic limits? What problems may result?

11 Summarize the following types of change goals and give at least one work-related example of each:

    a. strategic

    b. technological

    c. structural

    d. behavioral

    e. program

12 List at least three major reasons why people resist change.

13 Which three sources most often create communication conflicts? What can managers do to reduce the stress that results?

14 Differentiate between communication conflict and structural conflict. In your opinion, which type of conflict is most easily controlled by an individual manager? Why?

15   Propose at least seven things you can do to alleviate your own job stress. How does the comment, "It's easier said than done" apply here?

16   Review the methods of reducing stress that were presented in this chapter. How would you convince a spouse or family member who is under great stress to *try* one or more of these methods?

17   "She's unflappable; nothing can shake her up." Why might the speaker be wrong in this assessment of the person?

18   How can this chapter's information be used in choosing a college major? a career?

--------------------------------- CASES ---------------------------------

Case 16.1

In April 1979 General Mills reported the findings of a vast research project titled "Family Health in an Era of Stress." The research had been conducted by Yankelovich, Skelly and White. It was General Mills's third such survey. The first dealt with money management and the second with rearing children.

One of the findings of this study says 82 percent of adult Americans feel they are under too much stress to function properly. And inflation is the main worry creating this stress. A second finding suggests that since 1970 societal values have virtually turned away full face from the protestant work ethic. They found that Americans have shifted from self-denial to self. People are interested in "Who am I?"

Other findings show about 56 percent of Americans greatly fear cancer, but only 7 percent worry about becoming mentally ill. About 76 percent believe that technology solves more human problems than it creates. And although we are all under stress, single parents apparently have more anxiety than most.

Case Questions

1   Discuss the phenomenon of the "me generation" in which people have become extremely self-centered and dissociated with collective effort for shared or mutual benefit. In your opinion, what social conditions have prompted that attitude?

2   Do you believe that the trend away from work for work's sake is a fundamentally healthy one for a society? Why or why not?

3   What features of life in the United States contribute to the level of stress Americans encounter in their work and nonwork activities? What changes are needed to reduce the amount of stress-producing experiences in society as we know them in the United States? Do you believe it's feasible for influential leaders (in government, business, religion, education, etc.) to attempt to make these changes? Why or why not?

4   In your opinion, what other nations appear to have the least stressful social and work environments, and why?

Case 16.2

Dick Clements, a midwestern publishing company executive, was glad to hear from his long-time friend Ty Barclay. They had known each other for years.

"I'm heading up a new publishing company in Boston, Dick; it's really going to be a leader," Ty said enthusiastically. "I'm hand-picking my top people, and I want you on my team. Oh, I know you've been settled out there for almost ten years, but here's a chance to get back into action again. We're going to do great things! You can be a part of it."

"Exactly what do you have in mind, Ty?" Dick asked.

"You'll be one of my senior editors, scouting the market and signing authors to write books on specific subjects. You'll travel a lot like you did when we worked together at Intertext. I'll top any salary offer from your present employer, and I know our benefits are better than you're getting there. What do you say?"

Dick discussed the offer with his family. Moving meant separating from lifelong friends and buying a new home in an expensive area. In addition, Dick's wife Gwen would relinquish a solid career just two years short of qualifying for full retirement benefits.

"There's another possibility," Dick suggested. "I can take a room in Boston and you can maintain our base of operations here. The kids can graduate from high school with their friends and you can get your time in for maximum retirement. If we can live just two years like this, we'll be set. I'll be traveling so much that I can fly through and stop over for several days every month."

They talked this idea over and finally decided to see how it would work out. Dick welcomed the challenge and thrill of the job and of building a leading publishing company from the ground up.

As Dick's job took shape, it became so hectic and his travel plans were so compressed that he was away from his family for more than six weeks at a time.

Tonight he called his wife to tell her that he would not be home next week as expected. "It looks like it will be at least three weeks until I can get out there, Gwen," he complained. "I wish there was something else I could say. This job's stretching me pretty thin; I'm paying over $300 per month for a small apartment, and I'm very frustrated trying to hold my job and all of you together when we're separated by several thousand miles."

"Well, we're getting along fine," she assured him. "I've got the household bookkeeping in order. I haven't missed a single basketball game that the boys have played this fall. I'm taking a night course at the local community college, and I've even done some basic plumbing repair. All in all, this arrangement has made me see that I can do things I never dreamed I could handle before, and I'm becoming such a different person you'll hardly know me!"

"That's what concerns me," Dick answered. "This arrangement is really throwing a monkey wrench into our relationship. We both need to grow, but I don't want us to grow apart."

"Well, this is a concern of mine, too. Let's talk about this when you come home," she said.

Case Questions

1 What would you suggest to Dick Clements under the circumstances, and why?
2 Indicate some of the stressful events Dick is facing according to Exhibit 16.1. How might he alleviate one or more?
3 How might this experience actually strengthen the relationship between Dick, and his wife and children?

─────────────── NOTES ───────────────

1. Walter H. Gmelch, "Stress: Management's Twentieth-Century Dilemma," *Supervisory Management* (September 1978): 30.
2. Thomas H. Holmes and Richard H. Rahe, "The Social Readjustment Rating Scale," *Journal of Psychosomatic Research* 11(1967): 213–218.
3. Anthony Ramirez, "A Manager's Transfers Impose Heavy Burden on His Wife, Children," *The Wall Street Journal,* 28 February 1979, p. 1.
4. Lawrence Ingrassia, "Aftermath of Failure: The Collapse of a Man, The Agony of a Family," *The Wall Street Journal,* 23 October 1980, p. 1.
5. "Distiller Says Errors in Its Inventories Caused by Manager," *The Wall Street Journal,* 23 October 1980, p. 1.
6. Robert C. Shirley, "A Model for Analysis of Organizational Change," *MSU Business Topics* (Spring 1974): p. 62.
7. Chris Argyris, "Today's Problems with Tomorrow's Organizations," *Journal of Management Studies* (February 1967): 53.
8. Andrew J. DuBrin, *Fundamentals of Organizational Behavior—An Applied Perspective* (Elmsford, N.Y.: Pergamon Press, 1974), pp. 304–311.
9. James D. Thompson, "Organizational Management of Conflict," *Administrative Science Quarterly* 4(March 1960): 389–409.
10. Auren Uris, "How Managers Ease Job Pressures," *International Management* (June 1972): 45–47.
11. *The Wall Street Journal,* 20 March 1979, p. 1.
12. Uris, "How Managers Ease," pp. 45–47.
13. Herbert Benson, "Your Innate Asset for Combating Stress," *Harvard Business Review* (July–August 1974): 49–60.
14. Ruanne K. Peters and Herbert Benson, "Time Out for Tension," *Harvard Business Review* (January–February 1978): 124.
15. Ibid.
16. George S. Odiorne, "Executives Under Siege: Strategies for Survival," *Management Review* (April 1978): 7–12.

─────────────── SUGGESTED READINGS ───────────────

Beehr, Terry A., and Newman, John E. "Job Stress, Employee Health, and Organizational Effectiveness: A Facet Analysis, Model, and Literature Review," *Personnel Psychology* 31(1978): 665–669.

House, Robert J., and Rizzo, John R. "Role Conflict and Ambiguity As Critical Variables in a Model of Organizational Behavior," *Organizational Behavior and Human Performance* 7(1972): 467–505.

McGaffey, Thomas N. "New Horizons in Organizational Stress Prevention Approaches," *The Personnel Administrator* (November 1978): 26–32.

4

Human Relationships and Your Future

17

Values, Ethics, and Social Responsibility

When you complete your study of this chapter, you should be able to:

1　Assess your personal values for working,
2　Understand the need for sound ethical policies in business,
3　Establish a plan for raising the level of ethical responsibility in business, and
4　State the importance of business involvement in societal needs (i.e., its social responsibility).

———————————————— OPENING CASE ————————————————

Greg O'Keefe, a machinist, works on the first shift in the machine shop at Paragon Products, Inc. Paragon has several contracts to manufacture weapons systems and aerospace products for the Army, Navy, and NASA. In a single week Greg may work on as many as four government projects.

Most days are relatively routine for a skilled craftsman like Greg, but last Monday was unusual. It started with a brief conversation with Manny Dirkman, his foreman.

"Hey, guy," Manny said cordially, "I'm going on vacation next week, and I need our best machinist to look after things while I'm gone. No formal authority, mind you, just sort of a father figure for the rest of the guys."

"All right, Manny, I'll try to make you look good," Greg bantered back. "I save your job that way at least once a year."

"Hey, if you talk like that I won't buy the beer for our next fishing trip," Manny grinned. The monthly outings had been traditional for the past five years, and both men enjoyed each other's company considerably.

"Anything special that needs to be done?" Greg asked.

"Not really," Manny answered, "just a minor accounting detail. Make sure account number 11210 is on every job cost sheet that comes through here. That's all. Got it?"

"Sure, 11210," Greg confirmed. "No problem."

Greg had memorized most of the account numbers that were used to assign labor costs to the various government contracts, but 11210 was new. During a break he confirmed it with a call to a friend in the accounting department. "Sure," his friend said, "11210 is assigned to Nimrod—that new NASA satellite we're just starting up. Funny, though, I didn't think any Nimrod stuff would reach the shop so soon. We've only had the contract a month! It's a real plum, by the way. NASA pays our costs plus a profit."

Back in his work area, Greg pondered that information. All the military contracts were cut-and-dried. The company had to meet its original bid; if it didn't, it lost money. Nimrod, though, was different. NASA agreed to pay Paragon's full cost plus a fixed fee or profit. Looking at the jobs in progress around the shop, Greg didn't see a single one that looked new. He knew all the parts by sight; they were regular items that had been moving through the shop for months. Suspecting an error, he called Manny at home.

"No mistake, Greg," Manny confirmed. "It's 11210, like I told you. Now don't worry about it. Put that number on every job cost sheet until I get back, and everything'll be fine."

"But Manny, that's a NASA job; work hasn't even been released to the shop yet! We'll be charging our work on the military contracts to NASA's Nimrod, and the accounting will be all screwed up!"

"Greg, what can I say?" Manny persisted. "That account number came down from Ivan Key himself, the head of the accounting department! Just go ahead and do it, buddy!"

With a growing sense of uneasiness, Greg did one more thing: he called Ivan Key's office. After explaining his concern to a secretary, he was told Ivan Key was in a meeting and would contact him before the day was over. Within an hour Ivan strode through the shop door.

"What's the problem down here, O'Keefe?" he demanded. "Have I got to be called away from my desk by a machinist who won't follow his foreman's orders? If you won't, maybe we should find somebody who will!"

"Well, I was certain there was a mixup, and I wanted to get it straightened out. We're charging work on one project to a different one," Greg answered defensively.

"It's not your job to question management directives," Key stormed. "You'll hear more about this!"

The next morning Greg was called into the machine shop manager's office and fired for insubordination. "I've been a real dummy," he thought, gathering up his tools. "The company's charging its cost overruns on the other projects to Nimrod, because NASA will pay all the costs on that one plus a fat profit. What a sham! But here I am, a machinist at the bottom of a multimillion-dollar corporation. Who'd believe my word about what's going on? Besides, if I blow the whistle to anybody, Manny may get fired for not postponing this creative bookkeeping until he got back from vacation. The company will probably load thousands of dollars of cost overruns onto Nimrod before it's finished, and the taxpayers will suffer in the long run. I wonder what I should do."

At this point in your study of how to manage human relationships, you have developed skills and knowledge for handling the day-to-day people problems in business. You are now ready to practice these skills in the real world. Perhaps you lack as much experience as you want, however. One thing that is helpful is relating human relations knowledge to a specific job.

This will be discussed in Chapter 18. It will give you a look at your goals in life, ways to get that first job on graduation, and changes that await you. The concern, as throughout this text, will center on the continued need for effective interpersonal relationships. In this chapter we will deal with social responsibilities for business persons of the future. We will also discuss values and ethics that sustain a human relations philosophy.

The Public Be Damned

Unfortunately, many business people would probably agree with Manny and Ivan. They exist to make a profit, not to please the public. They do not see

Do you think there has been a decline in ethical behavior in the U.S.?

themselves as having any social responsibility. They profess belief in ecology, consumerism, and honesty, but they do not always practice what they preach. Thus in this last decade we have seen:

- Watergate and the conviction of high-level government employees,
- corporations caught breaking political campaign contribution laws,
- shoddy product quality,
- lack of concern for worker health and safety,
- mishandling of corporate pension funds, and
- corporate bribes to foreign officials made public.[1]

Such a decline in ethical behavior concerns many Americans. There is great opportunity for such unethical behavior at all organizational levels—from the top on down. Some studies of American industry suggest neither managers nor workers can state with certainty what is definitely right and wrong in all situations. Therefore, persons who practice or condone small unethical practices have a tendency later to attempt more serious unethical activities. They apparently feel since no repercussion occurred when something little was done there is no threat in attempting a more serious activity.

What has caused these declines?

What gives rise to this public-be-damned attitude? There probably are several indicators.

Money Talks

Money talks loudly. It is estimated, for example, that direct employee theft costs business $3 to $5 billion yearly; and internal theft outweighs external losses three to one.[2] When employees engage in theft they are depriving the stockholders, managers, and other employees of the right to decide what should be done with corporate profits. As another example, a *Fortune* survey of 1043 leading companies showed that more than 10 percent violated at least one major domestic law during the 1970s.[3] Offenses in foreign countries (such as bribing foreign officials) were not considered. Crimes fell into five categories: bribery, criminal fraud, illegal political contributions, tax evasion, and crimes in restraint of trade involving bid rigging and price fixing.

In addition, since most of our product choices relate to a particular supplier's making a profit, we, in one sense, have encouraged manufacturers to accommodate us so we can have more and more materialism. Thus, some business people would claim we have done it to ourselves. We created the climate for unethical behavior and therefore should not be surprised when it occurs. In the words of an age-old proverb, "He who sleeps with the dogs will get fleas." However, do such attitudes really justify unethical behavior?

Caveat Emptor

Historical acceptance of the caveat emptor principle (let the buyer beware) has encouraged business to produce and sell shoddy merchandise. Such activities have resulted in the establishment and growth of the consumer movement. The impetus for consumerism was Ralph Nader's attack on General Motors and other groups.

―――――――――――――――― Government Policies ――――――――――――――――

A third reason for the public-be-damned attitude probably resulted from ineffective and untimely government policies. The tentacles of government have reached almost every business concern and have enforced certain rules and standards. In many companies the increase in paperwork, hiring directives, and safety regulations increased production costs. These increases resulted in higher prices in the marketplace. Many business people felt justified in naming the public's interest in consumerism and lower taxes as the culprit. Thus, there is almost a sense of revenge in some arenas: "You did it to me and I'm going to do it to you."

Although we might hope such attitudes do not exist, in many instances even worse ones may prevail. And actions result from the values people hold about work.

―――――――――――――――― Values for Working ――――――――――――――――

Within any culture there can be widespread differences in the interpretation of ethics, values, and sanctions. For example, some think all behavior within the law is ethical. Others assume behavior that makes a person feel good is ethical. **Ethics** might be defined as a system of principles for moral conduct. Still others believe behavior reflecting the values of superiors is ethical. **Values** are premises that define appropriate behavior of a particular group. Some persons adopt an absolute standard or believe the same rules apply to every situation for all time. Others think ethics are relative; they depend on the situation. There are people who adopt the ethical sanctions of the group to which they belong, and those who accept a code for themselves alone. **Sanctions** are rewards or penalties that lead people toward ethical behavior or away from unethical behavior. Examples of these sanctions are the Judeo-Christian code or the philosophy of a particular governmental system.

Why do you behave the way you do?

ethics

values

sanctions

An example may clarify these views. Consider Ms. *A*, who works in sales and feels pressure from her superior to submit reports showing a growth in sales each month. Ms. *A* may be tempted in some months to doctor her sales report to show the necessary increase in sales. She would consider this act ethical if her view of what is ethical depends on the situation involved. She could also view this act as ethical if she feels that complying with a supervisor's request constitutes ethical behavior. She might take a different view of her behavior if she believes anything less than complete truth is unethical. Also, she might feel differently if the ethical code adopted by her group (for example, her church) did not condone such behavior. Therefore, the same act could be viewed differently by different people depending on their individual circumstances and ways of looking at the world. All of this makes any study of work ethics difficult.

Levels of Work Values

On which level of work values development do you exist?

What are your values about working? All workers exist at different levels of psychological development. These levels are expressed in the values they hold about work. Seven useful levels of development and work values are listed in Exhibit 17.1.

EXHIBIT 17.1

1 **Reactive.** This level of psychological development is restricted primarily to infants and people with serious brain deterioration and certain psychopathic conditions. Employees are not ordinarily found at this level.

2 **Tribalistic.** These employees are best suited to jobs that offer easy work, friendly people, fair play, and, above all, a good supervisor. Employees at this level believe they may not have the best job in the world, but they do as well as others with jobs like theirs. They like a supervisor who tells them exactly what to do and how to do it and who encourages them by doing it with them.

3 **Egocentric.** These employees see jobs as having two major requirements: they should pay well and keep people off their back. They do not care for work that ties them down, but they will do it if they must in order to make the money. Because of the raw, rugged value system of these employees, they need a supervisor who is tough but allows them to be tough too.

4 **Conformist.** These employees like a secure job where the rules are followed and no favoritism is shown. They feel they have worked hard for what they have and think they deserve some good breaks. Others, they believe, should realize it is their duty to work. They like a supervisor who calls the shots, isn't always changing his or her mind, and makes certain everyone follows the rules.

5 **Manipulative.** The ideal job for these employees is one that is full of variety, allows some free wheeling and dealing, and offers pay and bonus on the basis of results. They feel they are responsible for their own success and are constantly looking for new opportunities. A good supervisor for these employees understands the politics of getting the job done, knows how to bargain, and is firm but fair.

6 **Sociocentric.** A job allowing for the development of friendly relationships with supervisors and others in the work group appeals to these employees. Working with people toward a common goal is more important than getting caught up in a materialistic rat race. They like a supervisor who promotes working in harmony by being more of a friendly person than a supervisor.

7 **Existential.** These employees like a job where the goals and problems are more important than the money, prestige, or how it should be done. They prefer work of their own choosing, work that offers continuing challenge and requires imagination and initiative. To them, a good supervisor is one who provides access to the information they need and lets them do the job in their own way.[4]

As you look at the seven levels, where do you think you'd be most happy as an employee? Most employees might answer either level 6 or 7. If so, this puts most managers into a dilemma. Most supervisors and managers are managing at levels 4 and 5. Perhaps this should not be surprising in light of the history of management thought during the last seventy-five years. Managers and employees seldom seem to have an exact match of philosophies. For some reason they don't mesh on change, and often human relationships are tense.

Work Attitudes

Not everyone's values are the same. What may seem right to the employee may be wrong for the manager. That's why some people have suggested a need for a change from managing by the **Golden Rule:** "Do unto others as you would have them do unto you." This statement assumes all employees have the same work values. And that is not the case. Therefore, managers may need to consider managing by the **Platinum Rule:** "Do unto others as they would have you do unto them." Such a change in management philosophy could introduce a new work ethic into our society.

Golden Rule

Platinum Rule

Let's look more closely at your values and attitudes about work. Respond to the questionnaire in Exhibit 17.1. Your answers will reveal something of the way in which you value your present job. If you are not satisfied with the number of positive approaches you're taking toward work, begin a new self-improvement direction.

What are your attitudes toward work?

Business Ethics

If you were to compare your responses in Exhibit 17.2 with someone else's you might find several different responses. The same is true when you compare ethical beliefs and behavior. Not everyone agrees as to what is ethical in business. Let's look at what research says about business ethics.

Sound Ethics Is Good Business

Two studies have shown persons agree with the statement, "Sound ethics is good business." One study of readers of *Harvard Business Review* (HBR) found 99 percent of the executives responding to the poll agreed with this statement. Most stated they felt this policy made for good public relations, which is conducive to making money.[5] Another study, using MBA graduates from the American Assembly of College Schools of Business (AACSB) schools as a population, found 90 percent of these persons agreed with this statement.[6] Therefore, persons about to enter the business world as well as executives in the field indicate sound ethics is good business.

Is sound ethics really good business for today?

FIGURE 17.1

Work Attitude Survey

	Yes	No	Sometimes
1 Do you take a genuine personal interest in your work and in the company's affairs?	___	___	___
2 Or, is your real feeling one of "what's it to me"?	___	___	___
3 Do you feel the problems that arise in the operation of the business are none of your business as long as someone else is willing to handle them?	___	___	___
4 Do you take full advantage of every coffee break, rest period, et cetera, even though to do so may often interrupt something important on which you are working?	___	___	
5 Do you gossip about the organization, criticize its methods and its personnel to outsiders, even to fellow employees?	___	___	___
6 Do you do merely what you are told to do, or do you seek additional work and responsibility in an effort to be increasingly valuable to the company?	___	___	___
7 If occasionally you do things beyond the minimum requirements of your job, are you motivated by a sense of the *company's* welfare, or merely by the thought that such extra effort may improve your standing with your supervisor?	___	___	___
8 Do you withhold help and advice to other employees in your department because of a feeling that they may stand in the way of your own progress?	___	___	___
9 Are you profit-conscious to the point where you try to do everything you can to avoid waste and to cut expense?	___	___	___

		Yes	No	Sometimes

FIGURE 17.1 cont.

10	Or, is your attitude one of "that's not up to me; let the front office worry about it"?	___	___	___
11	If the absence of a fellow worker means someone must help out by taking over some of his or her work, are you one of the first to volunteer?	___	___	___
12	Or, do you wait for someone else to do so?	___	___	___
13	Do you check and criticize your own work and strive always for excellence?	___	___	___
14	Or, is your attitude one of "oh, I guess that will do"?	___	___	___
15	Do you know, or attempt to learn, anything about the operation of the company outside of your own area, so that if someone were needed in another department you could be of help?	___	___	___
16	Do you believe work is something you *have* to do to make a living?	___	___	___
17	Or, do you believe work is an opportunity to be of value to your employer, your family, your community, and yourself?	___	___	___
18	Are you inclined to be careless if you can get away with it and, if discovered, to alibi or pass the blame on to someone else?	___	___	___
19	Do you have the feeling that the company pays you less than you are worth?	___	___	___
20	Or, do you ever ask yourself whether you are giving the company as much as they are paying you for?	___	___	___

Source: Adapted from H. K. Dugdale, *Wanted! A New Attitude Toward Work* (Timonium, Maryland: Kirkley Press, 1964), pp. 8–10.

The Profit Motive

Does business exist to make a profit?

When asked whether profit alone is the motive for business activities, persons in three surveys agreed it was not. In the HBR study we just mentioned, 94 percent of the participants disagreed with the statement, "Business exists for only one purpose, to create and deliver value situations at a profit." A study of the same population fifteen years later showed only 69 percent of the group felt profit alone was not the determining factor in business situations.[7] Finally, the MBA graduates also were asked about the profit motive; 89 percent disagreed profit was the only legitimate business concern. This statement was made despite the fact that five of the leading economics textbooks listed profit maximization as the ultimate objective of persons in business.[8]

Despite the idea that profit is not the sole business motive, some persons feel a conflict between what is expected of them in order to show results and what is expected of them as ethical human beings. However, this feeling is decreasing. In 1961, three out of four individuals stated they experienced conflict between what was expected of them as "efficient, profit-conscious managers" and what was expected of them as ethical persons. This number decreased to four out of seven in 1976. There are two possible reasons for this decline: (1) Ethical standards have declined. (2) Situations once causing ethical discomfort have become accepted.[9]

General Foods Corporation stockholders have pressured the company to discontinue television advertising directed at children below nine years of age and to give greater emphasis to good nutrition in ad campaigns. Some Kellogg Company stockholders have endorsed a similar approach. The total shares involved were less than 6 percent in each case.[10]

Personal Standards

Do managers exert pressure on subordinates to compromise ethical practices?

Other studies indicate persons in the business world feel pressure to lower ethical standards to achieve necessary results. One study reveals 78 percent of the respondents agree with the statement, "I can conceive of a situation where you have sound ethics running from top to bottom, but because of pressures from the top to achieve results, the person down the line compromises." These feelings of pressure are keenly felt at the middle and lower management levels.[11]

This same pressure is felt by persons in both the private and public sectors. Sixty-four percent of private-sector employees and 60 percent of public-sector employees feel pressure to compromise personal standards to achieve organizational goals. Senior managers and persons with higher educational levels are less likely to feel this pressure.[12]

When managers at Uniroyal, Inc., and at Pitney Bowes were asked if they felt pressure to compromise personal ethics to achieve organizational goals, 70 percent and 59 percent respectively responded they were.[13] Only one study showed fewer than 50 percent of the respondents stating they felt no such pressure. This study polled members of the National Association of Purchasing Managers (NAPM). Only 27 percent of the respondents stated they felt internal pressure to behave unethically.[14]

Competition

Another cause often listed for unethical behavior is competition. Various businesses may be competing for the same dollar. Individuals in the same company may be competing for promotions and salary increases. Forty percent of the MBA graduates who were asked about profit motive (page 384) felt stiff competition could force business persons to resort to shady practices that become necessary for survival. Therefore, it would be logical to expect these same students to justify later behavior in business. Competition can encourage persons "to ignore ethical considerations relating to means and to justify any action on the basis of good ends."[15] Therefore, if the outcome of unethical activities (i.e., profits) seemed good, the whole behavior could be viewed positively.

Does competition cause shoddy business practice?

Competition between individuals within businesses and organizations also causes problems. Some of these problems are distortion of information, hiding of failures, falsification of figures, empire building, and mutual distrust.[16] All these problems could be viewed as unethical and perhaps could be avoided if less competition existed between individuals.

Pressure to Achieve Results

Like competition, pressure to achieve results can cause unethical behavior. In fact, all activities of superiors influence the ethics of employees' actions. This fact has been substantiated by a study of managers in an executive development program. Researchers found most of these persons felt "their ethical beliefs were highly congruent with those of their superiors."[17] The conclusion suggests top executives serve as a reference group for others in a company in the setting of ethical standards. A comparison between workers at Pitney Bowes and those at Uniroyal, Inc., also showed that young managers in these companies go along with superiors in order to show loyalty.

Are a subordinate's ethics similar to his or her manager's ethics?

This loyalty to or agreement with superiors' beliefs can cause both ethical and unethical behavior by subordinates. A majority of public-sector employees and private-sector employees felt obliged to go along with superiors and show loyalty even in unethical activities. Both groups felt pressure from superiors to achieve results and compromise beliefs.

In the HBR studies, the behavior of superiors was the primary factor influencing executives to make unethical decisions. The behavior of a person's supervisor was the second most likely influence in causing a subordinate to act ethically. Therefore, it can be seen that an ethical supervisor is an important factor in causing ethical behavior in a work group.

Loyalty to the Company

Does loyalty to an organization encourage abandonment of ethical principles?

Just as supervisors influence employees to act ethically and unethically, the way people relate to a company affects their behavior. We tend to view self-enhancement or harm to others as less moral if the people act on their own behalf rather than as agents or representatives of some group.[18] The implication is the more employees and managers are taught to identify with, represent, and have loyalty to their companies, the more they are being encouraged to abdicate personal responsibility for their actions.

What business employees are likely to behave ethically in the business world? The ones with well-defined personal codes. Persons with an ethical supervisor are also more likely to behave ethically. Also, ethics tend to be highest in the youngest employees and in those who are in the final decade of their careers.

Raising Ethical Standards

Can ethical standards be raised?

The preceding research poses an interesting question: Is it possible to raise the ethical standards of business people?

Several solutions have been proposed for dealing with unethical business behavior and helping define standards in the business world. The solution most often presented is to establish a code of ethics listing policy statements and sanctions, either for a company or for an industry as a whole. The National Association of Manufacturers (NAM) designed such a plan, the Code of Moral and Ethical Standards. However, this code proved ineffectual, because no enforcement provisions were included, and the language of the code was filled with generalities and platitudes that signified little but goodwill.[19]

Codes of Conduct

Does anyone use a code of conduct?

Despite the lack of success of the NAM Code, this solution is still given when business ethics are discussed. Seventy-three percent of the 241 firms polled in an Opinion Research Corporation survey have written codes of ethics, half of which were created during the late 1970s. However, less than 40 percent distributed copies to rank-and-file workers.[20]

In the HBR studies, over 50 percent of the respondents favored an industry-wide code. In 1961, 71 percent of the respondents favored the idea of a code. However, of that number, 87 percent felt a code would not be easy to enforce. Fifty-seven percent stated they would violate the code whenever they felt they could avoid detection. In 1976 the response was a little less enthusiastic for a code. Also, those favoring a code saw the same difficulties in enforcement and detection of violators.

Caterpillar Tractor Company has published a comprehensive ten-page code of worldwide business conduct addressing the following areas:

ownership and investment;	competitive conduct with dealers, suppliers, users, and competitors;
location of corporate facilities;	observance of local laws;
relationships with employees;	business ethics;
product quality;	relationships with public officials;
technology sharing;	public responsibility;
finance;	disclosure of information;
intercompany pricing;	international business; and
accounting and financial records;	procedures by which managers at various levels report their compliance with the code each year.
differing business practices among countries;	

Strongest research agreement to the idea of an industry-wide code comes from Uniroyal, Inc., and Pitney-Bowes. In 1976, 90 percent of the managers surveyed in these companies favored a code of business ethics. They also favored teaching ethics in business schools.[21] Bethlehem Steel also supports compliance with a code of ethics. Its managers suggest that maintaining Bethlehem's standards of honesty and integrity in business conduct depends on employee judgment and personal and ethical standards. Bethlehem's Code of Business Conduct states:

It is Bethlehem's policy to observe and comply with all laws, rules and regulations affecting the conduct of its business in all countries in which it operates and to require all Bethlehem personnel to avoid any activities which could involve or lead to involvement of Bethlehem or its personnel in any unlawful practice. The employment of Bethlehem personnel or the use of Bethlehem assets for any unlawful purpose is strictly forbidden.[22]

For many companies such a code has become an accepted part of their policy manuals. There are many who, like Bethlehem, have come to place great importance on a code. One reason for this is the tendency of some companies in recent years to ignore their corporate and social responsibility. Bethlehem, for instance, recently pleaded guilty in a New York City federal court to paying more than $400,000 to induce privately owned foreign ship representatives to steer their ship repair business to Bethlehem and to settle bills for such repairs when completed.[23] Since then Bethlehem has strengthened internal corporate controls, expanded internal audits, and

Does anyone ever follow a written code of conduct?

taken other appropriate actions. Such remedial action again suggests a need for trying to raise the ethical awareness of many business concerns. For other examples of codes of conduct, see Exhibit 17.3.

EXHIBIT 17.3

Kaiser Aluminum's Board of Directors' Resolution
Concerning Conflicts of Interest

RESOLVED, that it is the policy of this Corporation, for itself and on behalf of its subsidiary Corporations, to expect of its officers and employees their loyalty to the business interests of this Corporation and its subsidiaries, measured by high standards of law and ethics, thereby avoiding conflicts of interest situations, whether existing or as a latent possibility, and accordingly:

1   The officers and employees of this Corporation shall refrain from having a direct or indirect financial interest in the business of any supplier of goods or services to this Corporation or any customer of this Corporation when such interest creates or may reasonably be expected to create a conflict between the employee's interest in and loyalty to this Corporation and his interest in or loyalty to any such supplier or customer;
2   The officers and employees of this Corporation shall refrain from accepting any material gifts, gratuities, or loans from suppliers of goods or services to this Corporation or customers of this Corporation which might tend to influence improperly their judgment in favor of any such supplier or customer in any dealings with this Corporation;
3   The officers and employees of this Corporation shall not permit any influence, interest, or relationship to arise or exist which might conflict with the best interests of this Corporation or which might endanger or prejudice this Corporation's reputation for integrity and fair and open dealing; and
4   It shall be the continuing responsibility and duty of all officers and employees of this Corporation to report to the office of the Secretary at any time or from time to time any circumstances or situations whereunder any such officer or employee might find himself in a position where his own interests might conflict with the best interests of this Corporation, or whereunder some prospective circumstance or action might place him in such a position.

Complying with a Code

Can a manager improve her or his business behavior?

One proposal for raising ethical standards is to establish an association to promote the idea of responsibility and ethics in business practice. Persons representing moral concerns and views should be the founders of such an institute. These persons could include members from the business community as well as lawyers, clergy, and philosophers. Accrued benefits from the establishment of such an institute include (1) restored confidence in business by the improvement of performance as well as the improved image of business and (2) the possibility of fending off legislation by providing self-policing of the business community.[24]

Several ways managers can take the initiative in improving business behavior are listed in Exhibit 17.4.

EXHIBIT 17.4

- Realistic goals should be set by top management. These goals should be high enough to lead to better performance, but not so high that they create a climate of temptation for unethical behavior.
- Leadership for ethical behavior should start at the top, with senior officials setting good examples.
- A code of ethics should include sincere efforts to help employees know how to act in questionable situations.
- Violators of the code of ethics should be disciplined so all employees know the code truly represents company policy.
- An ethical advocate (i.e., someone to question management's decisions) should be appointed or hired to encourage management to act in a socially responsive way.
- A mechanism should be provided for employees to report unethical acts.
- Managers should be trained to recognize ethical problems and their solutions. These persons must be more ethics-conscious.[25]

Finally, managers should realize that they all have many persons to whom they are responsible. These persons include consumers, stockholders, members of the community, employees, peer groups, the supervisor, and professional associations. Any behavior in business influences the behavior of many other persons.

Social Responsibility

Would a sense of social responsibility help ethics?

Because business behavior influences so many others, there is a real need for businesses to have a social conscience. They must feel a sense of **social responsibility** to their clients and customers, suppliers, unions, and government. Each of these public groups has a claim on the firm and deserves to be treated justly and fairly. From that standpoint, we are dealing with the whole issue of human rights.

social responsibility

Pros of Social Responsibility

What are the advantages of social responsibility?

Many arguments could be cited in favor of or against social responsibility. The pros of social responsibility, however, follow five basic themes.[26]

1. Business, and any other institution, must meet the needs of society in order to survive. If business is not responsive to society's needs, it will

lose the power it derives from public support. As social problems become of more concern, existing institutions must be effective in dealing with these problems. Otherwise they will be replaced.

2. Not only is American society paying more attention to social problems, but society's expectations are that business will play a major role in solving these problems. This is reflected in legislation and the recently changing public attitudes and business people's responses. The changes, highlighted by consumerism, racial demands, and concern for the environment, are not temporary. They represent a major shift in public expectations. This shift has far-reaching implications for modern organizations. The social contract between business and society is changing. Society once looked to business to provide an abundance of products at low cost, but the competitive marketplace, with its emphasis on profit maximization, is not necessarily the forum for social justice. Society expects business to contribute to the quality of life in more than purely economic ways.

3. It is the long-term interest of business to maintain a favorable climate, including social values and conditions. An organization relies on the environment for its existence. Without suppliers, customers, and favorable political, economic, and social conditions, business cannot function. With such total reliance on a hospitable climate, business cannot ignore trends. This dependency implies that business should do what it can to mold an environment favorable to its future existence.

4. Business is a major form of social power in society; and it has social responsibilities commensurate with that power. Approximately 70 percent of the people who work are employed directly by business. A significant portion of their time is spent on the job. Furthermore, much of the productive capacity and managerial talent is under the control of business. All of this represents social as well as economic power.

5. Not only is business obligated to use its power to solve social problems; it also must use its know-how. Big business has capital resources, managerial talent, innovative skills, and a broad range of functional expertise. These need to be used in solving problems. Business should be expected to take the lead in areas such as training and finding employment for the hard-core unemployed, for reducing pollution, and for renovating urban areas.

Some businesses are using their resources in a socially responsible way. For example, Control Data Corporation's Fair Break program is designed to provide steady employment for the disadvantaged.[27] The program provides participants with support and assistance to overcome reading, writing, or mathematical deficiencies that are costing them jobs and offers counseling for personal, career, and other problems. Fair Break programs exist in almost fifty locations throughout the country.

Control Data also has responded to the plight of the hard-core unemployed by building four plants in inner cities. The plants have accumulated attendance, turnover, and profitability records at least equal to those in the company's other plants.[28]

---------------- Cons of Social Responsibility ----------------

Although the arguments in favor of social responsibility may outweigh those against it, there are also four basic reasons for restricting business's involvement in social affairs.[29]

What are the disadvantages of social responsibility?

1. Business is an economic institution. Corporations exist to earn a return on the investment of stockholders. Social responsibility subverts the basic purpose of business and reduces its profit motive.

A business must maintain a profit to survive, and incurring costs for social purposes will endanger the future of many organizations. Business investments successfully applied are self-renewing, but social outputs do not provide a direct economic return. Furthermore, many marginal businesses will be forced into liquidation if they incur significant social costs. Already many organizations have been forced to terminate their activities because they cannot afford the investment necessary to reduce their external pollution to meet government standards. The higher cost of doing business will also weaken international balance of payments, because it will increase the costs of exports, making them less attractive to foreign buyers.

2. There are dangers in blending roles of business and government. By accepting broad social responsibilities, business moves into the traditional realm of government. No institution can serve all society's needs.

3. Even if business has social responsibilities, business people are not trained or qualified to make social decisions. Their expertise is in economic affairs; others are more qualified to solve social problems. However, many environmentalists cite Pacific Gas and Electric, Armco, Owens-Illinois, and Atlantic Richfield for making impressive strides within their industries in implementing effective environmental pollution control measures, and consumerists have praised Levi Strauss and Cummins Engine for endorsing laws to ensure that consumers are represented at regulatory hearings.[30]

4. One potential danger of social responsibility is that it will make business even more powerful and tip the balance now existing among the many institutions forming our pluralistic society. If business became dominant in economic and social affairs, it could result in a concentration of power unequalled by other organizations. This would endanger our society as we know it, and introduce another form of the monolithic state.

---------------- CONCLUSION ----------------

After studying the pros and cons, management must determine the extent of its social involvement. This answer will, of course, depend on the situation. That is why it is to our advantage to examine our values and ethical standards now. If we recognize our convictions we may experience less vacillation and ambiguity when faced with stressful decisions. A strong ethical framework will help us make the decisions which will enhance our daily human relationships.

KEY TERMS

Ethics: a system of principles for moral conduct.
Values: premises that define appropriate behavior of a particular cultural group.
Sanctions: rewards and penalties that lead people toward ethical behavior and away from unethical behavior.
Golden Rule: do unto others as you would have them do unto you.
Platinum Rule: do unto others as they would have you do unto them.
Social Responsibility: business's sense of responsibility to clients, customers, suppliers, unions, and government.

QUESTIONS
---

1 Reread the opening case.
   a. If you were Greg O'Keefe what would you do?
   b. Consider the seven work levels discussed in this chapter. At which one would you place Greg? Manny? Ivan Key?
   c. How would you describe Paragon Products's social responsibility to its workers? its customers? the public at large?
2 Recall a recent ethical controversy in your location involving politicians, business leaders, government officials, or others. What principles or ethical standards were compromised, in your opinion? How did the matter surface? Do you believe it was resolved to the satisfaction of most citizens? Why or why not?
3 Discuss the three factors that promote a public-be-damned attitude. How are they related? In your opinion, which is the most significant? Why?
4 Construct your personal definition of ethical behavior. How might your opinion of ethical versus unethical conduct be altered by:
   a. your economic situation,
   b. the individuals involved (i.e., persons known to you as opposed to strangers),
   c. effect on others,
   d. the number of persons who would feel the effect, and
   e. the extent to which they would be affected,
   f. the likelihood that your actions would be discovered, and
   g. your conscience?
5 Defend the remark, "Ethics and values vary according to cultural setting."
6 Would you say that the United States legal system and the laws it intends to administer accurately reflect today's ethics, values, and sanctions? If so, why? If not, how would you suggest they be changed, if change is desirable?

7 Summarize each of the seven levels of work values. Which one do you presently occupy? Do you hope to move to a different level in the future? Why or why not?

8 Contrast the Golden and Platinum Rules. Describe the "faulty" premise on which the Golden Rule is based. What difficulties might a manager encounter when following the Platinum Rule?

9 "The different segments of society have become so complex and interdependent that business persons who ignore everything but the profit motive will probably encounter more problems than those who take a broader and more enlightened view of today's business environment." Do you agree with this position? Why or why not?

10 In your opinion, what factors are responsible for the pressure that middle and lower managers feel to achieve organizational goals? Why does this pressure subside as a manager nears the top of an organization? What kinds of programs or policies might decrease it for those at lower levels?

11 Discuss competition's effect on ethical behavior in each of the following jobs:
    a. department managers in a retail store,
    b. salespeople selling products to corporate purchasing agents, and
    c. managers at the vice presidential level.

12 How would you characterize "healthy" versus "unhealthy" competition? How is one's attitude toward competition affected by frame of mind? personal background and experiences? the attitudes of co-workers?

13 How might personal standards conflict with pressure to achieve results in each of the following jobs?
    a. quality assurance inspectors in manufacturing plants,
    b. salespeople,
    c. production managers, and
    d. assembly line workers.

14 Consider top management's role in promoting ethical conduct throughout an organization. How does the remark "Silence implies acceptance" apply to their role? What influence can the immediate supervisor have on an employee's ethical attitude and conduct?

15 How does the motto "The buck stops here" relate to ethical business conduct for each employee?

16 Consider a past or present employer that has a code of ethics. In your opinion, how well does it influence worker's conduct? How might this influence be enhanced?

17 Discuss the value of training techniques such as seminars and role-playing in raising managers' consciousness about ethical conduct.

18 Consider the various clients that a business serves: customers, governmental agencies, stockholders, the community, employees, and others. In your opinion, which would oppose and which would support the following top management actions, and why?
    a. price increase,
    b. price decrease,
    c. dividend postponed,
    d. dividend increased,
    e. major contribution made to a charitable organization, and

f.   product recalled voluntarily because of a suspected but unconfirmed quality problem.

19   Summarize the general arguments in favor of social responsibility. What are the five arguments used to oppose business's involvement in social issues? Considering these and your own feelings, what is your personal position on business's role in society?

-------------------------------------- CASES --------------------------------------

Case 17.1

Paul Moyer, a production planning management trainee, was employed three months ago by Interchem International, a large chemical firm in Maryland.

Paul circulates through every part of the plant, observes production runs, and checks on orders in process so their status can be relayed to the customer relations department and to salespeople in the field.

Although the company tries to mix the exact amount of chemicals needed for each order, invariably there are several gallons left over from each batch, and Paul began to wonder where these leftovers went. They could be anything from fertilizer to paint remover.

Last week he traced the drain pipes from the mixing vats to the outside of the building, where they emptied into a small stream meandering past the plant. The stream runs into a river several miles outside town.

When Paul mentioned hazardous waste disposal to his boss the next day he was assured, "The company's about as concerned as any other firm in the nation. That runoff from each batch is chicken feed. The sewage from a high-rise condominium would make that look like nothing at all, now wouldn't it? Besides, we've got an environmental compliance inspector—a full-time employee—who spot-checks every plant for safe disposal practices. The Environmental Protection Agency sends inspectors around, too. We're fine. Take my word for it."

On his way home yesterday, Paul noticed that the creek was filled with a noxious-looking chemical that spewed from the exit drain in a steady stream. Alarmed that someone had left a valve open, he drove back to the plant and hurried to the mixing area to alert the department manager and to shut off the flow. Instead, he discovered four burly workers systematically dumping drums of a recently banned insecticide into the mixing vats, where it drained out into the creek.

"What's going on, guys?" Paul asked, aware that his appearance would probably arouse some antagonism.

"Well, the EPA's put this stuff on its no-no list," one of the men explained, "so it's worthless to us now. We've got to have more space in the storage area, so out it goes!"

"Yeah, but that's running into the creek!" shouted Paul.

"Well, what would you have us do, kid?" asked another worker. "Do you want to pay some hazardous waste hauler $2,000 to get rid of it for us? Man, you college boys think this company's made of money!"

Paul went away, wondering what effect the chemical (about 500 gallons worth) would have as it found its way to the river and beyond. "I know I can turn them in," he thought to himself, "but that's no good unless they're caught in the act. Then too, *I'm* one of 'them'—I'm a member of management—and to discredit my company and my plant makes me feel like a traitor. Anyway, if an inspector did start asking questions, they'd probably figure that I blew the whistle, and I've got my job and my career to protect. Just what *do* the words 'ethics' and 'social responsibility' mean out here in the real world?"

Case Questions

1 If you were Paul, would you inform the EPA or the company's in-house inspector? Why or why not?
2 What could Paul do to alert management to what had happened without going outside the company or to the in-house inspector? List three possible results and how he should prepare to deal with each.
3 Recommend action his company could take to make it easier for people in his predicament to come forward without fear of reprisal.

Case 17.2

Roger Thornberg is a management consultant for Interco Management Systems, Inc., a management consulting firm with field offices throughout the country. Roger recently concluded a three-month consulting assignment in which he evaluated the personnel policies and compensation system used by Singleton's, a regional chain of retail department stores.

Yesterday he submitted a proposed draft of his findings and recommendations to his supervisor, Andy Maas. However, Andy seems to have something else in mind, which he raised in a closed-door meeting with Roger this morning.

"Roger, top management has taken a very hard line on profitability," Andy began. "All of us must put out 110 percent to round up additional business. That's why I'm talking to you now. Do you think we've done all we can for this Singleton client? Can we do any more studies or propose any additional work whatsoever before we terminate the engagement?"

"You mean, can I think of anything more to sell them that would run up our *bill?*" Roger asked incredulously.

"Don't be so indelicate," Andy replied. "This is a retail chain with twenty-six stores. Can we *really* stand behind our findings and recommendations without some additional work?"

"Andy," Roger said cautiously, "I'm comfortable with what I've done for Singleton's. I spent all the time I felt was necessary to research their systems, and I have a good sense of what they're doing with their personnel policies and pay scales. I couldn't suggest anything else that we should do before we give them our final report and close the file."

"I want you to think of something," Andy said, eyebrows raised knowingly. "We've got a multimillion-dollar business to sustain, and revenues are down 20 percent from last year due to the recession. At the field office management meeting last week the top brass pulled no punches: we're going to lay off people and close some offices if we don't generate $3 million more nationwide within the next three months!"

"Spell out what you're driving at," Roger said grimly.

"All right," Andy agreed. "I want you to rewrite this report to Singleton's top management and recommend that we do a comprehensive study of *all* policies in *every* area, not just in personnel. Use some buzz phrase; tell 'em we want to ensure a 'balanced organizational philosophy' or believe the 'structural integrity' of the company should be analyzed comprehensively for the sake of departmental interface. And Roger, who's to say we're not *right* to do that?" Andy asked. "We might find some holes in their system that your isolated study didn't identify. We can justify a more extensive engagement, one that may bill out at, say, $15,000. Here, take this report and have another run at it," said Andy, sliding it across the desk.

Roger looked at Andy skeptically as he picked up the report and got to his feet. "I know what you mean now," he said, "But I'll have to do some serious thinking about it. I'll get back to you tomorrow."

Case Questions

1 How would you summarize Roger Thornberg's dilemma?
2 What would you suggest to him, considering his boss's position?
3 Draft a code of ethics for Interco Management Systems and suggest how it should be implemented at field office locations such as Roger Thornberg's.

--------------------------------- NOTES ---------------------------------

1. W. M. Blumenthal, "Business Ethics: A Call for A Moral Approach," *Financial Executive* (January 1976): 32–33.
2. John W. Newstrom and William A. Ruch, "The Ethics of Management and the Management of Ethics," *MSU Business Topics* (Winter 1975): 30.
3. Irwin Ross, "How Lawless Are Big Companies?" *Fortune* (December 1, 1980): 56.
4. Vincent S. Flowers and Charles L. Hughes, "Why Employees Stay," *Harvard Business Review* (July–August 1973): 56.
5. Raymond C. Baumhart, "How Ethical Are Businessmen?" *Harvard Business Review* (July–August 1961): 18.
6. Robert M. Fulmer, "Business Ethics Present and Future," *Personnel Administration* (September–October 1971): 49.
7. Steven N. Brenner and Earl A. Molander, "Is the Ethics of Business Changing?" *Harvard Business Review* (January–Feburary 1977): 68.
8. Fulmer, "Business Ethics," p. 49.
9. Brenner and Molander, "Is Ethics Changing?" p. 59.
10. *The Wall Street Journal,* 26 July 1979, p. 1.
11. Archie B. Carroll, "Linking Business Ethics to Behavior in Organizations," *S.A.M. Advanced Management Journal* (Summer 1978): 8.
12. James S. Bowman, "Managerial Ethics in Business and Government," *Business Horizons* (October 1976): 50.
13. James S. Bowman, "The Pressure to Compromise Personal Ethics," *Business Week* (January 31, 1977): 107.
14. James S. Bowman, "Ethics: New Study Probes Gifts to Buyers," *Purchasing* (April 11, 1979): 19.
15. Ernest G. Borman, *Discussion and Group Methods* (New York: Harper and Row, 1975), p. 318.
16. Edgar H. Schein, *Groups and Organizations* (Belmont, Calif.: Wadsworth Publishing Co., Inc.), p. 548.

17. Newstrom and Ruch, "Ethics of Management," p. 32.
18. Schein, *Groups and Organizations*, p. 550.
19. Baumhart, "How Ethical?" p. 331.
20. *The Wall Street Journal*, 10 July 1979, p. 1.
21. Bowman, "Pressure to Compromise," p. 107.
22. Don Troutlein, "Dear Fellow Employee," *Bethlehem Review*, no. 169 (1980).
23. Ibid.
24. Blumenthal, "Business Ethics," p. 34.
25. Carroll, "Linking Business Ethics," pp. 8–11.
26. Howard M. Carlisle, *Management: Concepts and Situations* (Chicago: Science Research Associates, 1976), pp. 221–223.
27. Control Data Corporation advertisement, *The Wall Street Journal*, 17 February 1981, p. 7.
28. Adam Meyerson, "Social Responsibility," *The Wall Street Journal*, 6 October 1980, p. 1.
29. Carlisle, *Management*, pp. 223–224.
30. Meyerson, "Social Responsibility," p. 1.

SUGGESTED READINGS

Kimbrell, Grady, and Vineyard, Ben S. *Succeeding in the World of Work*. Bloomington, Ill.: McKnight, 1975.

Kohlberg, Lawrence. "The Cognitive-Developmental Approach to Moral Education," *Phi Delta Kappan* (June 1975): 670–677.

Nyquist, Ewald B. "The American 'No-Fault' Morality," *Phi Delta Kappan* (November 1976): 272–277.

18

A Look into Your Future

When you complete your study of this chapter, you should be able to:

1 Express your occupational goals in life,
2 Prepare a resume and write a job application letter,
3 Design a strategy for a job interview,
4 Describe the organizational and managerial changes predicted for the future, and
5 Recognize the necessity for flexibility.

—————— OPENING CASE ——————

Stacey Zimmerman is a marketing major at Midwestern College. Her courses emphasize retailing, marketing principles, consumer behavior, personal selling, and advertising. She has worked in the college bookstore for the past three years, served on the college yearbook committee, and been president of her sorority.

Despite this experience with human relationships, she was uncertain about what to expect at her first serious employment interview, scheduled for today. The company, Berne, Inc., is one of the nation's largest manufacturers of office machines and minicomputers. The campus recruiter, Scott Hughlett, introduced himself in the vestibule of the placement office and motioned Stacey to a secluded cubicle, where he invited her to sit down.

"Nice to be sharing some time with you, Stacey," he said warmly. "This is just an opportunity for us to find out more about each other. Tell me, what made you want to interview Berne?"

"Well," she answered nervously, "it was the information I discovered while doing a research paper not long ago. Several articles pointed out your exceptional market position and product line and well-funded research-and-development activities. Berne sounded like a market leader with a solid future, and that's the kind of firm I want to work for as a marketing representative."

"Wonderful," remarked Scott. "What do you expect us to do with you if you're hired?"

"Oh," Stacey responded. "Well, I'd expect you to give me good training . . . some kind of solid training. I wouldn't want, you know, to be thrown into the job to sink or swim."

"What kind of training did you have in mind?" Scott probed.

"Thorough training on your product line, the extent of your service capabilities, and whatever else is necessary to prepare me to represent your firm effectively," she responded, regaining her composure.

"That's definitely part of our orientation and training package for marketing representatives," Scott assured her. Glancing at his notes he continued, "Let me know how you'd react to an unusual customer encounter. What would you do if you walked into some small company to sell an electronic sales register and the hostile owner told you to clear out and not to come back, and said if you came back he'd call the police?"

"Good heavens!" Stacey exclaimed. "Well, ah, I guess I'd probably . . . No. Yes, I guess I would."

"Would what?" Scott asked.

"I'd do it. Leave, I mean. Like, who wants to have to fight with somebody to do an honest job, you know? If the guy didn't have the sense to listen to my sales presentation, he probably doesn't deserve to own a quality product like a Berne sales register," she concluded.

"All right, tell me something about your feelings on moving," said Scott. "You know, we have offices in every state. How would you respond if we asked you to move to a state several thousand miles away?"

"I'd be ready," Stacey affirmed. "If a company offers me the degree of opportunity I want, I'll go where it's located."

"And your long-term goals with Berne? Where do you expect to be within ten years?"

"I'm ambitious," Stacey declared. "I would hope to be at or near the vice presidential level by then. After all, Berne is the nation's leader in the office equipment industry."

"All right," Scott continued, "and how about activities after graduation. What do you have in mind as far as follow-up education, self-improvement activities, these sorts of things?"

"Really, I never thought about that that much," Stacey said. "I'll be glad just to get out of college, because it's been a long four years. But if Berne pays the tuition and books and if my working hours permit, I'd certainly consider going for a Master of Business Administration degree at a college where I was located, assuming I'd be in one spot long enough to complete the program. Tell me, is that likely?"

"We would postpone any transfers or promotions that required a move until you completed your degree," Scott confirmed.

"That certainly sounds fair," Stacey said.

"What were some of your favorite college courses?" Scott asked.

"Well, I liked all my marketing courses, but I also enjoyed courses in applied psychology and human relations. Of course, these subjects relate directly to success in marketing, as I'm sure you know," Stacey replied.

"Fine," Scott responded. "Well, our time's about up, and thank you for considering Berne as a potential employer. We have several other people to interview, but you'll receive word from us concerning a job offer within two weeks."

"Thank you," Stacey answered. "I'll look forward to hearing from you. Have a good day."

Do You Know Where You're Going To?

Where are you headed in life?

There are plenty of people in this world with no direction and no plans. There are people who seem to follow paths to self-destruction. Fortunately most people settle down to a normal life-style. A few years ago the theme song from the movie *Mahogany* asked the question, "Do you know where you're going to?" It was a good song and a good question. Do you know where you're headed? Are you prepared for the future? You've just spent several months studying a topic that proposes to make your future working relationships in this world a little smoother. Are you planning to use these skills? Where are you going? Do you know?

Managing Your Life by Goals

The best time to prepare for tomorrow is today. The really important questions are: Where do I want to go? What are my objectives, my goals? What is my purpose, my mission? Once one knows that, then one can ask a very practical question: How do I get there? Then, and only then, can one ask: What do I do *today*?

Are you prepared for tomorrow?

Goal Consciousness

If you don't know where you want to go, any road will get you there. That is why this chapter asks you to be introspective. You need to know who you are, how you see the world, what your needs and motivations are. If you don't know these things, you will be unable to set goals. You will be unable, in the final count, to understand and relate to others who have discovered themselves. So you need to become very purposive. You and those you work with need a sense of trying to achieve something that is worthwhile, to contribute in some meaningful way.

Do you know what you want out of life?

Dr. Charles A. Garfield, a clinical professor at the University of California at San Francisco Medical School and head of the Peak Performance Center at Berkeley, conducted a fifteen-year study of more than 1000 highly successful persons in all walks of life, including sports, business, education, and health care. These superperformers shared six characteristics.[1] They

- achieved progressively higher goals over a period of time,
- took their work seriously and did not grow complacent about their jobs,
- were motivated by self-set, personal objectives (rather than goals dictated by others) and worked for the pleasure of working,
- attacked problems rather than the persons who caused them,
- assessed the worst possible results of a risky situation before proceeding, and
- mentally projected themselves into upcoming situations, activities, or circumstances and role-played how they would react.

Although these practices or habits can be taught, Professor Garfield discovered that less successful individuals, regardless of their career fields, had no regular pattern of preparation, mental attitude, and methodology that they applied to life or work situations.

Thus, the initial step in becoming goal conscious is to look at oneself. We control the direction of our life. Our thoughts and attitudes place the limits on what we achieve. The positive thinkers have told us for centuries that we *can* if we *think* we can. Unfortunately, many students have simply not forced themselves to think hard enough or long enough when dealing with a personal problem or challenge. They have not unleashed the power that lies within themselves to alter the course of their lives for the better. We need to believe in ourselves and in what we're doing. We must set high goals and go after them. The stronger our faith in our goals, the sooner we will reach them. See Exhibit 18.1.

Career Counseling

If you don't know where you're headed, do you know where to get help?

If you are unsure of your future, however, or of your job potential, you should consider seeing a career counselor. There is probably a career counselor on your campus who could give you an occupational preference test or provide information about various careers. If you already have a full-time job, there may be a counseling psychologist at your company who could provide information. Don't be timid about seeing such a person. It could be a sound investment in your future. (However, major responsibility for your career development rests with you. Counselors can only offer help.)

Goal Classification

What are the differences between work goals and personal goals?

So far we have emphasized personal goals. However, there are also work goals. Personal goals are meaningful to the person who holds these goals. Work goals are meaningful to the work group or organization. Often these goals overlap. When they do, harmony and satisfaction can result. When they are in conflict, human relationships are in trouble.

personal goals

PERSONAL GOALS. Goal setting is a prelude to action. It affects people directly, as well as the future they create for themselves. To set **personal goals** (i.e., goals for yourself), consider five important steps:[2]

1. Crystallize your thinking. Define every goal you intend to achieve. You can't go anywhere until you know where you want to go. Once you've defined your goals, rank them.

2. Develop a written plan of action with deadlines. Set a date for achievement.

3. Develop a sincere desire for the things you want in life. Decide how honestly you want to achieve something.

—————————— EXHIBIT 18.1 ——————————

Don't Be Afraid To Fail

You've failed
many times,
although you may not
remember.
You fell down
the first time
you tried to walk.
You almost drowned
the first time
you tried to
swim, didn't you?
Did you hit the
ball the first time
you swung a bat?
Heavy hitters,
the ones who hit the
most home runs,
also strike
out a lot.
R. H. Macy
failed seven
times before his
store in New York
caught on.
English novelist
John Creasey got
753 rejection slips
before he published
564 books.
Babe Ruth struck out
1,330 times,
but he also hit
714 home runs.
Don't worry about
failure.
Worry about the
chances you miss
when you don't
even try.

Source: A message as published in *The Wall Street Journal* by United Technologies Corporation, Hartford, Connecticut 06101

4. Develop self-confidence. Change any habits and attitudes interfering with positive action. Believe in your ability to achieve.

5. Develop a dogged determination to follow through. Don't let the mediocre multitude's thoughts and criticisms deter you from success. Forget the word ''impossible.'' Believe you can, and you will.

work goals

WORK GOALS. Work goals concern quality or quantity of work, labor cost, job performance, and so forth. Such objectives focus on measurable achievements during a certain period. These work goals are crucial to success in any organization. (We discussed these in terms of MBO in Chapter 16.) The worker's personal goals should also be considered. Both are necessary for on-the-job happiness.

────────────────────── The Job Search ──────────────────────

Are you looking for a job?

With these personal and work goals in mind, let us look now at how to achieve them. During the last decade over 30 million young people entered the labor force. Competition for jobs in the 1980s is expected to be equally intense. Knowledge of the job application process can help. We will deal with four factors, all of which are important to job procurement—sources of job information, the resume, the application letter, and the job interview.

────────────────── Sources of Job Information ──────────────────

Where can I get information about job availability?

There are thousands of job openings every year. Your chance of getting the right job is increased if you know what to look for. Where are the jobs? Lists are published daily by newspapers, state employment agencies, private employment firms, and college and university placement offices. Some additional sources that provide clues about the job search are:

- *Occupational Outlook Handbook* (U.S. Bureau of Labor Statistics),
- *Dictionary of Occupational Titles* (U.S. Department of Labor),
- *Occupational Outlook Handbook* (U.S. Government Printing Office),
- *Occupational Outlook for College Students* (U.S. Government Printing Office),
- *National Business Employment Weekly* (*The Wall Street Journal*), and
- *College Placement Annual* (College Placement Council).

A number of books are published annually about the job search process. Several of these are listed in the Suggested Readings section at the end of this chapter. People who are already working can also provide good leads for jobs. Teachers and employers who visit your campus are other possibilities. Use every possible source to find the job you want. Then you can begin to put the written materials together to procure an interview. The first written item is your resume.

——————————— The Resume ———————————

A **resume** is your personal data sheet (Exhibit 18.2). It may also be called a vita. It is a brief account of your educational and professional experience, a summary of yourself, a review of your qualifications, and most important, a first impression. The main purpose of the resume is to help you get an interview.

resume

How do I put a resume together?

BASIC PRINCIPLES.   There are ten basic steps in writing timely resumes.[3] These steps provide a passport to better things.

1. *Do a little soul-searching before you start.* Ask yourself some penetrating questions: What does the company want? What do you have? Why would they want to hire you? What will they expect you to be able to do? What experience have you had that qualifies you for this job? Keep a list of the things that you know you do well and that could be expected of you on a job.

2. *Write your objective.* Decide where you want to go professionally. Write it down on your resume.

3. *Sell yourself.* In one or two paragraphs describe what you have done and can do. Try to make the reader feel you can do something for him or her.

4. *Be brief and nonrepetitive.* Devote brief paragraphs to describing your activities. Leave out the irrelevancies and repetitions. Combine data where it is possible.

5. *Write it yourself.* Most potential interviewers want to know about you *from* you, not from a disinterested third person who makes a living writing people's resumes.

6. *List the jobs you've held.* List your past employers, your job titles, the dates you worked for them, and the skills demonstrated in these positions. The titles will indicate opportunities for experience.

7. *Forget the references.* You wouldn't list a reference who wouldn't give you a positive recommendation. Most prospective employers will make their own checks on your past.

8. *Make it neat.* First impressions count, so present yourself as positively as possible. Messy resumes insult the reader. Have your resume duplicated on good paper by a quality machine.

9. *Put yourself into your resume.* Employers are going to hire the person they like best or see fitting their organization most effectively. Since the purpose of a resume is to get an interview, your resume must do that. A good one will.

10. *Write a neat, short personal letter.* Tell the reader why you're writing to her or him. Show you've done some research about the company and are really interested in it. (The cover letter will be discussed in more detail later.)

—————— EXHIBIT 18.2 ——————

A Resume

↳ PHILIP VERN
13902 Russ Drive
Houston, TX 77039
1-713-442-6866

WORK OBJECTIVE:

To obtain a job with challenge and advancement potential in personnel management. Eventual objective is managerial position.

MAJOR QUALIFICATIONS:

College education in personnel management and communications. Work experience in banking and retail sales, including training, purchasing, and supervising.

EDUCATION:

M.B.A., Denver University, Denver, Colorado. Emphasis, organizational behavior. G.P.A., 3.5 on 4.0 system. Available June 1.

B.S., Abilene Christian University, Abilene, Texas. Major, marketing; minor, English. G.P.A., 2.4 on 4.0 system.

EXPERIENCE:

1978–present, First National Bank, Westminster, Colorado; in charge of training all new tellers, plus working as a roving teller.

1975–78, S & Q clothiers, Abilene, Texas; management trainee responsible for sales and buying in college-age men's department.

1974–75, Graridge Corporation, Breckenridge, Texas; supervisor of six-man crew of house painters; two summers.

1972–73, United States Department of Agriculture, Eastland, Texas; worked as land measurer of peanut acreage allotments; two summers.

PROFESSIONAL MEMBERSHIPS:

American Personnel Association, American Society of Training and Development, and Academy of Management.

PERSONAL DATA:

Date of Birth: 3/27/57

Marital Status: Married, no children

Height: 6'2"   Weight: 195 lbs.

Health: Excellent

REFERENCES:

Available on request.

DATE OF AVAILABILITY:

June 1

IMPORTANT AND UNIMPORTANT ITEMS. The rewards of using these steps should be interview invitations. Therefore, it will help to know what managers enjoy seeing on a resume (Exhibit 18.3). A study of 205 personnel directors' responses found that the five most important items were an applicant's current address, past work experience, major in college, job objectives and goals, and date of availability for employment.

In addition, these personnel directors favored aesthetically pleasing, short (no more than two-page) resumes. They were impressed by typed resumes, as opposed to xeroxed copies. And they agreed a resume should

---

EXHIBIT 18.3

205 Personnel Managers' Ratings of Importance of Items in Resume

Rank	Important Items	Rank	Important Items
1	Current address	26	Class standing
2	Past work experience	27	Sources for financing college studies
3	Major in college		
4	Job objectives and goals	28	References
5	Date of availability for employment	29	Percentage of money earned for college
6	Career objectives	30	Computer programming skills
7	Permanent address	31	Birthdate and birthplace
8	Tenure on previous job	32	Membership in honorary societies
9	Colleges and universities attended	33	Membership in college social organizations
10	Specific physical limitations		
11	Job location requirements	34	Offices held in social organizations
12	Overall health status		
13	Salary requirements	35	Student body offices held
14	Travel limitations	36	Hobbies
15	Minor in college	37	Foreign language skills
16	Grades in college major	38	Marital status
17	Military experience	39	Complete college transcript
18	Years in which degrees were awarded	40	Height and weight
		41	Number of children
19	Overall grade point average	42	Typing skills
20	Membership in professional organizations	43	Spouse's occupation
		44	Spouse's educational level
21	Awards and scholarships received	45	Sex
22	Grades in college minor	46	Photograph
23	Offices held in professional organizations	47	Complete high school transcript
		48	Personal data on parents
24	Statistical or mathematical skills	49	Race
25	Spouse's willingness to relocate	50	Religious preference

Source: Adapted from Abbott P. Smith, "How to Make Sure Your Next Resume Isn't an Obituary," *Training HRD* (May 1977): 63–64.

—————————————————— EXHIBIT 18.4 ——————————————————

An Application Letter

202 Northwest Avenue
Raritan, New Jersey 08869
Date

Ms. Jane Kepper
Addend Data Corporation
Midtown, Rhode Island 02840

Dear Ms. Kepper:

I am interested in the position of programmer as advertised in *The New York Times*, Sunday, July 30th. My educational background in computer science and limited experience in assembly language should qualify me for an entry-level position. As stated in your advertisement, I am most interested in a position that will permit me to develop into "one of the top professionals in the field."

On August 11, 19—, I will receive my bachelor's degree from the Dallas Institute of Technology. My specific course work has been in computer science with strong complementary work in mathematics and statistics. In fact, these areas have been my forte since early high school days.

In addition to taking nearly all the math, statistics and computer science courses in the college catalog, I have applied what I learned in a part-time job with the college's technical assistance center. With a limited background of experience in the application of my textbook knowledge, this job helped me to apply what I learned in preparing programs for surveys and small business projects for three years.

Please grant me an interview so I can further explain how my qualifications meet your job requirements. Enclosed is my resume for your reference.

Thank you for your consideration.

Sincerely yours,

Carol S. Jannette

Source: Adapted from John L. Meyer and Melvin W. Donaho, *Get the Right Person for the Job* (Englewood Cliffs, N.J.: Prentice-Hall, 1979), p. 58.

focus on the highlights of the applicant's past activities, particularly work experience and education.

The Application Letter

After preparing a resume, the next important piece of writing is the cover letter for the resume. An **application letter** will let the employer know what you think of his or her company in personal terms. Because first impressions count, the application letter should also be carefully constructed. Letters that are carelessly worded, are poorly typed, contain misspelled words, are poorly organized, or state unclear goals will be rejected. It is probably fairly common for personnel directors to weed out half of the applicants on the basis of the appearance of the letter and resume. A well-written application letter is illustrated in Exhibit 18.4.

application letter

How do I write an application letter?

   The cover letter can help an employer identify the person who should be hired. It can whet the potential employer's appetite and can be tailored to a specific firm or industry. As a whole, a well-written letter should answer many of the questions in Exhibit 18.5.

EXHIBIT 18.5

- What is the initial visual effect? Does the applicant reflect care in writing? Is the letter neat and carefully typed? Is it free of errors such as misspelled words, grammatical errors, or inconsistencies?
- Does the applicant clarify his or her motivation for writing? Is the applicant changing careers? a new graduate? responding to a specific job advertisement?
- Does the applicant set forth clear job objectives or well-directed responses to a specific job advertisement?
- Does the applicant provide insight into her or his educational goals?
- Does the applicant provide insight into his or her previous experience?
- Does the applicant provide the data briefly, concisely, and yet adequately?
- Is the letter free of negative data that might exhibit the applicant's undesirability?
- For certain types of applicants, does the letter illustrate imagination, creativity, assertiveness?
- Is the letter free of negtive data that might exhibit the applicant's undesirability?
- Does the letter seem to reflect the applicant's personality and other characteristics positively?
- Does the applicant request an interview?
- Does the applicant state the date of availability?
- Are all enclosures identified?
- Does the applicant provide a suitable selection of references along with addresses and/or telephone numbers?
- Does the applicant reflect courtesy?[4]

job interview

Coupled with a good resume, an effective cover letter should get you an interview. The **job interview** will allow you to sell yourself in person and convince the employer you are the person for the job.

The Job Interview

What do I do if I receive an invitation for a job interview?

The employment interview is often fairly brief: twenty-five to thirty minutes. But it is an extremely important factor in the job search. It may determine one's future career. Certainly it is an opportunity to exchange vital information otherwise unnoticed. The employer has a chance to ask personal questions about information not in the cover letter or resume and to explore these answers in detail. The applicant can ask some specific questions regarding company policies and practices. Then, matching the applicant's personality with the job's needs, the employer can decide whether or not to offer a job. The applicant can decide whether to accept a job if the offer is made.

PREINTERVIEW RESEARCH.   The first major consideration in an interview is preparation. A potential job has been located and the necessary writing stages have been followed. Now comes an oral examination. Some interviewers will do all the talking and watch your reactions (the comprehension and intelligence you show). Others will say very little; you must sell yourself. Some interview tips are listed in Exhibit 18.6.

EXHIBIT 18.6

- Approach the interview with a positive attitude and sincere interest in the company.
- In appearance, good taste is your best guide. Simply remember that you are looking for a job.
- Arrive a few minutes early for the interview.
- Allow the interviewer to initiate the conversation.
- Be friendly, relaxed; be yourself.
- Maintain good eye contact.
- Be courteous at all times.
- Do not monopolize the conversation.
- Be an attentive listener when the interviewer is speaking.
- Respond to questions with more than a yes or no answer.
- Show interest through asking questions. Ask some definite questions about the company.
- Do not try to fill in the silent spots. You may tend to ramble.
- Display your personality and achievements; initiate as well as respond.
- Accentuate the positives. Be optimistic. Display self-confidence, ambition, and a competitive attitude. Be sure your good points get across to the interviewer.[5]

You can expect questions about your long-range goals, ambitions, and future plans. Employers may want to know why you chose your field of study and how you have prepared yourself for work. They may want to know why you want to work for them. They could ask what your major strengths and weaknesses are and what plans you have for improvement. They will be interested in what you know about their company and what questions you'd like to ask. Therefore, the Boy Scout admonition, "Be prepared," is excellent advice.

During the interview you can also expect questions concerning the organization and position. You should, therefore, be well informed about the organization interviewing you. Information can be obtained from several sources in addition to those listed earlier in this chapter: *Dun and Bradstreet Million Dollar Directory*, *Dun and Bradstreet Middle Market Directory*, *Fortune* magazine, or the organization's annual report.

However, these sources of information are most useful for large firms. Data about smaller local firms may be acquired by a telephone call or visit to that office. Learn all you can about the job and organization before the interview. Do your homework. Don't be like the young marketing graduate who was interviewing for a job in Wisconsin. The first question was, "What do you know about Wisconsin?" His reply after much uncertainty was, "Well, I understand you have lots of good cheese and milk there." That's not a very auspicious beginning for a potential job.

APPEARANCE. Although it would be ridiculous to suggest that appearance alone can get you a job offer, a bizarre or tacky appearance will get you rejected. As Malcolm Forbes remarked, "Looking the part helps get the chance to fill it."

Interviewing male seniors, especially business majors, should be meticulous about things such as shirt collar shape, executive-length (over-the-calf) socks, and other sartorial ingredients in their total appearance package.[6] Female seniors should consider a dark, suited skirt and jacket (without vest) with a contrasting blouse and perhaps a string tie or scarf.

Attention to detail isn't lost on corporate recruiters. Deviating from conservative or traditional dress raises some mental eyebrows. Recruiters prefer stylish but subdued outfits: two- or three-piece suits for men; tailored outfits with appropriate coordinated accessories and minimal make-up for women.

EMPLOYMENT-SCREENING CRITERIA. There are at least six screening criteria interviewers use during the job interview.[7] They are shown in Figure 18.1 and discussed below. They are integrity, general intelligence and knowledge, ability to communicate, maturely directed energy, ambition, and specific abilities.

What do employers look for?

Integrity. The first of the basic employment-screening criteria is integrity. The interviewer may begin by being concerned with the applicant's sincerity, morals, and honesty.

FIGURE 18.1
Employment
Screening Criteria,
and Their Relative
Importance

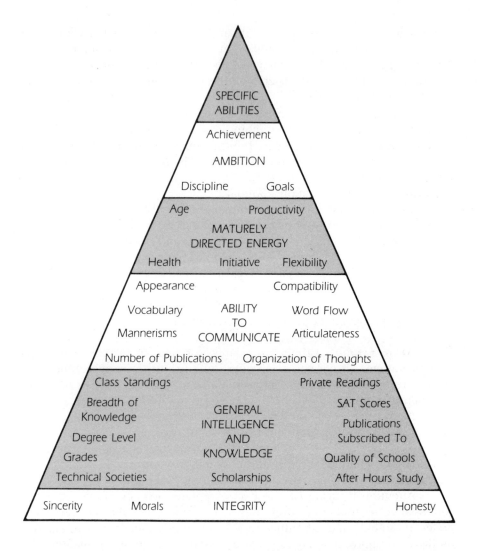

General Intelligence and Knowledge.   The second criterion may be the most important. Certainly one would not apply for a job if one did not have the proper level of general intelligence and the breadth and depth of knowledge within one's field. To judge an applicant's qualifications as they meet this criterion the interviewer may want to know something about class standing, breadth of knowledge, degree level, grades, technical society memberships, scholarships, private readings, SAT or ACT scores, publications subscribed to, quality of school, or after-hours study.

Ability to Communicate.   A person who has the knowledge but cannot communicate it might as well not have the knowledge. The result is about the same. Therefore, the interviewer will observe such things as appearance, vocabulary, mannerisms, compatibility, word flow, articulation, and organization of thoughts. Interviewers are impressed by pleasant, neat candidates who speak sensibly and can focus on the heart of the problem.

Maturely Directed Energy.   Interviewers can get a feeling for one's energy level by inquiring about or observing age, health, initiative, productivity, or flexibility. Thus, they will be interested in activities (on and off campus), rest requirements (type of vacation), and accomplishments (honors and awards).

Ambition.   Ambition is necessary for success, but interviewers do not always seek the most ambitious candidates. Sometimes ambition is a cover for impatience. However, the interviewer will be interested in an applicant's achievement, discipline, and goals.

Specific Abilities.   Specific abilities could include all kinds of basic attitudes, personalities, and personal philosophies. For example, Caterpillar Tractor Company looks for such things as:

- *Personality.* Be genuine, self-confident, pleasant and honest. Be yourself.
- *Articulateness.* Express yourself clearly and concisely. Answer questions quickly and in a candid manner.
- *Alertness.* Make your answers and questions relevant and intelligent. Develop your questions prior to the interview.
- *Enthusiasm.* Be enthusiastic, optimistic, and show an appropriate amount of eagerness.
- *Maturity.* Express clear professional goals. Know what you want. Conduct yourself as if you are determined to get the job you are discussing.
- *Motivation.* Show your incentive and willingness through your desire and interest in the job opportunity.
- *Compatibility.* Express, through your behavior, your ability to get along with others.
- *Preparation.* Know relevant information about the company—location, product, and general knowledge about its business purpose. The more you know, the greater impression you will make on the interviewer.[8]

The specific abilities of an applicant are only minor clues to the employability of an individual. Necessary specific skills can usually be learned on the job.

—————— Work, Human Relations, and the Future ——————

You now have the basic tools to find that job allowing you to practice your human relations skills and knowledge. However, the future is just around the corner, and today's answers may not relate to tomorrow's questions.

Are you ready now for the future?

Change is inevitable. Flexibility is a necessity. Automation, technology, and increasing computer use will drastically change the next twenty years just as it changed the last twenty years. For example, it is estimated that by the year 2000 more than 90 percent of the labor force will be employed in the services industries. Such changes will come about through the continued knowledge explosion and the quest for self-actualization. People who have any concern for their own future and the future of the world are concerned with personal growth and improvement. They search for new answers to age-old questions. They learn from their mistakes, and they press toward the future and the achievement of their goals.

--------------------------- The Occupational Future ---------------------------

What changes are you ready to face?

There will be many changes in people, power, and organizational values within the next twenty years. These changes will in turn precipitate other changes. Are you preparing for such possibilities? From a projection of current trends, and the potential interaction among these trends, we may predict the following changes by the year 2000.[9]

OCCUPATIONAL NEEDS WILL BE ANTICIPATED.   It is now impossible to predict accurately specific occupational skills needed in the future. Change is just too rapid. However, discontinuous change will force society to anticipate and to plan in order to avoid economic disruption. Thus we can expect to see a system developed to forecast occupational needs and to match human resources with available jobs.

BUSINESS WILL DEVELOP CLOSER TIES WITH NONCORPORATE ORGANIZATIONS.   Based on the planning for future occupational needs, a closer tie will be formed between business and government. Top leaders in the private sector may spend part of their business career in government. Business will likewise form closer ties with universities to gather research on the social and environmental consequences of their business actions. They will also operate more closely with labor unions as both attempt to establish long-range goals consistent with national people-power policies.

Will there be different organizational structures?

NEW ORGANIZATIONAL STRUCTURES WILL EMERGE.   Free-form (less pyramidal and more flexible) structures will be developed to replace the ineffective bureaucratic pyramid. Task forces composed of specialists who possess diverse skills for responding to changing conditions and problems will become more common.

matrix organization

One of the organizational changes predicted for the future is the development of project teams or task forces into a structure called a **matrix organization.** Such an organization involves units that cut across both the vertical and horizontal dimensions of the organization. A project team is

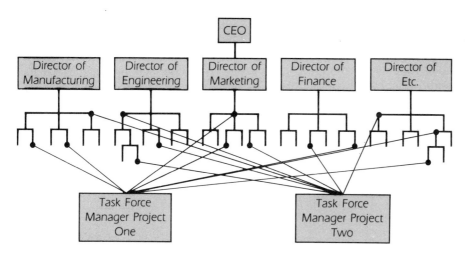

FIGURE 18.2
A Matrix Structure

composed of people from all the relevant managerial areas. These people are formed into a small group with the responsibility and power to solve a particular job. Once the problem is solved, the project team is disbanded. Since an organization could have many teams at one time, the result is an organization resembling a matrix (Figure 18.2).

The matrix organization is not just an extension of the formal hierarchical structure. Instead, it is often composed of five or more people who represent all levels of authority, thus creating an informal organization with formal responsibility and authority.

TECHNOLOGICAL CHANGE WILL ALTER WORK. The production of both goods and services will become more mechanized. Even certain non-manual jobs such as supervision, inspection, and materials handling will be replaced by automation. Thus many jobs will be altered. The level of skill required to do a job will rise. New technology will change workers' career patterns.

How will technology change the work environment?

WORKERS WILL BECOME MORE MOBILE. Workers will become less loyal to an individual employer or company. They will become more cosmopolitan and maintain their closest ties to their profession or skill. They may, however, be forced to alter their occupations and have several different careers during their lifetimes. They also will become more mobile as data systems are developed to match human resources with job needs. The values we hold about work will change.

THE MIDDLE MANAGER'S ROLE WILL CHANGE. New information-processing technology may eliminate middle managers or drop them to a lower rung. Many middle managers will work in relatively unstructured

Will managers manage differently?

positions as group leaders or as communication links between groups. They will probably spend much of their time managing by exception. Innovation and creativity will become more important. The middle manager will be concerned with promoting high levels of cooperation among technicians and with providing a work climate conducive to group collaboration.

TOP MANAGERS WILL TAKE A NEW APPROACH.   As information technology develops, top managers will have a much broader view of the organization and its relation to society. They will rely less on middle managers and will focus on determining organizational goals, establishing long-range plans, and facilitating organizational relations with the external environment. Emphasis will be placed on team management as managers of the future become more flexible and less authoritative.

How will training and development differ?

CONTINUAL EDUCATION AND TRAINING WILL BECOME VITAL.   Workers of the future must expect to be trained and retrained several times in their careers. Organizations will need to establish their own education centers with advanced educational technology and systems. Managers will need to be more broadly and intensively trained. At Bethlehem Steel, this prediction has already become reality.[10]

Bethlehem's innovative training program, the Loop program, has been touted for its practicality, organization, and ability to attract and hold top-quality college graduates.

Loopers, as the participants are informally called, are assured of an opportunity to enter management from their first day with the firm. The program's underlying assumption is that management qualities surface in students' backgrounds, activities, interests, and personalities by the time they reach the senior level. Thus it's assumed that loopers have the basic qualifications for success before they start work. More traditional companies adopt a wait-and-see policy that denies new graduates meaningful responsibility and exposure to operations until they've puttered around in relatively unimportant jobs for a year or two. Not so at Bethlehem.

Loop-course participants first receive two weeks of orientation at the company's home office in Pittsburgh, Pennsylvania, where they learn about the technical side of making steel and receive a comprehensive view of Bethlehem's operations. They then move to a plant or office, where they rotate through various departments. This is followed by two years of on-the-job training that includes performance evaluations every three months.

Bethlehem credits its Loop program with keeping management turnover low. Whereas most manufacturing companies lose half their college recruits within five years, fewer than a third of Bethlehem's Loop participants defect to another firm during that time. More than half the company's higher managers are Loop alumni, and in some subunits of the company (such as steel operations) nearly 80 percent of Loop graduates are still with the company.

WORK HOURS WILL DECREASE.   The average work week will decline until it is around twenty-eight hours instead of forty. Flextime will become more common, and formulas for work or vacation will disappear. People may have the choice of working forty hours a week for six months or four hours a day, year in and year out. However, as technology advances it will eliminate more jobs. Work could become scarcer. Workers could be forced to share jobs. And the added leisure time will allow people to develop avocational occupations.

Will I be able to work fewer hours?

CONCLUSION

The future holds much in store for you. It will change as no other period of time has changed. But whatever the cause of these changes may be, the future can be exciting if you're ready for it. With the skills you've developed through an intensive study of this book, you'll be ready to face the future world of work humanely and productively.

Good luck!

KEY TERMS

Personal Goals: goals relating to an individual.
Work Goals: goals relating to quality or quantity of work, labor cost, job performance, et cetera.
Resume: your personal data sheet, which provides a summary of your educational and professional experience.
Application Letter: a cover letter that accompanies a resume and lets a prospective employer know what you think of his or her company in personal terms.
Job Interview: an opportunity to sell yourself in person and to convince an employer you are the person for the job.
Matrix Organization: an organization involving units that cut across segments of both the vertical and horizontal dimensions of the organization.

QUESTIONS

1   Reread the opening case.
   a.   What did Stacey do well in this interview?
   b.   What could she have done better, and how?

    c. What additional areas should Scott Hughlett have questioned her about, and why?

    d. What suggestions would you offer to Stacey in preparing for her next on-campus interview?

2 Discuss the effect that the following persons have on your personal goals and attitude toward a career:

    a. friends,

    b. immediate family, and

    c. those whom you contact frequently (co-workers, supervisor, or others).

3 Which specific individuals in (2) influence you most positively toward personal goals? toward career goals? How?

4 Summarize the role that your frame of mind and inner self play in directing you toward success or failure in personal and working relationships.

5 React to the comment, "It's easiest to blame somebody else for your failure."

6 How does "You can lead a horse to water but you can't make it drink" relate to career planning and goals setting?

7 Identify at least one person whose life and attitudes would make good models for your own. Describe that person from the standpoints of

    a. determination,

    b. self-motivation,

    c. ambition,

    d. willingness to sacrifice, and

    e. self-discipline.

8 What is the relationship between personal goals and work goals? Do you believe one can be set independently of the other? Why or why not?

9 How do the following characteristics apply to work goals:

    a. participation,

    b. reach,

    c. realism,

    d. relative importance,

    e. need for revision, and

    f. limited numbers.

10 List at least three sources of job information contained in the library. Where else might you look for information? How might personal contacts be valuable?

11 What is the main purpose of a resume? List at least seven principles that you should follow when writing one.

12 List at least ten guidelines that you should follow when writing a cover letter to accompany a resume.

13 Why should a job interview be considered a two-way exchange? How should that affect your preparations for one?

14 List at least four sources of information on a corporate employer. How should that information be used to improve your success in an interview?

15 Summarize the effect that each of the following screening criteria has on your interviewing success:

    a. integrity,

    b. general intelligence and knowledge,

    c. communication ability,

    d. energy direction,

    e. ambition, and

    f. specific abilities.

16 Predict how each of the following aspects of work and human relations will change by the year 2000:

    a. predictability of occupational needs,

    b. relationship of business to nonbusiness organizations,

    c. organizational structures,

    d. technology,

    e. mobility,

    f. the role of middle management,

    g. the role of top management, and

    h. working hours.

17 What further changes seem to be on the horizon for human relations and the working environment, in addition to those referred to in (16)?

CASES

RESUME

Case 18.1

Norma Richert
710 S. Hillcrest Avenue
Tampa, FL 32305
(813) 324-0683

Birthday: August 10, 1960
Marital status: Single; no plans for marriage
Height: 5'10"
Weight: 115 lbs.
Health: Exceptional

WORK OBJECTIVE:

To become a Merchandising Management Trainee with Contemporary Stores, Inc.

MAJOR QUALIFICATIONS:

Bachelor of Science degree in Fashion Merchandising to be awarded from Independent Southern University in June of this year. Work as retail store sales representative.

MEMBERSHIP:

Collegiate chapter of the American Marketing Association, Independent Southern University.

EXPERIENCE:

1981–present, Sold advertising for student newspaper. Sharpened skills in dealing with the public and perceiving promotional needs of merchants who were asked to buy advertising in this once-weekly student publication (circulation: 9,000 per week).

1980–present: Retail salesperson, Grove's Fashion Center, Tampa, Florida. Worked after classes and on weekends selling women's fashion merchandise to higher income bracket consumers.

1979–1980. Retail sales clerk for Bargain Basement Discount House, Sarasota, Florida, while in high school. Ran sales register at self-service checkout lane.

EDUCATION:

B.S., Fashion Merchandising, Independent Southern University. Available June 1.

710 S. Hillcrest Avenue
Tampa, Florida 32305
March 15, 198_

Ms. Carol Coe
Human Resources Manager
Contemporary Stores
1387 - 16th Street
New York, NY 10007

Dear Mrs. Coe:

I plan to graduate from Independent Southern University in August of this year. Although graduate school looks tempting, I believe it's time to leave the academic world and settle down in a career position.

Since I'm a fashion merchanding major, I thought I'd qualify for a merchandising management trainee position with your firm. The College Placement Annual indicated you have a strong demand for them. I also have an intrest in working with disadvantaged teenagers, which I mention here because of a recent article I read that praised your companys' work in that area.

While a student, I marketed advertising for the student newspaper, a member of the student council, and belonged to our collegiate chapter of the American Marketing Association. Dean Roy Schultz and Ms. Patty Oberon in the President's office will provide you with references about my work on the newspaper and the Council.

A copy of my resume is attached for your reference. Please grant me an interview so we can discuss my future as a Merchandising Management Trainee for Contemporary Stores, Inc.

Sincerely,

Norma Richert

1   Critique Norma Richert's resume and cover letter.
2   Rewrite each of them to present the material accurately and effectively. Use your imagination to create any desired details that are now missing.
3   Assume Carol Coe's role. How would you react to the letter and resume as they now appear, and what would you answer in response to her request for an interview?

When Jan Cary graduated from high school, she hoped she was through with formal education. Her attitude was reflected in her grade average, although several teachers thought she had more potential. Said one, "She's a mental hobo; it's as though she doesn't have a care in the world."

Jan spent the first two months of her summer lying around the house in the morning, going to the beach every afternoon, and cruising main street at night. Her father urged her to get a job and suggested a few places she could go for interviews, but Jan convinced him she needed some time to unwind from high school. "Right now I need to relax and have some fun for a couple of months," she asserted. "I've got the rest of my life to worry about making a living!"

However, as August appeared Jan discovered that most of her friends would be attending State University in the fall. She'd be left without any beach or cruising buddies. With the help of her dad she managed to register for the fall semester to "get some more education."

Uncertain of a major, she decided to take only the core courses required of all freshmen and postpone serious thinking about a career path until her junior year. Her academic counselor helped her work out a schedule of morning classes, pointing out that "this will give you afternoons free for study and library research." Jan stifled a snicker at the thought of spending her afternoons in some stuffy library.

During the first couple of weeks Jan made several dormitory friends, and they formed a clique, even to the extent of adopting a slogan: "Protect wild life— throw a party tonight!" As Jan's social life picked up speed, she found less and less time for studying, and soon she began cutting at least one morning class because of her late hours at fraternity parties and other nonacademic pursuits. By the end of the fall semester she had received a passing grade in only one course—"Orientation to Campus Life."

When her father received a copy of her grades, he exploded. "What have you *done* up there?" he raged. "I've paid for you to make something out of yourself and you blew every cent. If you had to start supporting yourself tomorrow, exactly how would you do it? You've got one more semester to get your act together, and if you don't, you've had it! If college means nothing to you, then move out, get some nickle-and-dime job slinging hash, and see what life's like *without* college!"

1   Discuss the value of having students like Jan work in a full-time job for at least one year before entering college.
2   How would you summarize the problem that Jan Cary (and many other college freshmen) have adjusting to a collegiate environment?
3   What could her father have done to help her avoid the problem she encountered?
4   Summarize the indirect responsibility that students like Jan have toward
    a.   parents,

b. other students,
c. themselves, and
d. society at large.

What basic trait causes them to ignore that responsibility in your opinion? What remedy, if any, would be effective?

NOTES

---

1. Erik Larson, "Why Do Some People Outperform Others? Psychologist Picks Out Six Characteristics" *The Wall Street Journal*, 13 January 1982, p. 33.
2. Paul J. Meyer, "The Multiple Values of Goal-Setting," *Positive Living* (1978): 23.
3. Adapted from Abbott P. Smith, "How to Make Sure Your Next Resume Isn't an Obituary," *Training HRD* (May 1977): 63–64.
4. John L. Meyer and Melvin W. Donaho, *Get the Right Person for the Job* (Englewood Cliffs, N.J.: Prentice-Hall, 1979), p. 59.
5. Caterpillar Tractor Company, "Guide to the Interview."
6. Betsy Morris, "Students Seek Sartorial Edge in Job-Hunting," *The Wall Street Journal*, 9 November 1981, p. 31.
7. Robert A. Martin, "Toward More Productive Interviewing," *Personnel Journal* (May 1971): 359–363.
8. Caterpillar Tractor, "Guide."
9. G. Lowell Martin, "A View of Work Toward the Year 2000," *Personnel Journal* (October 1977): 502–504, 526.
10. Douglas R. Sease, "Graduates Trained for Fast Track at Bethlehem," *The Wall Street Journal*, 29 July 1980, p. 29.

SUGGESTED READINGS

Bolles, Richard Nelson. *What Color Is Your Parachute?* Berkeley, Calif.: Ten Speed Press, 1979.

Hawkins, James. *The Uncle Sam Connection.* Chicago: Follett, 1978.

Jackson, Tom. *Guerrilla Tactics in the Job Market.* New York: Bantam, 1978.

Lathrop, Richard. *Who's Hiring Who.* Berkeley, Calif.: Ten Speed Press, 1977.

Shingleton, John and Bao, Robert. *College to Career: Finding Yourself in the Job Market.* New York: McGraw-Hill, 1977.

Terkel, Studs. *Working.* New York: Avon Books, 1975.

INDEX